4

Schwartz, William
A.

The nuclear
seduction

$25.00

| DATE | | |
|---|---|---|
|  |  |  |
|  |  |  |
|  |  |  |
|  |  |  |
|  |  |  |
|  |  |  |
|  |  |  |
|  |  |  |
|  |  |  |
|  |  |  |
|  |  |  |
|  |  |  |

# The Nuclear Seduction

# The Nuclear Seduction

Why the Arms Race
Doesn't Matter—
and What Does

**William A. Schwartz
and Charles Derber**

with Gordon Fellman
William Gamson
Morris S. Schwartz
and Patrick W. Withen

*The Boston Nuclear Study Group*

UNIVERSITY OF CALIFORNIA PRESS
*Berkeley · Los Angeles · Oxford*

University of California Press
Berkeley and Los Angeles, California

University of California Press, Ltd.
Oxford, England

© 1990 by
The Regents of the University of California


Library of Congress Cataloging-in-Publication Data

Schwartz, William A.
  The nuclear seduction : why the arms race doesn't matter and what does /
William A. Schwartz and Charles Derber with Gordon Fellman . . . [et al.].
    p.   cm.
  Bibliography: p.
  Includes index.
  ISBN 0-520-06134-9 (alk. paper)
  1. Nuclear weapons.   2. Arms race—History—20th century.
3. Nuclear warfare.   4. World politics—1945–     I. Derber, Charles.
II. Fellman, Gordon.   III. Title.
U264.S37   1990
355.02'17—dc20                                              89-5028
                                                              CIP

Printed in the United States of America
1   2   3   4   5   6   7   8   9

The paper used in this publication meets the minimum requirements of American
National Standard for Information Sciences—Permanence of Paper for Printed Library
Materials, ANSI Z39.48-1984.                                            ∞

*For our parents*

*and for everyone working to save our planet*
*and the people of the Third World*
*from state violence*

# Contents

# Preface

In 1983 the Harvard Nuclear Study Group published *Living with Nuclear Weapons,* an authoritative statement of mainstream thinking about nuclear war and peace. Late that year, at the initiative of Gordon Fellman, the Boston Nuclear Study Group was formed with the original intention of answering the Harvard book. Our approach at that time was broadly sympathetic to the American anti–nuclear war movement's analysis of the nuclear problem, emphasizing dangers associated with new "destabilizing" weapons and defensive systems and the arms race generally, and hence advocating a halt to the arms race, weapons reductions toward "minimum deterrence" in the short run, and general nuclear disarmament whenever it might become possible.

On the verge of writing our rebuttal, we began to doubt whether, in following the well-worn paths of many nuclear analysts before us, we had really been asking the right questions. It seemed that perhaps the Harvard group *and* its critics were offering a misleading picture of the nuclear problem. We decided to put our writing on hold and reexamine the nuclear literature and nuclear-age history in the light of our new doubts and conceptions.

This study led us to the conviction that in fact the nuclear debate, in the United States and elsewhere, largely focuses on a set of marginal issues and with only a few exceptions ignores the real risk factors for nuclear war. This book is a statement of what we found.

William Schwartz did the writing and took the lead in formulating many of the book's ideas. Charles Derber collaborated intensively with him in developing the book's thesis, conceiving the arguments of each chapter, and thoroughly revising the manuscript. In many ways, their constant dialogue and debate made this book what it is.

With the indispensable assistance of Patrick Withen, W. Schwartz conducted the literature review and historical research on which the book is based. Derber and W. Schwartz interviewed several dozen high- and mid-level U.S. nuclear planning officials in the Pentagon, in the National Security Council, and on Capitol Hill. They also interviewed a number of former senior U.S. officials as well as peace movement leaders and scholars in Washington, New York, and Boston.

The group as a whole met weekly for several years and played a crucial role throughout the project. Only through our lengthy discussions did the idea for this book take shape. The group subjected conceptual outlines, and later chapter outlines—prepared by W. Schwartz—to continual challenge and debate. The members of the group also reviewed every chapter and suggested many important revisions. Derber, Fellman, Gamson, and M. Schwartz (no relation to W. Schwartz) each contributed $2,500 of personal funds to help support the project. The group provided a friendly but critical forum for the development of ideas that from the beginning were unsettling to us and to many others. This book reflects an exciting collective effort, all too rare in the academy today.

Naturally, within the group there remain many differences of emphasis and, in a few areas, of substantive position. We chose not to highlight these; our main purpose is to stimulate public debate through a clear and simple presentation of a new point of view. For the same reason we have tried to write a book that any literate, motivated person can read. We do not pretend to offer an academically exhaustive, definitive, or final analysis of the nuclear danger and the remedies for it.

We owe a great deal to those few thinkers, some of whom are mentioned in the introduction and throughout the text, who have had the courage and insight to challenge what has become conventional wisdom about the nuclear problem. This lineage dates all the way back to Bernard Brodie, author of the first and in many ways still the most perceptive study of the nuclear question. We owe a particular debt to George Rathjens, whose authoritative critique of what we call "weaponitis" influenced us greatly. We are also indebted to Noam Chomsky, whose writings and detailed comments on the manuscript were invaluable, and to the other scholars and activists who launched the idea of the "deadly connection" within the American peace movement.

For reviewing drafts or providing other encouragement and criticism, we also thank Gar Alperovitz, Michael Klare, Lynn Eden, Len Ackland, Robert Tucker, Bob Borosoge, Mark Sommer, Steven Kull, Paul Joseph, Hugh DeWitt, Randy Kehler, Randy Forsberg, Paul Walker, Marinel Mobley, Robert Jervis, Michael Howard, Bruce Birchard, and Ping Ferry. To all those who were interviewed in confidence and remain anonymous, we express our appreciation. The views presented here are, of course, solely our own.

We also thank the many family members and friends, too numerous to name, who kept us sane and smiling. For financial contributions we thank Ping Ferry, Sid Shapiro and the Levinson Foundation, the Tides Foundation, Carol Guyer, the Stern Fund, and Boston College. For providing space and collegial support, we thank the Boston College Department of Sociology and its students, staff, and faculty. We owe much to Beth Jacklin, Eleanor LeCain, and our other friends and office mates at the Exploratory Project on the Conditions of Peace. For publishing an earlier (March 1986) account of ideas that bluntly challenge some of its most basic premises, we thank the *Bulletin of the Atomic Scientists* and its editor, Len Ackland.

At the University of California Press, we thank our editor, Naomi Schneider, for aggressively sponsoring the publication of the manuscript; Steve Rice, Mary Renaud, and Betsey Scheiner for gracious and expert editorial work; and Amy Klatzkin for superb copyediting.

# Introduction

A nuclear sword, we all know, hangs over the earth. But where does the danger of nuclear war come from? What makes it worse? How can we reduce it?

For many years, a striking consensus has reigned: the nuclear arms race between the superpowers is the main source of danger. The arms race is "the central concern of the closing years of the century," the cause célèbre of our time. A U.S. senator says that "the very survival of our planet, the survival of the human race, is at stake," a common view.[1]

The right, the center, and the left disagree, of course, about how the United States should run the arms race. The right urges us to build weapons like the MX missile, the Stealth bomber, and "Star Wars"; the center, to sign arms control treaties like INF and START with the Soviet Union; and the left, to stop and then reverse the arms race through a test ban, a "freeze," and huge reductions in nuclear arsenals. But all focus on the hardware, the weapons themselves. Most of the nuclear debate concerns which weapons should be deployed and which destroyed.

But short of near-total nuclear disarmament, we believe that no change in the arms race can in fact make a profound difference. MX, Star Wars, INF, a freeze, or even a 90 percent reduction in nuclear arsenals cannot reliably change the horror of a nuclear war. They cannot much affect the risk that the nuclear states will plunge us into that horror. They cannot make the world much safer *or* more dangerous than it already is.

The nuclear danger is real—even more ominous, as we will show, than most people appreciate. But the fixation on weapons has obscured the real menace: the political conflict and violence raging around the world that could one day burn out of control and set off a nuclear cataclysm. As the world debates largely irrelevant missiles and arms control treaties, the superpowers are fanning the flames of conflict and war from Afghanistan to Nicaragua, Lebanon to Cambodia. Forty years of history reveal that such conflicts can suddenly veer out of control and even erupt into open superpower confrontation. Yet in a time of unprecedented public concern about nuclear war, few—even in the peace movement—protest the nuclear hazards of their governments' foreign intrigues and interventions.

Those of us concerned with the nuclear threat have long been like the apocryphal drunk who searches for his lost keys hour after hour under a lamppost—because it's light there. The giant weapons systems are seductive, the obvious place to look for answers to the nuclear peril. The light there is good. But there is little to be found. If we want the keys to a safer world, we must turn the light to the real conflicts and battlefields where the superpowers and their clients confront each other every day, often hidden from public view, and where they periodically collide in terrifying crises that threaten to provoke worldwide catastrophe.

## THE ABSOLUTE WEAPON

Public issues generally develop a "culture," a consensus about the key questions, the level of analysis, and the language of debate. Since these assumptions are shared, they rarely come up for discussion.

The common perspective that guides discourse on nuclear war and peace is what we call the "weapons paradigm." It magnifies the importance of the weapons themselves far beyond their real significance. It views weapons as the basic source of security or insecurity, power or weakness, peace or war. It pegs the arms race as the problem and some change in that race as the solution.

If nuclear weapons were like conventional ones, then their number and technical characteristics would of course matter. But nuclear weapons are different. They are so powerful that both superpowers long ago acquired the means to utterly destroy each other along with much of the rest of the planet. For decades the arms race and arms control have changed only the number of times that we can bounce the radiating rubble of the world.

Those who imagine that more missiles or fewer missiles can really change the nuclear peril simply do not appreciate the destructive power of what Bernard Brodie called, in 1946, "the absolute weapon."[2] In Hiroshima,

of the city's 76,000 buildings, 90% were destroyed along with most of their occupants. After the mushroom cloud formed, an oily, highly radioactive "black rain" fell for thirty to sixty minutes, bringing death to thousands outside the firestorm and the shockwave. Out of a resident population of 245,000 over 110,000 were killed. . . .

In the weeks, months, and years that followed, deaths continued. Leukemia, a variety of tumors, cataracts and cancers, diffuse hemorrhage, infection, uncontrollable vomiting were soon commonplace. Grotesque skin excrescences appeared, mental retardation, children were born with small heads. In the five years following the bomb, as many died in Hiroshima from cancer via radiation as were killed on that fateful morning. Thirty-five years after the explosion, 2,500 still die annually from the bomb's radiation.

The Hiroshima bomb was tiny by modern standards. Imagine that a large, twenty-megaton, warhead is dropped on Boston:

Within a radius of four miles . . . the city will literally disappear. It will be replaced by rubble. More than 750,000 will die outright, from concussion, heat, or fire. Many of them will be vaporized. Fire-wind storms . . . will originate in a fireball hotter than the sun, and will sweep a radius of twenty miles. Within that radius 2,300,000 will die outright. Another 500,000 will be disabled and in shock . . . anyone who looked at the explosion from a distance of forty miles or less will likely be blinded.

Epidemic disease, carried by radiation-resistant flies and mosquitos and by hunger-crazed animals, will end the suffering of more than 25% of the weakened survivors. In the judgment of several authorities, such diseases from the past as polio, dysentery, typhoid fever, and cholera will reappear.

Occupants of shelters will die in assorted ways. By crushing if the shelter is vulnerable to bomb blast. By incineration if the shelter is reached by firestorm, or by asphyxiation if the firestorm absorbs all available oxygen. By starvation or dehydration in the likely absence of radiation-free food or water. By radiation if the air within the shelter cannot be continuously filtered. Appearance outside a shelter for more than three minutes will produce fatal third-degree burns from intense ultraviolet light.

Of Greater Boston's 6,000 doctors, 5,100 will be incapacitated or dead. . . . Doctors will have to treat the maimed where they lie, in the radioactive rubble. And with little more than bare hands. There will be no anesthesia, no bandages, few drugs.

A one-megaton nuclear bomb "equals half of the total destructive power of all bombs used by the Western Allies in Europe during all of World War II. . . . It would take a train 300 miles long to transport the equivalent dynamite." If one such bomb is dropped on New York City, it is estimated that 2,250,000 will die, 1,000,000 of them within eleven seconds. Most will be vaporized. About 3,600,000 will suffer crushing injuries and ruptured internal organs.

The fireball, hotter than the sun, will be about one-and-one-half miles in diameter. The resulting firestorm will cover about 100 square miles. Third-degree burns are likely for those within a radius of 8 miles of the burst, second-degree burns will be common over an additional 250 square miles. Shelters in that area will become ovens, incinerating their occupants.

Skyscrapers will topple. It is unlikely that a single metropolitan hospital will remain standing. The city will be replaced by acres of highly radioactive rubble. There will be no communication, no transport, no medicines, no edible food, no drinkable water.

Some species will survive, notably cockroaches. They will be blind but they will continue to reproduce.

For any human survivors, other consequences over the years will include "genetic damage, abnormalities in new births, psychological trauma of every description, mental retardation, and concentration of plutonium in testicles and ovaries (for 50,000 years)." A twenty-mile-an-hour breeze "can carry lethal fallout hundreds of miles from the burst."[3]

A *single* Trident submarine, carrying twenty-four seven-warhead missiles, could destroy 168 Russian cities, "with each receiving at least ten times the megatonnage that fell on Hiroshima." According to a Pentagon estimate, only *one hundred* nuclear warheads "could *immediately* kill 37,000,000 and destroy 59% of Soviet industrial capacity." What would happen over the following days, weeks, years, and even generations, we can only guess. Independent studies recently confirmed that as few as "*one hundred* one-[megaton] weapons . . . could devastate the urban areas of either 'superpower.'"[4]

Today the United States and the Soviet Union each have about *twenty-five thousand* nuclear weapons. Would it matter if each had a million? Or only a thousand? Or if one side had a million and the other a thousand?

A GUIDE TO THE BOOK

The thesis of Part I is that the arms race has not much affected the nuclear threat for more than twenty-five years. Chained as it is to the pre–nuclear weapons paradigm, our thought just has not caught up with the power of our weapons. "The unleashed power of the atom," as Albert Einstein warned, "has changed everything save our modes of thinking."[5]

Chapter 1 explains in brief why the superpower arms race no longer matters. Chapters 2–5 (which some general-interest readers may want to skip) address common counterarguments that are strikingly parallel in the thinking of both the right and the left. Chapter 2 discusses the fear that "first-strike" weapons are destabilizing deterrence and in a crisis could tempt one side to try a massive knockout blow against the other. Chapter 3 takes up the purported need for new weapons to ensure the credibility of deterrence and the logically parallel fear that those same weapons can dangerously narrow the "firebreak" between conventional and nuclear war. Chapter 4 examines the argument that national leaders might irrationally *think* new weapons matter, which of course would make the weapons matter. Chapter 5 asks if the U.S. Strategic Defense Initiative, or Star Wars—presently the most hotly disputed weapons program—is an exception to the irrelevance of new weaponry, if it is really the nuclear savior or the nuclear devil that many claim it to be.

"A page of history," as a lawyer once wrote, "is worth a volume of logic."[6] To find the real sources of nuclear danger, we must consult the relevant historical record—not the chronology of the arms race that often passes for the history of the nuclear age, but the actual occasions on which the nuclear sword threatened to drop on humanity. As the review of those occasions in Part II reveals, since 1950 the arms race has rarely if ever endangered the world. But the same is not true of the superpowers' violent efforts to bring much of the planet under their political and economic control. Aggression, intervention, and threats by both the United States and the Soviet Union have regularly produced crises and confrontations that, as leaders on both sides have openly admitted, could have spun out of control and even ignited a final holocaust.

Danger loomed in Europe until the early 1960s and to an extent still does. But the main tinderboxes for nuclear war have always been in what is called the Third World—the real prize of the Cold War and the site of almost all actual superpower collisions. Chapter 6 reviews those shocking events in the Third World. Chapter 7 explains why local Third World conflicts with limited stakes have so often blown up into global crises and how such crises could degenerate into perilous confrontation and even nuclear war. Chapter 8 examines the worst nuclear crisis yet, the 1962 Cuban missile crisis, in the light of the argument of this book. "Those who do not remember the past," wrote George Santayana, "are condemned to relive it."[7] We do not remember, and we have not learned. The nuclear dangers lurking in the Third World today, as we will see, seem no less ominous than in the past.

The United States, of course, blames the Soviet Union for most Third World conflict and violence, just as the Soviet Union blames the United States. In reality, both superpowers and many other states and political movements regularly contribute to the tensions and conflicts that are ravaging the Third World and could one day destroy the whole world. The United States, however, has long been the leading world power, allied with some of the most violent, unstable, and repressive regimes in the Third World and, as the record will show, has with few exceptions demonstrated far more nuclear recklessness than the Soviet Union. Just as important, Americans can hope to influence the actions of our own government more than those of any other, especially since our democracy affords significant opportunities for public influence over foreign policy. Whether one supports or opposes U.S. actions in the Third World on political grounds, their dangers in the nuclear age should be the focus of the nuclear debate, in the United States at least. We hope that this book will help inspire citizens to learn about their government's role in perpetuating the nuclear threat and to organize to do something about it.

Part III discusses this and other political implications of our study. Chapter 9 considers the implications of Part I, asking if arms control can help make a safer future. Though the superpower arms control agenda, including the INF and START treaties, can do little to diminish the nuclear threat, another kind of arms control could—by reversing the pervasive nuclearization of the conventional fighting forces of both sides that (hard as it may be to believe) could allow an artilleryman, a ship's captain, or a jet pilot, in the chaos and horror of some future battle, to fire a shot truly heard 'round the world. Chapter 9 also examines the economic impact of arms control and asks whether treaties like INF actually do help prevent nuclear war, as widely assumed, by promoting better superpower relations or by paving the way for nuclear disarmament. Chapter 10 turns to the real challenge of the nuclear age: the changes in foreign policy required to prevent the kinds of Third World crises that have tempted fate so often in the past.

Logic and history both suggest that the arms race matters little to the danger of nuclear war. But it does of course matter in other ways. The arms race undermines us morally, as individuals and as a society, continually leading us to build weapons that, if used, would slaughter millions of innocent people and much of the natural order. The arms race wastes hundreds of billions of dollars on redundant weapons while millions starve, cities crumble, and the earth's environment succumbs to industrial assault, perhaps beyond redemption. The arms race prompts us to mass-produce pound after pound of radioactive substances that can kill in the most minute amounts; inevitably, some escapes—sometimes intentionally, as in the era of open-air nuclear test explosions and in the decades of planned radioactive releases at U.S. nuclear weapons plants, a policy finally acknowledged by the U.S. Department of Energy in 1988. Dr. John Gofman, director of biology and medicine at the Lawrence Radiation Center of the University of California, states that if only 2 percent of the plutonium manufactured by the year 2000 is released into the environment, "assuredly, we can give up on the future of humans."[8]

The arms race is vile. But concerned citizens must abandon the delusion that controlling, stopping, or even reversing it—*whatever the other benefits*—could help reduce the threat of nuclear war.

We do not try to explain the origins and history of the arms race *or* of the Third World policies of the superpowers. After reading this book, those who seek to prevent a final calamity will, we hope, want to learn more about the true nature of the Cold War, the record of and interests behind U.S. foreign policy, and the role the United States government plays in the Third World, topics well covered elsewhere.[9]

## NAGGING DOUBTS

Despite a near consensus that identifies the problem of nuclear war not with the violence actually occurring in the world but with the size, accuracy, and throw weight of redundant missile systems, a few voices have always raised doubts about the conventional wisdom. Bernard Brodie, the father of nuclear strategy, knew as early as 1946 that "margins of superiority in nuclear weapons or the means of delivering them might count for little or nothing in a crisis so long as each side had reason to fear the huge devastation of its peoples and territories by the other," a notion that "any reflective observer of the time would have found more or less self-evident." In 1978, near his death, he wrote: "I could never accept . . . that the balance of terror between the Soviet Union and the United States has been or ever could be 'delicate.'" To take another early example, in 1956 even Secretary of the Air Force Donald Quarles suspected that war had become an "unthinkable catastrophe" from which "neither side can hope by a mere margin of superiority in airplanes or other means of delivery to escape."[10]

As the arms race has produced ever more redundant increments of destructive power and technological wizardry, more nagging doubts have occasionally surfaced. For example, at the beginning of his 1983 book on nuclear command and control, Paul Bracken notes that "the arsenals of both countries are now so large that reductions in nuclear armaments, even deep reductions, would leave so many remaining weapons that the difference might be negligible should a war break out." His approach, far more reasonable than those focusing on the weapons hardware itself, is to analyze the "management of nuclear forces at the moment they would go on alert, and as they would perform during a war," with the hope that one could thereby "identify potential flashpoints and triggers that might lead to catastrophe."[11]

The Harvard Nuclear Study Group similarly cautions that "it is usually misleading to concentrate one's attention on the numbers of nuclear weapons when analyzing the likelihood of war." The group criticizes the "widely assumed" notion that "changes in the numbers of weapons in the superpower arsenals—either upward or downward—are the major determinant of the risks of war." But like Bracken and almost all other analysts, these authors attach great importance to the *characteristics* of new nuclear systems even though they recognize the irrelevance of raw numbers. Thus the "vulnerability of weapons" and other technical factors are central considerations. Indeed, despite their annoyance at the "common fixation on numbers of weapons," by far the greatest part of their book is about the composition of U.S. and Soviet nuclear arsenals.[12]

A later Harvard book on the nuclear problem exhibits a similar schizophrenia. The editors were quoted in the press as deeply critical of approaches that emphasize "the weapons themselves." The dean of Harvard's Kennedy School of Government, Graham Allison, asked rhetorically, "If the United States and the Soviet Union cut their nuclear arsenals in half, or if their arsenals were twice as large, would either of those events fundamentally change the shape of the problem?" Nevertheless, at least half of the book's "principles of avoiding nuclear war" entail proposals about nuclear weapons systems. There is no examination of the history or dangers of U.S. policies in the Third World or, with the exception of the Middle East, of the many international conflicts involving the United States that could spin out of control and result in a direct confrontation with the Soviets.[13]

In a few cases the doubts raised about the importance of weapons have been less nagging and more serious. Robert Jervis's book, *The Il-*

*logic of American Nuclear Strategy,* is a rigorous rebuttal to the idea that the "countervailing" nuclear strategy of the United States can escape the "nuclear revolution" that has made all societies existentially vulnerable to nuclear destruction regardless of the conventional or nuclear forces available for use. Jervis argues that both the nuclear balance between the superpowers and their meaningless quests for nuclear superiority no longer matter much to the actual conduct of international affairs.[14] In this respect Jervis has formalized a position already staked out, as we will see, by McGeorge Bundy, Robert McNamara, and other former high-level officials. But in directing their ire at nuclear weapons policy and strategic doctrine, even such astute critics further obscure the real point: that these no longer make much difference in a world of mutual mega-overkill.

By far the most forceful critique of nuclear "weaponitis," as we call it, has come from George Rathjens of MIT, a longtime distinguished member of the arms control community. In a courageous but little-noticed rebuttal to this mainstay of the establishment anti–nuclear war agenda, he argues that arms control's focus on weapons

> is deceptive to the point of almost being a gigantic fraud: there is the implicit suggestion that controls on weapons of the kind that have been tried will solve the problem—or at least make a big difference—when there is no real reason for so believing. . . . The negotiations have been predicated on a belief that numbers and detailed performance characteristics of weapons are important [and as a result] the importance of differences in capabilities have been exaggerated to the point where political leaders and the public have been led to believe that such differences could be exploited militarily, when almost certainly they could not be.[15]

To take one final example, in 1986 the noted military historian Michael Howard delivered a speech to the Council for Arms Control blasting the notion that arms control can substantially remedy the nuclear danger. Is it not, he asks, "the modern equivalent of the alchemist's search for a philosopher's stone which will turn the lead of international relations into the gold of perpetual peace?" Howard disputes the notion that " 'arms races' build up to war" and that "arms reductions . . . lead to peace." He argues that the profound benefit supposedly derivable from nuclear arms treaties is understood by those in government as no more than a Platonic "noble lie," a generous characterization.[16]

The nuclear hazards of conventional Third World militarism are slowly coming to light too. Appalled by the U.S. peace movement's silence about the U.S.-armed Israeli invasion of Lebanon and the considerable international dangers it entailed, the American Friends Service Committee brought together in 1982 a group of intellectuals and political activists to discuss the "deadly connection" between military intervention and nuclear war. This conference led to the publication of an important volume.[17] Covering the Middle East, Central America, southern Africa, Southeast Asia, Korea, and elsewhere, the participants discussed some of the past occasions on which Third World intervention moved toward a superpower showdown and warned that numerous conflicts around the world posed similar dangers today. Much of the U.S. antinuclear movement, including the largest organization, SANE/Freeze, has since adopted the "deadly connection" analysis as part of its official program. Despite widespread public opposition to U.S. military activities in Central America, southern Africa, and elsewhere, however, few protest the potential nuclear dangers of American involvement in regional conflicts around the world. Even obviously dangerous actions, such as outright U.S. interventions in Lebanon and the Persian Gulf, elicited little opposition. And numerous "covert" operations, such as American aid to the guerrilla coalition dominated by Pol Pot in Kampuchea and to the Islamic fundamentalist segment of the Afghan resistance, are rarely debated.

We hope this book will help transform the doubts that have long nagged nuclear scholars and activists into a basic shift in thought and action: from the details of redundant nuclear weapons to the real conflict and violence that could bring those weapons tragically into use.

# PART I

# Why the Arms Race Doesn't Matter

Everything about the atomic bomb is overshadowed by
the twin facts that it exists and that its destructive power is
fantastically great.

—*Bernard Brodie*

## CHAPTER ONE

# Why the Arms Race Doesn't Matter

A tired old Bear bomber, and a maneuvering hypersonic
re-entry vehicle . . . [either one] can destroy New York just
as well.

*—Admiral Noel Gayler, former commander
in chief of U.S. forces in the Pacific*

## THE FALLACY OF WEAPONITIS

The *existence* of nuclear weapons is a fundamental feature of the
modern world. Their possession—by the human race generally or
by any particular nation—definitively matters. They have completely
changed the consequences of full-scale war between the dominant world
powers, posing a threat to the very survival of civilization and the natural order. Correspondingly, international nuclear disarmament, or even
unilateral denuclearization of individual states, would be singular historical events.

The fallacy of weaponitis lies in attributing great significance to the
*size* and *technical characteristics* of the superpowers' nuclear stockpiles,
and especially to the *margins* of each arsenal—incremental additions to
or subtractions from the immense current force, such as building MX
missiles or removing Pershing II and cruise missiles from Europe.[1]

With *conventional* military technology, such concerns about weapons make sense. From the ancient discovery of the club, reenacted in
*2001: A Space Odyssey,* to the horrors of modern saturation bombing,
the types and quantities of conventional weaponry have undeniably
affected military and political power. Conventional arms races matter
because conventional wars are processes of attrition. The guns, tanks,
and planes of one side oppose and try to neutralize the weapons and
fighters of the other. One side's forces must deplete those of the enemy
before a threat of destruction can be posed to the enemy's inner society.

13

Because no single weapon or small arsenal of weapons determines the result, the quality and size of the overall fighting forces matter.

The side with more or better weapons does not always win, of course, because technical factors must share the military stage with psychological, social, economic, and political ones. In modern guerrilla warfare, for example, primitively armed local organizations sometimes defeat huge, highly advanced military powers. But the military balance has determined much of human history. Firearms helped European settlers conquer Native Americans. Germany's buildup of naval power prior to World War I increased the military threat to Britain. Large, technically advanced interventionary forces supported American power in Korea and other Third World conflicts after World War II.

At the beginning of the nuclear age, too, the weapons paradigm made sense. The atomic bomb was a new weapon, and it revolutionized war and politics. The reason was the immense power of an individual atomic weapon, especially the later hydrogen weapon—so powerful that a single warhead could destroy a city. As Bernard Brodie wrote in 1959: "People often speak of atomic explosives as the most portentous military invention 'since gunpowder.' But such a comparison inflates the importance of even so epoch-making an event as the introduction of gunpowder."[2]

Consider what a single large warhead could do to Chicago:

> One twenty-megaton nuclear bomb explodes just above ground level, at the corner of LaSalle and Adams. In less than one millionth of a second the temperature rises to 150,000,000 degrees Fahrenheit, four times the temperature of the center of the sun. A roar follows but no one is alive to hear it.
>
> Chicago has disappeared. The crater is 600 feet deep, one-and-one-half miles in diameter. Within a five-mile radius, skyscrapers, apartment buildings, roads, bridges, trains, subways, planes, hospitals, ambulances, automobiles, gas mains, trees, earth, animals, people—all have vanished. . . .
>
> The fireball is hotter than five thousand suns. The firestorm roars out in all directions, absorbing all available oxygen, thereby suffocating or incinerating all the living in its path. Before it burns out it will devastate 1,400,000 acres and most of the people on them.
>
> The firestorm is followed by the shockwave, the latter at close to the speed of sound. Then the mushroom cloud, reaching twenty miles in height, and the beginning of lethal radioactive fallout.[3]

All weapons are subject to diminishing returns, but with weapons this powerful the point of saturation—when increasing the number or quality of weapons adds little to military potential or risks—was reached very soon, perhaps as early as 1955 and no later than the early

1960s, although the date is unimportant now. Both sides had by then acquired so much destructive power that only secondary importance would attach to any further quantitative or qualitative improvements in the leading weapons of the day. The same was true for even large reductions in weapon stockpiles. The weapons paradigm was already obsolete.

For with nuclear weapons, a nation's armed forces no longer must be defeated, or even seriously confronted, before its inner society can be destroyed, because the penetration of so few warheads is needed to accomplish the task.[4] General war would no longer be a drawn-out process of attrition but an orgy of mutual devastation. Additional weapons on one side could do little to inflict greater damage on the other.

Even modern air attack with huge conventional bombs does not dispense with the task of defeating the enemy's armed forces. For example, the Allied bombing of German cities during World War II killed hundreds of thousands of people but did not make a decisive difference in the war. In more recent memory, the heavy bombardment of cities such as Hanoi and Beirut caused unimaginable human horror, but even in combination with the extensive bombing and shelling of other cities and villages, it did not completely destroy Vietnamese or (at least so far) Lebanese society.

In contrast, as McGeorge Bundy writes, "a decision that would bring even one hydrogen bomb on one city of one's own country would be recognized in advance as a catastrophic blunder; ten bombs on ten cities would be a disaster beyond history; and a hundred bombs on a hundred cities are unthinkable." Herbert York, another former high-level American official, concurs: "From one to ten are enough whenever the course of events is being rationally determined." Yet we urgently debate the composition of nuclear arsenals that now number not in the tens but in the tens of thousands. As the military historian Michael Howard notes, the amount of damage to be expected from a war that employs such weapons is so insensitive to the sizes of the nuclear arsenals held by the opposing powers that "the nuclear arsenals of the superpowers could be reduced by a factor of a hundred without affecting their capacity to destroy each other, and probably the rest of the world as well."[5]

## THE EXISTENTIAL BALANCE OF TERROR

Overkill in itself did not make the arms race irrelevant. The arms race would matter had it produced either (1) a way to defend society against nuclear weapons or (2) a way to control nuclear war and prevent escalation to all-out carnage. In either case, leaders might believe that their nations could survive or even win a nuclear war and hence might be more inclined to fight one. But because of the great power of the individual hydrogen weapon, no arsenal can provide an effective defense or a reliable means to prevent escalation.

Brodie predicted, almost from the beginning, that an effective defense would be impossible. To those who said that every new weapon always brought forth a suitable defense, he retorted that "after five centuries of the use of hand arms with fire-propelled missiles, the large number of men killed by comparable arms in the recent war indicates that no adequate answer has yet [been] found for the bullet." When a single warhead can demolish a city, a meaningful defense of society must be nearly perfect—a goal that no military technology, including President Reagan's Star Wars plan, can achieve (see Chapter 5). As former secretary of defense James Schlesinger—hardly a nuclear dove—said without qualification: "There is no realistic hope that we shall ever again be able to protect American cities."[6] If we *could* build weapons to protect cities, these weapons would certainly matter. Since we cannot, MX missiles, orbiting battle stations, and arms control treaties are irrelevant; everything will probably be destroyed with or without them once the missiles are launched—unless, that is, nuclear war could be kept limited.

If a nation *could* build weapons or other devices to reliably control escalation, then even without a defense, leaders might imagine surviving or even winning a limited nuclear war. But the hydrogen weapon is too powerful to be controlled by any known means. Through blast, heat, radiation, and electromagnetic pulse, even a few nuclear weapons could destroy the leaders, organizations, and communication devices needed to control nuclear war. As we shall see, no one has devised a weapons system, a command mechanism, or an arms control treaty that could give leaders reliable control over events after a nuclear war erupted or one that could reliably prevent escalation once leaders lost control.[7]

Noted strategic analyst John Steinbruner observes that "regardless of the flexibility embodied in individual force components, the precariousness of command channels probably means that nuclear war would be uncontrollable, as a practical matter, shortly after the first tens of weapons are launched, regardless of what calculations political leaders might make at the time." Desmond Ball's thorough study agrees that "control of a nuclear exchange would become very difficult to maintain after several tens of strategic nuclear weapons had been used." The conservative strategic theorist Colin Gray regards the effort to wage nuclear war in controlled steps as little more than "suicide on the instalment plan."[8]

Once central control of a nuclear war is lost, the fate of the earth will be left to dozens, perhaps hundreds, of isolated commanders with nuclear weapons at their disposal. No one can say what they will do. As Michael Howard observes: "The length of the war and the destruction it causes would be determined not by the number of weapons available but by the readiness of the belligerents to endure punishment in the hope of ultimate victory. A few missiles directed against carefully selected targets might cause the moral collapse of one belligerent, or indeed both; or they might fight on as grimly among the radioactive ruins as did the Russians in the ruins of Stalingrad or the Germans in the ruins of Berlin."[9]

Leaders, then, cannot know just what will happen if nuclear war breaks out, regardless of the state of the arms race. They know only that they will probably not be in control and that mutual annihilation may well occur. That risk, that uncertainty, is what frightens and deters them. It may or may not be enough to prevent a holocaust. But pending the abolition of nuclear weapons, an effective defense against them, or a way to curb the risk of escalation, further arming or disarming cannot affect the terrible uncertainty that produces the balance of terror. That terror, as Brodie noted, is not at all delicate; it is existential, inherent in the existence of the "absolute weapon."[10]

The nuclear warhead is the ultimate blunt instrument of human violence whose effects cannot be calculated in advance and whose use always risks the destruction of far more than is originally intended. After four decades of effort and hundreds of billions of dollars of investment, no one has found a way to sharpen the weapon to eliminate or even greatly reduce this risk. That much is well known. In a 1984 survey 90 percent of Americans agreed that "we and the Soviets now have enough nuclear weapons to blow up each other several times over"; 89 percent said that "there can be no winner in an all-out nuclear war; both the U.S. and the Soviet Union would be completely destroyed"; 71 percent believed that "there is no defense in a nuclear war"; and 83 percent thought that "a limited nuclear war is nonsense."[11]

McGeorge Bundy coined the term "existential deterrence" to describe the implications of these basic nuclear realities. He observes that the "terrible and unavoidable uncertainties in any recourse to nuclear war" invalidate all strategies based on specific weapons and scenarios.[12]

All that matters is the possibility of uncontrolled escalation once the nuclear shooting begins. No one knows the likelihood of escalation or how
to prevent it. So real political leaders, as opposed to abstract models of
nuclear strategists, concern themselves only with the gross fact that catastrophic escalation could occur—that is all that they really know.

The whole complex labyrinth of nuclear hardware and the doctrines
governing its use thus collapse to a single easily understood fact: each
side has "large numbers of thermonuclear weapons that could be used
against the opponent, even after the strongest possible preemptive attack." This reality is "essentially unaffected by any changes [in weapon
deployments] except those that might truly challenge the overall survivability of the forces on one side or the other."[13] The remote likelihood of such a challenge (see Chapter 2) makes deterrence inherent in
the existence of the weapons.

If the strength of deterrence—the main force preventing nuclear
war—is existential and thus relatively independent of the arms race,
then logically the risk of nuclear war should be also. Like most nuclear
doves, however, Bundy is well known for his opposition to "the competition in weapons systems," which, he dramatically writes, "is now itself
becoming the largest single threat to peace." Similarly, George Kennan
writes that "today we have achieved, we and the Russians together, in
the creation of these devices and their means of delivery, levels of redundancy of such grotesque dimensions as to defy rational understanding";
that "the nuclear bomb is the most useless weapon ever invented"; and
that "the relative size of the arsenals has no serious meaning." But Kennan too looks to these "redundant" and "useless" weapons for solu-
tions to the nuclear problem, most dramatically with his well-known
advocacy of a mutual 50 percent across-the-board cut in superpower
nuclear arsenals.[14] Yet if this "modest proposal" were ever carried out,
could Kennan claim that deterrence and the risks of war had been fundamentally altered—rooted as they are in a "redundancy of grotesque
dimensions" that even a 50 percent cut would hardly begin to undo?

The right, the center, and the left seem equally misguided in attaching
great significance to which nuclear weapons are deployed or destroyed
by the superpowers. Because no realistic changes in the pace, balance,
or even direction of the arms race can alter the basic conditions of our
nuclear existence, they should make little difference to the incentives to
start nuclear war, the damage we can expect should a war occur, or the
division of international political power. Even major steps by the superpowers to rearm (including Star Wars) or to disarm (including the nu-

clear freeze or large cuts in nuclear arsenals) would leave the nuclear problem essentially unchanged, as we argue in more detail in succeeding chapters. The common tendency to identify the *problem of nuclear war* with the *nuclear arms race* is a logical fallacy that dangerously distorts nuclear politics by promoting technical fixes to what is overwhelmingly a political problem.

## CHAPTER TWO

# What About First Strike?

What do Soviet leaders think U.S. submarine crews are going
to do if they learn that the United States has been destroyed?
Go to Tahiti and retire?

*—Frank von Hippel*

FIRST STRIKE, YOU'RE OUT

Many people who understand the uncertainty and terror of any nuclear war continue to worry about the arms race, fearing that "first-
strike" weapons may undermine the mutual vulnerability on which
stability depends. If one side could strike hard and fast enough to
effectively disarm the enemy, then it could wage nuclear war *without*
inviting its own destruction as a nation. Hawks worry about Soviet first-
strike weapons, doves about American ones. The argument is the same.
Only the names change.

This striking parallelism came dramatically to light in 1985 with the
publication of two articles—one in a conservative journal, the other in a
progressive one. They appeared at the same time (July 1985) with
nearly the same title ("First Strike, You're Out" and a slight variation),
and they mirrored each other's arguments down to details. Daniel O.
Graham and Gregory A. Fossedal warned in the *American Spectator*
that "nuclear weapons are not unusable, not if you have enough of
them, with enough accuracy, plus the capacity to find the necessary
military targets and defend against the handful that survive." They worried that "it is now at least plausible that the Soviets will have a first-
strike capability by 1990, and it is likely by 1995—unless there is a
change in U.S. nuclear strategy and weapons programs." Daniel Ellsberg warned in the *Progressive* that "with a combination of Trident II
and MX and Pershing II, plus our anti-submarine warfare, one side—

namely, the United States—would . . . have total coverage of the other side's retaliatory capability." Similarly, Howard Moreland wrote in the *Nation* several months earlier of "a U.S. first-strike capability" that "would upset the nuclear balance and could provoke the Russians to launch a pre-emptive strike." "The only way to avoid that situation," he said, "is to cancel the MX, Trident D-5, and Midgetman missile programs, and negotiate a mutual, easily verifiable moratorium on all ballistic missile flight tests."[1]

## YOU CAN RUN BUT YOU CANNOT HIDE

Despite all the worry, the fact remains that hydrogen warheads are too powerful, nuclear weapons platforms too diverse and well-defended, and societies too fragile for one side to rob the other of retaliatory capability. A successful first strike would require an overwhelming, near-simultaneous threat to almost all nuclear delivery vehicles or, even less plausibly, to warheads after launch. Even one surviving ballistic-missile submarine or a few dozen ICBMs or strategic bombers would sustain the essential risk—destruction of the attacking nation. First-strike weapons may add something to abstract military capabilities and even betray evil intent, but they cannot change the balance of terror.

First, neither side can find and destroy enough enemy weapons to even begin to prevent retaliation. Nuclear weapons platforms are diverse and highly protected: missile silos are very "hard," bombers can fly off on warning into the sanctuary of the air, and submarines, while "soft," are so difficult to locate in the open oceans that they are "immune to surprise attack."[2] In theory, of course, future advances in technology could dangerously increase the vulnerability of submarines and other strategic weapons. But no such advances are in sight, and should they develop, countermeasures will probably be found to further hide and protect nuclear forces.

Even if one side could theoretically destroy all the enemy's strategic weapons, massive uncertainty—the key feature of deterrence—would still accompany any nuclear first strike. Except for the dropping of two atomic bombs on nearly defenseless Japanese cities over forty years ago, there is no operational experience with nuclear attack. Yet a successful first strike depends on the correctness of dozens of assumptions, many of which are, as MIT physicist Kosta Tsipis describes, "uncertain," "questionable," and "untestable." Everything must go according to plan the very first time, with nearly 100 percent effectiveness. Tsipis asks, "If we cannot predict the performance of one missile against one silo with the kind of precision the formula for calculation implies, what if anything can we say ahead of time about the outcome of an attack against, say, 1,000 silos with warheads carried by several hundred missiles?"[3]

Vital but untested human and political calculations must also play out as expected. The missile operators of the attacking nation must all faithfully execute the launch orders, knowing what the consequences will be for millions of people, and they must do so with perfect timing. And the enemy, after detecting the strike, must *not* launch its weapons on warning, which would doom even a technically perfect attack.

Mathias Rust, a West German student, dramatically demonstrated how fictional the supposed Soviet first-strike threat is by safely flying not an advanced B-1 or Stealth bomber but a defenseless private plane, with no cloaking devices, all the way to Red Square. He could have leveled Moscow if his plane had carried only one nuclear bomb. As the most conservative nuclear strategist we interviewed readily admitted: "Neither side can ever take away the other side's ability to destroy its cities and industries. If you have to you can do that with bombs in suitcases."[4]

A Soviet first strike against the United States could succeed only if whoever survives to command U.S. forces decides not to destroy the Soviet Union *and* if the many lower-level U.S. commanders with control over nuclear weapons that can strike the Soviet Union decide the same thing. As the Soviets know, the chances of that are remote (and have little to do with the technical characteristics of the weapons anyway). A major study recently concluded that "a large-scale [first-strike] attack on strategic forces would cause so many civilian casualties that it would be difficult to distinguish from a deliberate attack on the population."[5] Hence, vengeful retaliation is almost certain.

Thomas Schelling, perhaps the dean of strategic analysts, observes that "over a protracted period, both sides in a strategic nuclear war would preserve a more than sufficient capacity to do horrendous damage, and neither could hope to gain even a 'bargaining advantage' with any confidence." Most fears of a Soviet first strike, he points out, derive from nothing more than the existence of theoretically vulnerable, fixed land-based missiles in the United States. The remainder of the U.S. deterrent force has acquired a bizarre "vulnerability by association." Schelling knows there is no real first-strike danger to worry about, but he proposes the elimination, unilateral if necessary, of land-based missiles in order to "clean the atmosphere psychologically."

> If we unilaterally abolished our land-based missiles, we would instantly deprive a large part of the Soviet land-based missile force for [*sic*] its raison d'être. It might look to them as if they had much less to preempt. They actually would not, because the U.S. missiles they might have preempted were redundant in the first place. Looking over a seascape inhabited by U.S. submarines and at bombers likely to be launched on warning, they would see, without the smoke and ruins, what would have been left over after they preempted.[6]

In other words, the fear of a Soviet first strike has become so irrational that *reducing* the American deterrent force would help calm it!

Those who warn of an *American* first-strike threat are as misleading as those who warn of a Soviet one, and for the same reasons. When the new generation of U.S. strategic weapons is fully deployed, the United States may in theory pose a greater threat to the Soviet deterrent than the Soviets can pose in return, particularly considering U.S. advantages in antisubmarine warfare. But no matter how many MX and D-5 ballistic missiles, B-1 and Stealth bombers, air-launched cruise missiles, and other weapons the United States builds, striking first still means almost guaranteeing America's own destruction in return.

A major study by analysts at the Brookings Institution and the Lawrence Livermore National Laboratory recently confirmed that neither superpower has even the remotest ability to achieve a disarming first strike against the other, and that neither is in any danger of acquiring such an ability. Based on the superpower arsenals of early 1986, the study was designed to *overestimate* the first-strike capability of each side by a wide margin. The calculations unrealistically assume, for example, that the attacker's forces are *100 percent* reliable and are *all* on full alert for war; that *none* of the victim's forces are at an unusual state of readiness; and that the attacker succeeds in destroying *all* of the enemy missile silos it attacks.[7]

Nevertheless, the study found that "either side as the aggressor would have to face retaliation by at least roughly 3,000 surviving warheads." That is enough to utterly destroy either society many times over. In fact it is doubtful, as the study notes, that either side even has 3,000 targets its opponent's military would consider worth retaliating against; beyond 1,500–2,000 targets, "the marginal contribution to the overall effect would be so small that a prudent military command would presumably choose to preserve any remaining weapons rather than to expend them in redundant and unnecessary retaliation." An aggressor would also have to assume that after detecting the attack, the victim would launch at least some missiles before they were destroyed, an action that would increase the retaliatory threat even further. No numerical change in superpower forces or technological development now on the horizon would greatly change the threat of cataclysmic retaliation following a first-strike attempt. And as we will see in Chapter 9, even reductions in the superpower arsenals far greater than any now contemplated likewise would change little about the feasibility of a first strike. As George Kennan writes, "The fact is that there are today, in this threatened world of ours, no 'windows' of vulnerability that could be opened or closed. We are vulnerable—totally vulnerable. There is no way that could be changed."[8]

Though the public debate focuses on so-called first-strike weapons, specialists warn of other technical factors that supposedly produce additional "incentives" for launching nuclear weapons first. The current fashion in strategic analysis is to warn of the dangers of "decapitation"—that is, attacking the enemy's nuclear command and control network. Though as we have seen, neither side can even begin to destroy enough of the other's missiles and bombers to significantly affect its military capabilities, either side could quickly devastate the other's system for commanding and controlling those forces. A few high-altitude nuclear bursts, for example, could knock out radar and communications through electromagnetic pulse and other effects. Shortly thereafter direct attacks on ground-based radar and communications facilities could finish the job. Attacks on Washington and Moscow could kill national leaders and destroy command centers such as the Pentagon. Most other command centers are equally vulnerable, and though both sides have alternative command arrangements, including airborne command posts and hardened communications devices, none would likely survive long in the event of a large-scale strategic war.[9]

Many scholars argue that in a crisis the fear of sudden decapitation could give either superpower a reason to launch first in an effort to destroy the enemy's command system while its own is still intact. John Steinbruner, for example, writes that the vulnerability of command and control "is probably the single most important and dangerous . . . incentive" to launch first, and that modernizing the command system could reduce that incentive.[10] Though not strictly an instance of weaponitis (since command and control systems are not technically weapons), that view is simply another version of the fallacy that technological factors can significantly stabilize or destabilize the nuclear stalemate.

Obviously, trying to decapitate the enemy is no less foolishly suicidal than trying to disarm it. As seventeen highly regarded strategic analysts (including Steinbruner) write, even after a completely successful surprise decapitation attack

> there is every reason to believe that there would be retaliation. . . . The U.S. government has often stated that provisions are always in place that guarantee large-scale retaliation under the most dire of circumstances. Given the vast forces (primarily those at sea) that would survive any attack on command, the possibility of predelegated contingency arrangements, the possible existence of high-level command elements and communications links of which the attacker has no knowledge, and the multitude of communication channels that are likely to survive or that could be established, these official statements should be taken at face value by a potential attacker.[11]

Even if *no* command channels survived, at least some of the many commanders with nuclear weapons at their disposal would almost certainly launch their weapons on their own authority. As Frank von Hippel asks, "What do Soviet leaders think U.S. submarine crews are going to do if they learn that the United States has been destroyed? Go to Tahiti and retire?" In fact, isolated commanders acting chaotically, without central coordination, might well inflict far *greater* damage on an attacker than an intact central command would order. Retaliation following a decapitating first strike could "actually result in the 'assured destruction' of Soviet society—in contrast to the less apocalyptic retaliatory options that are likely to receive serious consideration in a 'deliberate' centrally coordinated response following full assessment of an attack." The same applies in reverse; Soviet leaders, like their American counterparts, need not fear that an American decapitation attack would rob them of the ability to retaliate in kind.[12] No plausible development in the arms race could make decapitation or indeed any first strike other than what it is today: suicide.

## SUICIDE FOR FEAR OF DEATH

Still, specialists claim that in at least one extreme circumstance a first strike might logically be considered a rational move: when one side feels that nuclear war is inevitable no matter what steps it takes. If a nuclear war cannot be avoided, the argument goes, then preemption—striking before the enemy does—might be the best way to fight it. Richard K.

Betts argues that "there are few plausible circumstances in which striking first could seem to make sense—at least for the superpowers. . . . when one believes the enemy is about to strike . . . is the only situation in which the initiator would have reason to believe that starting a nuclear war could cost less than waiting to try other options."[13]

But as Stansfield Turner writes, "I cannot imagine a Director of Central Intelligence [Turner's former position] ever having anything approaching 100 percent confidence in his prediction that the Russians were truly going to attack. The President would be faced with a choice between the total probability of nuclear destruction" if he launched a preemptive strike that brought down the almost inevitable Soviet response and "some lesser probability" if he waited. Richard Ned Lebow, in an unusually sensible discussion of first strike, agrees that "the judgment that the other superpower is about to strike can never be made with full certainty. . . . the side that strikes first risks making its fear of nuclear war unnecessarily self-fulfilling. . . . preemption is an altogether irrational act."[14]

Preemption is, in Bismarck's phrase, "suicide for fear of death." No arms control treaties are needed to ensure that preemption is suicidal and totally irrational, and this reality cannot be altered by any plausible development in the arms race. It is an existential fact of life in the nuclear age.[15]

## ITCHY FINGERS ON THE BUTTON

Finally, we must consider perhaps the most horrifying scenario: One side receives evidence that its enemy has *already* launched a nuclear attack. Satellites report missile launchings, radars warn of missiles en route, and—in the worst case—leaders receive reports of actual nuclear explosions. In that event, if in no other, many observers contend, the hardware deployed by each superpower could prove fateful—strongly influencing whether the side receiving the warning of attack would make a hasty decision to launch its own strategic nuclear weapons.

The seventeen strategic analysts quoted earlier, for example, state that because of the extreme vulnerability of nuclear command and control, the United States has been "forced" to seriously consider "a prompt launch" of its strategic forces (very "prompt," within several minutes) should it receive warning of a Soviet attack in progress. Why? Because waiting until the attack is over "runs the risk that the command system may not have sufficient coherence . . . to execute a *coordinated* counterattack."[16] That is, even if national leaders survived, they would probably not be able to communicate with and control their forces well enough to determine precisely what *kind* of retaliation took place—for example, how many weapons were fired and where they were aimed. Devastating retaliation would, as we saw, almost certainly take place; but it would not be under firm central control. To ensure that retaliation occurs *under* central control, the analysts contend, it should perhaps be ordered almost immediately after warning of an enemy attack.

The seventeen analysts recognize that if leaders decide to launch hastily, they would probably feel strong pressures to do so massively, with "thousands of nuclear warheads." Leaders would not receive reliable estimates of the extent and nature of the attack in the few minutes available for decision before they are killed or control otherwise disintegrates; "too much would be at stake to give the attacker the benefit of the doubt." Furthermore, because of "the limited endurance of the backup command network, decision makers could not expect to employ withheld forces in a coordinated fashion. In all likelihood, the selection of a small [attack] option would mean that all other strategic options would be relinquished forever . . . [which] would encourage selection of a major attack option."[17]

In discussing prompt launch, like so many other questions, so-called experts dispense dangerously misleading analyses that fly in the face of common sense. The danger of losing central control over nuclear forces is hardly a rational reason to launch the missiles hastily, virtually *guaranteeing* devastation on a planetary scale on the basis of *warning* of an enemy attack. Such a warning, of course, can always be mistaken or misleading, even after indications that nuclear explosions have actually occurred. Conceivably, technical malfunctions could produce a warning of attack when no attack was in fact occurring. A limited attack—perhaps even accidental—could also be misinterpreted as a full-scale first strike in the few frenzied minutes available for analysis. As Lebow points out, prompt launch demands

> an organizational capacity to make an almost instantaneous decision to respond to attack coupled with an entirely foolproof mechanism to safeguard against false alerts. Both requirements are unrealistic. There is no way of guaranteeing that a complex system of sensors, computers, related software, and human operators can function error-free all of the time. . . . A hairtrigger—and this is a fair description of quick-launch options—would multiply the probability of error by several orders of magnitude [that is, a hundred times].[18]

To fire thousands of strategic nuclear weapons suddenly because one *thinks* the enemy has launched a major attack would be the greatest war crime in history, and perhaps the last one. It would also be totally irrational, even from the most amoral, self-interested point of view, particularly since, as we saw, devastating retaliation is virtually assured *no matter what* leaders decide.

The complex analyses of first strike by the right, the left, and the professional experts have only obscured the simple truth. No state *ever* has the slightest rational incentive to launch strategic nuclear weapons first or in haste, and certainly not before confirming *beyond any doubt* the explosion of many nuclear warheads on its territory. Even in that instance elementary morality would dictate that retaliation be withheld, since it would be little more than the mass murder of innocents—on a scale that would make the Nazi slaughter seem modest by comparison—with no prospect of accomplishing any legitimate goal. Of course the *threat* of retaliation may be important to mutual deterrence and the prevention of nuclear war; but that threat, as we emphasize throughout this book, is existential, inherent in the existence of the weapons. The threat to launch *first* or to launch *hastily* is not important to deterrence. Does it matter if an attacker is destroyed minutes, hours, days, or even weeks after it launches its missiles? Morton Halperin gives much wiser advice: *avoid* launching nuclear weapons suddenly, perhaps by making it physically impossible, while maintaining the option of retaliating after considerable time for reflection and perhaps negotiation.[19]

The best way to reduce the danger of a first strike is to encourage wider recognition that launching nuclear missiles first or launching them precipitously is insane *regardless* of the hardware on either side. In addition, our overwhelming concern should be to avoid the extreme *political* conditions in which Soviet or American leaders could actually believe that their counterparts had decided to launch World War III—when leaders, seduced by the prevailing nuclear nonsense, might make a split-second decision that could terminate human civilization. In the nuclear age, the desperate feeling that the ax is about to fall is the key factor—not the size, speed, or accuracy of the ax.

## CHAPTER THREE

# What About Credibility and the Firebreak?

| | |
|---|---|
| SENATOR GLENN: | I get lost in what is credible and not credible. This whole thing gets so incredible when you consider wiping out whole nations, it is difficult to establish credibility. |
| SECRETARY [OF DEFENSE] BROWN: | That is why we sound a little crazy when we talk about it. |

—*Senate Committee on Foreign Relations,*
Hearing on Presidential Directive 59,
*September 16, 1980*

## NUCLEAR CREDIBILITY: DO WE NEED OR WANT IT?

During the brief American nuclear monopoly after World War II, many believed that the United States might use nuclear weapons again in a war or political crisis. No country could retaliate, and the 1945 nuclear attacks on two defenseless Japanese cities as well as the earlier killing of hundreds of thousands of German and Japanese city dwellers with conventional weapons showed that moral considerations might not inhibit American actions.

As the Soviets developed their own nuclear arsenal, however, American strategists worried that the fear of retaliation could reduce the United States to a hobbled nuclear giant. They became obsessed with what was politely termed the "credibility" problem: how to make the world believe that American nuclear threats might actually be carried out even though the result could be the destruction of the United States. The belief that special weapons are required to solve this problem is one of the major driving forces of, and rationales for, the nuclear arms race.

In most cases, however, credibility is not problematic and does not in fact require special weapons. Should any country launch a general nuclear attack on the United States, few have ever doubted that the U.S. military would do its best to return fire in kind, regardless of the weapons available. There would be little left to lose. Here the credibility problem reduces to the technical matter of whether retaliation would be

29

possible in the rubble and chaos. It would (as we argued in Chapter 2), if only through the vengeance of surviving nuclear weapons commanders on land or at sea. Even a *limited* Soviet first strike on the United States would probably kill millions of Americans; the United States would surely retaliate and would have many credible options for doing so regardless of the details of its nuclear arsenal.

No great credibility problem attends the defense of Western Europe, either. The specter of a Soviet blitzkrieg is by now, certainly, largely mythical, and in any case no new or special weapons are necessary to deter it. The Soviet Union has little to gain and everything to lose by invading its powerful trade and financial partners in Western Europe. The Soviets have enough trouble controlling their Eastern European satellites, such as Poland, and could not even conquer Afghanistan. NATO has consistently outspent the Warsaw Pact, enjoys a large technological lead, and would occupy the favorable position of defender in the event of a Soviet invasion. The Warsaw Pact's much ballyhooed numerical superiority in tanks and troops means little when readiness, technology, and alliance loyalty are considered.[1]

Besides, invading Soviet generals would face more than one thousand European-owned nuclear warheads, which are slated for major expansion and improvement over the next few years. Many in the United States dismiss the comparatively small French and British nuclear arsenals. That is pure weaponitis. No country actually faced with the possibility of a nuclear attack by France or Britain (or any other nuclear power) would take the prospect lightly. And, as Earl Ravenal observes, "even the whiff of American nuclear retaliation is probably enough to keep the Soviet Union from invading Western Europe."[2]

The United States, however, wants its nuclear weapons not only to defend itself and its European allies but also to project American power into the Third World. One example, among the many discussed in Chapter 6, is the 1973 U.S. nuclear alert during the Arab-Israeli war. Nuclear threats in the Third World may indeed pose credibility problems. But should we seek to make such threats more believable? Obviously, even a noble goal, such as defending a small country against aggression, does not justify endangering the planet. And, as we will argue, U.S. motives have often been less than noble—as in 1973, when Henry Kissinger *created* a crisis by giving Israel permission to violate the cease-fire he had just negotiated in Moscow.

Special efforts to enhance nuclear credibility seem to us either unnecessary or illegitimate. But for the purpose of argument let us grant that there is a real credibility problem and see if special weapons can solve it.

## RATIONALIZING THE IRRATIONAL

Allan S. Krass and Matthew Goodman write that for nuclear threats to be credible, "the capability and the will must exist for carrying them out. . . . Nuclear threats cannot be a rational tool of policy unless nuclear war itself is also rational" or at least appears to be. "This defines the problem that nuclear strategists have been trying to solve since 1945: *can nuclear war be made rational?*" Colin Gray, among others, argues that only when "victory is possible" will American nuclear threats appear rational and believable, because unless the U.S. homeland is defensible, carrying out the threats would amount to suicide. With the right weapons (strategic defenses and missiles aimed at the Soviet state apparatus), he contends, the United States could survive all-out nuclear war and hence credibly threaten to use nuclear weapons.[3]

Other observers, who recognize that victory is in fact impossible, seek only, as Earl Ravenal explains, to "limit damage to 'tolerable' levels of casualties and destruction . . . so an American president can persuade others that he would risk an attack on the U.S. homeland, or that he could face down a threat to attack that homeland."[4] But of course the damage cannot be made tolerable. No matter what weapons each side fields, large-scale nuclear war will probably destroy both superpowers and much more; hence threats to unleash it are altogether irrational and, in all but the most dire circumstances, incredible. Other strategists thus contend that the only way to make nuclear threats believable is to threaten action that is *not* suicidal—that is, to threaten a very *limited* nuclear war and to suggest that it can be kept limited. In the words of Robert Osgood, credibility "requires that the means of deterrence be proportionate to the objectives at stake."[5]

One approach to enhancing "limited nuclear options," as former secretary of defense James Schlesinger called the doctrine, is to reduce the yields of the weapons so they do less damage. Another approach is to deliver them more accurately, which minimizes collateral damage and permits the use of smaller-yield warheads. One can redesign warheads to reduce collateral damage—the essential purpose of the neutron bomb. One can aim weapons away from population centers, and so on. But because no one knows how to keep nuclear war limited, credibility remains as problematic as ever. There is, however, another way to achieve it.

## THE DOOMSDAY MACHINE

In the black-comedy film *Dr. Strangelove,* a Soviet "doomsday machine" automatically destroys the planet when American nuclear bombers, launched by a deranged general, attack the Soviet Union. That neatly solves the credibility problem. Of course, as far as we know, there is no isolated contraption consisting of nuclear weapons wired to an automatic tripping device. But according to Paul Bracken and others, current nuclear command and control procedures may have created, in effect, a doomsday machine.

In Europe, Bracken contends, "the NATO strategy of relying on nuclear weapons is politically and militarily credible because the governing command structure is so unstable and accident-prone that national leaders would exercise little practical control over it in wartime." That is, the nuclear command structure and the weapons it controls are not so much "designed to gain battlefield advantage through attrition of enemy forces" as to "enforce deterrence by necessitating that any war be nuclear." Nuclear weapons are thoroughly integrated into NATO (and Warsaw Pact) conventional forces, including, by one estimate, several hundred nuclear land mines, over one thousand nuclear artillery rounds, several thousand surface-to-surface missile warheads, several thousand more nuclear bombs and missiles for delivery by aircraft, hundreds of surface-to-air missiles and aircraft-launched antisubmarine weapons, and, for a while, Pershing II and cruise missiles.[6] U.S. naval forces in the area are assumed to carry enormous tactical nuclear arsenals as well. Many individual fighting units, which could easily become isolated in wartime, are equipped to fire nuclear weapons.

In peacetime most nuclear warheads are stored at special sites to avoid accidental or unauthorized use. But because the stored weapons are vulnerable to preemptive destruction, during the development of a crisis "there are likely to be strong pressures within NATO for a general release of weapons to NATO military forces assigned the task of using these weapons," spreading six thousand nuclear warheads "from the North Sea to the plateaus of eastern Turkey." Since the Soviets could paralyze the command system, thus preventing the transmission of the codes needed to fire NATO's weapons, Bracken believes that "a strong pressure exists to release any needed codes at the same time that the weapons are dispersed from their storage sites."[7] Field commanders could then launch nuclear weapons on their own initiative early in a conflict. The same is presumably true of Soviet nuclear forces.

Compounding the problem, a number of nations in addition to the United States could fire NATO nuclear weapons in their possession without the U.S. approval theoretically required. Indeed, during the 1974 Turkish invasion of Cyprus, the Pentagon prepared U.S. marines for a helicopter assault on nuclear warhead storage facilities in Turkey, if necessary, to ensure U.S. physical control over the weapons. The warheads normally stored aboard quick-alert aircraft in Greece and Turkey were removed to safe storage. In wartime the United States might be unable to hold on to nuclear weapons deployed on allied territory if local forces were determined to seize them. And if the warheads were intentionally dispersed, it might be impossible to get them back where they belonged.

Under mutual high-alert conditions, as Bracken warns, "a single Turkish pilot could trigger World War III, as could a Soviet naval officer in charge of a Shaddock cruise missile." What we have is "a strategy of deterrence by massive duplication of a nuclear hair trigger."[8]

Others besides Bracken have noticed the doomsday threat, and it is by no means limited to Europe. In a 1985 review of "Who Could Start Nuclear War," the widely respected Center for Defense Information (CDI), composed largely of former high-ranking American military officers, observes:

> There is a wide discrepancy between those people, primarily government officials, who have the *authority to order* a nuclear attack, and those persons, primarily military officers, who actually have the *physical capability* to fire nuclear weapons. . . . During a military crisis, many people in the U.S., U.S.S.R., Britain, France, and China will likely have the authority to order a nuclear attack or the physical capability to start a nuclear war. In a surprise attack, government officials in the U.S. and U.S.S.R. may not have time to decide whether to order a retaliatory nuclear strike before their own nuclear forces are hit and they themselves are killed. Even if the order to retaliate is given by the political leadership, destruction of communications channels might impede transfer of the launch order to the appropriate military commanders. Prudent military doctrine suggests, therefore, that each nuclear nation has developed procedures for the transfer of authority to release nuclear weapons to others below the highest government officials.

As CDI notes, "commanders would have the tendency to issue [the codes needed to unlock nuclear weapons] early, before an actual attack against civilian and military officials occurred. Once unlocked, the

weapons would be ready for use by lower level military personnel."
Moreover, "there are no [electronic locks on] any of the U.S. sea-
launched nuclear weapons," which can be carried by 85 percent of U.S.
ships. "A captain and several officers on any of the U.S.'s 37 ballistic
missile submarines could launch their nuclear weapons at any time
without receiving permission from the President or NCA [National
Command Authority]."[9] So could the crew of other nuclear-armed U.S.
Navy ships, including the aircraft carriers that are routinely rushed to
Third World crises and war zones.

Another group of respected mainstream analysts notes that "the U.S.
nuclear weapons deployed in densely populated Europe are numerous,
diverse (both in warheads and delivery systems), and integrated into
conventional units." They conclude that "negative control is therefore
complex and difficult"—where "negative control" means "preventing
the unauthorized or accidental use of nuclear weapons." They add that
what Bracken terms the "regional doomsday machine" in Europe is
really a planetary doomsday machine: "Because the loss of $C^3I$ systems
in the theater would undoubtedly affect strategic operations on both
sides—and because theater war could easily spill over onto Soviet territory—rapid escalation to strategic conflict must be considered a *very
likely* possibility if deterrence were to fail."[10]

To cite only one more study, Barry Posen suggests another reason to
suppose that a doomsday machine of some kind exists. He observes that
Soviet strategic nuclear forces, both on land and at sea, would probably
be attacked, or would justifiably fear attack, by NATO forces during a
large-scale conventional war in Europe, regardless of whether NATO
intended such attacks. For example, whereas U.S. strategic-missile submarines hide in the open sea for protection, two-thirds of the Soviet
Union's strategic submarines are believed to be stationed in a defended
sanctuary in the Barents Sea, protected by two-thirds of the Soviet nu-
clear-powered attack submarines as well as by their best surface vessels.
In the event of a conventional war, NATO would almost certainly hunt
down Soviet attack submarines there to protect vital sea-lanes. Soviet
attack subs are so difficult to distinguish from Soviet strategic nuclear
missile subs that some of both types would probably be sunk by NATO
forces. The U.S. Navy might deliberately attack strategic subs in any
case since, in addition to long-range ballistic missiles, they carry torpedoes and mines capable of sinking NATO attack subs and surface ships.
Also, the chance to degrade Soviet nuclear capabilities under the cover of
conventional operations might be too great to resist. As the Navy's direc-

tor of Command, Control, and Communications once acknowledged, "In a conventional war all submarines are submarines. They are all fair game." Posen comments: "The Soviet Union could see . . . sinkings [of nuclear missile submarines] as a deliberate attempt to degrade the Soviet Union's *nuclear* retaliatory capability rather than as 'accidents' to be accepted with equanimity."[11] In the context of a growing conventional threat to their other nuclear forces as well, the Soviets might be tempted to use nuclear weapons in a desperate attempt to stop the war and save their nuclear deterrent.

According to Posen, part of the doomsday problem results from reckless NATO conventional war plans, which grant little or no attention to the avoidance of inadvertent nuclear escalation. Those plans are perhaps one more element of a *deliberate* strategy to ensure that any war must be nuclear, thereby shoring up the credibility of the nuclear deterrent. As Posen writes, "The 'threat to lose control' is an important element of NATO's flexible response strategy."[12]

THE FIREBREAK

Before examining whether the arms race really matters much to nuclear credibility, we must mention the nuclear "firebreak," the conceptual prism through which much of the arms control community and the peace movement view the issues under discussion. Michael Klare writes:

> The only existing barrier to . . . escalation [from conventional to nuclear war] is a moral and psychological firebreak—the widely shared perception that nuclear weapons are different from all other weapons, and that their use could unleash a chain reaction of strikes and counterstrikes leading to total world destruction. So long as this firebreak remains wide and secure, so long as the distinction between nuclear and conventional arms remains sharp and unambiguous, potential combatants will retain an incentive to stay on the non-nuclear side of the divide, no matter what their prospects are on the conventional battlefield. But if that distinction were to fade or disappear, the inhibition against nuclear escalation would decrease and the risk of global annihilation would skyrocket.

The conventional/nuclear firebreak is crucial, because as Alain Enthoven observed in 1965, "There does not appear to be another easily recognizable limitation on weapons—no other obvious 'firebreak'—all the way up the destructive spectrum to large-scale thermonuclear war."[13]

Klare contends that the superpowers are eroding the firebreak from both ends. Near-nuclear conventional weapons such as precision-guided munitions, cluster bombs, and new explosive technologies "could possess a destructive potential comparable to that of low-yield nuclear munitions." Low-yield tactical nuclear weapons are simultaneously reducing the destructiveness of nuclear warheads to near-conventional levels. The neutron bomb behaves even more conventionally, killing soldiers but minimizing collateral damage. Dual-capable weapons span the firebreak by permitting the same weapon to shift easily between conventional and nuclear ammunition. For example, tactical aircraft (such as F-4, F-15, F-16, A-6, A-7) can carry both kinds of bombs, tactical missiles (such as Lance, Terrier, ASROC, Tomahawk, Nike-Hercules) can fire both kinds of warheads, and artillery pieces (such as 155-millimeter and 8-inch guns) can lob both kinds of shells. As U.S. Army General Louis Wagner told Congress in 1980, "We use the same troops and we have the same cannons available to do the conventional and nuclear job." Klare believes that the growing deployment of such weapons "diminishes the problems involved in moving from the conventional to the nuclear realm—thus narrowing the 'pause' or discontinuity that separates one from the other."[14] Similar trends can be observed in Soviet forces.

By now almost all types of conventional weapons—from the giant strategic bomber to the lowly land mine—have nuclear counterparts. The military can wipe out tanks and soldiers, sink ships, shoot down planes, interdict supplies, disrupt command, and do almost everything else with nuclear weapons. Tactical nuclear weapons systems are generally deployed with or made available to U.S. conventional military forces wherever they are based on land or at sea, effectively rendering the entire U.S. military dual-capable.

THE TWO SIDES OF THE COIN

Credibility and the firebreak both come down to the same question: Can nuclear war be made to resemble conventional war? Conventional war, even with modern weapons, is *limited;* it is unlikely to end up in the complete physical destruction of either side.[15] The question is whether nuclear war can be limited in this way, whether the gulf that separates it from conventional war can be narrowed.

If so, then nuclear threats, like conventional ones, can be credible, for they are not threats to commit suicide. And the firebreak will be narrow, because nuclear and conventional war will not seem so different. Conversely, if the gulf between the two kinds of war stays wide, then nuclear threats lack plausibility unless a state's survival is threatened, and the firebreak will be vast and clear. To put it another way, narrowing the firebreak enhances nuclear credibility. Widening it undercuts nuclear threats. The nuclear weapons systems that some advocate to boost credibility are precisely the same ones that others criticize for eroding the firebreak (e.g., the neutron bomb).

The debate about such matters, then, does not involve fundamentally different ways of looking at nuclear war. The main point of contention is *values*. Those concerned about credibility want to have a real non-suicidal option for starting nuclear war so they can plausibly threaten it not only to strengthen deterrence but also to advance American military and political goals. Those concerned about the firebreak want to make it as difficult as possible for anyone to start a nuclear war and do not want states threatening such a war for political purposes. Both groups are discussing the same thing: the width of the gulf between conventional and nuclear war. One group wants it narrow, the other wide.

## SUICIDE ON THE INSTALLMENT PLAN

But the gulf between conventional and nuclear war cannot in fact be made much narrower *or* wider than it already is. Hence, neither a continued arms race nor further arms control—with an important exception—can much affect the level of nuclear credibility or the width of the nuclear firebreak. Credibility is inherently questionable and the firebreak inherently wide because nuclear war *is* different from conventional war. The gulf between the two is intrinsically huge since any extensive use of nuclear weapons would be, as McGeorge Bundy said, "a disaster beyond history."[16] Even a very limited nuclear attack would inescapably risk escalation to total annihilation, whereas the use of conventional weapons does not.

As we have said, no one has devised a way to control a nuclear war and thereby confidently prevent escalation to large-scale nuclear exchanges, and no one has found a way to defend society against such exchanges.[17] If the arms race or arms control ever *do* produce a way to reliably control escalation or defend society—both remote prospects—then the firebreak *might* narrow and the credibility of nuclear threats *might* increase (although probably not by very much, given the uncertainties and the destructiveness of nuclear weapons).

We consider the prospects for a defense against nuclear weapons in Chapter 5. As for controlling escalation, "is it realistic to expect that a

nuclear war could be limited to the detonation of tens or even hundreds
of nuclear weapons, even though each side would have tens of thousands of weapons remaining available for use?" As we have seen, "The
answer is clearly no," because, as former secretary of defense Robert
McNamara explains, expecting nuclear war to remain limited

> requires the assumption that even though the initial strikes would have in-
> flicted large-scale casualties and damage to both sides, one or the other—
> feeling disadvantaged—would give in. But under such circumstances, lead-
> ers on both sides would be under unimaginable pressure to avenge their
> losses and secure the interests being challenged. And each would fear that the
> opponent might launch a larger attack at any moment. Moreover, they
> would both be operating with only partial information because of the disrup-
> tion to communications caused by the chaos of the battlefield (to say nothing
> of possible strikes against communications facilities). Under such conditions,
> it is highly likely that rather than surrender, each side would launch a larger
> attack, hoping this step would bring the action to a halt by causing the oppo-
> nent to capitulate. . . . It is inconceivable to me, as it has been to others who
> have studied the matter, that "limited" nuclear wars would remain limited—
> any decision to use nuclear weapons would imply a high probability of the
> same cataclysmic consequences as a total nuclear exchange.[18]

Klaus Knorr agrees that "a large risk of continuous escalation, intentional or inadvertent, cannot be excluded once nuclear exchanges begin.
Initiation means accepting that risk of unwanted escalation." As Leon
Wieseltier writes, "The worst may not happen first, but it may happen
fast." General David C. Jones, former chairman of the Joint Chiefs of
Staff, concurs: "I don't see much of a chance of nuclear war being limited or protracted."[19]

Unless someone finds a defense or a means of control, nuclear war
cannot be made to resemble conventional war. It cannot be made rational in any sense. No amount of weaponry can allow a nation to win a
nuclear war, to fight one like a conventional war, or to limit damage. It
*is* possible, as the flexibility advocates argue, to start a nuclear war without *immediately* destroying everything. But that ability has always been
available to any substantial nuclear power. One always has the option
of firing fewer or more weapons, and relatively low yield weapons have
been available from the beginning. The bomb that destroyed Hiroshima
yielded only about 12–15 kilotons, very little by today's standards.
During the 1950s the United States deployed warheads with yields in
the low kiloton and even subkiloton range, easily small enough to provide limited and flexible nuclear options.[20]

And the real issue is not how the war *begins* but how it ultimately will *end*. As Desmond Ball concludes,

Given the impossibility of developing capabilities for controlling a nuclear exchange through to favourable termination, or of removing the residual uncertainties relating to controlling the large-scale use of nuclear weapons, *it is likely that decision-makers would be deterred from initiating nuclear strikes no matter how limited or selective the options available to them.* The use of nuclear weapons for controlled escalation is therefore no less difficult to envisage than the use of nuclear weapons for massive retaliation.

Although, as we shall see, decision makers may in fact initiate nuclear strikes, Ball is surely correct to insist that for practical purposes limited nuclear options differ little from unlimited ones and are only marginally more credible. The fundamental problem that has dogged credibility— the suicidal nature of any threat to start nuclear war—remains. In brief, "the problem of making nuclear war rational has no solution at all."[21]

Those worried about the firebreak also exaggerate the consequences of changes in weapons. With or without fuel-air munitions and neutron weapons, any decision to go to nuclear war is unmistakably a decision to court mutual suicide. True, Ronald Reagan once proclaimed the neutron bomb "conventional." But, as we discussed in Chapter 4, that does not necessarily mean he would underestimate the consequences of actually using it in a war with the Soviet Union. In any case, as Klare emphasizes, the firebreak is ultimately psychological and moral. Whatever technological developments occur, it could become stronger or weaker depending on how leaders think about nuclear war. Long before the neutron bomb was developed, American leaders were publicly calling nuclear weapons conventional to lend credibility to nuclear threats. In 1955 President Eisenhower said that he saw no reason "why [nuclear weapons] shouldn't be used just exactly as you would use a bullet or anything else." Richard Nixon, then vice president, added that "tactical atomic weapons are now conventional and will be used against the targets of any aggressive force."[22] The answer to such statements now, as in the 1950s, is to insist on the truth—nuclear war is inherently irrational, uncontrollable, and unwinnable—and to ensure that civilian and military leaders recognize it.

The only technical factors that can greatly alter credibility and the firebreak are those that are responsible for the doomsday machine: (1) the fragility of nuclear command and control and (2) the presence of nuclear weapons at the front lines in Europe, Korea, and the Middle

East, at sea, and elsewhere. As we have seen, not much can be done about the fragility of command and control. As Ball's painstaking study concludes, "Command-and-control systems are inherently relatively vulnerable. . . . The allocation of further resources to improving the survivability and endurance of the strategic command-and-control capabilities cannot substantially alter this situation. . . . The capability to exercise strict control and co-ordination would inevitably be lost relatively early in a nuclear exchange." In Europe, another group of experts adds that "conditions . . . are not congenial to major improvements in $C^3I$."[23] And whatever can be done has less to do with the race to build or control weapons—the focus of the nuclear debate—than with the *organization* of the command system. For example, NATO presumably could make it much more difficult for field commanders to obtain the authority and technical ability needed to detonate nuclear warheads in the event of a war in Europe.

Much more can be done about the way nuclear weapons systems are scattered around the globe. Although modest changes would not make much difference, radical changes could. If NATO units guarding the central European front did not have nuclear weapons, then their involvement in conventional battles could not erupt spontaneously into nuclear war. If American aircraft carriers were not dual-capable, or if they were not sent into war zones, their commanders could not ignite a cataclysm. A thorough removal of tactical nuclear weapons from flash points for conventional war could significantly widen the nuclear firebreak, though possibly at the expense of credibility. Ironically, this one aspect of superpower arms control that bears directly on the risk of global holocaust has received almost no attention during the public debate in the United States.

## THE POLITICS OF CREDIBILITY

The debates about credibility and the firebreak, like first strike, have been suffused with weaponitis. The most important factors, as usual, are not technological but political. States will consider crossing the nuclear firebreak, and their threats to do so will be taken seriously, so far as (1) they believe vital interests are at stake and (2) they do not mind risking the lives of hundreds of millions of people to pursue those interests. As Blechman and Hart observe,

> Only in certain places and very special circumstances might attempts to manipulate the risk of nuclear war be credible. For the United States, these

probably include military contingencies involving Europe, Japan, and Korea, for which a willingness to make first use of nuclear weapons has long been articulated policy. Elsewhere, such U.S. threats probably would only be credible in the Middle East (including the Persian Gulf), and only when taken in response to Soviet, not local, actions. For the Soviet Union, military challenges to its position in Eastern Europe would no doubt trigger credible threats of nuclear war, as would a serious military confrontation with China in Central Asia. In all other places, Soviet nuclear threats would only be credible in the context of direct military confrontation with the United States and, even then, would depend on the circumstances which precipitated the conflict to begin with.[24]

The historical record shows that confrontation actually can erupt in surprising places because the definition of vital interests is not straightforward. Witness the willingness of both superpowers to go to the brink over Soviet nuclear weapons in Cuba, which, as we show in Chapter 8, had little military significance for either side. Vital interests are subjectively defined by the people who run governments. In the case of Cuba, as in many others, the true vital interest judged worthy of defense at any cost was not something concrete, such as territory or natural resources, but the *perception of resolve*—the state's reputation for standing firm when challenged. Many accept the U.S. government's long-standing contention that any capitulation on a matter that has been declared important compromises all future commitments and invites further challenges to the government's power. On such a theory, *anything* can be instantaneously transformed into a "vital interest" by nothing more than a *statement* that it is one.

Blechman and Hart conclude from the 1973 Middle Eastern nuclear crisis that

> within fairly permissive boundaries, the effectiveness of nuclear threats may not be influenced by the *aggregate* strategic balance. The threat is not so much to go deliberately to nuclear war as it is to participate and persevere in an escalatory process, even though it might *result* in nuclear war. Accordingly, the credibility of the threat would not, from a first approximation, be influenced by calculations of just how badly off each side would be if the escalation ran its course, presuming, of course, that both sides had maintained substantial forces. Its credibility would depend on the ability of the nation making the threat to demonstrate convincingly that it perceived such vital interests at stake that it was even prepared to fight a nuclear war, if that became necessary.

The numbers and performance characteristics of the weapons are again irrelevant. Indeed, beyond promoting the doomsday effect, particular

weapons are at most only symbolic contributors to images of resolve.
An Aspen Institute report observes:

> Deployments of U.S. nuclear weapons in and around Europe—designed for
> tactical and intermediate-range missions—serve a preeminently political
> purpose: to symbolize the American commitment to the defense of Europe,
> and to demonstrate in a concrete way that any large-scale Soviet attack
> would risk escalation. In large measure, then, their contribution to security
> stems simply from their presence. Their ostensible military role—to bolster
> NATO's conventional insufficiencies—remains open to debate, since Soviet
> nuclear capabilities in the region ensure that any use of nuclear weapons by
> the West could also risk the destruction of Europe.

Indeed, former assistant secretary of state Richard Burt, responding to a
possible delay in Pershing II deployment because of technical problems,
reportedly said, "We don't care if the goddamn things work or not. . . .
What we care about is getting them in."[25] We find it remarkable that
both supporters and opponents continued to debate the range, speed,
and accuracy of this missile after Burt's statement.

No matter what interests are at stake, morally responsible leaders
could never credibly threaten the existence of life on a planetary scale.
At the other extreme, viciousness or insanity undoubtedly promote nuclear credibility. Schelling speaks of "the rationality of irrationality," the
enhancement of credibility that comes from instability and unpredic-
tability. Nixon spoke more bluntly of the "madman theory."[26]

The United States, the Soviet Union, and other nuclear powers have
long been governed by men and women prepared to endanger the planet
periodically for the goals of their states. Consequently, to use Schelling's
phrase, a "competition in risk taking" has become the way to resolve
the most extreme conflicts between them. Each side takes actions that
*could,* through a chain of ensuing events, lead to the destruction of
everything. As in the teenage game of chicken—where two cars speed
toward each other until one driver "chickens out" and turns away—
states ratchet up the chances of disaster until one saves itself, and the
planet, by giving in. The outcome is determined not by the meaningless
details of the arsenals that would bring about the holocaust but by the
leaders' willingness to run the ultimate risk.


THE PARADOX OF DETERRENCE

What if a development in the arms race someday does what now
seems impossible: truly narrows the gulf that separates conventional

from nuclear war? The credibility of nuclear threats would increase; hence potential combatants would be more cautious about starting a conventional crisis or war. But the firebreak would narrow; hence if war broke out anyway, the use of nuclear weapons would be more tempting. The net effect on the risk of nuclear war is unclear.

For example, assume (falsely, in our view) that if deployed in Europe the neutron bomb would significantly lower the nuclear threshold, increasing the credibility of NATO's threat to use nuclear weapons by decreasing the firebreak between conventional and nuclear war. If the Soviet Union contemplated an invasion of Western Europe, it would presumably be deterred by the increased credibility of NATO's nuclear guarantee, as theorists from the nuclear right and mainstream often argue. But should the Soviets decide to invade anyway, the existence of the neutron bomb would accomplish what much of the nuclear left and the arms control community say it would, namely, increase the likelihood that NATO would actually use nuclear weapons. After all, the credibility of NATO's nuclear guarantee only increases because NATO appears more likely to use the weapons. Thus even if the neutron bomb did significantly narrow the firebreak and boost NATO's nuclear credibility, its effect on the risk of nuclear war would be unclear.[27]

The same is true for almost all other new weapons that might be invented and almost all nuclear arms control treaties that might be negotiated. Since most weapons and treaties cannot greatly alter credibility and the firebreak and in any case produce contradictory effects on the risk of nuclear war, they are of little significance.

What about technical changes in the doomsday machine, which *can* significantly affect credibility and the firebreak? If we removed tactical nuclear weapons from Europe, Korea, Navy ships, and so on, would we, by widening the firebreak, reduce the credibility of deterrence and thereby invite conventional war? In situations where there is any real chance of war—that is, where the superpowers believe vital interests are at stake—the answer is no. Here there is no great credibility problem to begin with. Both sides know that superpower combat would pose a terrifying risk of nuclear escalation *regardless* of the doomsday threat, since either side might deliberately use nuclear weapons rather than concede defeat. In Europe, for example, doomsday weapons are superfluous to deterrence.

Where the superpowers do *not* claim vital interests, the credibility of threats to deliberately use nuclear weapons is of course inherently low. Here doomsday weapons—weapons that might be launched in combat *without* an executive order—probably breed caution on both sides. But war is quite unlikely anyway in such situations, and in any case the creation of a doomsday machine is indefensible given the unthinkable consequences should something go wrong.

Unlike other nuclear arms control measures, then, those designed to reduce the "massive multiplication of a nuclear hair trigger" are of great importance. But even these measures could be only partially effective because any conventional conflict involving the superpowers poses an inescapable risk of sparking an unauthorized or unplanned holocaust, as we discuss in Part II. Preventing conventional conflicts must be the first priority of any serious effort to avoid nuclear war. But removing the nuclear weapons most likely to be used first when crises occur would be a hopeful sign of nuclear sanity.

## CHAPTER FOUR

# What About Misperceptions?

I don't know any American officer, or any Soviet officer, who
really believes either superpower can achieve a true first-strike
capability, that one side could ever so disarm the other as to
leave it without the ability to retaliate. . . . [Both] strongly
agree that neither side can win a nuclear war in any meaningful sense.

*—General David Jones, former chairman of*
*the Joint Chiefs of Staff*

## ARE LEADERS MISINFORMED
## ABOUT NUCLEAR WAR?

One of the most basic objections to our argument is that the people
in charge of nuclear weapons might not understand it. Weapons might
matter, if only because people think they do and act accordingly. The
realities we have described may be unimportant if irrational perceptions
actually govern the decisions of real national leaders.

The nuclear establishment takes this possibility seriously. As psychol-
ogist Steven Kull shows, "perception theory" has dominated establishment thinking for years.[1] The idea that one side or the other could
achieve objective, militarily useful advantages in the nuclear balance has
been widely, though not totally, discredited. Yet influential theorists argue that because the Soviets and other key audiences may misperceive
the meaning of new weapons, we must build them to *appear* strong even
if they do not really make us any stronger or protect against any real
threat. One version of this argument is that the Soviets mistakenly believe that nuclear war can be fought and won and that they will soon be
confident of the capability to do so unless the United States takes strong
actions to disabuse them of this notion. Thus if MX or Star Wars or
Trident II makes the Soviets reconsider their reckless position, it must be
built whether or not it has real military value. Even if the Soviets might
not actually start a nuclear war, the argument goes, their confidence

about winning one, should it occur, could strengthen their hand in political conflicts with the West.

As Warner Schilling explains, "Throughout the 1970's, the United States has been concerned with the appearance of the strategic balance, as well as with its reality, and has been intent on maintaining forces that are not only equal to those of the Soviet Union but are perceived as equal." Schilling believes that "this concern with perceptions is the result of the fact that the pace of the Soviet build-up has enabled the Soviet Union, over time, to surpass the United States in such measures as the total number of missiles, the total number of delivery vehicles, and the total amount of megatonnage," which must then be judged against U.S. advantages in the total number of warheads. As we have seen, such measures have little meaning. In most cases American "disadvantages" resulted from unilateral U.S. decisions to limit force levels to avoid gross redundancy—for example, to let the total megatonnage of the U.S. nuclear stockpile decline from a historical high of around 8,000 equivalent megatons in the early 1960s to about half that today, and to let the total number of U.S. warheads shrink from a high of 32,000 in 1967 to around 26,000 in 1983. Yet "Soviet numerical advantages have led many Americans to fear that the Soviet Union might be tempted to use the threat of nuclear war to intimidate or blackmail the United States, its allies, or other states." Worse, "allies or other states, believing that the Soviet Union has the superior nuclear force, might be led to yield or accommodate to Soviet interests, and the Soviets could gain the political results of nuclear superiority without even having to threaten, much less fight, a nuclear war."[2] A recent version of this fear concerned the Soviet deployment of more SS-20s aimed at Europe—a militarily meaningless addition to the vast Soviet nuclear threat, but one widely predicted to intimidate U.S. allies in the absence of a compensating U.S. deployment of Euromissiles.

In our view, the left exhibits its own version of perception theory in arguing that even if the Pentagon's new weapons do not actually give the United States a first-strike option, the generals, the national security adviser, and the president might not recognize this reality. With MX, Trident II, and the Stealth bomber in hand, they might foolishly press the button under the delusion that victory is finally possible. Howard Moreland, for example, acknowledges that "to launch a first strike would be risking suicide." But he argues that since "the only discernible military purpose of the nuclear arms race in the 1980's is to acquire a first-strike capability or to prevent the enemy from acquiring one," leaders apparently do not understand the risk.[3]

U.S. weapons programs, then, are taken as a signal of a U.S. *perception* that a successful first strike may be achievable. The problem therefore lies not in MX and Trident II, which do little to change meaningful U.S. nuclear capabilities, but in the leadership's misperception of them. The Soviets may also be misinformed. If they come to believe that the U.S. arsenal poses a real threat of disarming them—or that American leaders believe it does—then in the heat of a crisis they might preempt, desperately and senselessly using their weapons rather than risk losing them.

As we have seen, others fear that nuclear innovations at the *low* end of the destructive spectrum, such as the neutron bomb, could promote the dangerous misperception that nuclear war can be fought and contained like conventional war. Michael Klare, for example, worries that if, irrationally, the distinction between conventional and nuclear weapons faded in leaders' minds, "the inhibition against nuclear escalation would decrease, and the risk of global annihilation would skyrocket."[4]

## NUCLEAR SCHIZOPHRENIA

There is little solid information about how leaders in various countries perceive the importance of new weapons systems—a scandalous omission since purported misperceptions have become a central part of the official case for more U.S. nuclear weapons. As Schilling writes, there is

> very little knowledge about how perceptions of the strategic balance are actually influenced (if at all) by such household words as throw-weight, one-megaton equivalents, or prompt hard-target kill capability. The Soviets keep their perceptions to themselves. . . . As for allies and other states, there is no evidence that the United States government has engaged in any systematic research as to how relevant foreign elites reach their judgments about the state of the strategic balance or even what those judgments are.[5]

But there has been sufficient real-world experience with nuclear weapons in international affairs to suggest the probable role of perceptions. True, leaders on both sides urgently decry the dangers of their opponent's nuclear weapons and constantly seek new systems of their own. In the peacetime budgetary and domestic political process, weapons certainly matter to them. But leaders do not necessarily *act* in the international arena on the basis of these exaggerated assessments of the weapons' import.

Historical experience suggests that military and political leaders on both sides have a "schizophrenic" view of nuclear weapons. For in real foreign policy decisions and in the handling of real crises, their behavior does not appear to be affected by which weapons each side has built. They may still be willing to run the risk of nuclear war—as we document in Part II—but when they do so the details of the nuclear balance do not influence them and certainly do not delude them about the risk they are running.

At the time of the Cuban missile crisis, for example, the United States had a far larger and more advanced nuclear arsenal than the Soviets and had a highly evolved counterforce strategy for launching a disarming attack against Soviet nuclear facilities. If differences in hardware affect leaders' perceptions, then that would have been the time. Many assume that a widespread perception of American nuclear superiority was in fact decisive—motivating Chairman Khrushchev to put nuclear missiles in Cuba; leading President Kennedy to demand the missiles' removal to avoid an unfavorable change in the nuclear balance of power; and allowing the United States to prevail in the crisis. But as we will see in Chapter 8, Khrushchev and Kennedy considered the missiles important not for military reasons but mainly for symbolic ones. Kennedy certainly knew full well that the missiles caused no significant change in the nuclear balance of power.

Six of the president's senior advisers at the time—Dean Rusk, Robert McNamara, George Ball, Roswell Gilpatric, Theodore Sorensen, and McGeorge Bundy—wrote in a *Time* essay in 1982, "American nuclear superiority was not in our view a critical factor, for the fundamental and controlling reason that nuclear war, already in 1962, would have been an unexampled catastrophe for both sides." Existential deterrence was in place despite the great asymmetries in nuclear forces. American leaders, at least, perceived clearly that "the balance of terror so eloquently described by Winston Churchill seven years earlier was in full operation," and they had little doubt that the Soviets knew it, too. The former advisers reported: "No one of us ever reviewed the nuclear balance for comfort in those hard weeks. The Cuban missile crisis illustrates not the significance but the insignificance of nuclear superiority in the face of survivable thermonuclear retaliatory forces." Other factors determined the real balance of power in the conflict, especially the "clearly available and applicable superiority [of the United States] in conventional weapons within the area of the crisis."[6]

In a comprehensive study of newly released documentation of the missile crisis, historian Marc Trachtenberg provides strong additional evidence that American decision makers *did not even consider* the nuclear balance in their extensive deliberations:

> There is no evidence that President Kennedy and his advisers counted missiles, bombers, and warheads, and decided on that basis to take a tough line. . . . One of the most striking things about the October 16 transcript [of key off-the-record White House meetings between the president and his senior advisers] is that no one even touched on the issue of what exactly would happen if the crisis escalated to the level of general war. . . . One does come away from the transcript with the sense that even rough calculations of this sort were not terribly important.[7]

Despite the Kennedy administration's urgent peacetime concern about deficiencies in the strategic balance and its fancy new theories of nuclear strategy, in the actual crisis none of them mattered. Trachtenberg reports that "no one discussed what American counterforce capabilities were—that is, how well the United States might be able to 'limit damage' in the event of an all-out war. It was as though all the key concepts associated with the administration's formal nuclear strategy, as set out for example just a few months earlier in McNamara's famous Ann Arbor speech—in fact, the whole idea of controlled and discriminate general war—in the final analysis counted for very little." The president himself said in one of the October 16 meetings: "What difference does it make? They've got enough to blow us up now anyway." At the point of command decision, he needed no lessons in existential deterrence.[8]

The same schizophrenia between peacetime rhetoric and crisis actions apparently operated during the next great nuclear confrontation, the Middle Eastern superpower crisis of October 1973, which we discuss in Chapter 6. The United States undertook the most urgent military alert, both conventional and nuclear, since the Cuban crisis and obliquely threatened direct American military action if the Soviets intervened in the Middle East war. Military confrontation between the superpowers loomed. Nixon later wrote that "we neared the brink of nuclear war."[9]

Like Kennedy before him, Nixon was deeply concerned about the nuclear weapons balance and sought new American weapons to improve it. Yet during an actual crisis neither he, Kissinger, nor other key leaders appear to have paid any attention to the specific nuclear weapons on either side that so obsessed them before and afterward. Nowhere in Nixon's or Kissinger's memoirs can one find any reference to considerations of the nuclear balance in making these fateful decisions. Trachtenberg's conclusions about the Cuban crisis seem equally relevant here. One gets the impression that the humiliating events of Watergate had more to do with the decision to demonstrate "our ability to act" and our "resolve" than any count-up of nuclear warheads.[10]

Other accounts confirm this picture of the crisis. Barry M. Blechman and Douglas M. Hart, for example, characterize the nuclear alert as an effort to communicate to the Soviets that "if you persist in your current activity, if you actually go ahead and land forces in Egypt, you will initiate an interactive process between our armed forces whose end results are not clear, but which could be devastating. . . . The United States is prepared to continue escalating the confrontation up to and including a central nuclear exchange between us, even though we understand that the consequences of such an interaction potentially are 'incalculable.'" The results "could" be devastating, and the consequences are "incalculable"—an assessment consistent with an understanding of existential deterrence. As these authors confirm, Nixon did not misperceive what nuclear war would mean or what new weapons could do for the American position in such a war. Blechman and Hart emphasize that "the Soviet Union clearly did not back down because the United States had an edge in strategic weaponry and could 'win' a nuclear exchange. . . . Neither side possessed the capability for a disarming first strike, and each would have expected to suffer devastating retaliation if it launched nuclear war." Richard K. Betts agrees that the nuclear balance was unimportant: "Kissinger's public remarks at the time of the crisis made not the remotest suggestion of U.S. nuclear advantage and referred only to the awesome danger of mutual annihilation." If American leaders "sensed some significance in a marginal U.S. nuclear advantage, it could not have seemed more than a remote and trivial one."[11]

Other crises and foreign policy initiatives have followed the same pattern. As Bundy points out, contrary to the right's fears, "there has been no Soviet action anywhere that can be plausibly attributed to the so-called window of vulnerability." In our interviews with Pentagon and National Security Council officials, we often heard that the Soviets "might well" derive political advantages from that window, opened by their prodigious new nuclear systems. But when challenged for evidence, not one could connect Afghanistan, Central America, the Middle East, or the conflicts of any other region with the nuclear tally sheet. As

Raymond Garthoff sensibly observes: "An American warning to the Soviet Union not to intervene in Hungary in 1956 would not have been heeded, despite the clear American strategic superiority. The Soviet stake in Hungary was great if not vital; the American was not." And the Soviets enjoy tremendous conventional military superiority in their border areas; hence any threat of provoking a major crisis would lack credibility. "For the same reason, *not* because of changes in the strategic balance, the Soviet leaders ignored repeated warnings from the United States not to intervene in Afghanistan in 1979, and not to build a base in Vietnam in the same year."[12]

Similarly, American militarism and foreign policy have not borne a clear relation to weapons balances or arms negotiations. No one has plausibly demonstrated that American power concretely benefited anywhere in the world from an American strategic edge since at least 1950. As Henry Kissinger asked rhetorically in his memoirs: "What in the name of God is strategic superiority? What is the significance of it, politically, militarily, operationally, at these levels of numbers? What do you do with it?" The Center for Defense Information notes that in the late 1960s, "when the U.S. still had so-called 'strategic superiority' over the Soviets, it was unable to translate that into political or military clout in the Vietnam War." More recently, as Bundy writes,

> It is not self-evident, to put it very gently, that the "victory" of December 1983, and the safe arrival in Europe of the first ground-launched cruise missiles and Pershing II's, has left the [NATO] Alliance stronger and more self-confident than it would have been if it had been decided in 1977 and thereafter that there was nothing in any new Soviet deployment of any sort that required a change in the decision of the 1960's that the right place for American mid-range nuclear weapons supporting NATO was in submarines at sea.[13]

The nuclear weapons balance does not seem to have affected the outcome of superpower confrontations or the division of real power in the world. Bundy believes that even during the four years of U.S. nuclear monopoly, 1945–1949, "aside from the debatable European case, there is very little evidence that American atomic supremacy was helpful in American diplomacy. . . . To whatever degree atomic diplomacy may have tempted this or that American leader at this or that moment in those years, it did not work."[14] World opinion alone proved an enormous barrier not only to actual nuclear use but also, as Truman and Eisenhower discovered, to believable nuclear threats.

American leaders understood as soon as Soviet nuclear weapons appeared in 1949 that the U.S. lead in the arms race might be of little value when weighed against the destructive potential of even a few Soviet atomic warheads. Betts writes: "There was never a time when leaders were *confident* that the United States could wage nuclear war success-fully . . . restricting damage of the West to 'acceptable' levels." From the start, American leaders worried about both conventional and nuclear Soviet retaliation against Europe, and "U.S. leaders also had no confi-dence, even in the early period, that they could prevent significant Soviet nuclear retaliation against the American homeland." Even in 1949 the U.S. Joint Chiefs of Staff estimated that Soviet bombers could "reach every important industrial, urban and governmental control center in the United States on a one-way mission basis." Army Intelligence told the National Security Council that just eighteen Soviet nuclear weapons could "wipe out one-third of U.S. steel and iron production, cripple governmental operations in Washington, and hamper and delay mobi-lization and retaliatory efforts." Secret testimony in 1951 congressional hearings asserted that already the Soviets could obliterate American cities.[15]

At the beginning of the Eisenhower administration, in 1953, Paul Nitze told Secretary of State Acheson of a National Security Council study revealing that "the net capability of the Soviet Union to injure the United States must already be measured in terms of many millions of casualties"—in fact, 22 million casualties for a postulated Soviet attack with 150-kiloton weapons. In 1954 Eisenhower said, "Atomic war will destroy civilization." An elaborate 1955 nuclear war simulation sug-gested that fifty-three American cities could be bombed, causing 8.5 million immediate fatalities, leaving an equal number injured, and de-priving 25 million of food and shelter. Reportedly, "the president's one comment was: staggering." Eisenhower's diary for January 23, 1956, records his impressions of an Air Force briefing on the consequences of a hypothetical Soviet surprise attack: "The United States experienced practically total economic collapse. . . . A new government had to be improvised by the states. Casualties were enormous . . . something on the order of 65% of the population would require some kind of medical care, and in most instances, no opportunity whatsoever to get it." Even when the scenario gave the United States a month of warning and had the Soviets concentrate on American air bases rather than cities, the president wrote, "there was no significant difference in the losses we would take." Eisenhower was so disturbed by such findings that he asked the National Security Council to study how much destruction the United States could "absorb and still survive."[16]

By 1957 Eisenhower was talking about 25 million American dead and 60 million injured. The Joint Chiefs of Staff suggested that estimate might be optimistic: considering the effects of radioactive fallout, between 46 million and 117 million Americans could die. In 1960, when Eisenhower was told of possible plans for sharp increases in strategic nuclear weapons, he reportedly responded sarcastically: "Why don't we go completely crazy and plan a force of ten thousand?" (Ironically, that is about the number of U.S. strategic weapons today.) How many times, the president asked, "could [you] kill the same man?" The Air Force estimated in 1960 that a Soviet first strike could kill 150 million people, three-quarters of the American population; even Soviet retaliation after an American first strike could kill 110 million. John F. Kennedy reportedly absorbed the figure of 150 million dead from his first briefing by the Joint Chiefs of Staff. By that time the Soviet Union had so much nuclear megatonnage that Khrushchev announced cutbacks in production of some missiles because rockets "are not cucumbers, you know—you don't eat them—and more than a certain number are not required to repel aggression." Nuclear war, he said, "is stupid, stupid, stupid! If you reach for the button, you reach for suicide."[17] Existential deterrence was securely in place and both sides knew it.

Garthoff, who has painstakingly studied the history of U.S.-Soviet relations, writes, "The global strategic balance is much less important in deterring or resolving crises than many have assumed, because the prospect of nuclear war deters even leaders who command an overwhelming superiority, as shown in 1962, and all the more so leaders on both sides with larger but more equal forces, as demonstrated ever since." If the Cuban missile crisis recurred, he believes that "the outcome today under strategic nuclear parity could be the same. . . . The mere possibility of nuclear war was the deterrent."[18]

Referring to the great Suez, Berlin, and Cuban crises, Bundy similarly asserts: "In none of the three cases, I feel confident, would the final result have been different if the relative strategic positions of the Soviet Union and the United States had been reversed." In all three, the United States enjoyed an immense superiority in nuclear hardware. But it counted for little, since the Soviets had enough to pose an unacceptable threat to New York, Washington, Chicago, and other U.S. cities. As strange as it may seem, if the United States had been the laggard in the nuclear arms race its power would not have been less, because "a stalemate is a stalemate either way around."[19]

In a major study of American military operations, *Force Without War*, Barry Blechman and Stephen S. Kaplan also conclude: "Our data would not support a hypothesis that the strategic weapons balance influences the outcome of incidents in which both the United States and the U.S.S.R. are involved." To the contrary, in surveying dozens of incidents from 1946 to 1975, they found that, from the point of view of American objectives, "short-term outcomes were positive 43 percent of the time when the U.S. strategic advantage was 100 to 1 or greater, 82 percent when the U.S. strategic advantage ranged between 10 and 99 to one, and 92 percent when the U.S. advantage was less than 10 to 1. . . . If we look at [only] those incidents in which the Soviet Union used or threatened to use force, these figures were 11, 50, and 90 percent, respectively." These conclusions cover not only the period of existential deterrence but also the earlier period of enormous American nuclear superiority. The numerous detailed case studies in *Force Without War* likewise "provide little support for the notion that decisions during crises are strongly influenced by aggregate strategic capabilities."[20]

We likewise found no evidence of even the most casual discussion of relative nuclear strength or the characteristics of nuclear weapons systems during the many superpower crises and confrontations discussed in Part II. This neglect stands in surreal contrast to the near obsession with the numbers and performance characteristics of nuclear arms in noncrisis times documented throughout Part I. It is as if everyone takes a powerful weaponitis pill on the days when the world is relatively safe and an equally potent reality pill when it is not. Thank goodness it is not the other way around.

Some conservative analysts, such as General Daniel Graham and Richard Pipes, continue to insist that the Soviets reject existential deterrence. According to them, the Soviets believe that in the nuclear age, as in previous ages, war is just a "continuation of politics," that it can be won, and that "socialism" will be victorious. In this view, Soviet restraint so far reflects only their analysis that the "correlation of forces" has not yet moved in their favor. This restraint could change after the Soviets complete their nuclear rearmament unless the United States undertakes several major new offensive and defensive nuclear programs. Other students of Soviet military thought, such as George Kennan, dismiss as farfetched the idea that the Soviets believe they could fight a nuclear war without risking unacceptable damage and casualties.[21]

Apparently, Soviet leaders are as schizophrenic on nuclear issues as their American counterparts. In public pronouncements, Soviet leaders often stress the importance of preparing for nuclear war and building the weapons that would permit them to fight it. But they do not necessarily act in international affairs on this basis or even privately harbor delusions about what nuclear war would mean. Robert L. Arnett concludes his careful study of Soviet attitudes as follows: "What Soviet spokesmen have been saying about nuclear war does not support the claims of various Western analysts who argue that the Soviets believe they can win and survive a nuclear war." Rather, as in the United States, public pronouncements reflect only half of a split view, one shaped largely by domestic ideological needs. "Publications written for internal consumption," however, "contend that nuclear war cannot serve as a practical instrument of policy, and they continually talk about the dire consequences of such a war." Similarly, David Holloway's authoritative study argues that underneath their rhetoric the Soviets understand that their relationship with the United States "is in reality one of mutual vulnerability to devastating nuclear strikes. . . . There is little evidence to suggest that [the Soviets] think victory in a global nuclear war would be anything other than catastrophic." Bundy agrees that despite the continuing search for "marginal benefits," *both* sides ultimately recognize that "effective superiority is unobtainable."[22]

The most objective analysts observe that Soviet strategic policy advocates *preemption,* not premeditated first strike, and does not reflect a victory-is-possible mentality. As Leon Wieseltier (no admirer of the Kremlin) emphasizes, this policy "means only that the Soviet Union would fire its missiles first if a crisis with the United States reached the point at which a nuclear exchange seemed inevitable"—a position identical to that advanced by American officials and reflected in U.S. nuclear policy. Soviet policy is indeed "a provision for the brink of war, not the breaking of the peace. There is no evidence at all that the Soviets believe in 'first strike,' or that they have plans to start a nuclear war, or that their nuclear strategy is, as Pipes put it, 'not retaliation but offensive action.'"[23] And as we saw in Chapter 2, preemption, whatever its merits, has little to do with weapons balances and everything to do with political conditions and the perceived risk of war.

In honest moments outside the budgetary process, senior professional soldiers on both sides sometimes acknowledge that nuclear weapons hardware does not really affect basic military realities. Marshal Ogarkov, commander in chief of the Warsaw Pact, said in a May 1984 interview in the Soviet press that "the deployment of U.S. intermediate-range missiles in Western Europe did not increase the possibility of a 'first strike' against the Soviet Union. Both sides fully recognize the inevitability of a retaliatory strike." General David Jones, former chairman of the Joint Chiefs of Staff, agreed: "I don't know any American officer, or any Soviet officer, who really believes either superpower can achieve a true first-strike capability, that one side could ever so disarm the other as to leave it without the ability to retaliate . . . [both] strongly agree that neither side can win a nuclear war in any meaningful sense."[24] In other contexts each man has undoubtedly denounced the first-strike weaponry of his enemy and urged new weapons systems for his own side. Yet clearly on another level they both understand the meaninglessness of this constant arming and counterarming.

Steven Kull provides still more evidence of nuclear schizophrenia in a series of interviews with high-level military and civilian nuclear planners and strategists. He examines the extent to which planners "conventionalize" nuclear weapons by viewing a nuclear war in the same light as a conventional war that can be limited in scope, meaningfully won, and deeply influenced by the relative armaments of the contending powers. Although the academic literature often suggests that the military wildly conventionalizes scenarios of nuclear war, "even among those who overtly conventionalized, the majority of people [Kull] interviewed, when questioned directly, did recognize the key elements of the nuclear revolution." Most "shifted between a mindset that conventionalized and another that recognized key features of the nuclear revolution," suggesting "a fragmentation or lack of integration."[25] Respondents often began by railing against the dangers of Soviet nuclear weapons systems and the need for American systems to counter them. But under Kull's questioning, they would quickly acknowledge, as any informed person must, that both the United States and the Soviet Union are completely vulnerable to nuclear destruction, that none of the new weapons on either side has changed this vulnerability, and that it will remain in place for as long as anyone can foresee.

Even in peacetime national leaders and others involved with the nuclear issue are schizophrenic, sometimes recognizing the fallacy of weaponitis. "Virtually all respondents," Kull reports, "would at some points recognize that, given the military realities of the nuclear era, the policies they were proposing were questionable or even invalid. To elicit this second perspective, I simply had to direct their attention to key features of nuclear reality that they were ignoring or suppressing. . . . not a single respondent consistently presented a conventional mindset perspective; all would at some point recognize the key features of nuclear reality." Kull found, for example, that among the eighty-four former and present U.S. military officers, civilian security officials, congresspeople, and nuclear strategists he interviewed, "the vast majority . . . readily recognized that . . . both sides have the capability, even after absorbing an all-out first strike, to retaliate in such a devastating fashion that neither side could meaningfully benefit from such a first strike." Moreover, "it was frequently stated that it would be impossible to keep a nuclear war limited and, sometimes, that anybody who thought so was crazy." Kull is "convinced that, perhaps with the exception of a few . . . individuals the defense establishment as a whole does fully perceive the American population as fundamentally vulnerable." "It was particularly striking," he observes, "how easily many individuals, even members of the current administration, would blithely dismiss the military value of weapons proposed or currently being deployed."[26] Those weapons, they realize, cannot really alter the superpower nuclear stalemate for better or for worse.

Kull found a similar schizophrenia among Soviets: "In every case the clear implicit message was that they were fully aware that the military rationale for maintaining the balance [of nuclear weapons between the superpowers] did not really make logical sense. They also seemed to feel that I should know that they understood this, and they thought me a bit thick-headed for being so impolite as to force the issue." "The dominant theme of the answers," Kull writes, "was that any superpower war would almost certainly be all out and both sides would be effectively annihilated. Soviet civil defense efforts were dismissed as simply the result of 'bureaucratic inertia' or efforts to 'calm down the population.'"[27]

George Rathjens and Laura Reed ask, "Can one really believe that an American president (or the Soviet leadership, or that of a third country) would behave very differently in a crisis if the United States had no MX missiles, or a thousand instead of the number now envisaged; or if the Soviet Union had never developed the SS-20, or alternately had thousands of them?" They are on firm ground when they answer, "It is unlikely."[28]

A DRAWING-ROOM COMEDY

Bernard Brodie would be disappointed to see how little progress has been made since he noted a quarter century ago that "eager acceptance of the new is coupled, not only within the same organizations but often within the same persons, with stubborn insistence upon retaining also much of the old." The nuclear schizophrenia of leadership partly reflects this inner split that Brodie noticed. In the calm peacetime budgetary process, many officials get caught up in the old thinking: the weapons paradigm. But in a crisis involving much higher stakes, when abstract analysis must give way to practical command decisions, leaders are much more influenced by common sense. They recognize that it does not much matter who has what nuclear weapons at this point in the arms race since everything will probably be destroyed anyway in the event of a nuclear war. "In even contemplating a first strike," as John Steinbruner writes, leaders "would not be very sensitive to the fine details of the technical force balance. The destructiveness of nuclear weapons delivered in retaliation, even in modest numbers, is compelling enough to dominate [their] attention and behavior. . . . even clearly demonstrable technical advantages would have very little effect on this basic result."[29]

As Brodie wrote in 1978, "The defense community of the United States is inhabited by peoples of a wide range of skills and sometimes of considerable imagination. All sorts of notions and propositions are churned out, and often presented for consideration with the prefatory words: 'It is conceivable that . . .' Such words establish their own truth, for the fact that someone has conceived of whatever proposition follows is enough to establish that it is conceivable."[30] When asked why he spent so much effort and money on military capabilities he knew were marginal, if not utterly unrealistic, one high-level nuclear war planner told us that it was his job to take no chances when it came to deterrence. He asked, "Do you want me to play 'you bet your country'?"

Such "marginal thinking" resembles what defense critics call "worst-case thinking." Near the end of his life, Brodie developed a profound distrust for it: "The thinking up of ingenious new possibilities is deceptively cheap and easy, and the burden of proof must be on those who urge the payment of huge additional premiums for putting their particular notions into practice."[31] But regardless of its merits, it can logically coexist with an understanding that in the big picture the weapons balance is almost irrelevant. Marginal thinkers can work hard to get the weapons they want to achieve marginal benefits. They can then, without inconsistency, ignore those weapons when they make major foreign policy or military decisions that are logically based not on the margin but on the core of the military and political balance.

Moreover, many officials and strategists hope that over many years numerous improvements in weapons, each marginal by itself, will add up to something significant. Although they consciously exaggerate the significance of individual weapons systems, such as the MX, to get public and congressional approval for them, the real agenda is a much longer term shift in strategic posture. But again, when they must make major foreign policy decisions, they recognize that the marginal improvements do not in fact amount to much and therefore that the real strategic balance is the same as always.[32]

At one level, then, nuclear schizophrenia reflects flawed styles of thinking—internal confusion and obsession with marginal military capabilities—that lead officials to seek new weapons in the vain hope of increasing real military capabilities. But nuclear schizophrenia is also a deliberate strategy designed in part, as Warner Schilling explained earlier, to deal with others' supposed weaponitis by feigning one's own. Kull found that though most American officials know that new weapons cannot change the nature of nuclear war, they suspect that Soviet and other foreign leaders might not understand that. Hence they act *as if* the nuclear balance mattered, buying weapons to impress those leaders—in part to discourage any lingering misperception that a successful first strike against the United States is possible and even perhaps to *encourage* the misperception that a successful U.S. first strike against the Soviet Union *is* possible. If foreign perceptions of American military power (however unfounded) grow, then—as American officials have publicly argued—so will America's ability to intervene abroad without interference. The Soviets, as Kull found, follow a similar strategy—building weapons to counter supposed *American* misperceptions.

"The situation resembles nothing so much as a drawing-room comedy," Kull observes. "All of the key characters know a certain secret—that strategic asymmetries are militarily irrelevant in an age of overkill—but because they think that others do not know the secret they act as if they do not know the secret either. A farcical quality emerges as all the characters, more or less unconsciously, collude to establish a norm of behavior based on a failure to recognize the secret."[33] But in crises leaders—all of whom *do* know the secret—do not consult the nuclear balance or indulge in the fantasy that either side can actually use its new nuclear systems without inviting worldwide destruction.

As Robert Jervis observes, "There is little evidence that European or Third World leaders pay much attention to the details of the strategic balance." In 1977 the Pentagon sponsored a rare effort to gather such evidence through a conference on "International Perceptions of the Superpower Military Balance." It provided scant support for the actors in this "drawing-room comedy": "In the overall strategic-nuclear area . . . the Soviets, the [French] *Défense Nationale* writers, and the Arabs gen-

erally characterized [the superpowers] as equal, with many of the last
two groups believing it moot to ask, 'Who is ahead?' in a situation of
mutual nuclear overkill. These individuals saw the superpowers as func-
tionally equal regardless of which had the quantitative or qualitative advantage." The conference findings also refer to the "oft-stated French
belief . . . that overall strategic inventory totals have lost their significance due to the 'balance of terror.' It is generally assumed that both
sides have more than enough." Just as important, the studies also failed
to find evidence that international leaders believe "accommodations"
with the Soviets should be sought because of "recent perceived shifts in
some balances away from U.S. favor." Contrary to the argument that
international elites mistakenly attach importance to the nuclear weapons constructed by the superpowers, at least in some cases they do not
even bother to monitor these developments. One study of Arab newspapers concluded that they "do not follow the details of new weapons
developments." Concluding that no one in the world seems impressed
by all the weapons built for that purpose, Kull comments: "What is particularly striking [in the drawing-room comedy] . . . is that when the
main character—in this case the Defense Department—is informed
that, in fact, everybody knows the secret, it stiffens its resolve to maintain the charade." [34]

The Pentagon maintains the charade perhaps partly to convey the impression that American leaders are dangerously irrational by building
first-strike and other weapons that only lunatics would try to use. As
Joseph Gerson explains, "If the Soviets believed that our leaders thought
they could launch a first-strike blow—Nixon's 'madman' theory—they
would use extreme caution in countering U.S. moves." Hence, as many
on the right hope and many on the left fear, continual nuclear weapons
modernization might be able to "shield" or "cover" U.S. intervention
abroad even though everyone knows that the technical arms race is in
fact permanently stalemated. Kull found that

> such thinking has continued in defense circles. . . . Some analysts or former
> officials explicitly described how they would actively work to create these
> irrational images. One analyst described his goal of making Americans ap-
> pear "wild and crazy" and imagined—with apparent delight—the effect of
> articles about winning nuclear war on Soviet analysts. . . . He also credited
> some of his well-known hawkish friends with intentionally appearing irra-
> tional as part of an unofficial role they had designed for themselves in the
> service of the United States Government. [35]

The madman strategy, like the other sources of peacetime weaponitis
mentioned earlier, produces apparent schizophrenia. To appear danger-

ously irrational, government officials publicly convey the belief that their new weapons actually give the United States usable new nuclear options. But well aware that is not really the case, in crises leaders do not waste time thinking or talking about those apocryphal options.

## SELF-INFLICTED WOUNDS

What should be done if—despite the evidence cited earlier—serious misperceptions about nuclear weapons either linger from the prenuclear era or emerge from the superpowers' loud claims that their new nuclear weapons actually provide new and usable military power? Potentially catastrophic misperceptions have certainly occurred before. For example, recent interviews with four of the most important U.S. Air Force generals of the early nuclear age elicited some eerie reflections on the Cuban missile crisis. The generals did not—and to this day do not—concur with the realistic assessment of President Kennedy and his top civilian advisers that even in 1962 nuclear war would have been a total catastrophe for both superpowers and much of the rest of the world. General David A. Burchinal, a former Strategic Air Command (SAC) wing commander, chief of staff of the Eighth Air Force, and senior staff of Air Force Headquarters and the Joint Chiefs of Staff, insisted that

> the Kennedy administration . . . both the executive leadership and . . . McNamara . . . did not understand what had been created and handed to them, and what it had given them. SAC was about at its peak. We had, not supremacy, but complete nuclear superiority over the Soviets. . . . Our politicians did not understand what happens when you have such a degree of superiority as we had, or they simply didn't know how to use it. They were busily engaged in saving face for the Soviets and making concessions, giving up IRBMs, the Thors and Jupiters deployed overseas [see Chapter 7]—when all we had to do was write our own ticket.

General Curtis E. LeMay, father of the Strategic Air Command and Air Force chief of staff during the crisis, added: We could have gotten not only the missiles out of Cuba, we could have gotten the Communists out of Cuba at that time." "You bet we could have," agreed General Leon W. Johnson, with the National Security Council at the time. According to LeMay, when a U.S. fighter plane strayed into Soviet airspace near the height of the crisis, potentially provoking an accidental war, Defense Secretary McNamara rushed to "apologize to the Russians" [see Chapter 7], but the Joint Chiefs of Staff said, "No. Tell them, don't touch that thing, or they've had it."

These men believe that at least for that brief time the United States could really have fought a nuclear war with the Soviet Union without risking devastating destruction. Indeed, LeMay contends that the United States had nothing at all to fear: "During that very critical time, in my mind there wasn't a chance that we would have gone to war with Russia because we had overwhelming strategic capability and the Russians knew it." Burchinal is puzzled that in "publications about the Cuban missile crisis all claim that we were so close to nuclear war; ninety-nine percent of the people who write about it don't understand the truth." He even claims that "we were never further from nuclear war than at the time of Cuba, never further." But even Burchinal recognizes that "as the Russians built up their capacity during the 1960's and into the early 1970's, that situation [of overwhelming superiority] no longer obtained."[36]

Even today the superpowers' propaganda about their new weapons may foster dangerous misperceptions about nuclear war. The political and military institutions of both sides may, too. The Soviet Union and the United States have long planned, equipped, and trained their forces to fight a nuclear war like a conventional one. Both countries promote elaborate strategies for limiting a nuclear war and trying to win it. For example, a U.S. Army field manual published in 1980 states: "The U.S. Army must be prepared to fight and win when nuclear weapons are used."[37] Military bureaucracies, then, may be institutionalizing dangerous misperceptions. In crises to come, as in crises past, some military officers and civilian officials may urge the U.S. president or the Soviet general secretary to enact such war plans in the insane belief that they could actually be carried out without risking everything.

Irrational beliefs about nuclear war certainly persist among professional nuclear analysts and could be dangerous if these analysts got the ears of top national leaders. Today most (but not all) reputable analysts recognize that neither side can gain a meaningful advantage by launching a first strike. Most (but not all) also recognize that a nuclear war cannot confidently be kept limited and could well lead to the total destruction of both superpowers and much more. Still, as we have seen, the so-called nuclear experts, exhibiting their own schizophrenia, often speak of "incentives" for getting in the first blow or of the possibility of using "limited nuclear options" to influence the outcome of a crisis. And in some areas the experts flatly express dangerous misperceptions. An important example, which we noted in Chapter 2, is the seventeen highly regarded specialists who write that an American leader (perhaps Bush or Quayle) must make a *split-second* decision about whether to launch *thousands* of warheads in the event of a *warning* that the Soviets have already pushed the button.

Even if leaders do harbor dangerous misperceptions about nuclear war, however, building or opposing weapons systems is not the answer. Ironically, that can easily reinforce the very misperceptions that one is trying to counter. When the U.S. government argues for new weapons to create an image of strength, for example, it decries glaring weaknesses in American forces to justify these weapons to Congress and the public. This outcry actually fosters an image of weakness, not of strength, as Kull points out. The Pentagon-sponsored review of the evidence on Soviet, French, and Japanese perceptions of the nuclear balance acknowledged that "the tendency of many U.S. spokesmen (particularly government officials at budget time) to emphasize Soviet strengths and U.S. weaknesses often had a negative impact on the perceived U.S. standing." The former secretary of defense James Schlesinger calls these "self-inflicted wounds," by-products of taking false fears seriously and thereby reinforcing them.[38]

The Soviet government plays the same crazy game. It fears that new U.S. weapons, though militarily irrelevant, will create a perception of American gain. So it denounces the weapons and vows to build its own to counter them. But this response plays into the Pentagon's hands—reinforcing the perception that the United States has shifted the balance of power. The U.S. air-launched cruise missile, for example, was supposed to counter perceptions of American strategic inferiority. "Whether or not such perceptions" of new American strength are warranted, writes Richard K. Betts, "they should be enhanced by the Soviet Union's vigorous complaints about the new threat they feel from the U.S. cruise missile."[39]

The peace movement likewise opposes so-called destabilizing weapons, in part to prevent the misperception that the United States is acquiring a first-strike knockout capability. But to succeed, the peace movement must decry the dangers of first-strike weapons, thus unwittingly adding legitimacy to the erroneous and dangerous idea that in nuclear war it matters who strikes first. George Rathjens is one of the few critics of American nuclear policy who grasps this problem. He writes that he opposed the MX "only with great diffidence and selectiv[ity]," not because he doubted the valuelessness of the weapon but because in making the standard arguments against it he did not want to "concede implicitly that there was some legitimacy to the 'window of vulnerability' claim and/or that 'first strike' attacks were a very serious problem—

when . . . there were many problems more demanding of attention."
With the same logic Rathjens "chose not to testify for or against" SALT
II: "To do either with vigor would have suggested the agreement more
significant than I believed it to be."[40]

The only sensible way to counter dangerous misperceptions about
nuclear war is to correct them. Concerned citizens and specialists alike
must challenge false statements about nuclear war wherever they appear, whether in newspapers, academic publications, classrooms, government press releases, or the annual report of the U.S. secretary of
defense. That is a big job, and a crucial one; as we have seen, most
academic and political commentary about nuclear war, befuddled by
weaponitis, continues to suggest that some technological deficiency or
advancement could give a state a rational reason to fire nuclear weapons
first or to fire them in haste. We must also work to unmask and replace
the many military officers and civilian leaders who spout nuclear nonsense. During his 1979–1980 campaign for the Republican presidential
nomination, for example, George Bush had the following interchange
with journalist Robert Scheer:

SCHEER:    Don't you reach a point with these strategic weapons where we can
           wipe each other out so many times and no one wants to use them
           or be willing to use them, that it really doesn't matter whether
           you're 10 percent or 2 percent higher or lower?

BUSH:      Yes, if you believe there is no such thing as a winner in a nuclear
           exchange, that argument makes a little sense. I don't believe that.

SCHEER:    How do you win in a nuclear exchange?

BUSH:      You have a survivability of command and control, survivability of
           industrial potential, protection of a percentage of your citizens,
           and you have a capability that inflicts more damage on the opposi-
           tion than it can inflict on you. That's the way you can have a
           winner.[41]

We must also challenge the institutional sources of nuclear misinfor-
mation, exposing and rebutting official U.S. plans for nuclear "war
fighting," "controlled escalation," "prevailing," or "damage limitation." And we should work to change those absurd plans, not indirectly,
by opposing the weapons requested to implement the plans, but directly: by insisting that official nuclear strategy reflect the obvious fact
that nuclear war cannot be fought without seriously risking the destruction of everything. Then the government would not be training thousands of soldiers to think about nuclear war and conventional war in
the same way.

If *foreign* leaders should misperceive, say, the importance of Soviet advantages in throw weight or megatonnage, then "the appropriate American response," as Schilling argues, "is not to add to some component of its strategic forces in order to change the direction of a curve on a chart, but to explain to its allies and friends (and to the Soviet Union if need be) that the numerical differences in question would have no significant bearing on the outcome of a nuclear exchange."[42] The same explanation is in order if the Soviets or anyone else should fear that *American* innovations or numerical advantages allow the Pentagon to launch a successful first strike or to control nuclear war.

As for the madman strategy, American and Soviet leaders may indeed try to convince each other, and others, that they are crazy enough to launch the missiles if challenged in the Third World. But even if the strategy works, the actual possession of giant new weapons is not the main reason for success. Hence working to stop those weapons or even the arms race generally may do little to stop the diabolical psychological game.

No amount of MX and Trident II missiles is likely to convince the Soviets that American leaders fail to recognize the probable result of launching thousands of such missiles in an attempted first-strike knockout: a global calamity with no winners. The same is true in reverse. The balance of terror is, by now, too obvious for either side to imagine that the other would not realize the catastrophic consequences of large-scale nuclear war.

Of course, the first-strike risk cannot be totally discounted by those who would be the victims. But more plausible by far, and the real heart of the madman strategy, is that leaders would attempt a *very limited* use of nuclear weapons if seriously challenged in the Third World or elsewhere—not because of a wild misperception that one side could actually win a large-scale nuclear war should it come to that, but simply because of *recklessness:* a mad willingness to run the risk of escalation and total mutual destruction.

As we will see in Part II, American and to a lesser degree Soviet leaders have repeatedly rolled the nuclear dice in past Third World conflicts to intimidate each other, taking actions they *knew* would raise the risk of a mutually unsurvivable holocaust. No matter what the state of the essentially irrelevant nuclear arms race, neither superpower is likely to underestimate the possibility that the other would go even further in the future, actually using a small number of nuclear weapons in an extreme crisis.

True, appearing mad enough to use nuclear weapons may be somewhat easier if one is constantly spending billions on building up and improving those weapons. But what really makes an impression on people around the world are the mad actions that have actually propelled the superpowers toward confrontation many times. Even after a START treaty or a nuclear freeze, the superpowers could maintain the madman strategy, since the details of the nuclear armories are not really its basis. To the extent that particular nuclear weapons do reinforce the madman strategy, it is not the so-called first-strike weapons but the small doomsday weapons (discussed in Chapter 3) that would probably be used first on some future superpower battlefield. Those doomsday weapons, as we have argued, are in fact dangerous and should be abolished, unilaterally if necessary.

To denounce as dangerous other nuclear weapons systems, which in reality add little to the nuclear danger, may seem to the Soviets and others as only more evidence that perhaps those weapons really *do* pose a new threat in the hands of lunatic American leaders. The most realistic answer to the madman strategy is to counter it directly by preventing madmen from becoming leaders and, failing that, by imposing large political costs on leaders who say or do crazy things in the nuclear age.

Pretending that weapons matter is thus in every way more dangerous than the weapons themselves. Such a pretense—whether by the superpower governments or by the peace movements opposing those governments—can only confuse people about the existential risks and horror of a war fought with *any* nuclear weapons. This pretense also distracts attention from the occasional new weapon that actually adds to the risk of nuclear war. The furor over so-called U.S. first-strike weapons, for example, has almost totally eclipsed discussion of the real hazards of the U.S. sea-launched cruise missile (discussed in Chapter 9).

If the arms race doesn't matter, we should simply say so, point out the genuine exceptions, and confront all who harbor or spread misperceptions or who speak and act like madmen. Otherwise we only add to the confusion, and to the danger.

## CHAPTER FIVE

# What About Star Wars?

Every new weapon will eventually bring some counter
defense to it.
      *—Harry Truman, addressing the*
      *U.S. Congress, October 1945*

After five centuries of the use of hand arms with
fire-propelled missiles, the large number of men killed by
comparable arms in the recent war indicates that no
adequate answer has yet [been] found for the bullet.
      *—Bernard Brodie,* The Absolute Weapon, *1946*

## NUCLEAR SCIENCE FICTION

In a fund-raising letter for Americans for Democratic Action, Isaac
Asimov writes that the Star Wars plan for defending the United States
by shooting down Soviet nuclear missiles is nothing but "Hollywood
science fiction." He warns, nevertheless, that Star Wars is "dangerous"
and "destabilizing," and even "a threat to world peace" and "to our national security." But how can a fictional weapon endanger the survival
of the real world? Similarly, Harrison Brown, then editor in chief of the
*Bulletin of the Atomic Scientists,* reveals that on learning of Star Wars
he "laughed" and is "quite certain that [his] laughter blended with that
of thousands of other scientists and engineers," because the design of an
impenetrable nuclear shield is "virtually impossible." But if, as Brown
believes, the Star Wars concept is "reminiscent of the concept of perpetual motion," how can it also carry "unprecedented dangers," and
why does he say that "those of us who laughed when the Star Wars concept was first suggested should be crying"?[1]

This strange contradiction is at the heart of the debate about the Strategic Defense Initiative (SDI), otherwise known as Star Wars. Almost
everyone now accepts that SDI cannot defend America from nuclear
war. The world's premier scientific journal, *Nature,* stated flatly that

"the scientific community knows that [Star Wars] will not work." The Pentagon nevertheless insists that SDI is essential for U.S. security. Moscow incorporated opposition to Star Wars into the new Communist party program, thereby making it "one of the most basic precepts of the party." And the American peace community, having worked diligently to prove Star Wars impractical, continues denouncing it as an unprecedented threat to peace and committing many precious resources to stopping it.[2]

The preoccupation with Star Wars is perhaps the classic case of weaponitis. Star Wars cannot shift the nuclear equation, for better *or* for worse, any more than a perpetual-motion weapon could if President Reagan had gone on national television to announce that the United States was determined to build it.

Let us examine three of the central claims made about Star Wars: (1) it will protect people from nuclear war, (2) it will make nuclear war either more likely or less likely, and (3) it will radically transform the nuclear arms race.

A NUCLEAR UMBRELLA?

President Reagan's original vision, presented in his startling speech to the nation of March 23, 1983, was apparently of an impenetrable shield that could repel any offensive nuclear barrage, protect the U.S. population, and even "give us the means of rendering . . . nuclear weapons impotent and obsolete." A 1985 fund-raising letter of the Citizens for a High Frontier was in full agreement: "This plan . . . [will] make all of us safe from nuclear missile attack . . . [because] it will actually render harmless virtually all nuclear missiles anyone might fire at us."[3]

No one doubted that it was possible to shoot down ballistic missiles—and had been since the original ground-based antiballistic missile (ABM) weapons of the 1960s. But soon after the first ABMs were deployed, most authorities agreed that actually protecting populations and industry was well beyond their means. Indeed, the ABM treaty of 1972 was essentially a formal recognition by both sides that a practical and economic missile defense of society was unreachable in the 1970s.

The prognosis is unlikely to change in the 1990s or even in the twenty-first century. Former secretary of defense James Schlesinger writes that "there is no realistic hope that we shall ever again be able to protect American cities" because a single hydrogen warhead can destroy one. As McGeorge Bundy, George Kennan, Robert McNamara, and Gerard Smith point out, "even a 95-percent kill rate would be insufficient to save either society from disintegration in the event of general nuclear war." To work effectively, the shield cannot leak, but as the entire history of military technology shows, "there is no leak-proof defense."[4]

No complex technology works perfectly, and Star Wars would be by far the most complex ever attempted. But it "must work perfectly the very first time [it is used], since it can never be tested in advance as a full system." A true operational test would require an actual Soviet attack. As prominent software engineers have pointed out, even if the gamut of exotic Star Wars hardware by some miracle performed flawlessly in its first full-scale use, the unprecedentedly large software programs that control it would not, since it is impossible to build large "bugless" programs. David Parnas, a computer scientist on the president's Strategic Defense Initiative advisory panel, resigned with the following explanation: "Because of the extreme demands on the system and our inability to test it, we will never be able to believe, with any confidence, that we have succeeded."[5]

In fact, a leak-proof shield against current Soviet nuclear forces would be only the beginning, and possibly the easiest part, of strategic defense. For "any prospect of a significantly improved American defense is absolutely certain to stimulate the most energetic Soviet efforts to ensure the continued ability of Soviet warheads to get through." This is the answer to those who compare the prevailing skepticism about Star Wars' feasibility to that about putting a man on the moon in the 1960s: "The effort to get to the moon was not complicated by the presence of an adversary. A platoon of hostile moon-men with axes could have made it a disaster."[6]

One way to foil Star Wars is simply to attack it. Schlesinger predicts that "an effective opponent will develop defense suppression techniques and will punch a hole through any space-based defense that is deployed." And "no one has been able to offer any hope that it will ever be easier and cheaper to deploy and defend large systems in space than for someone else to destroy them. The balance of technical judgment is that the advantage in any unconstrained contest in space will be with the side that aims to attack the other side's satellites."[7]

The Soviets could also expand and improve their offensive nuclear strike forces until they could overwhelm, elude, and spoof the defensive screen. A study for the U.S. Office of Technology Assessment (OTA) by Ashton Carter, a Pentagon systems analyst in the first two years of the

Reagan administration, concludes that "for every defense concept proposed or imagined, including all of the so-called 'Star Wars' concepts, a
countermeasure has already been identified"; that these "could be implemented with today's technology, whereas the defense could not";
that "in general, the costs of the countermeasures can be estimated and
shown to be relatively low, whereas the costs of the defense are unknown but seem likely to be high"; and that "in general, the future technologies presupposed as part of the defense concept would also be potent weapons for attacking the defense." To take just one example, leaks
of a classified Defense Intelligence Agency study revealed Pentagon evidence that by 1993 the Soviets could build "fast-burn" rocket boosters
able to evade the critical "boost-phase" intercept by U.S. space-based
weaponry. That phase is the only chance to attack Soviet missiles before
they decompose into numerous warheads and decoys. The new Soviet
rockets would "burn out" so fast after leaving the earth's protective atmosphere that space-based weapons would not have enough time (less
than one minute) to destroy many of them before the hot exhaust used
to track them was gone.[8]

Even with a near-perfect antimissile defense—a technical absur-
dity—America would remain absolutely vulnerable to nuclear devastation; ballistic missiles are only one of many ways to deliver nuclear warheads. Others include air-breathing delivery vehicles (manned bombers
and cruise missiles) and covert delivery by commandos, infiltrators, and
saboteurs. Former secretary of defense Caspar Weinberger suggested
that Star Wars would defend against these threats as well, but that
hardly seems credible. Schlesinger points out that "the United States Air
Force has long argued that air defense systems [against manned bomb-
ers] are penetrable and will always be penetrable. . . . The United States
has long seacoasts. In contrast to the Soviet Union, the bulk of our
population lies along the coast." (Indeed, the United States long ago dis-
mantled the bulk of its air-defense system because of its impracticality
in the nuclear age.) Furthermore, "there is no foreseeable way that we
can preclude [cruise] missiles' impacting on our cities—even if we had a
perfect ballistic missile defense." The Carter OTA background paper
adds that "a desperate Soviet Union could introduce nuclear weapons
into the United States on commercial airliners, ships, packing crates, diplomatic pouch, etc." And it notes that even if all these methods somehow
failed, "other methods of mass destruction or terrorism would be feasible for the U.S.S.R., including sabotage of dams or nuclear power
plants, bacteriological attack, contaminating water, producing tidal
waves with near-coastal underwater detonations, and so on."[9]

As Bundy and his colleagues observe, "the overwhelming consensus of the nation's technical community is that in fact there is no prospect whatever that science and technology can, at any time in the next several decades, make nuclear weapons 'impotent and obsolete.'" Ashton Carter's OTA background paper, based on "full access to classified information and studies performed for the executive Branch," concludes as follows: "The prospect that emerging 'Star Wars' technologies, when further developed, will provide a perfect or near-perfect defense system . . . is so remote that it should not serve as the basis of public expectation or national policy." Even Lieutenant General James Abrahamson, former commander of the Star Wars program, has flatly stated that "a perfect defense is not a realistic thing." Under Secretary of Defense Richard DeLauer, the department's senior technical official, admitted in congressional hearings that "there's no way an enemy can't overwhelm your defenses if he wants to badly enough." The Reagan administration suppressed one of its own high-level technical reports that came to the same conclusion about SDI: "The report doesn't boldly state that the plan is idiotic. But after reading the list of disadvantages, only a fool could come to the wrong conclusion." [10]

Reactions such as this prompted several new twists in the president's argument to shore it up politically and lend it at least minimal scientific credibility. It was necessary to show how an *imperfect* defense might still protect Americans in a nuclear attack—a very small one, that is, launched by terrorists, a minor nuclear power, or even by the Soviet Union if it heavily cut back its offensive nuclear forces or made a small accidental launch. This justification is reminiscent of one rationale for the original American ABM of the 1960s: the need to defend against the nascent Chinese nuclear threat.

An imperfect defense against a small-scale attack is a far less demanding goal than foiling a large-scale attack and could possibly be achieved to an extent. But the importance of such a defense should not be exaggerated. A "mad captain" on either side might be able to launch an unauthorized attack—but an attack by even a single modern nuclear submarine would not in fact be very small and probably would not be calmly regarded as accidental by the nation at the receiving end. And as Ashton Carter argues, "Emerging nuclear powers or terrorists would be unlikely to use ICBMs [what Star Wars defends against] to deliver their small nuclear arsenals to the United States." [11]

A committed nuclear attacker or terrorist will probably always be able to detonate one or more warheads on American soil no matter what defenses are built. And Rathjens and Ruina note that "a reasonably thin area defense intended to protect against some unauthorized, accidental, or third-country attacks can be developed with existing technology. With time, such systems can surely be improved, but we need not await breakthroughs in technology resulting from the SDI program to address realistically the question of the net benefits of such a defense and to decide whether it should be deployed." Noted weapons scientist Richard Garwin asks, "If protecting the United States against accidental launches of Russian ICBMs is truly important, why wait for an elaborate defense? The United States and the Soviet Union could more easily and cheaply protect themselves against accidental launches by installing the command-destruct radio receivers commonly used in test firings of their operational missiles." Physicist Sherman Frankel points out that Star Wars only "detracts from getting on with deploying" such devices "on our huge arsenal of missiles."[12]

Fred Hoffman told a Senate armed services subcommittee in March 1985 that the inability of Star Wars to defend U.S. cities is irrelevant since the Soviets, for fear of retaliation in kind, probably would not attack cities. A Soviet attack on U.S. *military* targets, Hoffman contends, may "leave the bulk of Western civil society undamaged." Hence even an imperfect defense could increase the number of survivors. But as Sidney Drell and Wolfgang Panofsky point out, "While neither the United States nor the Soviet Union has made the destruction of enemy populations in response to enemy attack an explicit policy objective, both recognize that should a large fraction of the superpowers' arsenals be used—under any doctrine, any choice of pattern of attack, or for any purpose—then the threat to the survival of the two societies is very grave indeed."[13] In fact, Star Wars could easily *increase* the number of Soviet missiles hitting the United States if, as is likely, the Soviets acted on worst-case assumptions about the defense, building and firing more missiles than they otherwise would have, and if, as is also likely, the defense did not in fact work.

Most of the technical debate about Star Wars is simply beside the point. There is no way to defend populations against hydrogen weapons, period. It does not matter whether nuclear-pumped lasers, orbital battle stations, and the like can be made to work. The issue of the "pop-up" defense—Star Wars satellites that would be launched into orbit just before use to replace those destroyed by Soviet antisatellite weapons—illustrates how absurdly technical the debate has become. During 1984 Senate hearings, Harvard's Albert Carnesale conjectured that "if we could deploy a popup system, they could probably deploy a popup system to destroy ours." Senator Paul Tsongas asked the next logical question: "But you could not assure us that we could not develop an anti-popup popup system?"—that is, a way to pop up American satellites to destroy the satellites the Soviets popped up to destroy the satellites the United States popped up to destroy the missiles the Soviets popped up to pop the United States![14]

## A SHIELD FOR USING THE SWORD

As Schlesinger writes, the debate about Star Wars has undergone a "remarkable transformation": "The argument is no longer that somehow we can protect American cities perfectly. Instead the argument has become that maybe, not definitely but maybe, strategic defense would permit us to improve deterrence—and that the mix of offense and defense would lead to a more stable world."[15] The rationale is no longer that Star Wars can reduce the *consequences* of a nuclear war, but rather that it may reduce the *risk* by decreasing the incentives for a Soviet first strike.

In July 1985, for example, former national security adviser Zbigniew Brzezinski called in the *New Republic* for "reformulating [SDI] politically and strategically." He argued that "the U.S. should drop or at least de-emphasize President Reagan's idealistic hope for total nuclear defense for all our population." The goals, rather, should be to "reinforce deterrence and promote nuclear stability." On the anniversary of Hiroshima, the *Economist* wrote that "the case for Star Wars" rested not on a "wildly implausible" defensive screen for American society but on "the possibility of a defensive screen capable of stopping quite a lot of the Soviet warheads aimed at America's nuclear forces and command centres," which "would make it almost impossible for the Russians to risk a disarming first strike against America."[16]

The new goal of SDI, according to Gerold Yona, the Pentagon's chief Star Wars scientist, is to make "leakage of such low military value as to discourage a first strike." The Defense Department general counsel, William H. Taft IV, wrote that "the purpose of the President's initiative is to strengthen our ability to deter . . . to reduce the likelihood of war" and *not* to "save lives in time of war." Physicist Robert Jastrow ("the single most influential proponent of SDI outside the government") contends that Soviet first-strike weapons have "knocked the stuffing out of deterrence" and that only Star Wars can restore stability. Jastrow actually denies that President Reagan ever claimed that Star Wars was intended to defend American cities. The purpose of Star Wars, for now at least, is to "strengthen and preserve the American deterrent to a Soviet attack."[17]

Star Wars advocates claim, then, that the system will stabilize deterrence by discouraging a first strike. But critics counter that Star Wars will *destabilize* deterrence by encouraging a first strike. Schlesinger, for example, worries that Star Wars would "create instabilities during the entire period of deployment. . . . The advantage of striking first, for either side, would be greater than is the case for terrestrial capabilities." The late Herbert Scoville, president of the Arms Control Association and former high-level official of both the CIA and the Arms Control and Disarmament Agency, agreed that "developing defenses encourages a first strike." Harvard's Stanley Hoffmann, writing in the *New York Review of Books*, called Star Wars "a major threat to stable deterrence."[18]

The anti-SDI pledge, signed by most of the faculty of the nation's top-ranked physics departments as well as by many in other science and engineering departments, says: "The program is a step toward the type of weapons and strategy likely to trigger a nuclear holocaust." Hundreds of prominent scientists, including dozens of Nobel laureates and a majority of members of the National Academy of Sciences, signed a Union of Concerned Scientists appeal stating that space-based missile defenses and related antisatellite weapons "would increase the risk of nuclear war." The Mobilization for Survival's anti–Star Wars literature quotes the extraordinary claim of Robert Bowman, head of the Air Force advanced space programs between 1976 and 1978, that all Star Wars proposals "would be extremely destabilizing, probably triggering the nuclear war which both sides are trying to prevent." Writing on behalf of the same organization, Benjamin Spock warns that "our very survival depends on" stopping Star Wars.[19]

So we are told on the one hand that Star Wars is required to prevent, and on the other that it would trigger, nuclear war. Both claims, fortunately, are wildly overblown. Star Wars probably cannot affect the risk of nuclear war one way or the other. Because Star Wars cannot change the probable outcome of a nuclear war, it should not change the incentives on either side to start one.

As we saw in Chapter 2, a successful first strike by either side is simply impossible. Star Wars cannot change that. The American deterrent force does not need to be protected more than it already is. Considering in particular the invulnerability of U.S. strategic submarines, further protection of U.S. land-based missiles is of little importance. And

Star Wars would be perhaps the least plausible and most expensive way to approach the job. The United States could protect its missiles by superhardening their silos, moving them around on railways or on roads (as with the Midgetman missile), or defending them with simple ground-based antiballistic missiles (ABMs).[20] As for protecting command and control, as Charles Glaser points out, there are fewer than one hundred critical U.S. command and control points, and many of them are very fragile; hence "even very effective [ballistic missile defense] could not deny the Soviet Union the ability to destroy these targets with a first strike."[21]

The fear of an *American* first-strike capability, backed by Star Wars, is as baseless as the fear of a Soviet one. Many argue that while a leaky space umbrella is indeed no good in a downpour (that is, a Soviet first strike), it can help a lot in a drizzle (that is, ragged Soviet retaliation following an American first strike). But against hydrogen warheads that can each level a city, a leaky umbrella is meaningless in either case. Even after absorbing an American first strike, the Soviet Union could send off enough ballistic missiles (to say nothing of bombers and cruise missiles) to utterly destroy the United States no matter what defenses we build.

As E. P. Thompson acknowledges, with or without Star Wars a successful American first strike is nothing more than an "ideological fiction."[22] Both sides recognize this. True, the Soviets fear Star Wars. But what they really fear is losing a Star Wars technology race (which could give the United States a big advantage in spin-off technologies) and being forced to develop expensive countermeasures (a hedge against the small chance that Star Wars will actually work to a significant extent). The Soviet Union, we should recall, expressed urgent fear about many previous American nuclear systems, such as MIRVed missiles and the Pershing II and cruise Euromissiles. The United States has expressed similar fears about many Soviet systems, from sputnik to the "window of vulnerability." But these systems never tempted either side to preempt or even to take other steps—such as adopting a policy of launch on warning or putting bombers on airborne alert—that would indicate a genuine fear of first strike. Star Wars will not tempt them either.

As George Rathjens writes, the effects of Star Wars on crisis stability are "only of academic interest. . . . The prospects for a technically effective defense are so poor that I cannot imagine deployments in this century that would make a difference to the outcome of a nuclear exchange." Rathjens and Jack Ruina add that "there is no realistic prospect of defenses . . . even . . . being perceived as that effective."

None would be sufficient to affect "the behavior of nations in times of crisis." And even if we grant the improbable idea that Star Wars could slightly alter strategic stability or perceptions of it, we still cannot know the direction of the change. As Glaser observes, any U.S. nuclear defense program would probably be matched by the Soviets, and in that case "an attacker would face greater uncertainty about both the effectiveness of his attack *and* the effectiveness of the adversary's retaliation. The net effect of defenses is, therefore, indeterminate."[23]

Star Wars *could* change the amount of warning time between the detection of a possible Soviet missile attack and the decision about whether to respond. The best way to shoot down Soviet missiles would be to attack them from space within minutes of launch—so-called boost-phase interception—before they decompose into numerous warhead-carrying reentry vehicles and decoys. With time so short, many fear that U.S. commanders may panic or take a fateful step based on incomplete information, or even that the United States might computerize the split-second decision and thereby invite an accidental war.

But the exotic technology required to attempt boost-phase interception does not exist and may never be perfected. And activation of a boost-phase interception system, whether by accident or following a false alarm of Soviet attack, would probably mean nothing more than laser beams or other weapons shooting harmlessly into empty space. That should in no way be confused with the firing of Minuteman missiles after a false alarm, which would of course be a catastrophe but has nothing to do with Star Wars.

But what if Star Wars is really an offense masquerading as a defense? Could it then contribute to an American first strike? One study by R & D Associates, a Marina Del Ray think tank, warns that "in a matter of hours, a laser defense system powerful enough to cope with the ballistic missile threat can also destroy the enemy's major cities by fire—each city perhaps requiring only several minutes for incineration." An Argonne National Laboratory physicist adds that the fires caused by such an attack might "generate smoke in amounts comparable to the amounts generated in some major nuclear exchange scenarios," possibly triggering "a climatic catastrophe similar to 'nuclear winter.'"[24] These are appalling prospects, to be sure, but they have nothing to do with a first strike, and the superpowers can of course incinerate each other's cities and perhaps blacken the atmosphere in well under thirty minutes with technology already at hand.

Star Wars might also be used offensively, many critics contend, to attack Soviet satellites—a logical first step in a U.S. first strike. But as Ashton Carter points out, the loss of photoreconnaissance, communications, and even early warning satellites may seem dramatic but still cannot make a successful first strike possible and hence would not increase the incentives to preempt.[25]

In 1986 Robert English, a former Pentagon policy analyst, proposed the ultimate scenario for a U.S. first strike using Star Wars. It begins with a lightning "laser attack on the other side's communications networks and early-warning systems, including satellites." High-altitude nuclear explosions would "further paralyze command and control systems" through electromagnetic pulse. Then, "with the victim effectively blinded," the coup de grace: "the launch of space-based missiles against such targets as silos, command bunkers, airfields, and other military facilities. . . . Lasers might also be used to pin down missiles in their silos until the silos could be destroyed." Thus, "in a matter of minutes, the victim of such an attack might find the bulk of his ICBM and bomber force gone and his command systems in disarray—without having endured any significant damage to his cities and industries."[26]

True, there would be little if any warning of such a science fiction attack from space, but of course the victim could still destroy the attacker, if only from submarines that would remain invulnerable. Unsavory as offensive weapons in space may be, they seem unlikely to upset the nuclear stalemate any more than weapons on land have.

A LOGICAL CIRCLE

Though Star Wars cannot reduce the damage or change the likelihood of nuclear war, it may well transform the nuclear arms race. Advocates contend that the United States can ultimately bargain it away in return for dramatic Soviet concessions on offensive missiles, perhaps as part of grand strategic reductions along the lines of the START treaty. Critics predict the opposite: the demise of arms control, a runaway offensive arms race, and a new arms race in defenses and the militarization of space as the Soviets scramble to counter the American program. Four former high-level U.S. officials wrote in *Foreign Affairs* of "the president's choice: Star Wars or arms control."[27]

Whoever is correct, nothing of importance to deterrence is likely to change. Many times in the past the experts on nuclear war have attributed to some new weapon a decisive importance, either positive or negative, and when that proved difficult to sustain they have backtracked to the argument that even inconsequential new systems will set off a cycle of responses and counterresponses that *will* make a difference. As Richard K. Betts points out, concerns about the arms race have mostly been "future-oriented." Thus, "during the 'missile gap' controversy, the issue was whether the Soviets might achieve superiority a few years later. In the late 1970's the raging controversy was whether the 'window of vulnerability' would open by the early 1980's." Yet "when the early 1980's arrived, and the actual operating balance of intercontinental launchers and warheads had moved further in Soviet favor, U.S. concern evaporated because [of] Reagan's *plans* for strategic modernization and buildup."[28] Few notice that the feared or hoped-for developments never materialize because deterrence is in fact existential.

Perhaps someday the United States or the Soviet Union will build a weapon that actually changes the nuclear peril. But that is a remote prospect. In the meantime the superpowers are periodically endangering the planet, as they have over the past forty years, through different actions. To these we now turn.

# PART II

# How the Superpowers Roll the Nuclear Dice

If men could learn from history, what lessons it might teach us! But passion and party blind our eyes, and the light which experience gives us is a lantern on the stern, which shines only on the waves behind us!

—*Samuel Taylor Coleridge*

## CHAPTER SIX

# The Real History of the Nuclear Age

Ours is a world of nuclear giants and ethical infants.
—*General Omar Bradley*

In the early years after World War II, the United States considered using its massive nuclear advantage to reduce the Soviet Union to "a smoking radiating ruin at the end of two hours." [1] But the rapid development of the Soviet existential deterrent in the 1950s made the United States vulnerable to devastating retaliation. Since then, with the nuclear balance of terror firmly in place, a military advantage or disadvantage in the arms race—the main concern of the nuclear debate—has in fact *never* tempted the superpowers to attack each other and has *never* caused or even seriously contributed to an actual superpower crisis that threatened war, for the reasons explained in Part I.

American and Soviet leaders *have* repeatedly and intentionally risked nuclear war, but for a different reason—to back up foreign intervention and the division of the world into superpower-dominated spheres. In the early years, the superpowers clashed several times over the division of Europe. But the Berlin crises of 1958–1959 and 1961 showed that further confrontation on the continent would be far too dangerous. Neither side has provoked a crisis there since, and they probably will not in the future. As Noam Chomsky observes:

Some years ago it was perhaps realistic to suppose that Europe was the "tinderbox," but such a judgment hardly appears accurate today. If war does break out in Europe, it will probably be in reaction to conflicts arising elsewhere. Brutal repression will no doubt continue under Soviet rule, but it is extremely unlikely that it will lead to Western intervention; the day is long past when the U.S. was actively supporting guerrilla armies established by

Hitler in the Carpathian mountains or attempting to carry out coups in Albania, as part of its "rollback strategy." . . . It is also hardly likely that the U.S.S.R. would intervene within Western domains, even at or near its borders, any more than it has in the past: e.g., when the U.S. was engaged in destroying the former anti-Nazi resistance in Greece in the late 1940's, or backing the restoration of fascism in Greece in 1967, or supporting a ruthless military dictatorship in Turkey since 1980. Nor is it likely that either superpower will launch a military attack in Europe, or that either will attack the other directly.[2]

The restraints of the Cold War in Europe, however, did not apply to the Third World. There, the superpowers have continually used and sponsored enormous violence and, as we describe in this chapter, they have moved toward confrontation many times—in some cases waging tense crises, making nuclear threats, preparing nuclear weapons for use, and even considering whether to cross the nuclear brink.

In most cases, to be sure, the chance that a nuclear war would actually erupt seemed small at the time and still seems small in historical perspective. Even in the most serious crises, neither side has apparently come close to actually launching nuclear weapons or even to intentionally taking actions that could have directly precipitated such a calamity. To this degree leaders have been cautious, and the reason is clear: as we saw in Chapter 4, on both sides they have long recognized that a nuclear war would probably lead only to unimaginable destruction on a worldwide scale.

Nevertheless, a degree of nuclear peril is always present when the superpowers move in the direction of political or military confrontation, and certainly when one side actually prepares nuclear weapons for use or entertains the thought of using them. Each such incident is a nuclear gamble with uncertain odds, a roll of the nuclear dice. Again and again history has shown that no one can predict where crises involving states with massive nuclear-armed military forces will end.

The leaders of the nuclear states, as we will see, have long recognized the potential hazards of their Third World adventures. They have openly acknowledged that their actions could provoke a series of desperate reactions that, combined with unanticipated miscalculations, errors, and foul-ups, could produce a mad slide toward disaster. Today, as we will see, that danger is still real, perhaps more so than in the past. To see it we need only review the real history of the nuclear age—not the oft-told story of the nuclear arms race, but the hidden history of reckless Third World violence, intervention, confrontation, and crisis that has continually tempted fate since 1950. Our point is not that such adventures pose an enormous risk of nuclear war, but that *whether large or small* the nuclear danger primarily lies here, as it has for many years.

Much of the danger, as we show, has resulted from error, miscalculation, and leaders' inability fully to understand or control complex, violent crises. But the problem is deeper and more troubling. American, and to a lesser extent Soviet, leaders have on numerous occasions *intentionally* raised the risk of nuclear catastrophe when they thought that could help them achieve their goals. On the American side, at least, that strategy has been explicit. One of the key U.S. foreign policy planning documents of the postwar era, NSC 68 (enacted in 1950 and declassified in 1975), reveals the American plan to give the Soviet Union "evidence . . . that we may make any of the critical points [in the world] which we cannot hold the occasion for a global war of annihilation."[3] That is, where diplomatic and conventional military means were inadequate, the United States would use the danger of nuclear war to intimidate the Soviet Union into accepting American designs for various regions of the world. American leaders have repeatedly reaffirmed that intention in word and, much more significantly, have followed the dictate of NSC 68 in deed—providing ample "evidence" that conflict throughout the Third World, if not resolved to American satisfaction, could in fact end up in a global war of annihilation.

## KOREA, 1950–1953

Referring to the Korean War, U.S. Air Force General Jack J. Catton notes that

> General MacArthur and later General Ridgway [had] the atomic capability of a unit of the 43d Wing. . . . Those were B-50-A's, atomic-capable. . . . We could have atomic weapons very reliably and very accurately delivered within a period of about sixteen hours. We exercised that capability constantly throughout the war, of course on a simulated (but very realistic) basis. . . . That capability was there to be used and would be highly effective if our national command authority chose to do so.

The Strategic Air Command was alerted twice early in the war when U.S. ground forces got into trouble at Pusan and Yalu. Truman mentioned the nuclear option at a November 1950 press conference the day after Chinese troops surrounded U.S. marines at the Chosin Reservoir, bringing an alarmed British Prime Minister Atlee "scurrying across the ocean," in Dean Acheson's words. "Diplomatic hell broke loose . . . the news conference set off alarm bells abroad about the danger of World War III. . . . The U.S. chargé in London cabled Washington that British public opinion was 'deeply troubled' that escalation in Korea could ignite 'general atomic war.'"[4]

"In the desperate days of December 1950," writes Richard K. Betts, "General Douglas MacArthur . . . requested thirty-four [nuclear] bombs for use against retardation targets, invasion forces, and targets of opportunity." Truman wrote in his diary for January 27, 1952, that the "proper approach now would be an ultimatum" that could lead to "all out war" destroying "Moscow, St. Petersburg [Leningrad], Vladivostok, Peking, Shanghai, Port Authur, Dairen, Odessa, Stalingrad, and every manufacturing plant in China and the Soviet Union."[5]

Eisenhower's memoir, *Mandate for Change,* states that in case of a "major offensive" by the United States, "the war would have to be expanded outside of Korea"—to China—and that "to keep the attack from becoming overly costly . . . we would have to use atomic weapons. . . . We would not be limited by any world-wide gentleman's agreement. . . . we dropped the word, discreetly, of our intention. We felt quite sure it would reach Soviet and Chinese Communist ears." Declassified minutes of the National Security Council meeting of February 11, 1953, reveal that Eisenhower "expressed the view that we should consider the use of tactical atomic weapons on the Kaesong area. . . . Secretary Dulles discussed . . . Soviet success to date in setting atomic weapons apart from all other weapons as being in a special category. It was his opinion that we should try to break down this false distinction." Eisenhower was well aware of the terrible damage that even the primitive Soviet nuclear capabilities of the time could do. His memoirs note that if the United States used nuclear warheads, then there could be "problems . . . not the least of which would be the possibility of the Soviet Union entering the war. In nuclear warfare the Chinese Communists would have been able to do little. But we knew that the Soviets had atomic weapons in quantity and estimated that they would soon explode a hydrogen device."[6]

"Throughout the spring of 1953," Betts observes, "nuclear use in one form or other dominated the planning" for escalation of the war. "The principal division between the president and his military advisers . . . was on the *range* of nuclear options." In "a climactic May 20 meeting," after swearing the National Security Council to secrecy, Eisenhower approved a Joint Chiefs of Staff plan. That plan, "as Eisenhower later wrote, was to mount nuclear strikes against North Korea, Manchuria, and the Chinese coast." Indeed, "the president often went to great lengths in the secrecy of NSC consultations to promote explicit plans for employment of nuclear ordnance." Even after the armistice, the NSC continued its nuclear planning, forseeing "large-scale nuclear strikes against China" if the war reopened. "The principal targets were to be all forward airbases, with Eisenhower personally envisioning one atomic bomb on each field."[7]

Russell Weigley's *History of the United States Army* claims that 80-millimeter atomic cannons were actually sent to Korea. That report has not been verified, though Dulles announced at a December 7, 1953, meeting that the United States "had already sent the means to the theater for delivering atomic weapons." Eisenhower was later asked why the Chinese had finally settled. He answered, "Danger of an atomic war."[8]

## VIETNAM, 1954

Soon after the end of the Korean War, the United States again entertained the nuclear option—this time in Vietnam. A Pentagon study group concluded that three tactical nuclear weapons could relieve the French forces besieged at Dien Bien Phu. The Joint Chiefs of Staff thought that if the United States intervened, then atomic weapons should be used "whenever it is to our military advantage."[9]

French Prime Minister Bidault claimed that on two separate occasions in 1954 Dulles actually offered him tactical nuclear weapons— once for use against China, which was supplying the Vietminh, and once to rescue the French troops at Dien Bien Phu. Dulles denied making the offers. Bidault said he declined them. In Richard Nixon's description, Bidault told Dulles that "it would be impossible to predict where the use of nuclear weapons against Red China would end, that it could lead to Russian intervention and a worldwide holocaust." The U.S. Air Force chief of staff, General Nathan Twining, was not afraid:

> I still think it would have been a good idea [to have taken] three small tactical A-bombs—it's a fairly isolated area, Dienbienphu—no great town around there, only Communists and their supplies. You could take all day to drop the bomb, make sure you put it in the right place. No opposition. And clear those Commies out of there and the band could play the Marseillaise and the French could march out of Dienbienphu in fine shape. And those Commies would say, "Well, those guys might do this again to us. We'd better be careful."[10]

## QUEMOY AND MATSU, 1954–1955, 1958

An extremely serious Third World nuclear crisis occurred in 1954–1955 during a military conflict between mainland China and Taiwan over the tiny islands of Quemoy and Matsu. Occupied by Chiang Kai-shek's Nationalist forces as they fled to Taiwan, but always claimed by the People's Republic of China, the islands are, as Eisenhower described, practically within "wading distance" of the mainland.[11] This crisis rehearsed key elements of the Cuban missile crisis and later crises— among them American leaders' willingness to consciously risk nuclear holocaust for minor goals of foreign policy; their efforts to quell the popular fear of nuclear war in order to run these risks; and the role of little more than luck in preventing a lurch toward disaster.

After heavy Chinese shelling of Quemoy and possibly preparations to capture the islands, the United States decided to support Chiang's defense of them, bringing the United States and mainland China to the "edge of war," as Eisenhower acknowledged. As historian Gordon Chang persuasively demonstrates on the basis of newly available documentary evidence, "Eisenhower actually brought the country to the 'nuclear brink,' far closer to war than a distraught public feared in 1955, closer than Eisenhower acknowledged in his own memoirs, and closer than most historians have heretofore even suspected." He "was privately determined to defend the islands, and to use nuclear weapons if necessary."[12]

Details of the documentary record make shocking reading. The chairman of the Joint Chiefs of Staff (JCS), Admiral Arthur W. Radford, totally supported U.S. defense of the islands and the use of nuclear weapons in case of a major Chinese assault, as did the rest of the JCS.[13] By February 1955 the JCS ordered the Strategic Air Command to begin, on an "urgent basis," selecting targets for an "enlarged atomic offensive" against China. A memorandum by Secretary of State Dulles on a meeting with Eisenhower on March 6, 1955, records the two men's agreement that "the use of atomic missiles" would be required to defend the islands. On March 10 Dulles told the National Security Council (NSC) that war with China was "a question of time rather than a question of fact" and that he agreed with the military brass that it would rapidly go nuclear.[14]

On March 25 Admiral Robert Carney, chief of naval operations, publicly revealed (apparently without authorization) that he expected war with China by April 15 and that the United States was planning extensive nuclear attacks. On March 31 General Curtis LeMay, commander of the Strategic Air Command, provided eerie details in a cable to the head of the Air Force, General Twining, noting that one wing of bombers was already "in pos at Guam" with others on alert in the United States. The bombing plan was "ready for immed execution," he wrote; "target selections have been made, coordinated with other responsible comdrs and asgd to B-36 crew." McGeorge Bundy writes that in addition to nuclear-armed naval and air units in the area, "eight-inch howitzers that could have been supplied with nuclear warheads . . . were landed at Quemoy."[15]

On March 28 Secretary of State Dulles and his brother, Alan, director of the CIA, met with advisers to plan strategy. After the secretary proposed a "generalized" conventional and nuclear attack on China, "Robert Bowie, head of the Policy Planning Staff, and generally considered one of the administration's more moderate elements toward China, suggested that the United States announce it would 'from time to time' drop nuclear bombs on [Quemoy and Matsu] if they were captured by the Communists." Secretary Dulles thought that this plan would entail a "considerable waste" of valuable weapons and that the United States should not "splurge" its nuclear stockpile.[16]

Shortly after the publication of Chang's study, the Associated Press asked for comment from "a former senior counselor to President Eisenhower," who confirmed that "the President was definitely considering" the use of atomic weapons. The source gave details of a plan to drop several "small" (i.e., Hiroshima-size) atomic bombs on coastal Chinese air bases in the vicinity of Quemoy and Matsu, adding that Eisenhower and his aides understood that civilian casualties from such an attack could number "in the millions." The CIA had estimated that nuclear attacks on airfields and artillery opposite Quemoy would in fact cause twelve to fourteen million civilian casualties.[17]

Although the thought of these millions of potential innocent victims apparently did not bother American leaders, they realized that the populace at home and abroad might respond in horror. Dulles dryly noted at a National Security Council meeting on March 10, 1955, that the "United States and world public opinion must be prepared" for the use of nuclear weapons, and that much had to be done within the "next month or two." Indeed, he wanted to delay what he regarded as a nearly inevitable war with China in order to "create a better public climate for the use of atomic weapons." Admiral Radford "heartily endorsed" this position, although, understandably, "the rest of the NSC was practically speechless." Dulles was afraid that if public aversion to nuclear arms were allowed to grow, "we might wake up one day and discover that we were inhibited in the use of these weapons by a negative public opinion." As Chang notes, Eisenhower too had long "wanted to change public attitudes about the atomic bomb" and "the widespread public squeamishness about its use." The president stunned the world at a news conference on March 16 by announcing that he saw no reason "why [nuclear weapons] shouldn't be used just exactly as you would use a bullet or anything else." The next day, Vice President Nixon said that "tactical atomic weapons are now conventional and will be used against the targets of any aggressive force." On March 12 Secretary Dulles made the outrageous claim that American scientists had developed "new and powerful weapons of precision" that could "utterly destroy military targets without endangering unrelated civilian centers" and that these might be used in case the Quemoy-Matsu crisis erupted into war with China.[18]

Remarkably, the administration "virtually ignored the Soviet Union's potential responses," despite both superpowers' recent development of hydrogen weapons. Agitated, the British (among others) "feared that American belligerence would lead to world war." In reality, as historian H. W. Brands notes, "American leaders could not tell whether socialist fraternalism extended to a Soviet willingness to go to war over the off-shore islands." The Soviet ambassador officially noted the possibility, warning that in case of a U.S.-Chinese war the Soviets would face a "terrible dilemma. . . . Confronted with a choice between involvement in a war in which they had no direct interest and abandonment of their chief and possible only real ally in [the] world, it is impossible in advance to say which decision would be made." Eisenhower, of course, was well aware of the Soviet "nuclear umbrella" for China, and in November 1954 told the NSC, "When we talk of general war with Communist China, what we mean is general war with the U.S.S.R. also."[19]

Eisenhower resisted the most extreme advice of the military, such as Admiral Radford's suggestion that the United States preemptively bomb mainland air bases to give the Chinese a "bloody nose." Aware of the looming dangers, Eisenhower and Dulles agreed on a new proposal to offer Chiang Kai-shek: if the Nationalists withdrew from Quemoy and Matsu, the United States would blockade hundreds of miles of the mainland Chinese coast to prevent a military buildup that could threaten Taiwan. As Karl Rankin, the U.S. ambassador in Taiwan, understood it, the U.S. Navy would interdict all traffic of "a contraband or war-making character" and would "lay mine fields which would force coastwise junk traffic to come out where it also could be intercepted and controlled." Dulles even proposed putting nuclear weapons on Taiwan.[20] Chang relates that

> Rankin, who usually favored an aggressive policy toward the Chinese Communists and had supported the idea of a Nationalist blockade of the coast, was aghast. This proposal meant war. . . . How could the Communists accept a blockade of their coast or the mining of their own territorial waters? Radford agreed with Rankin's characterization of the proposal, adding that it would only be a matter of time before Chinese aircraft attacked American ships. Radford said he had fully informed Eisenhower of this probable outcome.

Chang agrees that "war would certainly have come if [Chiang] had accepted the evacuation-blockade plan."[21]

As Brands observes, that war was avoided "owed as much to luck as to skill, as [Dulles and Eisenhower] privately admitted." To the consternation of the Americans, Chiang, for his own reasons, flatly refused their offer, stating that "soldiers must choose proper places to die. Chinese soldiers consider Quemoy [and] Matsu . . . proper places for them." Unwittingly, Chiang probably averted a major, potentially nuclear, war by rejecting the reckless U.S. plan. Of course, Chiang's refusal to compromise on the status of Quemoy and Matsu created its own dangers of continued confrontation. But the People's Republic suddenly changed course, proposing negotiations rather than war and effectively ending the crisis. The reasons for this historic decision are unknown.[22]

Dulles later bragged: "Of course we were brought to the verge of war. . . . If you run away from it, if you are scared to go to the brink, you are lost." Three years later, in 1958, this logic produced a rerun of the Quemoy-Matsu crisis that again brought the United States and China "nearly to war." Again Eisenhower sent a directive to the JCS to prepare for imminent use of nuclear weapons in case of a Chinese attack on the islands, and again the Soviets explicitly threatened to intervene in case of an American attack on China and to respond in kind if the United States used nuclear weapons.[23]

SUEZ, 1956

During the serious 1956 Suez crisis, after the French-British-Israeli attack on Egypt, Eisenhower again sent Strategic Air Command nuclear bombers to forward bases and U.S. aircraft carriers with nuclear bombers aboard toward striking range of the Soviet Union. While avoiding provocative military actions, the Soviets pointedly reminded the three attackers that they were vulnerable to "rocket weapons." Soviet Premier Nikolai Bulganin sent a note to British Prime Minister Anthony Eden warning that "if this war is not stopped it carries the danger of turning into a third world war." The French foreign minister, according to CIA agent Chester Cooper, told the Israelis, "We have no defense against missiles. I suggest that you do not belittle Bulganin's warning." Cooper reports that his British counterparts were "ashen" after hearing the Soviet warning. Eisenhower took the danger seriously, too. He told a White House assistant, "If those fellows start something, we may have to hit 'em—and, if necessary, with *everything* in the bucket."[24]

## LEBANON, 1958

During one more Third World nuclear incident of the Eisenhower years, the 14,000-man American invasion of Lebanon in 1958, nuclear-armed ships patrolled offshore and Eisenhower again "ordered a world-wide military alert of U.S. forces." "Strategic Air Command planes were prepared for takeoff if necessary." According to William Quandt, "nuclear-capable howitzers were even landed in Lebanon," although others claim that nuclear ordnance remained aboard ship.[25] The chairman of the Joint Chiefs of Staff, General Nathan D. Twining, "was ordered to 'be prepared to employ, subject to [Eisenhower's] approval, *whatever* means might become necessary'" to achieve American objectives. "It seems clear," Quandt writes, "that Eisenhower was referring to the possible use of nuclear weapons, an issue that was discussed several times during the crisis." According to Eisenhower's memoirs, these events again posed a risk of "general war with the Soviet Union," when Soviet nuclear capabilities were even greater than in the previous crises. Egypt's President Nasser requested assistance from Moscow, but Khrushchev told him, "We are not ready for World War III."[26]

## CUBA, 1962

The 1962 Cuban missile crisis is generally considered the great watershed of the nuclear age and is discussed in detail in Chapter 7. President Kennedy thought the chances of a superpower war were "between one in three and even." "One group, which included the majority of President Kennedy's advisors, believed we should seek to destroy the missiles by an air attack" even though "such an attack would almost certainly require a follow-up ground invasion that might result in twenty-five thousand U.S. casualties and a corresponding number of Cubans dead or wounded" and even though "it was believed that . . . the Soviet Union would very likely respond by military action against the flanks or even the center of NATO"—that is, by an all-out East-West showdown. As it was, President Kennedy chose the less aggressive tactics of quarantining Cuba, forcing "five or six" Soviet submarines to surface, and ultimately coming close to invading Cuba anyway. Like other presidents before and after him, Kennedy knew that public fear of nuclear war could constrain his freedom of action; he kept the entire affair secret until the decision to blockade Cuba, which he could not hide. As Raymond Garthoff, a participant in these events, recalls approvingly, Kennedy wanted to be "free of public pressure . . . free from external and domestic political pressures." Robert McNamara, then secretary of defense, recalls, "I feared I might never live to see another Saturday night on October 27."[27]

The standard view is that the shock of this crisis led both superpowers to a deep reevaluation of foreign policy and a commitment to avoid further nuclear danger points. Two noted Harvard scholars, for instance, write: "Since that time, both governments have exercised extraordinary caution about all things nuclear, circumventing interests in order to avoid fundamental clashes, cooling conflicts that might erupt."[28]

The historical record does not support such claims. Although both superpowers have certainly exercised some caution and no subsequent crisis has moved so near the brink as the Cuban confrontation, they have repeatedly come far closer to war in the Third World than most people appreciate. In some cases they actively *sought* confrontation for political purposes. Indeed, recklessness, not "extraordinary caution," may be the real legacy of the Cuban missile crisis, the official postmortem of which "concluded that the principal error of the president and his advisers was that they had worried *too much* about the danger of nuclear war."[29]

## MIDDLE EAST, 1967

Only five years after the Cuban shock, during the 1967 Arab-Israeli war, then secretary of defense Robert McNamara recalls that "once again the superpowers . . . moved close to confrontation." Indeed, the Soviets used the new hot line for the first time on June 5, the day after the lightning Israeli attack on Egypt, and again on June 6. Despite this dramatic evidence of Soviet concern and President Johnson's awareness that "the danger implicit in every border incident in the Middle East was not merely war between Israelis and Arabs but an ultimate confrontation between the Soviet Union and the United States and its NATO allies," the president sent the U.S. Sixth Fleet steaming toward the conflict zone.[30]

There the Sixth Fleet played a naval cat-and-mouse game with Soviet warships in which "the risk of U.S.-Soviet combat was often uncomfortably high." In one instance, on June 8, two Soviet warships "repeatedly intruded into the [American aircraft carrier] *America* formation, at times on a collision course with U.S. units." A Soviet patrol boat was observed "twisting in and out around the 77,000-ton carrier in dangerous maneuvers, attempting to force her to alter her course." These actions "continued for several hours, despite repeated demands by U.S. commanders that the Soviet ships withdraw."[31]

That same day President Johnson received word that the American intelligence ship *Liberty* had been attacked in international waters near the war zone, with much loss of life. As Johnson recalls, "For seventy tense minutes we had no idea who was responsible." McNamara "thought the *Liberty* had been attacked by Soviet forces." Armed American planes rushed toward the scene, while Johnson used the hot line to contact the Soviets. "Fortunately the episode occurred on the fourth day of the war when U.S.-Soviet tension was at a reduced level. Had *Liberty* been attacked earlier, before the hot line and other diplomatic exchanges had made the superpowers' intentions clear to each other, or later, when the threat of Soviet military intervention in Syria arose, the possibility of a sudden exchange between the superpower fleets might have been greater." One officer on board the *Liberty* wrote that the American F-4s "might have saved the ship, or they might have initiated the ultimate holocaust." McNamara has since said, "Thank goodness our carrier commanders did not launch immediately against the Soviet ships who were operating in the Mediterranean." As it turned out, the Israelis, not the Soviets, had attacked the American ship (officially an accident, but by some accounts a deliberate attack to make certain that military intelligence from the ship did not reach the Arab states).[32]

Such an accident or miscalculation was not the only possible spark for a world war. Some evidence suggests that in 1967 "Israel possessed at least a handful of nuclear weapons." Moreover, Anthony Wells notes, "As one Soviet writer later stressed, Washington would not have allowed Israel to be beaten, while in the White House there was concern over 'what Moscow might do if the Arabs were defeated. The Russians had planted stories to the effect that they would not permit Syria to be taken over.'" Amid reports of Israeli advances toward Damascus and bombing of the city, Kosygin again used the hot line, on June 10, in effect threatening, according to McNamara, "If you want war, you will get war." According to Johnson, Premier Kosygin "said a 'very crucial moment' had now arrived. He spoke of the possibility of 'independent decision' by Moscow. He foresaw the risk of a 'grave catastrophe' and stated that unless Israel unconditionally halted operations within the next few hours, the Soviet Union would take 'necessary actions, including military.'" Johnson observes that "in an exchange between heads of government, these were serious words: 'very crucial moment,' 'catastrophe,' 'independent decision,' 'military actions.'" On the basis of interviews with key participants, Wells reports:

> The [Soviet] threat was taken seriously in Washington. Helmut Sonnenfeldt, a key U.S. official involved with the crisis, has stressed that the Soviets were at the limits of tolerance: their hotline talk indicated that, if the Israelis did not desist, Moscow did in fact mean business, in the form of a massive airborne landing or drop. Dean Rusk, then Secretary of State, recalls the White House expectation that the Soviets were on the verge of using their Airborne Troops: he and President Johnson "had never assumed any other."[33]

Acutely aware of the unfolding dangers, Johnson tried to get the Israelis to stop advancing on Damascus. According to Moshe Dayan, "Secretary of State Dean Rusk got in touch with our foreign minister, Abba Eban, and our ambassador in Washington and asked them in near panic where we thought we were heading." At the same time, escalating tensions and risking further American engagement in the war zone, Johnson ordered the Sixth Fleet to steam rapidly to the Syrian coast, changing its orders to permit an approach to within fifty miles. Johnson says that his purpose was to send a "message" to the Soviets that "no translator would need to interpret to the Kremlin leadership": "that the United States was prepared to resist Soviet intrusion in the Middle East," even an "intrusion" to defend the capital of an ally from attack by an invading American client. Additional hot-line exchanges continued "throughout the morning."[34]

Fortunately a new cease-fire was soon negotiated, and with the war essentially over the superpower crisis subsided. Rusk's "feeling at the time was one of despair if the cease-fire had not held and the Israelis not halted when they did." McNamara recently agreed that "if the Israeli-

Syrian cease-fire had failed, superpower military intervention in the region would have become a reality." Johnson wrote that "the peace of the world walked a tightrope between June 5 and June 10, 1967." When Algerian leader Houari Boumedienne visited Moscow in 1967 and complained about Soviet caution in the war, Brezhnev replied, "What is your opinion of nuclear war?"[35]

SUEZ, 1970

In 1970 *three* separate crises erupted that American leaders believed to pose risks of superpower confrontation. The first was the bloody 1969–1970 War of Attrition between Israel and Egypt along the Suez Canal. In January 1970, after much violence on both sides, "Israeli planes [U.S.-supplied Phantom jets] began to stage a series of lightning attacks against missile sites and other military targets deep in the Egyptian heartland, bombing the very outskirts of Cairo" and in one case killing "70 civilians and wounding many more." Egypt succeeded in getting new Soviet military equipment to deal with the Israeli threat, and "in April Soviet fighter pilots were noted for the first time helping defend Egyptian airspace," a step that William Quandt notes "greatly raised the risk of superpower confrontation." The Soviets also "began to man SAM [antiaircraft] sites, and they began to staff Egyptian army units down to the company level." In a "momentous decision to employ Soviet combat forces on a large scale for the first time outside the Eastern bloc," the Soviets ultimately "deployed large numbers of air defense aircraft and missiles to Egypt and 10–15,000 combat and support personnel to man them." These forces "were clearly prepared to fight a major battle if circumstances had required" and "may have incurred risks that far exceeded any before (or since) in their diplomacy in the Third World." One of these was "a direct confrontation between the superpowers over interests that were important but not vital."[36]

Indeed, Kissinger writes of bluntly drawing a parallel to the Cuban missile crisis with the Soviet ambassador, Dobrynin, who could hardly have missed the point given Dobrynin's vital role in that earlier crisis. Far from concluding that this parallel demanded extreme caution, Kissinger decided that the main task was to "face down" the Soviets and "the Arab radicals." Incidentally, Kissinger's biographers, Kalb and Kalb, note that, at this point at least, Kissinger knew "next to nothing" about the Middle Eastern conflicts and that "he often admitted his limitations in this respect."[37]

Golda Meir threatened Nixon in a personal note stating that if the United States did not supply enough weapons to Israel, irrational actions by her government could not be ruled out, and "one cannot overstate the seriousness of the situation that will result." Kissinger believed that dogfights between Soviet and Israeli pilots became "a virtual certainty" by late April, but rejected what he derides in his memoirs as "the political strategy" recommended by the experts. Rather, in late May he told a meeting of the Senior Review Group: "What will discourage the Soviets is fear of confrontation with us. We have to have thought of how to convey that idea to them." By July 1 Prime Minister Meir was telling Nixon that she would soon feel compelled to bomb Soviet air defense installations, a move that Kissinger realized could produce "a direct clash between Israel and the Soviet Union," with obvious international dangers of the highest order.[38]

Although all parties to the conflict evidently made efforts to avoid such a clash, incidents that could have led to an Israeli-Soviet war did occur. On the night of June 29–30, Soviet SA-2 antiaircraft missiles "were moved forward, set up, and fired at dawn against attacking Israeli aircraft," with "two F-4's downed, the first losses of F-4's in combat. The Israelis were to lose two more by the middle of July and a third in the first weeks of August—severe losses given their small inventory and the American refusal to provide replacements." As Alvin Rubinstein observes, "The nearer Soviet crews and pilots drew to the incendiary canal area, the more ominous became the potential for a Soviet-Israeli crisis." Indeed, raising "the possibility that [the Soviets] might commit their own forces to the battle," SA-3 antiaircraft batteries moved to within range of the canal in early July, "presumably still manned by Soviet crews." In addition, "Soviet fighter operations intensified and began to take place . . . over the northern and southern flanks of the canal front. . . . Their presence aloft only a few minutes flight time from [the main Israeli-Egyptian combat] area raised the possibility that an air engagement would occur." Finally, on July 30, "Israeli Mirages ambushed a flight of Soviet-piloted MiGs south of Suez City, downing four."[39]

By this time, if not in 1967, Israel had probably developed atomic weapons. Peter Pry's study of the Israeli nuclear program concludes that although definitive information is unavailable, "by or before the early 1970's Israel [had] probably . . . armed itself with nuclear weapons." He notes that "some CIA analysts seem to believe that Israel had several bombs as early as 1968. . . . Tahtinen, in *The Arab-Israeli Military Balance Today*, suggests that Israel had actually built 'five or six' devices of

19 kiloton yield by 1969." Pry adds that CIA director Richard Helms, "speaking before the Senate Foreign Relations Committee on 7 July 1970 . . . testified that the Israelis at that time had the means to build an A-bomb."[40] If true, this means that in the tense 1970 conflict two nuclear-armed states were engaged in open combat, as in the Sino-Soviet border clash of 1969. Even ignoring the risk of direct U.S. intervention and superpower confrontation, then, a nuclear war was possible. Fortunately a cease-fire prevented additional Soviet-Israeli combat.

## JORDAN, 1970

Another crisis was brewing. On September 15 King Hussein "placed Jordan under martial law and replaced his civilian government with generals." Two days later, in what Palestinians remember as the Black September, Hussein's army launched a "massive drive" against the large Palestinian forces then based in Jordan. Meanwhile, a Palestinian faction staged a major hijacking and held hundreds of hostages.[41]

Nixon was aware "that a crisis in the Middle East could lead to a superpower confrontation." He observes in his memoirs that "the potential for a confrontation between the United States and the U.S.S.R. loomed large. If the Soviets were committed to Arab victories, and we were committed to Israeli victories, it did not require much imagination to see how we both might be drawn in even against our wills—and almost certainly against our national interests." But as Seymour Hersh writes, "Nixon was determined to have his crisis and prove his mettle, as John F. Kennedy had in the Cuban missile crisis."[42] He and Kissinger ordered U.S. naval forces to the area.

Amid Israeli and Jordanian reports that Syrian tanks had crossed the Jordanian frontier to help defend the Palestinian fedayeen, more American military forces, notably including the 82d Airborne Division, were alerted on September 19. "Then airborne units in West Germany were moved to airfields, crossing the Autobahn in so conspicuous a fashion that the Russians could not fail to pick up the signals. 'We wanted to get picked up,' Kissinger told us."[43] Large forces of ships, subs, and marines, including several aircraft carriers, moved to the area.

U.S. government specialists on the Middle East were skeptical about the reports of major Syrian intervention. As one of Kissinger's National Security Council aides reports, "We were relying on [information from] the Israelis, who had a vested interest, and Hussein, who was panicked." Andrew Killgore, a U.S. State Department desk officer in charge of the area at the time, notes that the United States had no direct sources of intelligence: "It was like the dark side of the moon." Killgore told Hersh that while some tanks (some, at least, with Palestinian Liberation Army markings) apparently did cross into Jordan from Syria, "we started getting these reports as if . . . they were invading in full force." Killgore and the National Security Council aide thought Israel had fabricated the intelligence reports to justify intervening and seizing the strategic Irbid Heights in Jordan. Hersh reports that both Nixon and Egyptian Foreign Minister Riad thought the Israelis were looking for a pretext to attack Syria as well, perhaps decisively. That action would likely have provoked Egypt to move into the Sinai and, Riad thought, into a new Middle East war.[44]

The United States likewise had no firm grounds to believe that the Soviet Union was encouraging a Syrian intervention. A National Security Council aide, observing that the Soviets were probably not involved, recalls: "We always seemed to be dragging the Soviets into crises. It's almost as if the Soviets weren't there, but we were going to discover them anyway." This aide briefed Nixon on events as they unfolded and reports, "I'd walk in and begin to give a specific listing of what'd happened overnight and Nixon would interject, 'Bomb the bastards,' or some other wild remark." Kissinger would then escort the aide out of the room.[45]

The United States and Israel discussed plans for military operations, including air strikes against Syrian forces and even deployment of U.S. ground forces directly into Jordan. Speaking to reporters, Nixon earlier "said that the United States might have to intervene in Jordan if Syria or Iraq threatened Hussein's regime." He "reportedly said that it would not be such a bad thing for the USSR to believe that the United States was capable of 'irrational action.'" Quandt reports that "the USSR clearly took the threat of U.S. intervention seriously." Kissinger, according to his memoirs, favored letting Israelis rather than Americans do the fighting, except for rescuing American hostages. But Nixon adamantly supported the direct use of American forces, even as "Soviet warships were beginning to shadow our Sixth Fleet off the coast of Lebanon." According to Kissinger, the dramatic show of American force "appealed to [Nixon's] romantic streak," leading the president to remark, "the main thing is there's nothing better than a little confrontation now and then, a little excitement."[46]

As for where "a little excitement" might have led, Nixon observed in retrospect that "the possibility of a direct U.S.-Soviet confrontation was

uncomfortably high. It was like a ghastly game of dominoes, with a nuclear war waiting at the end." Kissinger evidently took the possibility
seriously enough to wonder how the endgame might work out. According to Hersh: "In 1972, citing Jordan as an example of the impotence of
American nuclear planning, Kissinger asked senior Pentagon officials to
study new options for the use of such weapons. . . . Kissinger's com-
plaint was that if he was unable effectively to threaten the use of nuclear
weapons in such crises, 'we weren't getting our money's worth out
of them.'"[47]

Kissinger recalls that his "biggest problem . . . was to keep [Nixon's]
courage from turning into recklessness and the firmness into bravado."
His own, more moderate, view was that at the moment of confrontation
the national leader "must be prepared to escalate rapidly and brutally to
a point where the opponent can no longer afford to experiment." In "his
real baptism of fire in a crucial crisis management situation," Kissinger
"leaned over large maps, moving toy battleships and aircraft carriers
from one end of the Mediterranean to the other, arguing with admirals,
expounding on military tactics and then picking up the phone to order
the JCS [Joint Chiefs of Staff] to change the deployment of the Sixth
Fleet. The World War II sergeant had become all at once a general and
an admiral and, during that crisis, a kind of deputy Commander in
Chief." One top official explains: "Henry adores power, absolutely
adores it. To Henry, diplomacy is nothing without it."[48]

He got his chance to use it. At a New York party the night of September 20, Kissinger conveyed to Rabin and Meir a "critical" request by
King Hussein for Israeli intervention against the Syrian tanks. While the
Israelis pondered it, "five U.S. divisions, based in West Germany, were
put on full, ostentatious alert. The Sixth Fleet was expanded from two
to five carrier task forces," though "it was clear that most of Western
Europe [notably including Britain, the former great power in the area]
opposed American intervention." Nixon "could have gone to the people,
as Kennedy had done during the Cuban missile crisis, but he chose, four
months after Cambodia, to keep this crisis as muted as possible."[49]

The "diplomatic approach" suggested by Secretary of State Rogers,
perhaps with joint superpower efforts to end the crisis, was rejected. Instead, the Soviets were "again told that there would be an acute danger
to peace unless the Syrian tanks retreated. No option would be ruled
out." The Soviets in turn warned against "all" outside intervention.[50]

Hussein's forces reportedly stopped the Syrian advance. But the danger had not passed. "The Israeli Cabinet reached a decision. If . . . addi-

tional Syrian tanks moved [into Jordan], *with or without the Russians,* then Israel would intervene." Rabin told Kissinger that in addition to air strikes, Israel reserved the right to send ground troops into Jordan, and even into Syria itself, if necessary to secure the "political goal" of saving Hussein's regime. But "the Israelis attached a very significant condition that could have involved the United States in a Middle East war." Rabin insisted that the U.S. promise to deter, and if necessary meet with force, any Soviet intervention against the Israeli attack.[51]

The Defense Department expressed the fear that the Soviets would in fact respond to Israeli intervention with air strikes against Israel, a horrifying scenario almost certain to produce an extreme superpower confrontation. (And recall that Israel may have had its own nuclear weapons at the time.) Nixon simply "snorted" and responded, "I don't believe it." On September 21, when a small number of new Syrian tanks reportedly crossed the border, he unilaterally approved Israeli ground actions against the Syrians after being awakened by an early morning phone call from Kissinger and engaging in "a few moments" of discussion.[52]

Even Kissinger, eager for a showdown, was disturbed by this cavalier action. He recalls: "I was not about to let the President run the risk of a major confrontation with the Soviet Union without consulting his senior advisors. An Israeli ground operation could produce a Mideast war." After such a consultation, according to Kissinger, the decision was suspended for debate, which if true could have been a fateful step. Other accounts suggest that Israeli ground actions may indeed have been authorized. Quandt writes, "It appears . . . that agreement was reached late on September 21 that Israel would be prepared to intervene in Jordan by air and ground if Hussein's position were to deteriorate further." Kissinger reports, in any event, that "our government was united on approving Israeli air attacks."[53]

Most important, in "potentially one of the most critical decisions Nixon had to make," the president gave the Israelis the remarkable assurances that they sought, paving the way for perhaps the most feared of all international events, a direct superpower clash in the Middle East. The significance was not lost on the Kalbs: "Their understanding was stark and historic: Israel would move against Syrian forces in Jordan; and if Egyptian *or Soviet* forces then moved against Israel, the United States would intervene against *both.*"

> Israeli tanks, in great number, moved toward the Jordan River. The Golan Heights came alive with visible preparation for war. At military airfields throughout Israel jet engines were revved up and missile racks and bomb

bays were loaded. An American aircraft carrier eased to within sixty nautical miles of the Israeli coastline.[54]

The Russians watched.

Just in time, on September 22, reports arrived that Hussein's air force and army had hurt the Syrian tanks badly and sent some retreating home. By the following day the crisis was over, though the timing was so close that Quandt refers to Israeli or American military intervention as a "near thing." Quandt also notes "the virtual unanimity" within the Nixon administration over the goal of preparing for Israeli, American, or joint military intervention despite a clear awareness of the terrible risk involved.[55]

Even without direct intervention, the tension of the crisis could have produced a superpower clash. In his memoir, *On Watch*, Admiral Elmo Zumwalt describes how "Soviet ships equipped with cruise missiles trailed U.S. carriers around the clock . . . we . . . assigned ships armed with rapid fire guns to trail the trailers . . . to prevent them from preventing us from launching our planes by knocking out most of their cruise missiles before many of them took off."[56] In one case,

> a [Soviet] *Kynda*-class SSM [surface-to-surface missile] cruiser and a *Kashin*-class SAM [surface-to-air missile] destroyer, probably reacting to low-altitude, high-speed surveillance by three U.S. carrier-based aircraft, went to battle stations, trained their guns on the U.S. destroyer trailing them, ran surface-to-air missiles out on their launchers, and appeared to track the departing U.S. aircraft with their fire control radars. Fortunately, the U.S. destroyer did not respond to these gestures, and no more aircraft were dispatched to the scene.

Despite this warning of the dangers of superpower naval jostling, "the intermingling of Soviet and U.S. forces in postures of high readiness lasted until the end of October, although the crisis began to wind down on September 25."[57]

Nixon, we should add, "did not go to great lengths to communicate with the Soviet leaders," ignoring another supposedly well-learned lesson of the Cuban missile crisis. Indeed, though the hot line had been created after the 1962 scare to reduce the nuclear hazards of just this kind of situation, it "was not used during the crisis."[58]

## CUBA, 1970

At the height of the Jordanian crisis, H. R. Haldeman writes, Kissinger burst into his office with reconnaissance photographs of the Cuban port of Cienfuegos. Kissinger announced: "The Cubans are building soccer fields. . . . These soccer fields could mean war, Bob." When Haldeman asked why, Kissinger answered: "Cubans play *baseball*. Russians play *soccer*." Thus began yet another Soviet-American crisis "with prospects of direct superpower confrontation."[59]

For Kissinger, the soccer fields were evidence of a large Soviet base under construction—one that could repair and refuel nuclear missile submarines, and in a debatable interpretation, might violate the vague, unofficial understandings that ended the Cuban missile crisis. Cubans have played soccer, however, since at least 1924. They compete for the World Cup. Although the Soviets were apparently constructing something, "intelligence experts in the State Department, the CIA, and even the Pentagon saw no tangible evidence of a major installation." But "State Department officials did not realize that Kissinger was eager for a confrontation, whether justified or not."[60]

Nixon had his own interest in Cuba. During his 1960 television debate with John F. Kennedy, he recalls in his memoirs, "Kennedy conveyed the image—to 60 million people—that he was tougher on Castro and communism than I was." As Kissinger notes, "Nixon was determined that no one would ever be able to make this charge again." Kalb and Kalb comment: "Nixon had lost to Kennedy in 1960; he was not going to lose to Kennedy's ghost in 1970."[61]

Nixon's reflections on the 1962 comparison in his memoirs are frighteningly explicit on this point. He criticizes Kennedy for going public with the Soviet nuclear deployments early in the original crisis because doing so allowed "the universal fear of war to put pressure on Kennedy," preventing him from taking more forceful actions. "So instead of dealing with Khrushchev from the position of immense nuclear superiority that we still held in 1962, Kennedy ended up by agreeing to refrain from any anti-Castro activities in return for Khrushchev's removal of the Soviet missiles from Cuba"—apparently a humiliating show of weakness, in Nixon's opinion. "In view of what had happened in the 1962 crisis," Nixon writes, "I decided that I . . . would not deal with the Soviets from anything less than a position of unyielding strength."[62]

At the same time, "for all Nixon knew, [the Jordanian crisis] might trigger a showdown with the Soviet Union." Nevertheless he ordered contingency plans for military actions against Cuba, including the "tailing of Soviet ships." He also sent Kissinger to tell Dobrynin that the United States viewed the sub base "with the utmost gravity"—a clear reference to the White House's willingness to provoke an extreme crisis, if necessary, to remove the base. The Russian turned "ashen" (exactly the word used to describe Dobrynin's reaction on learning of Kennedy's decision to initiate the first Cuban missile crisis eight years before!). Dobrynin "understood the deeper meaning of Kissinger's warning. Not only would progress toward Soviet-American détente be halted, but an updated 'missile crisis' could easily result." Kissinger urged Nixon to "face the Soviets down." He believed that "we were close to . . . [a] confrontation" with the Soviets.[63]

Nixon reports that he ordered complete secrecy about these events, even as they were beginning to leak out, on the logic that as in 1962 "a serious war scare would sweep the country if the real story of Cienfuegos hit the headlines." Indeed, "some critics were already beginning to suggest that the President was 'manufacturing' confrontations with the Russians merely to demonstrate his machismo." Aware of the dangers, the American people might not approve of Nixon's confrontational actions, especially since (as we explain in Chapter 7) the sub base in question had little military significance. The people were not to know of the possibility, as Nixon candidly writes, of "what would have been known as the Cuban Nuclear Submarine Crisis of 1970 . . . which, like its predecessor, might have taken us to the brink of nuclear confrontation with the Soviet Union."[64] For although the general population had been terrified by the close call in 1962, the leadership was determined to continue brinksmanship diplomacy in the nuclear age. Secrecy was the only way to accomplish it.

Kissinger "solemnly warned the Russians that the President would regard the construction of a nuclear submarine base in Cuba as a 'hostile act'"—an interpretation he surely hoped the Soviets would not lend to the numerous American nuclear weapons bases around the periphery of their country. Secretary of State Rogers "was baffled by Kissinger's warning and criticized him for 'engaging in Cold War rhetoric.' . . . He refused to draw the apocalyptic conclusions about Soviet intentions." Quite correctly, "he did not think a sub base at Cienfuegos would upset the balance of forces in the Caribbean." Tad Szulc reported in the *New York Times* that U.S. intelligence sources said "they were at a loss" to explain the White House's aggressive actions.[65]

The Soviets quickly promised not to operate nuclear missile submarines out of Cuba. But that did not satisfy the White House, which insisted that not even repair and tending vessels for nuclear subs could operate from Cuban bases. Kissinger told Dobrynin that any servicing of subs in or from Cuban ports would "lead to the most grave situation between the United States and the Soviet Union"—language uncannily reminiscent of the ultimatums of the original Cuban missile crisis.[66] The Soviets again relented. Had they not, it is clear that Nixon and Kissinger would have taken extreme steps, perhaps any steps, to keep the bases out of Cuba.

INDIA AND PAKISTAN, 1971

A short time after the three 1970 crises, the Indo-Pakistani war provided another opportunity for crisis, this time involving the forces of no fewer than four nuclear-armed states: the United States, the Soviet Union, Britain, and China. On March 25, 1971, Pakistani General Yahya Khan

> imposed martial rule on East Pakistan, separated from [West Pakistan] by one thousand miles of hostile Indian territory. He was hoping to nullify the results of an election that clearly expressed the desire of the local population—the Bengalis—for political autonomy and, by military means, to put an end to the rebelliousness of the more populous eastern half of Pakistan. The result was a bloodbath. Yahya's soldiers embarked on what the Bengalis and their Indian supporters described as a ruthless campaign of murder, rape, and other atrocities against unarmed civilians in villages and towns throughout East Pakistan. By autumn, over ten million terrified Bengalis had fled across the border to India, which was ill-equipped to handle the flood of refugees.[67]

India threatened to intervene to defend the Bengalis, a predictable action that raised the possibility of a big war with superpower involvement. Meeting with Prime Minister Indira Gandhi on November 4, Nixon recalls: "I said that in some respects the situation was similar to that in the Middle East: just as American and Soviet interests were involved there, so Chinese, Soviet, and American interests were at stake in South Asia and the Indian subcontinent. 'It would be impossible to calculate precisely the steps which other great powers might take if India were to initiate hostilities.'"[68]

That month "border confrontations—mortaring and shelling, tank engagements, and jet aircraft duels—between Pakistani and Indian troops along the eastern border had become frequent." Finally, on December 3, after "a major [Pakistani] air and ground offensive on Indian military forces stationed along the West Pakistan–India border," Mrs. Gandhi sent troops into East Pakistan, and hostilities also erupted on the border with West Pakistan.[69]

Contrary to "the State Department's best judgment" that India's war aims were limited and that the Soviets and Chinese would keep clear, Kissinger feared that India, egged on by the Russians, would "dismember" Pakistan and deal a strategic blow to the United States. He recalls that Nixon summoned the surprised Soviet minister of agriculture to the Oval Office early in December and told him that "if India moved forces against West Pakistan, the United States would not stand by," adding pointedly that the Soviets had treaty obligations to assist India, and the United States to assist Pakistan. Emphasizing the potential nuclear danger of the crisis, much as Kennedy did in 1962, Nixon says he told the Soviet to convey to Brezhnev "my seriousness in saying that it was incumbent upon the two of us as the leaders of the two nuclear superpowers not to allow our larger interests to become embroiled in the actions of our smaller friends."[70]

Rejecting what he terms the "bland assessment" of the State Department, Nixon, "in a display of old-fashioned gunboat diplomacy aimed at India and Russia," sent an aircraft carrier task force toward the Bay of Bengal "to give emphasis to [U.S.] warnings against an attack on West Pakistan" and "to have forces in place in case the Soviet Union pressured China."

> The four Soviet ships already in the Bay of Bengal were overshadowed by U.S. Task Force 74 of the Seventh Fleet. . . . It consisted of the *Enterprise*, the world's largest attack carrier, with seventy-five nuclear-armed fighter-bombers on board; the amphibious assault carrier *Tripoli*, carrying a Marine battalion-landing team of 2,000 troops and twenty-five assault helicopters; three guided-missile escorts . . . four gun destroyers . . . and a nuclear attack submarine.

As Morton Halperin observes, "Since the [U.S.] fleet was equipped with nuclear weapons, and since it had little effective conventional capability to prevent an Indian invasion, some observers have viewed this action as constituting an implicit nuclear threat." The Soviets, for their part, assembled a naval force that included a minesweeper, a destroyer, a conventional attack submarine, a tank-landing ship augmented by a cruise missile–armed cruiser, and a sub equipped with antiship missiles. Later another Soviet anticarrier naval force was dispatched, amid Soviet guarantees to India that, according to the CIA, "the Soviet Union [would] not allow the [U.S.] Seventh Fleet to intervene" and "would open a diversionary action" in Xinjiang if China (by then a nuclear power) intervened against India.[71]

Beneath the "apparent calm" of the superpower naval comingling "was considerable tension," and "as in earlier confrontations, the conditions existed for an accidental combat exchange." One fear was that the Indian Navy would make a show of force, which could have been extremely dangerous because Indian Foxtrot-class submarines were, as far as U.S. observers knew, indistinguishable from those that the USSR had already deployed on the scene." Like others before it, this crisis also showed that superpower naval posturing, "once initiated, can take on a life of its own, largely independent of the crisis which started it. The Indo-Pakistani War was over on December 17, but the intense phase of the naval interaction did not *begin* until December 22, when elements of the first Soviet augmentation group arrived in the vicinity of [the American aircraft carrier] *Enterprise*. The naval interaction continued until *Enterprise* left the Indian Ocean on January 8, 1972."[72]

Drawing on its own intelligence as well as U.S. official statements, India also feared that the United States might try to use its warships to evacuate Pakistani soldiers trapped in East Pakistan. This "was cause for grave concern, for it would place India in the position of having to initiate military action against nonbelligerent American forces," leading to the possibility of a much wider crisis in which the Soviet Union might feel pressed to intervene. "To prevent any such peaceful evacuation the Indian Air Force was quickly ordered to destroy all ships in East Pakistani harbors, to keep all East Pakistani airports under constant attack to deter possible helicopter landings," and, more ominously, "to make preparations to sink any Pakistani troop ships attempting to link up with the U.S. task force."[73]

In the Nixon administration's first use of the hot line, the president sternly warned the Soviets, "I cannot emphasize too strongly that time is of the essence to avoid consequences neither of us want." Nixon understood "the danger of a great power confrontation" but accepted Kissinger's analysis: "We don't really have any choice. We can't allow a friend of ours and China's [Pakistan] to get screwed in a conflict with a friend of Russia's [India]."[74]

Kissinger's memoirs reveal extreme concern over an American suspicion that the Chinese were about to intervene in the war on behalf of Pakistan: "If so, we were on the verge of a possible showdown. For if China moved militarily, the Soviet Union—according to all our information—was committed to use force against China. . . . Nixon decided—and I fully agreed—that if the Soviet Union threatened China we would not stand idly by." Here is another dramatic war-and-peace decision, this time involving a three-way conflict between nuclear powers, that Nixon made "without informing either his Secretary of State or Secretary of Defense." Nixon then ordered the carrier task force previously dispatched to steam right into the Bay of Bengal, a dramatic step in the midst of war that led to another use of the hot line. When the Chinese intention not to intervene became clear, the task force was halted and then, after further hot-line discussion, redispatched into the bay. Kissinger claims that the goals were to warn the Soviets "that matters might get out of control on our side too" and to prepare U.S. forces "to back up the Chinese if at the last moment they came in after all." Hall believes that "an [Indian] attack on West Pakistan . . . would have posed a serious risk of Chinese intervention," noting that China conducted "troop movements along India's northern border and had issued two sharp warnings to New Delhi on the morning of December 16." Nixon concluded later that "we had . . . once again avoided a major confrontation with the Soviet Union." During secret 1975 grand jury testimony to the Watergate Special Prosecution Force, Nixon "shocked the lawyers" by stating—albeit with some exaggeration—that the United States had come "close to nuclear war" in the 1971 crisis. One attorney recalls his claim that "we had threatened to go to nuclear war with the Russians." In his 1985 interview with *Time*, Nixon said that had the Chinese intervened and the Soviets reacted, he would have used nuclear weapons against the Soviet Union.[75]

As Hall observes, the Indian government was confused about the purpose of the U.S. naval task force and failed to grasp that its mission was to deter Indian moves against West Pakistan. "For some four days Indian defense officials pondered the likely purpose of the U.S. task force; apparently they never reached a definitive conclusion. . . . Few Indian officials seem to have given serious thought during the war to the possibility of a link between the movements of U.S. naval forces and the principal Nixon-Kissinger objective of impressing New Delhi with the dangers of any major military action against West Pakistan." And in the end "Soviet and Indian support for a cease-fire was *not* the result of U.S. military pressure generated by Task Force 74." Nixon and Kissinger did not acknowledge the failure of their strategy, for as Hall observes, "few political executives can be expected to have both the intellectual detachment and political courage to state publicly that the risks of escalation associated with U.S. military deployment were assumed unnecessarily."[76]

VIETNAM, 1968–1972

Unsurprisingly, the Vietnam War, which proceeded throughout the period under discussion, provided many opportunities for superpower confrontation. One was the 1968 siege of American marines at Khe Sanh, when General Westmoreland wanted a contingency plan for a nuclear strike to save the unit. Westmoreland reflects:

> Because the region around Khe Sanh was virtually uninhabited, civilian casualties would be minimal. If Washington officials were so intent on "sending a message" to Hanoi, surely small tactical nuclear weapons would be a way to tell Hanoi something, as two nuclear atomic bombs had spoken convincingly to Japanese officials during World War II and the threat of atomic bombs induced the North Koreans to accept meaningful negotiations during the Korean War. It could be that use of a few small tactical nuclear weapons in Vietnam—or even the threat of them—might have quickly brought the war there to an end.[77]

So it might, and much more too.

Morton Halperin notes that "Nixon campaigned for the presidency in 1968, as Eisenhower had in 1952, with the promise of a secret plan to end the war. It was the same plan: a nuclear threat." Nixon told *Time* magazine in 1985 that when he took office he considered the use of tactical nuclear weapons in Vietnam.[78]

In 1969, as H. R. Haldeman reports, Nixon threatened the North Vietnamese with massive escalation of the war, possibly including the use of nuclear weapons, if they did not accept his negotiating terms. Haldeman's memoirs describe what must be the most outrageous version of "good cop–bad cop" ever conceived:

> We [he and Nixon] were walking along a foggy beach after a long day of speechwriting. He said, "I call it the Madman Theory, Bob. I want the North Vietnamese to believe I've reached the point where I might do *anything* to stop the war. We'll just slip the word to them that, for God's sake, you know Nixon is obsessed about Communism. We can't restrain him when he's angry—and he has his hand on the nuclear button—and Ho Chi Minh himself will be in Paris in two days begging for peace."

The man who "slipped the word" to the North Vietnamese was "a brilliant, impulsive, witty gentleman with an engaging German accent— Henry Kissinger." According to Ellsberg, Robert Morris, who worked with Kissinger on these plans, "reports seeing the actual mission folders, including photographs, for the nuclear targets recommended to the president; one of them was a railhead in North Vietnam a mile and a half from the Chinese border." So much for moderation and prudence after 1962.[79]

Some of Nixon's aides believed the madman theory was more than bluff. Hersh reports Charles Colson's recollection that "one night while sipping Scotch, [NATO ambassador] Bob [Ellsworth] said, 'The Old

Man . . . [will] drop the bomb before the year is out and that will be the end of the war.'" Apparently Kissinger even asked two scientists who had studied nuclear options in Vietnam for President Johnson to review the nuclear target folders. According to Hersh, they were "distressed at the nuclear option" and asked biochemist Paul Doty, a friend of Kissinger's, to discourage it. One of the scientists knew Haldeman and approached him as well. Haldeman said he also opposed the nuclear option "on the simple grounds of election politics." "Using nuclear weapons in the Vietnam War," Hersh observes, "would not help elect Richard Nixon in 1972."[80]

Sometime in October 1969, Hersh writes, "Nixon and Kissinger decided to send a direct military signal to the Soviet Union and its allies. . . . The Strategic Air Command was ordered to place its nuclear-armed B-52 aircraft on 'combat ready status'—a full alert." Ray B. Sitton, then a Strategic Air Command colonel known in the Pentagon as "Mr. B-52," comments that "the guy on the other side [the Soviet Union] saw what looked like a DefCon I"—the highest possible alert. Even in the darkest days of the Cuban missile crisis, the Strategic Air Command only went as far as Defcon II. The "guy on the other side" wisely declined to respond in kind. The alert "lasted an almost unbelievable twenty-nine days without public knowledge." It finally ended, according to Hersh, only because SAC commanders complained that their B-52s could no longer handle the strain.[81]

Former aides to Kissinger, Hersh adds, recall talk about using nuclear weapons "throughout the Vietnam war." In early 1971, when the South Vietnamese were building up forces to invade Laos, "that possibility was repeatedly raised by the President in his late-night telephone calls to Kissinger." Ross Terrill reports that the Chinese became concerned that Nixon might actually use nuclear weapons at that time and placed forces on alert in the border province of Yunnan. Though Hersh found no direct evidence of an imminent use of nuclear weapons, a CIA official then stationed at the agency's operations center told him that the Air Force had issued a top secret "stand-down" order banning all U.S. operations in and over a certain part of North Vietnam. "It's a standard indicator for a nuclear attack," the CIA official said. "We were talking about it—that if the Soviets had done this on the Chinese border, we'd be scared stiff." CIA officials assumed that a stand-down order meant "that they'[d] reached the point of activating" a nuclear weapon.[82]

The United States perhaps tempted fate on other occasions in Vietnam as well—for example, in the lethal bombing in 1972 of four Soviet merchant ships in Haiphong harbor (officially by accident). Nixon found it "interesting—and important—that [Soviet] protests were kept relatively low-keyed," as they also were when the United States bombed Hanoi, mined Haiphong harbor, and even bombed North Vietnam while Soviet Premier Kosygin was in the country.[83]

## MIDDLE EAST, 1973

The Arab-Israeli war of October 1973 produced several serious nuclear danger points, including the most explicitly nuclear, and most bizarre, superpower confrontation since 1962. The war began on October 6, that year a holy day for both Muslims and Jews, when Egyptian and Syrian units attacked Israeli forces stationed on territories captured by Israel in the 1967 war.[84] Peter Pry writes that "the decision to launch the October War was evidently based on a miscalculation that nearly resulted in a nuclear catastrophe. Israel apparently was prepared to retaliate with atomic force." In 1976 *Time* magazine reported:

> At the start of the 1973 October War . . . the Egyptians had repulsed the first Israeli counterattacks along the Suez Canal, causing heavy casualties, and Israeli forces on the Golan Heights were retreating in the face of a massive Syrian tank assault. At 10 p.m. on October 8, the Israeli Commander on the northern front, Major General Yitzhak Hoffi, told his superior: "I am not sure that we can hold out much longer." After midnight, Defense Minister Moshe Dayan solemnly warned Premier Golda Meir: "This is the end of the third temple." Mrs. Meir thereupon gave Dayan permission to activate Israel's Doomsday weapons. As each bomb was assembled, it was rushed off to waiting air force units. Before any triggers were set, however, the battle on both fronts turned to Israel's favor.[85]

According to Amos Perlmutter, Michael Handel, and Uri Bar-Joseph as well, "It seems that a decision to consider the use of a nuclear threat was made by Israel's top establishment officials. There are indications that Dayan gave an order secretly to put in combat readiness, for the first time, Israeli-made Jericho SS missiles, carrying nuclear warheads, as well as Kfir and Phantom bomber fighters equipped with nuclear devices. Altogether, 13 Israeli-made nuclear weapons were put on alert." Leonard Spector reports that "former and current U.S. officials" he interviewed recently "confirmed that Israel secretly readied nuclear weapons for possible use at this time."[86]

During the fighting, each superpower supplied its allies with military equipment and "alternated between urging a prompt cease-fire and using delaying tactics to postpone one, depending on the tide of the battle and estimates of the course of further hostilities."[87] By October 11 the Israelis were pushing deep into Syria, and Defense Minister Moshe Dayan publicly said he was going all the way to Damascus.

Soviet Ambassador Dobrynin told Kissinger the obvious: that the USSR "could not be indifferent to threats to Damascus" and that "matters might get out of hand." In his memoirs, Kissinger (who appears to have been in charge, with Nixon distracted by domestic events) reflects at this point on the merits of "intransigence in the face of menace"— even as the Soviets were complaining about Russian casualties in Israeli attacks on civilian targets in Syria and Egypt and on a Soviet merchant ship. Dobrynin brought a message to Kissinger warning: "The Soviet Union will of course take measures which it will deem necessary to defend its ships and other means of transportation."[88] On the very day that Congress passed the War Powers Act, intended to restrict executive authority for unilateral war making, Kissinger told Dobrynin that the United States would intervene militarily if the Soviets did.

Soviet and American warships were, as Kissinger lightly puts it, "milling around" together and, as in previous crises, could have engaged each other through accident or miscalculation. The chief of naval operations, Admiral Zumwalt, later wrote, "I doubt that major units of the U.S. Navy were ever in a tenser situation since World War II ended than the Sixth Fleet in the Mediterranean was for . . . [that] week." Though both sides took care to avoid naval violence, potentially dangerous incidents did occur. "There were instances of Soviet ships training their guns on U.S. ships, shining searchlights on U.S. ships at night, firing flares near U.S. patrol aircraft, and maneuvering close to U.S. ships," all of which "caused concern in the U.S. units involved." On October 25 U.S. "aircraft detected two small, high-speed surface craft approaching the [U.S. carrier] *Independence* task group. The group assumed a defensive posture, but fortunately the craft were identified as Israeli before stronger action became necessary." For the first time in a superpower crisis, Soviet ships also took actions that "had an immediate connection with the war" in progress and thus risked coming under attack by Israeli forces. They evacuated Soviet personnel from Egyptian and Syrian ports, maintained intelligence ships near the war zone, provided protection for the Soviet sealift and airlift of military cargo to Arab states, and evidently even used regular Soviet Navy ships to move some supplies. The Israelis did not challenge Soviet warships, despite their important role in keeping the Arab states equipped to fight. But the

Israelis did bomb a Soviet cultural center in Damascus as well as Soviet transport aircraft in Syria, and they sank a Soviet merchant ship in the port of Tartus, leading the Soviets to warn of "grave consequences for Israel itself."[89]

Kissinger told Alexander Haig that it might soon be time to mount an all-out airlift to Israel "no matter what the risk of confrontation." As cease-fire efforts were breaking down, he told the British, "I think developments now are going to drive us towards a confrontation." He reflects in his memoirs that "once a stalemate had become apparent, either by Soviet design or confusion, we moved decisively, even brutally, to break it." And he remarked to Brent Scowcroft, "Since we are going to be in a confrontation we should go all-out."[90] Ironically, in the midst of the raging Middle Eastern war and tense superpower standoff, and with a major nuclear crisis attributable mostly to Kissinger only days away, the secretary of state was awarded the Nobel Peace Prize on October 16.

The following day Brezhnev informed Washington that he had no interest in a direct showdown. On October 21 in Moscow, Kissinger and Brezhnev negotiated a cease-fire arrangement (the day after the "Saturday Night Massacre" in Washington, when Nixon fired Special Prosecutor Archibald Cox, and Attorney General Elliot Richardson and Deputy Attorney General William Ruckelshaus resigned in protest during the Watergate affair). Each superpower then sought the acquiescence of its client—a process that nearly led to disaster.

The Soviets gained Sadat's approval of the plan "only after Brezhnev assured him that, if necessary, the U.S.S.R. would act unilaterally to ensure Israel's observance of the cease-fire." Kissinger flew directly to Israel. "About halfway to Tel Aviv," he writes, "it dawned on me that we were heading into a war zone." Perhaps this insight was mostly of personal significance, or perhaps Kissinger realized that the downing of the U.S. secretary of state's plane might raise the kind of wider danger normally found only in spine-tingling adventure novels. In any case, he decided that "it might be a good idea to arrange some protection by aircraft from the US Sixth Fleet," a "large number" of which escorted him from Cyprus all the way to Tel Aviv. Evidently, he did not consider that this idea might have dangers of its own.[91]

Kissinger secured Israeli acceptance of the cease-fire despite "grumbles about how Egypt's Third Army might have been fully encircled and destroyed in another *three* days of fighting." In *Years of Upheaval* he openly admits: "I had indicated that I would understand if there was a few hours 'slippage' in the cease-fire deadline while I was flying home." That is, he gave the Israelis permission to continue attacking the Third Army after the cease-fire went into effect, violating the solemn assurances he had just given the Soviets. Furthermore, "informed Israeli accounts make clear that Kissinger was even more explicit, commenting, for example, 'Well, in Vietnam the cease-fire didn't go into effect at the exact time that was agreed on.' Moreover, he intentionally scotched efforts to provide U.N. supervision for the cease-fire, knowing that the Israelis had been pressing for more time to destroy the Egyptian Army."[92]

As Israel continued "an offensive of critical significance," the crisis ignited again in a far more ominous way. The Soviets realized that Kissinger had double-crossed them, and they had made a fateful promise to Sadat. Brezhnev complained urgently over the hot line. Sadat took the extraordinary step of requesting American intervention to stop the Israelis, who finally did offer to stop, but only after achieving their objective: cutting off the Third Army and thereby posing "a potential threat to Cairo itself." As Kissinger writes: "Starving the Third Army out would be a slower process than destroying it militarily. But it would lead to the same result and was almost certain to bring about a confrontation with the Soviets. They could not possibly hold still while a cease-fire they had cosponsored was turned into a trap for a client state." Nevertheless, another cease-fire on this basis went into effect on October 24.[93]

Fighting broke out again almost immediately, including an Israeli attack on an Egyptian naval base in the city of Suez. Sadat repeated his plea for American action to rein in Israel. The Soviets publicly warned Israel of the "gravest consequences" if it did not desist. Later that day, a desperate Sadat requested *joint* superpower intervention to enforce the cease-fire, an idea that the Soviets said they would bring to the U.N. Security Council. Kissinger writes, "We were determined to resist by force if necessary the introduction of Soviet troops into the Middle East regardless of the pretext under which they arrived"—the "pretext" being a request by President Sadat for *both* Soviet and U.S. troops to station themselves on sovereign Egyptian territory to enforce a U.N. cease-fire that the United States had helped negotiate and that a U.S. client was flagrantly violating.[94]

By this point Nixon, enmeshed in the Watergate scandals, was evidently under enormous psychological strain and was possibly unstable. "We were," Kissinger writes, "heading into what could have become the gravest foreign policy crisis of the Nixon Presidency—because it involved a direct confrontation of the superpowers—with a President overwhelmed by his persecution. . . . [He was] as agitated and emotional as I had ever heard him." Nixon even "expressed the hope that at a briefing scheduled for the next morning I [Kissinger] would tell the Congressional leadership about his central, indispensable role in managing the Mideast crisis. He had already urged me to call some Senators to make this pitch—a symptom of the extremity in which this proud man felt himself." Kissinger quotes him as saying, in reference to his domestic critics: "They are doing it because of their desire to kill the President. And they may succeed. I may physically die."[95]

The White House told Sadat, "Should the two great nuclear powers be called upon to provide forces, it would introduce an extremely dangerous potential for great-power rivalry in the area." Over the telephone, Dobrynin told Kissinger that the Soviets might introduce the U.N. resolution if the nonaligned countries did not. Kissinger writes: "I told him not to push us to the extreme. We would not accept Soviet troops in any guise. Dobrynin replied that in Moscow, 'they have become so angry, they want troops.'"[96]

Brezhnev wrote a letter supporting joint intervention to enforce the cease-fire and added, "I will say it straight that if you find it impossible to act jointly with us in this matter, we should be faced with the necessity urgently to consider the question of taking appropriate steps unilaterally." Kissinger called the full message "one of the most serious challenges to an American President"; Senator Fulbright called it "urgent"; Senator Jackson called it "brutal, rough."[97]

American intelligence picked up what one analyst terms "ambiguous, but alarming" evidence of Soviet preparations for intervention—possibly to deal with the situation on the Suez, but perhaps simply to save Syria in case the Israelis drove into Damascus as threatened.[98] Reportedly, the Soviets put their air force and all seven of their airborne divisions (totaling only about fifty thousand men) on alert, established an airborne command post, and prepared to move their forces.[99] Seven Soviet amphibious assault vessels and two helicopter carriers arrived in the Mediterranean, putting the Soviet fleet there at the "unprecedented" level of eighty-five ships. American intelligence reportedly noted unusual Soviet activities and communications that appeared to indicate an imminent major operation. By noon on October 24, as Blechman and Hart recount, "a large portion of the Soviet airlift fleet could not be located by U.S. intelligence systems, electronic intercepts indicated that Soviet flight plans for the next day were being changed, and certain 'communications nets' showed a surge in activity, indicating that a major change in Soviet operations could be expected soon."[100]

Journalist Elizabeth Drew calls the following hours "Strangelove Day." Kissinger, evidently in collaboration with Alexander Haig, decided not to wake the president to inform him of Brezhnev's crucial letter. Instead Kissinger called an urgent meeting of the Washington Special Action Group, which in Nixon's absence, ordered American military forces worldwide, both conventional and nuclear, to go to a Defcon III alert—the highest since the Cuban missile crisis—around midnight that night. Defcon V is normal peacetime status, though some forces, such as the Strategic Air Command, were routinely kept at Defcon IV. As Kissinger explains, "Defcon I is war. Defcon II is a condition in which attack is imminent. Defcon III . . . is in practice the highest state of readiness for essentially peacetime conditions."[101]

Yet "something more was necessary." Sixty B-52 nuclear bombers moved from their Guam base to the United States and joined the Strategic Air Command alert of American strategic nuclear forces to "give the Soviets another indication that we were assembling our forces for a showdown." Several aircraft carriers steamed toward the conflict zone, and the 82d Airborne, with fifteen thousand troops, was ordered to be "ready to move" by 6:00 A.M. the next morning. According to one participant, "we decided to alert everything but the kitchen sink." ("Alaska and Panama were the kitchen sink.") The president of the United States "knew nothing about the alert until it appeared in the morning newspapers."[102]

Following the pattern described above, the White House tried to keep the alert secret, ordering that the Defcon III command be implemented "with minimum public notice." The secrecy had nothing to do with security. The United States *wanted* the Soviets to become aware of the alert almost immediately. It was the American people the White House wanted to keep in the dark. Officials were afraid of awakening the inconvenient "universal fear" of war that had so bothered Nixon in the 1970 Cuban crisis—afraid, as Blechman and Hart put it, of "engendering a serious public debate in the United States." It is safe to assume that even more "universal fear" would have surfaced had the public known of the ideas Kissinger was entertaining during the crisis, revealed in the remark at this point in his memoirs that "two could play chicken."[103]

In the midst of preparations for war on both sides, Kissinger refused Dobrynin's "repeated" attempts to communicate, again throwing aside one of the great lessons supposedly learned in 1962: the need for timely superpower contact to avoid misunderstandings during crises. Kissinger also told the Israelis that the United States would not pressure them to return to the cease-fire line originally agreed on—even though the continued Israeli attack on the surrounded Third Army, in clear violation of the U.S.-brokered agreement, was *the* reason for the nuclear crisis.[104]

Finally, a message to Brezhnev, drafted at the meeting but evidently sent in Nixon's name while the president slept,[105] stated bluntly that "we must view your suggestion of unilateral action as a matter of the gravest concern, involving incalculable consequences." Ironically, the message made an oblique reference to the Agreement on the Prevention of Nuclear War, signed that very year, and then ominously repeated: "We could in no event accept unilateral action. . . . As I stated above, such action would produce incalculable consequences which would be in the interest of neither of our countries and which would end all we have striven so hard to achieve." At noon the next day, Kissinger reemphasized the nuclear danger during a press conference, noting the "very special responsibility" of the superpowers, since "we possess, each of us, nuclear arsenals capable of annihilating humanity. We, both of us, have a special duty to see to it that confrontations are kept within bounds that do not threaten civilized life."[106]

Though it is far from clear that the alert played a major role, the Israelis soon relaxed their attacks on the Third Army, the Egyptians duly withdrew their request for superpower troops, and the Soviets stopped pushing for bilateral superpower intervention. Brezhnev told the White House that he would send in only an observer team. The timing was tight: "One Soviet aircraft touched down at the Cairo West airfield in the early morning hours [of the 25th], but returned home almost immediately. It was as if this aircraft, containing the lead element of the interventionary force, had been caught en route when the Kremlin decided the risk was too great and reversed course."[107]

But the Israelis would not fall back to the original cease-fire line, and, "determined to starve out the Third Army," they blocked food, water, and medical supplies. Kissinger recognized that eventually "what [would] happen [was] another maximum Soviet demand." Yet he promised the Israelis: "You won't be pressured one second before [the starvation of the Third Army] becomes inevitable." Finally, almost two full days after the nuclear alert, Kissinger contacted the Israelis ("on behalf of Nixon. I do not remember checking in advance with the President")

and insisted that they allow humanitarian supplies to reach the trapped
Egyptian Army, a step that evidently did not occur for two more days,
when a single convoy was given access.[108]

Meanwhile, in a now familiar pattern, superpower naval forces continued aggressive operations against each other in the tense aftermath of
the nuclear alert, even after it "became clear that the new cease-fire . . .
would hold." For instance, Soviet anticarrier exercises—"the Soviet
Navy's equivalent of training its guns on the U.S. fleet" and "the most
intense signal the Soviets had ever transmitted with their naval forces in
a crisis"—went on until November 3.[109]

There is no way to know just how close to war the superpowers came
that weekend. But plausible scenarios could have led to it. As Blechman
and Hart ask:

> What if the Soviets had decided to intervene in a more direct way in the war?
> Or what if the Israelis, fearing that such a direct intervention might occur,
> chose to attack Soviet transports as they entered the war zone? (Note that
> Israeli aircraft deliberately provoked a battle with Soviet aircraft in 1970,
> when Soviet air defense units were deployed in Egypt [during the War of At-
> trition crisis, discussed earlier].) Or what if the Soviets, believing that the
> United States would interfere with Soviet transports during their vulnerable
> landing period, chose to attack the U.S. Sixth Fleet preemptively, perhaps
> along with Israeli Air Force facilities? What then? Where would the conflict
> have ended?

As these authors conclude from the 1973 record, "once the threshold of
active military involvement is crossed, finding a stopping point becomes
far from easy. By raising the specter of nuclear war at the onset of the
confrontation, the United States made more difficult the termination of
any escalatory process which might have ensued short of the use of nuclear weapons."[110]

In a revealing aftermath to the 1973 crisis, in the spring of 1974,
Kissinger reportedly "asked the JCS [Joint Chiefs of Staff] to devise a
limited nuclear option that the President might order in the hypothetical
case of a Soviet invasion of Iran." Kissinger, as we saw, was frustrated
about the lack of a limited nuclear war plan in the 1970 Jordanian crisis. Likewise, he must have wondered what he would have done next in
1973 if, during the massive U.S. nuclear alert, Israel had continued to
destroy the Third Army and the Soviets had actually intervened. "The
JCS solution was to fire nearly 200 nuclear weapons at military targets,
air bases, bivouacs and so forth—in the southern region of the U.S.S.R.
near the Iranian border." Not at all pleased, Kissinger responded, "Are

you out of your minds? This is a *limited* option?" Sent back to the drawing board, the generals returned in a few weeks and suggested the use of
three nuclear weapons to destroy two roads leading from the USSR to
Iran. This time Kissinger asked, "What kind of nuclear attack is this?"
Apparently he judged it a puny act from which Brezhnev would conclude that the president was "chicken."[111]


CUBA, 1979

Though it was far from a full-fledged crisis, the strange 1979 case of
the Soviet "combat brigade" in Cuba deserves a brief mention, if only to
show how little it can take to cause a potentially dangerous superpower
conflict. On August 30 the noted dove Senator Frank Church called a
dramatic press conference at his home to announce that American intelligence had observed a brigade of several thousand Soviet troops in
Cuba. He said, "The United States cannot permit the island to become a
Russian military base 90 miles from our shore," and asked the president
to demand "the immediate withdrawal of all Russian combat troops
from Cuba." Secretary of State Vance pointed out that the brigade had
evidently been in Cuba since at least the mid-1970s and its presence certainly did not violate the 1962 or 1970 Soviet-American agreements on
Cuba. But he insisted nonetheless that he would "not be satisfied with
maintenance of the status quo." As Garthoff notes, "Vance did not explain why, if the brigade had been there at least since the mid-1970s and
did not contravene any bilateral understandings, the status quo should
not be satisfactory, but instead constitute a serious concern 'affecting
out relations with the Soviet Union.'" Indeed, as McGeorge Bundy later
reported, in 1963 the United States had actually acquiesced to the presence of Soviet ground forces under the 1962 agreements.[112]

On September 7 President Carter reassured the American people that
the little brigade was "not an assault force," since "it [did] not have airlift or sea-going capabilities and [did] not have weapons capable of attacking the United States"—irrelevant facts when a few thousand troops
could hardly pose a serious threat to the United States even with all
those things. Yet he too added, "This status quo is not acceptable."
On September 9 Senator Richard Stone went so far as to suggest that
the Soviet brigade was comparable in importance to the original Cuban missile crisis: "By implication he was calling for the same kind of
military-political confrontation with the Soviet Union." Senator Church
went on to say that the entire Soviet-American relationship was "at

stake." As it turns out, Church had felt personally burned in the 1962 Cuban crisis: on the basis of information from the Kennedy administration he had publicly denied the presence of Soviet missiles in Cuba.[113] Like Nixon in 1970, Church in 1979 did not conclude from the experience of 1962 that superpower confrontation in Cuba should be avoided; on the contrary, that bad memory made them both *want* another confrontation in which the United States would act *more* aggressively than it had in 1962.

Vance pressured the Soviets to get Ambassador Dobrynin, a veteran of the 1962 crisis and many others since, to return to the United States from Moscow, where his parents were on their deathbeds. Unsurprisingly the Soviets refused to remove or reorganize the brigade. Indeed, "the main reaction in Moscow must have been puzzlement, soon to give way to suspicion about the U.S. purpose in stirring up a crisis without cause." On September 25 Carter admitted that the Soviet soldiers posed "no threat to our Nation's security," but he dramatically warned that if the Kremlin did nothing, "*we* [would] take appropriate action to change the status quo."[114]

Zbigniew Brzezinski, Carter's national security adviser, was upset that Carter had made such a threat and then did not follow through. He writes in his memoir, *Power and Principle,* "This was the only time that I ever thought seriously of the possibility of resigning." In Cuba, as in certain earlier incidents of the Carter administration, "for the first time since World War II the United States told the Russians . . . that we take great exception to what they are doing, that there will be negative consequences if they persist in their acts . . . and then we did nothing about it." He reports that the president "looked quite furious, and told me that he had no intention of going to war over the Soviet brigade in Cuba." Brzezinski comments, "I did not advocate that we go to war, but that we lay it on the line more explicitly in regard to Soviet adventurism around the world"—whatever that means.[115] All this fuss was over a perfectly legal group of Soviet soldiers so small that American intelligence did not notice or report them in Cuba for perhaps seventeen years! Cuba, 1962, 1970, 1979: history can indeed repeat itself—as farce—several times.

## LEBANON, 1982–1983

The 1982 Israeli invasion and occupation of Lebanon was much more dangerous than the botched 1979 Cuba affair, and not only for its tens of thousands of direct victims. The war brought important American and Soviet allies into direct combat, raising the possibility of "a generalized war," as the foreign ministers of the European Community warned. Exceeding Israel's stated war aim of securing a limited "security zone" in southern Lebanon, the Israelis drove once again to within shelling distance of Damascus, suggesting the possibility of a replay of the 1967 crisis. As Noam Chomsky observes, "If Israel's attack on Syrian forces had continued and the fighting escalated a notch or two higher, the USSR might have made some move in defense of its Syrian ally, a step that surely would have brought about a U.S. military response and possibly a superpower confrontation."[116] Indeed, one senior Soviet official "expressed concern that the Mideast fighting may provoke a full-scale confrontation between Israel and Syria, triggering greater Soviet involvement," and it is alleged that "the Russians had threatened to intervene militarily, if the fighting [between Israel and Syria] did not stop."[117] In a severe provocation to the Soviet Union, the Israelis shelled and "heavily damaged" the Soviet Embassy and later occupied a consulate building on the embassy grounds in Beirut, which are considered sovereign Soviet territory. U.S. Assistant Secretary of Defense Richard Perle later revealed that Israeli planes killed eleven Soviets who were investigating an Israeli reconnaissance plane shot down in Lebanon.[118] Ambassador Ghassan Tueni of Lebanon was correct when he noted at the United Nations General Assembly session on disarmament in June 1982 that "the war in Lebanon was becoming a danger not to Lebanon alone, but to others as well, and probably to the entire world."[119]

New dangers attended the United States' direct military intervention in the conflict in 1983 with ground troops, a large naval force, and heavy bombing and shelling from the largest conventional guns in the world, the sixteen-inchers on the newly reactivated battleship *New Jersey.* American ships on the scene were equipped to fire nuclear weapons, and some of them probably carried warheads aboard.[120] Before withdrawing, the United States lost several planes and hundreds of marines and could have ended up at war with Syria—or worse, if the Soviets had challenged the American intervention as America had challenged them when they appeared ready to intervene in the Middle East ten years earlier. According to William Ury, a specialist on negotiation and crisis control, "The Soviet description of Berlin in 1958 as a 'smoldering fuse connected to a powder keg' could have applied just as well to Lebanon in 1983."[121]

## AFGHANISTAN, 1979–1988

The Soviet invasion of Afghanistan did not produce a serious Soviet-American crisis, but the huge Afghan war posed real dangers that both superpowers greatly intensified through reckless actions. As Selig Harrison writes, "The Afghan case underlines the built-in danger that pursuit of the Reagan Doctrine [of militarily opposing Soviet-supported governments] can lead to a direct Soviet-American confrontation."[122] As the major base for U.S.-sponsored Afghan rebels battling the Soviet occupation and the Afghan puppet government, Pakistan was the ultimate source of thousands of attacks on both Afghan and Soviet forces. Unsurprisingly, the Soviets responded by carrying the war directly into Pakistan, one of the United States' most important client states.

Adding to heavy Soviet-Afghan shelling of Pakistan, jets bearing Afghan Air Force markings strafed and bombed refugee camps, guerrilla bases, and villages within Pakistan hundreds of times, in some cases penetrating thirty or forty miles. Five Afghans who claimed to be defectors from the Afghan Air Force said in September 1988 that Soviet pilots flew such missions because the Soviet Union did not trust Afghan pilots to do so, fearing they might "defect or fail to accomplish their mission." In 1984 Pakistani officials "reported sixty-three such incursions." By early 1987 Pakistan was repeatedly battling the intruding jets with its U.S.-supplied fighters. Pakistan reportedly shot down several planes (in at least one case capturing the Soviet pilot) and in turn lost at least one F-16 to Afghan or Soviet fire.[123] A Soviet-Pakistani war, with terrifying possibilities, could not be ruled out.

Neither could an internal upheaval in unstable Pakistan, which might have tempted either superpower, and perhaps both, to intervene. The U.S.-sponsored rebels' drug dealing and gunrunning (making "Pakistan the world's largest drug supermarket" and fueling ethnic violence), together with the cross-border attacks and tension between Afghan refugees and the Pakistani population, "turned the Northwest Frontier Province into a powder keg which could [have blown] up the regime of Gen. Mohammed Zia ul-Haq." In late 1986 an opposition Pakistani politician warned: "You have all the ingredients for a civil war now. We have become another Lebanon."[124]

Alarmed by Pakistan's inability to defend itself against Soviet attacks, Zia, his prime minister Mohammad Khan Junejo, and then U.S. secretary of defense Caspar Weinberger all publicly mentioned the possibility of having *American* pilots fly U.S. reconnaissance missions on the explosive Afghan-Pakistani border—a step that could have led to the first direct combat between Soviet and American forces in the nuclear age. Meanwhile, the rebels and possibly Pakistan itself reportedly launched terrorist attacks against Afghan airliners and other civilian targets in Kabul and throughout Afghanistan, and the Afghans and Soviets apparently ordered hundreds of terrorist bombings in Pakistani cities. The U.S.-sponsored rebels have openly called for rebellion and even "liberation" of Muslim-dominated republics in the Soviet Union (parts of which were seized from Afghanistan by czarist Russia). The rebels have reportedly even attacked *Soviet territory*. For example, in March 1987 they fired rockets on a rayon factory during a festival, resulting in loss of life—thus violating the most elemental tenet of superpower restraint in the nuclear age: never launching or sponsoring direct attacks on each other.[125] Imagine the response in the United States if guerrillas funded and armed by the KGB attacked Texas from Mexico.

By 1988 the Soviets finally realized that they could not defeat the rebels as long as Pakistan remained a sanctuary for rebel bases and supply. Unwilling to run the risk of a major attack on Pakistan—probably the only way for them to prevail—the Soviets finally decided to withdraw from Afghanistan. But what if they had made the other choice, concluding (as the United States did in Vietnam) that even a risky escalation was preferable to a humiliating retreat? Only Gorbachev's accession to power may have prevented such a decision. If after the failure of the air raids Soviet ground forces had swept into Pakistan to destroy rebel bases and supply lines, Pakistan might well have demanded direct U.S. intervention, leading to an extreme crisis—perhaps, as Laurence Martin warned, even involving Pakistan's longtime enemy India, which has its own reasons (including a territorial dispute in Kashmir) for wanting Pakistan's military damaged or destroyed.[126]

Both the Soviet Union and India, of course, are nuclear armed, and Pakistan apparently is too. As Leonard Spector reports, as early as July 1986 "a series of press stories . . . citing Reagan Administration sources, stated that Pakistan was considered to have the capacity to build nuclear arms or to be on the verge of having that capability, with one account stating that all that remained was for Pakistan to assemble the components." By early 1987 "it appeared Pakistan had decided to declare itself a nuclear power." In March 1987 Senator John Glenn announced his belief "that all the components and the means for assembling a working nuclear explosive device are in Pakistan's possession." In March 1988 Hedrick Smith wrote in the *New York Times Magazine* that Paksitan had enough nuclear materials for four to six nuclear weapons. Smith "made it clear that Pakistan could rapidly deploy nuclear weapons in any future conflict."[127] Thus the Soviet-Pakistani border violence was apparently one of the few instances in history in which nuclear-armed states have fought each other.

If the Afghan war had exploded into Pakistan, one of the countries might have considered a lightning preemptive attack, perhaps nuclear, on India's or Pakistan's suspected nuclear weapons facilities. The United States reportedly has nuclear weapons in Pakistan too. According to Lawrence Lifschultz, at Cambridge University, since 1983 the United States has secretly used Pakistani air bases for operations by P-3 Orion planes equipped to carry B-57 nuclear depth charges. These weapons have an explosive power only slightly less than the bomb that destroyed Hiroshima. Moreover, in "the single largest coordinated [military] construction program undertaken outside the United States since the end of the Vietnam War," huge bases have been constructed in Pakistan to support U.S. forces in case of direct intervention in the region. This construction is "taking place primarily in the sparsely populated province of Baluchistan, which borders Iran and Afghanistan," and according to the former chief minister of Baluchistan, "the most significant facility under construction is an enormous air base in the Chagai region, near the Afghan border."[128]

Moreover, "the multiservice U.S. Central Command [i.e., the nuclear-armed Rapid Deployment Force] . . . has included Pakistan and Afghanistan among the nineteen countries within its "area of responsibility." As Harrison adds:

> American capabilities for combat intervention and intelligence surveillance in South Asia have improved dramatically since President Richard Nixon sent the aircraft carrier *Enterprise* to the Bay of Bengal in 1971. As the U.S.-Soviet military competition has escalated in the Indian Ocean and the Persian Gulf, the United States has deployed most of its additional increments of naval strength in the immediate vicinity of Pakistan. An American carrier battle group with nuclear-equipped aircraft usually is on permanent patrol in the northern Arabian Sea and the Gulf of Oman. On the Indian Ocean island of Diego Garcia alone, the Deployment Force maintains seventeen giant military container ships loaded with enough tanks, rocket launchers, and amphibious armored personnel carriers to enable 12,500 U.S. Marines to fight for thirty days without resupply.

Writing shortly before the Soviet withdrawal, Harrison comments: "The possibility of American military intervention on the Pakistan-Afghanistan border has grown steadily as Moscow has deployed more of its troops near the border, as Washington has stepped up its weapons aid to the resistance, and as the diplomatic stalemate has dragged on. . . . Worst case scenarios envisage direct 'hot pursuit' by Soviet commandos to destroy base camps in Pakistan." The dangers of such an action—direct Soviet attack on a key American client state—should not be underestimated. Indeed, "should American combat forces come to the aid of Islamabad, some influential U.S. military analysts have even suggested that the United States might have to use tactical nuclear weapons."[129]

The ingredients existed, then, for a conflict involving *four* nuclear-armed states—five if we include China, which would probably feel a vital stake in any major crisis on the subcontinent. As Spector notes, the "cold peace" between India and Pakistan following the 1971 war "came to an end in 1983, when bilateral relations turned increasingly hostile. An uprising of separatists in Pakistan's Sind Province in August 1983 sparked accusations by Islamabad that India was aiding and encouraging the rebels. Over the following year, New Delhi, in turn, accused Islamabad of fomenting unrest by Sikh nationalists in India's Punjab region and of making incursions into Kashmir, which had led to a series of border clashes." Indeed, in the fall of 1984, around the time the Soviets were conducting air raids into Pakistan, "general war [between India and Pakistan] was considered a distinct possibility." At the end of 1986, "by which point Pakistan had apparently acquired its first stocks of weapons-grade uranium[,] Indo-Pakistani relations deteriorated seriously, and major Indian exercises near the Pakistani border, known as Operation Brass Tacks, led to a series of mobilizations and counter-mobilizations that some feared might lead to war."[130]

With only a few barely noticed exceptions like Harrison, the U.S. press, the mainstream foreign policy intelligentsia, and even the peace movement had little to say about the potential nuclear perils of the U.S. role in Afghanistan—just as they had been largely silent about Lebanon in 1983 and other crises past. Ironically, it was left to the CIA not only to warn of the Afghan danger but also to repeatedly try to forestall it— even, in some cases, by effectively disobeying White House orders. According to the *Wall Street Journal,* the agency strongly resisted the Reagan administration's State Department–led conversion of Pakistan into a base for the Afghan rebels because, despite the CIA's usual enthusiasm for covert military operations, it was "wary of provoking Soviet retaliation against Pakistan" and even of "precipitating a superpower showdown."[131]

As Harrison explains, "The CIA program during the early years of the war was designed [to avoid] a provocative, overt U.S. role that might prompt Soviet retaliatory pressures against Pakistan." Even after a spring 1985 presidential directive ordered a major expansion of the Pakistani operation, the *Journal* reports, "the CIA moved cautiously. . . . It assigned to Pakistan just three officers, none of them paramilitary experts, to manage the secret operation." For defense against deadly Soviet helicopters and planes, the CIA initially provided the rebels with only British-made Blowpipe missiles "because they couldn't be traced to the U.S." When these proved ineffective, Pakistan's General Zia told a U.S. congressional delegation in summer 1985 that the rebels needed the Stinger—a highly effective shoulder-fired U.S. antiaircraft missile. "The CIA station chief in Islamabad . . . relayed the request to CIA headquarters, but senior agency officials decided to sit on it, intelligence sources say." In fact, "William Casey, the agency's late director . . . and other high CIA officials delayed for about a year giving the Afghan guerillas the weapon now credited with turning the tide against the Soviets [the Stinger]." The CIA, according to the *Journal,* even misled the White House in late 1985 by claiming that Pakistan did not *want* Stinger missiles going to the Afghan rebels. Finally, President Reagan directly ordered the agency to provide Stingers. "But even the president's order wasn't enough to overcome the resistance from the CIA," which delayed for months on the pretext of testing the weapon against new Soviet helicopter defenses. The CIA finally delivered Stingers only in the summer of 1986.[132]

The CIA's fear that the Stingers might provoke the Soviets to make a dangerous move such as attacking Pakistan was well founded, for in the hands of the Muslim guerrillas the weapon proved devastating. According to U.S. Congressman Charles Wilson, "a pair of captured Soviet pilots told Pakistani interrogators that the best defense against the Stinger is to 'read the first two pages of the Koran.'" Ahmed Rashid, Pakistan correspondent for the London *Sunday Observer* and *Independent* and a writer for the *Far Eastern Economic Review,* reports that "the C.I.A.'s delivery of Stinger missiles . . . was seen by many Pakistanis as a provocation of the Russians." Indeed, as Harrison reports, some "foot-dragging" Pakistani leaders delayed delivery of the Stingers; they "feared Soviet retaliation." Anwar Khan, a Pakistani scholar of Soviet history, said in April 1987: "The Soviets are attacking [Pakistan] because they want to seal the border and stop the transport of these weapons. They want to get the Stingers."[133]

Astute American officials have long taken seriously the prospect of a crisis on the Afghan-Pakistani border. Perhaps the most graphic reminder of how they think is the remarkable photograph that Zbigniew Brzezinski permitted while he was in Pakistan in 1980: it shows him "at the Khyber Pass with Afghanistan in the background—and in the foreground, in his hand, a Chinese-made AK-47 assault rifle." Those who doubt that the events described earlier could in fact have provoked a severe crisis should recall this *Los Angeles Times* report in 1980: "White House and other senior officials dealing with national security" said in a press backgrounder that "if the Soviet Union carried its expansionism into Iran or Pakistan, the United States would have little choice but to oppose it militarily." Such an event, the officials said, "would almost certainly become a nuclear war."[134]

## CHAPTER SEVEN

# Third World Violence, Nuclear Danger

Why work with the Soviets to reduce the store of dynamite
and then do nothing about the blasting caps?
—*Bernard Avishai and Avner Cohen*, Boston Globe

Except for the Cuban missile crisis and possibly one or two other cases, most scholars and commentators deny, explicitly or implicitly, that the incidents we described in Chapter 6 posed notable nuclear dangers. Hence, they imply, the nuclear states can continue to practice violence and destabilization in the Third World without inviting a worldwide disaster. Even those who are well aware of the consequences of a nuclear war and of the relevant history often express such complacency.

McGeorge Bundy, for example, writes that since 1962 the superpowers "have continuously kept a decent distance from the nuclear danger that any confrontation between them must always present. . . . There are episodes in this period that have been said to have such a color to them, but closely examined they show much more prudence than menace, and on both sides." The only episodes that have such a "color" for Bundy are several occasions during the Vietnam War, the 1969 border conflict between China and the Soviet Union, and the October 1973 crisis in the Middle East. Bundy's close examination of them discovered "great caution on the part of all states possessing nuclear weapons, caution not only with respect to their use, but also with respect to any step that might lead to a level of conflict in which someone else might be tempted to use them." As for all the other incidents that might be thought to have had a "color" of nuclear danger, "caution on the American side has been so visible as not to require detailed study."[1]

Bundy is aware that "the most important thing that the United States and the Soviet Union can do to stay clear of the 'nuclear tornado' is to see to it that they have no war of any kind with each other" and that "the avoidance of war means the avoidance of all steps that can bring Soviet and American forces into open conflict with one another." Nevertheless, based on his happy reading of the historical record, Bundy quickly adds: "This leaves room for contests in which each of the superpowers supports some other combatant, and even for conflicts in which one side is directly engaged against forces supported by the other, as in Korea, Vietnam, and Afghanistan." On the front between the two Koreas (with numerous American nuclear weapons deployed in the south), Bundy reassures us, "the situation is not comfortable, but it is stable." As for the rest of the Third World, "the study of nuclear danger can tell us very little about such hard areas for American policymakers as the Middle East or Central America or the Philippines, just as it cannot tell the Politburo how to handle its overextension in Afghanistan and Africa." Bundy likewise finds "no" danger of a nuclear war arising from events in Eastern or Western Europe.[2]

The view that a proper respect for the nuclear danger "leaves room for" widespread superpower adventurism, including outright intervention with massive, nuclear-capable forces (as in Korea, Vietnam, and Afghanistan), is perhaps the most dangerous prevailing idea about nuclear war. The historical record, we believe, speaks for itself about the "prudence" and "caution" of the leaders of the nuclear states and about the safety of perpetual violence and intervention in a world peppered with enough nuclear weapons to destroy us all many times over.

To repeat, we do not claim that such actions necessarily made a nuclear war *probable* in the past or that they will make one probable in the future. We claim only that the nuclear danger is real—far too real for civilized people to accept—and that it lies here rather than in the arms race.

In truth, no one can estimate with any confidence the likelihood of a nuclear war. Given the historical record and the possible finality of a nuclear disaster, it is simply reckless arrogance to assume that there is "no" danger and to act accordingly. The people of the world have not given superpower leaders a license to make that judgment. Even the population of the United States, as we saw, has often been kept in the dark and excluded from any role in judging American actions with potential dangers on a planetary scale. A few considerations may help show that those dangers are in fact real.

## LOOSE CANNON
## ON THE NUCLEAR DECKS

Accidents and miscalculations during a crisis could lead to a nuclear disaster that neither side anticipates or wants. In peacetime, Paul Bracken writes, "with so many checks and balances, procedures for authentication of orders, and independent human interventions overlaid onto the control system for strategic weapons, the likelihood of accidental or inadvertent [nuclear] war is very, very low." But "the situation becomes very dangerous . . . when the [accidental] stresses occur in the midst of a Soviet-American crisis."[3]

In the tension and chaos of an extreme confrontation, thousands of soldiers, sailors, and pilots could ignite a superpower war—and as we showed in Chapter 3, dozens, perhaps hundreds, might be able to actually launch nuclear weapons—*no matter what the leaders of either side desired or ordered*. As Barry Posen writes, "Conventional war rolls the nuclear dice."[4] So does any conflict or crisis that could escalate to combat between the superpowers.

The Kennedys, for example, had no illusions about their ability to prevent the Cuban missile crisis from careening out of control. In one incident, a Soviet submarine escorting merchant ships approached the U.S. quarantine line around Cuba; a U.S. carrier was under orders to force it to the surface, if necessary with small depth charges. As Robert Kennedy writes, the president wondered: "Was the world on the brink of a holocaust? . . . President Kennedy had initiated the course of events, but he no longer had control over them."[5]

Admiral Anderson, then chief of naval operations, later called the missile crisis "perhaps the finest opportunity since WWII for the U.S. naval antisubmarine forces to exercise at their trade [and] to perfect their skills." They did so all too well. According to the Department of Defense's "postmortem," the American destroyer *Cecil* "forced a Soviet submarine to the surface" on October 30. Indeed, the Navy succeeded "in surfacing five or six Soviet Foxtrot-class diesel-attack submarines in or near the quarantine zone," in at least one case reportedly by a depth-charge attack—that is, by fighting between major U.S. and Soviet naval combatants. According to an American admiral, one Soviet sub was crippled, could not submerge, and was forced to steam home on the surface.[6] What if a Soviet sub had been sunk? Or what if a Soviet sub captain, to protect the lives of his crew, had returned fire in self-defense, sinking a major American vessel and causing many injuries and deaths? Such events can lead to war.

Equally alarming, in the North Atlantic U.S. antisubmarine forces hunted Soviet submarines equipped with nuclear cruise missiles, "which at the time were the principal element of the Soviet strategic nuclear deterrent forces." Attacks on them would have essentially constituted a first strike against the Soviet deterrent. This activity was "much more provocative than anything the President and his advisors had either approved or wanted." As John Steinbruner notes, despite "an extraordinary effort to co-ordinate the actions of the government and to subject those actions to exhaustive deliberation," "the efforts to bring American policy under central direction must be said to have failed."[7]

The Navy ran further risks. An American intelligence vessel steamed "just off the Cuban coast," and two warships, which "had the usual authority to fire at any hostile aircraft that approached them," crept to "within five or six miles of the Cuban coast." The Air Force sent a U-2 reconnaissance plane to the periphery of the Soviet Union on a supposedly routine mission during the crisis. When it "strayed" over Soviet territory, Soviet fighters scrambled to intercept it, and American jets were blithely dispatched to rescue it. On learning of this incident, Secretary of Defense Robert McNamara reportedly "turned absolutely white, and yelled hysterically, 'This means war with the Soviet Union.'" Khrushchev later wrote to Kennedy:

> The question is, Mr. President: How should we regard this? What is this, a provocation? One of your planes violates our frontier during this anxious time we are both experiencing, when everything has been put into combat readiness. Is it not a fact that an intruding American plane could be easily taken for a nuclear bomber, which might push us to a fateful step; and all the more so since the U.S. Government and Pentagon long ago declared that you are maintaining a continuous nuclear bomber patrol?[8]

Even the CIA got a chance to provoke fighting. Operation Mongoose, the agency's anti-Castro sabotage campaign, actually "ordered teams of covert agents into Cuba in order to support an invasion if it took place." On October 25, near the height of the crisis, the Cuban government foiled a sabotage attempt at the Matahambre copper mine. Amazingly, not until October 30 did the United States suspend Operation Mongoose attacks within Cuba—"once it had accidentally been learned that they were still going on!" But three six-man units were already in Cuba, and on November 8, in the midst of tense negotiations to end the crisis, "a

Cuban covert action sabotage team dispatched from the United States successfully blew up a Cuban industrial facility."[9]

Unanticipated dangers, as we have seen, shadowed other crises as well, often, as in 1962, at sea. Kaplan notes that, "generally speaking, after 1962 superpower military confrontations—at least in terms of the nearness of military units to each other—took place at sea." Blechman and Kaplan observe that the U.S. Navy, using "warships [that] often have nuclear warheads on board . . . has been the foremost instrument for the United States' political uses of the armed forces: at all times, in all places, and regardless of the specifics of the situation." The respected strategic analyst Desmond Ball points out: "There is probably a greater likelihood of accidental or unauthorized launch of sea-based nuclear weapons [than others], and the constraints on the authorized release of nuclear weapons are possibly more relaxed than those that pertain to land-based systems. . . . It [is] likely that any major conflict at sea would escalate to a strategic nuclear exchange relatively quickly."[10]

Even in calm times, the danger of accidental nuclear war lurks on and under the seas. Many collisions between Soviet and American warships have occurred, some during games of chicken. "Any one [of them]," Admiral Zumwalt writes, "could lead people to shoot at each other with results that might be by that time impossible to control." Harassment, some forms of which "are difficult to distinguish from preparations for hostilities," is also common, and "countermeasures to these provocations, such as maneuvering away from the threatening vessel, jamming or deceiving the adversary's electronic equipment, or directly harassing the threatening forces, could increase apprehensions on the other side, and thus 'prompt the very preemptive attack that they were meant to avoid.'" Soviet-American agreements have reduced the number and severity of serious incidents at sea, which in the late 1960s exceeded one hundred per year, but "serious collisions continue to occur at a rate of about half a dozen a year."[11]

American submarines on "Holystone" surveillance missions in and near Soviet territorial waters have come close to trouble many times. One "is reported to have collided with an E-class submarine in Vladivostok Harbor in the mid-1960's when photographing the underside of the Soviet vessel." On another occasion, in November 1969, "the U.S.S. *Gato* is reported to have operated as close as one mile . . . off the Soviet coast; later on the same patrol the *Gato* collided with a Soviet submarine 15–25 miles . . . off the entrance to the White Sea, in the Barents Sea off the northern U.S.S.R." These and other similar collisions—"together with more than a hundred other Holystone intrusion missions that were probably detected by Soviet forces but that they were unable to locate— could have been the catalyst for a chain of events that might have run from a localized engagement involving the intruding submarine to a full-scale nuclear exchange." Ball adds, "The general orders for Holystone missions reportedly state that, if threatened, the submarines 'have authority to use weapons.'" Incredibly, "in the November 1969 incident, the weapons officer of the *Gato* prepared to arm a SUBROC (UUM-44A) anti-submarine rocket (which carries a 1-5 kt W55 nuclear warhead) and three smaller nuclear torpedoes, and the submarine was 'maneuvered in preparation for combat.'" Reportedly "only one authentication—either from the ship's captain or her executive officer— was needed to prepare the torpedoes for launching."[12]

During crises, the risk of unplanned nuclear war greatly increases: "Having nuclear weapons close at hand obviously makes it much easier to consider their employment—particularly in situations in which their use might provide the only means of achieving a particular objective or preventing one's own destruction." As Ball notes, "It is difficult to imagine a commander on an ASW [antisubmarine warfare] mission, having exhausted his supply of conventional depth charges and related antisubmarine munitions, not being seriously tempted to break open his cache of nuclear depth-charges." Though the sources of inadvertent nuclear escalation at sea could be reduced to some degree, "others are essentially immutable," and "it would be realistic to expect that any war would have a significant naval component." Therefore "even a conventional conflict should not be joined without national decision-makers having clearly and consciously determined that the purpose served by such action justifies the real risk of an all-out nuclear exchange."[13]

Even if leaders retain effective control over their forces in the midst of conventional violence, they might decide to use nuclear weapons anyway, as irrational as this may sound. Psychopathology cannot be ruled out, especially given the bizarre 1973 record. In peacetime a destabilized leader would probably find it difficult to convince his subordinates to start World War III out of the blue. Lyndon Johnson reportedly remarked, "Some people wonder what would happen if I just woke up on the wrong side of the bed one day, decided I'd had it with the Russians, called the commander of SAC, and said, 'General, go get 'em!' You know what the general would say? 'Screw you, Mr. President.'" Gerald Ford recalls that "in the wake of Nixon's resignation, the newspapers were full of bizarre stories about his conduct in the final days. Some of them indicated that [then secretary of defense] Schlesinger was so concerned about Nixon's mental stability that he had taken steps to make sure the President couldn't give orders to the Armed Services unilaterally."[14] But in the midst of a tense crisis or war, such checks on an erratic executive may not be so easy to apply. Would the commander of SAC have said, "Screw you, Mr. President," to Nixon in October 1973?

## BRINKSMANSHIP FOREVER

Even supposedly sane leaders, as we saw, have knowingly risked nuclear war in the Third World, often over even the most trivial stakes. Why? American, and to a lesser extent Soviet, leaders have long regarded Third World crises not as local matters of limited importance but as epic tests or challenges that can affect their nation's global reputation and power for years to come.

As Robert Jervis writes, "Throughout history, and especially for the great powers since 1945, states have often cared about specific issues less for their intrinsic value than for the conclusions they felt others would draw from the way they dealt with them." Leaders have therefore been obsessed with the need to constantly demonstrate "resolve," to project a strong "image," to establish intimidating "precedents," to show a willingness to run risks, even nuclear ones, and, above all, to make others believe that they will go to any lengths to "win" future Third World confrontations. That the local stakes in a crisis may be small makes no difference—because local stakes simply are not the point. Kissinger's memoirs explicitly disparage the "unwillingness to confront seemingly marginal challenges, depicting them as unworthy because they appear not to encapsulate the ultimate showdown."[15]

The classic case is probably Quemoy and Matsu, the two "insignificant specks of land" over which the United States nearly went to nuclear war *twice* in the 1950s. As Brands observes, "Dulles and Eisenhower recognized that the U.S. was . . . approaching the brink of nuclear war over strategically trivial islands. However, they appeared to believe that U.S. credibility was on the line, and that if their approach didn't succeed, their entire defense policy might be undermined." Eisenhower expressed concern about the "psychological consequences" of letting the Chinese retake the islands and characterized the matter as a "concrete test" of his administration's resolve.[16]

President Kennedy's real concern during the Cuban missile crisis, as I. F. Stone wrote in 1966, was prestige. Remarkably, Kennedy's performance has become a model of how to conduct superpower foreign policy in the nuclear age. Richard Ned Lebow notes that Kennedy's "success" in the Cuban crisis "led responsible political analysts to exaggerate the efficacy of . . . demonstrations of resolve. . . . Political scientists enshrined the need for resolve at the core of widely-accepted theories of deterrence and compellence."[17]

Nixon writes that during the 1970 War of Attrition crisis, he dictated a memorandum to Kissinger stating that he planned to "stand up" to the Soviet Union in Vietnam, Europe, and the Middle East: "It is a question of all or none. . . . This is it cold turkey." Later, after *Syria* intervened in the Black September conflict in Jordan and Kissinger duly "drafted a very stern note and delivered it to the *Soviets,*" Nixon says he told Kissinger, "They're testing us." The president reportedly told a National Security Council meeting: "There comes a time when the US is going to be tested as to its credibility in the area. The real question will be, will we act? Our action has to be considered in that light. . . . Is the question really a military one or is it our credibility as a power in that area?" A member of Kissinger's staff professed, "The precedent is what will worry them most of all, and the demonstration that we could and will use our air power and naval presence will cast a shadow over their calculations about how far we might go in support of Israel at a later date in a new crisis, and our international posture generally." Kissinger, according to the Kalb brothers, believed "that the United States would never become 'credible' to the Kremlin, the Middle East or anywhere, for that matter, unless it was prepared to show power—and use it—in defense of its interests." As Quandt concludes, "the United States treated the Jordan crisis as a superpower test of wills."[18]

Referring to the 1970 Cienfuegos crisis, Kissinger writes, "I saw the Soviet move as going beyond its military implications; it was a part of a process of testing underway in different parts of the world." On the Indo-Pakistani war of 1971, he comments:

> The victim of the attack was an ally—however reluctant many were to admit it—to which we had made several explicit promises concerning precisely this contingency. Clear treaty commitments reinforced by other undertakings dated back to 1959. One could debate the wisdom of these undertakings (and much of our bureaucracy was so eager to forget about them that for a time it proved next to impossible even for the White House to extract copies of the 1962 communications), but we could not ignore them. To do so would have disheartened allies like Iran and Turkey, which sympathized with Paki-

stan, had the same commitment from us, and looked to our reaction as a token of American steadiness in potential crises affecting them. High stakes were therefore involved.

That Pakistan was then engaged in a major massacre, which had prompted the "attack," could on this logic be overlooked (especially considering that "allies like Iran and Turkey" were also prone to murdering their own people). Kissinger adds that "a reputation for unreliability was not something we could afford": "We had to act with determination to save larger interests and relationships . . . if we collapse now the Soviets won't respect us for it; the Chinese will despise us and the other countries will draw their own conclusions." Kissinger writes of ensuring that "the Russians retain their respect for us" and of "establishing an historical record of toughness . . . [that] might be used later to demonstrate that one's associates had wavered while one stood like a rock in a churning sea." Kissinger even complains about "the majority of informed opinion," which foolishly "sought to judge the confrontation on the subcontinent on the merits of the issues that had produced the crisis," including the fact, which Kissinger grants, that the American ally, Pakistan, "had unquestionably acted unwisely, brutally, and even immorally." After the crisis Nixon told the British prime minister: "The Soviets have tested us to see if they could control events . . . you have to consider the much bigger stakes in the Middle East and Europe." Nixon writes in his memoirs that "if we failed to help Pakistan, then Iran or any other country within the reach of Soviet influence might begin to question the dependability of American support."[19]

In 1973 the logic of testing and image led directly to the nuclear alert. According to Kissinger, "We could not sit on the sidelines if the Middle East should rage out of control; the world would view it as a collapse of American authority, whatever alibi we put forward." Describing events as they started to become tense, he reflects: "I had learned in Nixon's first term, largely under his tutelage, that once a great nation commits itself, it must prevail. . . . However ambivalently it has arrived at the point of decision, it must pursue the course on which it is embarked with a determination to succeed. Otherwise it adds a reputation for incompetence to whatever controversy it is bound to incur on the merits of its decision." He agrees with Nixon that "we were now in a test of wills" and that "that's what we [were there] for." Nixon expressed his "grasp of the situation," as Kissinger put it, very simply: "This is bigger than the Middle East. We can't allow a Soviet-supported operation to succeed against an American-supported operation. If it does, our credibility everywhere is severely shaken." [20]

As Richard Ned Lebow observes, Moscow "has been chary of using its military might as a means of sending signals to the United States." By contrast, American military displays have "become standard operating procedure in times of crisis. When a president confronts a foreign threat, he reaches almost by reflex for a carrier group or a fighter squadron to send to the troubled area," often against the advice of military officers, who prefer to use force only to achieve a concrete objective. "Gunboat diplomacy," Lebow adds, "may be the accepted American way of dealing with adversaries, but it is a dangerous atavism in the late twentieth century. For very little in the way of apparent political return, it raises the risk of war." [21]

Once defined as a historic test of wills, any conflict can quickly become a game of chicken in which neither side will back down. Each may then feel that even a terrible risk is better than defeat and humiliation. To terminate a crisis, a leader may decide to make the ultimate show of resolve, the use of nuclear weapons. Although such nuclear use might be limited at first—perhaps the "demonstration shot" discussed early in the Reagan administration, perhaps the use of several tactical nuclear weapons on a remote battlefield, perhaps the sinking of a single enemy ship with a nuclear warhead—escalation, as we have seen, cannot be fully controlled once the nuclear threshold is crossed. Even if command and control remain intact and even if an accidental or unauthorized catastrophe is avoided, the victim of a nuclear attack might believe that to back down now would be the ultimate signal of susceptibility to nuclear blackmail, leading to a global loss of prestige and power or even to further nuclear attacks. Escalation could easily continue until central control finally disintegrated and all-out nuclear war erupted.

READYING FOR ARMAGEDDON

American and Soviet leaders, as we saw, have already threatened to use nuclear weapons during numerous Third World conflicts, and in some cases the United States has actually put its weapons on alert and readied them for launch. Nuclear threats and alerts carry inherent risks of escalation and, again, could help produce a nuclear disaster that neither side intended.

As Daniel Ellsberg notes, on many occasions "U.S. nuclear weapons

*have* been used . . . in the precise way that a gun is used when you point
it at someone's head in a direct confrontation, whether or not the trigger
is pulled. . . . every president from Truman to Reagan, with the possible
exception of Ford, felt compelled to consider or direct serious preparations for possible imminent U.S. initiation of tactical or strategic nuclear
warfare, in the midst of an ongoing, intense, non-nuclear conflict or crisis." A major Brookings Institution study counts nineteen incidents between 1946 and the 1973 Middle Eastern war in which American strategic nuclear forces were actively involved in a political incident "in
such context that a nuclear signal of some type could be inferred."
These include four cases of "overt and explicit threat": Suez, 1956;
Lebanon, 1958; Cuba, 1962; and Sinai, 1973.[22]

The parallel Brookings study of Soviet military activities found that
although verbal nuclear threats were common, particularly during the
Khrushchev era, "in only one instance were data found confirming that
the USSR had actually raised the alert status of forces presumably included in plans for nuclear attack upon the United States, Europe, or
China." The stated exception is the Cuban missile crisis, though as
Garthoff authoritatively reports, "while Soviet and Warsaw Pact alerts
were prominently announced on October 23, they were in fact minimal
in impact, mainly involving largely symbolic measures such as cancel-
ling leaves. There were no major redeployments or high-readiness measures of the strategic missile force, air force, army, or navy." Moreover,
"no information was discovered that would indicate that the USSR has
ever redeployed strategic bomber units during a crisis," unlike the United
States, which did so ten times between 1946 and 1973. Even in October
1973, by which time U.S. nuclear superiority had long given way to
strategic stalemate, the Soviets did not respond in kind to the American
Defcon III alert. The lack of Soviet nuclear alerts in crises is all the more
remarkable considering that "the normal [noncrisis] levels of alert of Soviet strategic forces are much lower than those of U.S. strategic forces."
The apparent explanation is simply that, unlike American officials in
crises, "Soviet leaders may have been very anxious to restrict the risk of
accident or unauthorized action." The Soviets, of course, may not be so
cautious in the future. As Scott Sagan writes, there was "a dog that
didn't bark" in both 1962 and 1973:

> Certainly one of the significant reasons why both the 1962 and 1973 crises
> were resolved short of war is that Moscow quickly backed down rather than
> escalate the conflict. Especially with respect to predicting what would hap-
> pen if there was a mutual high level nuclear alert in a future superpower cri-

sis, therefore, a simple reading of the past could be highly misleading . . . relative Soviet acquiescence when confronted with American nuclear threats in the past . . . cannot confidently be expected to be repeated in the future.[23]

As Blechman and Hart write, "one cannot have the ostensible benefit of a nuclear threat without running its risks"—that is, one cannot intimidate an adversary unless the threat truly raises the chance of nuclear war. And threats do raise the risk because there is an enormous pressure to carry them out if their conditions are not met. Otherwise the state gets a reputation for crying wolf. "The result could be disastrous—U.S. policymakers being faced with the choice of admitting the emptiness of the nuclear threat, and thus undermining the credibility of fundamental U.S. commitments, or actually employing nuclear weapons."[24] Thus nuclear war could conceivably break out simply because a superpower leader said it would—much as Kennedy went to the brink to remove Soviet missiles in Cuba largely because he had threatened to do so, and Nixon in turn demanded the removal of the Cuban submarine base in 1970 largely because he believed that Kennedy had implied that this is what the United States would do (see Chapter 8).

Nuclear threats remain a backbone of U.S. foreign policy, and not only with respect to Europe. President Carter, for example, said in his 1980 State of the Union address that "an attempt by any outside force to gain control of the Persian Gulf region will be regarded as an assault on the vital interests of the United States of America, and such an assault will be repelled by any means necessary, including military force."[25] The administration made clear that "any means necessary" not only *included* the use of nuclear weapons but essentially *meant* nuclear war. As Ellsberg notes, "In the weeks before and after Carter's State of the Union message . . . the White House almost jammed Washington talk shows and major front pages with authorized leaks, backgrounders, and official spokesmen all carrying the message that the president's commitment . . . was, at its heart, a threat of possible initiating of tactical nuclear warfare by the United States." A key highly classified Pentagon study of military options in the region was leaked to *New York Times* correspondent (and later high Reagan administration official) Richard Burt within days. He summarized its conclusion "that the American forces could not stop a Soviet thrust into northern Iran and that the United States should therefore consider using 'tactical' nuclear weapons in any conflict there." In a television appearance that week, Assistant Secretary of State for Public Information William Dyess underlined that the United States refused to rule out the option of initiating nuclear war, noting dryly: "The Soviets know that this terrible weapon has been dropped on human beings twice in history and it was an American president who dropped it both times. Therefore, they have to take this into consideration in their calculus." In January 1981 departing Secretary of Defense Harold Brown (widely considered unusually progressive and thoughtful) reaffirmed that in the 1980s what will discourage the Soviets from moving on Iran or other parts of the Middle East is "the risk of World War III." In February, during Reagan's first week in office, the new president made clear that he subscribed to this policy. Acknowledging that "we know we couldn't" stop a major Soviet attack with conventional military means, he explained that the policy is "based on the assumption—and I think a correct assumption—the Soviet Union is not ready yet to take on that confrontation which could become World War III."[26]

The Carter Doctrine was more than just words. The so-called Rapid Deployment Force (RDF), a reorganized unit for quick U.S. military intervention abroad, is evidently intended to make the threat plausible. Too small to do much good in a major conventional war, its key feature is probably the potent and little-known nuclear arsenal it would carry to a conflict. As Christopher Paine explains: "The RDF is designed as a 'tripwire'—to signal U.S. determination to escalate to nuclear weapons as much as to cope directly with opposing conventional forces. The RDF can serve as a sort of 'doomsday device' which an opponent dares attack only at risk of triggering a mutually destructive war." It comes complete with a wing of twenty-eight Strategic Air Command B-52H bombers (which, as General Richard Ellis of SAC lamented, cause "a great deal of problems" with allies, since "B-52s seem to have a stigma"). The RDF also carries an immense tactical nuclear arsenal, including nuclear-capable tactical jets, artillery pieces, and howitzers, not to mention the nearly unlimited nuclear firepower available from the U.S. Navy. Ellsberg calls the RDF a "portable Dienbienphu"—a reference to the besieged French base in Vietnam that John Foster Dulles wanted to "save" with three tactical nuclear weapons—whose rescue could serve as a justification for using nuclear weapons anywhere in the world.[27]

Nuclear alerts constitute de facto nuclear threats and so share all their risks. But unlike simple threats, alerts also entail changes in the deployment and operation of nuclear weapons that greatly increase the chances of unintended or uncontrolled use. As Joseph Kruzel observes: "Something is far more likely to go wrong when forces are springloaded for action than when they are at rest. An unauthorized or accidental launching of nuclear weapons à la *Dr. Strangelove* is more likely in a force at high readiness than in one at low readiness." Scott Sagan— who wrote the Harvard Nuclear Study Group's *Living with Nuclear Weapons* and subsequently became a Pentagon nuclear planner—agrees that "any decision to place nuclear forces on alert in the future will be an extremely dangerous step" because the predelegation of nuclear launch authority to lower-level commanders during an alert "would produce serious problems with respect to controlling or terminating a nuclear exchange once begun and at least would raise the possibility of accidental war occurring through a warning or assessment failure during a superpower crisis." Indeed, Sagan recognizes that in the future "keeping the alert at the desired level will be extremely difficult, and the degree of further grave escalation uncertain."[28]

Yet, remarkably, he rejects a "no-alerts" policy on the grounds that "the failure to alert nuclear forces in a severe crisis, especially one in which Soviet strategic forces were moving to a higher state of readiness, might tempt the leadership in Moscow to continue escalating the crisis in the belief that the United States was willing to back down"—that is, it would show an unwillingness to compete in risk taking right to the brink, an unacceptable practice if you wish above all else for your state to win each confrontation. Many in government hold this view, though Sagan articulates it with unusual candor. As Lebow, who does not approve of using nuclear alerts for political purposes, notes, "The American defense establishment still conceives of nuclear alerts as an effective means of demonstrating resolve." Indeed, "this was the 'lesson' they learned from the 1962 and 1973 crises."[29]

## WHERE WILL THE NEXT GREAT CRISIS BE?

Almost *any* local conflict, as we have seen, can become a stage on which each superpower attempts to prove its toughness and resolve to the world and thereby enhance its credibility and power "everywhere," as Nixon put it in 1973.[30] If Quemoy and Matsu could become the unlikely proving ground for superpower prestige in 1954 and 1958, Cuba in 1962 and 1970, and the Indian subcontinent in 1971, who can say where the next great crisis will be?

U.S. officials have repeatedly discussed the option of blockading Nicaragua, an act that, as former U.S. secretary of the Navy John Lehman acknowledges, could lead to a superpower naval conflict. The Navy, Lehman notes, "cannot conceive that a naval conflict which engaged

Soviet forces could be localized"; it would be "instantaneously a global war."[31]

As a coda to the war in Afghanistan or as an extension of their own bitter conflict, India and Pakistan could well go to war again. This time, as Leonard Spector notes, both will almost certainly "have all the essentials needed to manufacture atomic bombs and to deliver them by aircraft during any crisis lasting more than several weeks," and perhaps much faster. In fact, "by 1991, Pakistan could have as many as 15 Hiroshima-sized devices, while India could have produced more than 100." As we noted in Chapter 6, many feared that the two countries neared war amid major military mobilizations in December 1986 and January 1987. Each continues to accuse the other of fomenting ethnic unrest, and either could suffer a major internal conflict, perhaps even a civil war. Spector highlights "the risk of political instability in Pakistan, which could lead to nuclear weapons (or highly enriched uranium) becoming bargaining chips in a struggle for domestic power. Episodes of this kind appear to have occurred during periods of internal unrest in France and China during the 1960s and are not as far-fetched as they may first appear."[32]

In Southeast Asia an American-backed guerrilla coalition dominated by Pol Pot's Khmer Rouge continues to battle the Soviet-backed Vietnamese occupation of Cambodia. The involvement of the U.S.-backed regime in Thailand poses particular dangers, such as an escalation of the periodic border and naval skirmishes to a Thai-Vietnamese war into which the superpowers could quickly be drawn. China, also aligned with the United States in these matters, could further internationalize the conflict—for example, by repeating its 1979 invasion of Vietnam—and thereby provoke Soviet involvement.

Elsewhere in Asia, more than 40,000 U.S. troops, "reportedly armed with some 150 tactical nuclear weapons . . . sit between 480,000 North Korean and 360,000 South Korean soldiers dug in along the DMZ." The U.S. troops constitute "an American nuclear tripwire stretched across the Korean peninsula," where "a second war could likely trigger an American nuclear attack on North Korea." Nuclear-armed Soviet naval forces in the North Pacific watch while enormous political upheaval and government repression continue to rack South Korea even after its nominal transition to democracy. The entire Pacific region, in fact, has become such a vast and unstable arena of nuclear-armed "eyeball-to-eyeball" superpower confrontation that "it is as likely that

World War III could begin in the Pacific as in Europe or the Middle East." For

> while Cold War blocs have remained steady in Europe, they have shifted dramatically in the Pacific. Two major land wars and a host of bloody insurrections and heavily armed repressive governments have erupted in less than half a century. Communist, democratic, and nationalist insurgencies, as well as continuing conflicts between nations, will continue to make the region politically turbulent into the foreseeable future, heightening the possibility of superpower intervention. Should their interventions overlap, the superpowers could clash and escalate to nuclear war.[33]

Southern Africa today is a bloody tangle of military conflicts, with Cuban troops defending Angola (and American oil interests) from U.S.-backed guerrillas, Zimbabwe helping Mozambique fend off South African–sponsored Renamo guerrillas, South African forces fighting rebels seeking an independent Namibia, and the antiapartheid struggle continuing within South Africa, which could well explode into civil war. One or more of these could lead to a major regional war in which both superpowers would feel some stake. Is it inconceivable, for example, that a rapidly deteriorating South African government, facing escalating cross-border guerrilla attacks, would expand its periodic attacks on its neighbors into a full-scale conquest of Mozambique or Angola, or even Zimbabwe? Would the Soviets necessarily stand aside, and would the United States sit back if they did not? Potentially dangerous incidents have occurred. On June 5, 1986, South Africa attacked three Soviet ships in the Angolan harbor of Namibe, sinking one of them. How many Americans have even heard of this significant event, much less heard their columnists and leaders condemn the dangers? Meanwhile Cuban soldiers and Soviet advisers in Angola continue to face South African attacks.[34]

For all practical purposes, South Africa has had a nuclear weapons capability for about a decade. As Spector reports, "U.S. analysts now date South Africa's status as a state capable of producing nuclear weapons from 1980–1981." Pretoria may have had as many as "fourteen to twenty-three weapons as of the end of 1987," a significant problem considering South Africa's continual militarism and the seriousness of its internal instability. Spector warns of

> the possibility that nuclear weapons or nuclear weapons material produced by South Africa's current regime might . . . fall into the hands of a radical faction—black or white—which had gained control of the government and

which might then use or threaten to use these nuclear assets to advance extremist objectives. Indeed, should domestic order crumble, governmental authorities could lose control over nuclear weapons or highly enriched uranium, which a non-governmental group might seize to create domestic or international turmoil or possibly sell or take into exile in order to lay the base for a return to power.[35]

The simultaneous presence of Israeli and Syrian forces in Lebanon poses a constant risk of another Arab-Israeli war—all previous instances of which since 1956, as we have seen, have led to actual or threatened superpower intervention and a significant risk of nuclear crisis. The ongoing conflict over Palestinian self-rule, as Bernard Avishai and Avner Cohen point out, "cannot be indefinitely contained to the West Bank and Gaza" and could lead to "a conflagration that not only could engulf Israel and her neighbors, but also has the potential to draw the superpowers into an unprecedented round of nuclear brinksmanship." Others believe that "a new war in the Middle East would probably be interpreted by both sides as something of a final test—like two boxers struggling near the fifteenth round with a feeling that up to this point the match had been a draw. . . . In a sense, nuclear war could erupt at any time in a fifth round of fighting between Israel and the Arab states because the enemy would be *figuratively,* if not literally, at the capital gates."[36]

Nuclear weapons will inescapably play at least an off-stage role in any future Middle East conflict. Much evidence suggests that Israel has a substantial and growing nuclear arsenal of "at least fifty to sixty nuclear devices—perhaps, significantly more—some of which are of an advanced design that makes them many times more powerful than the atomic weapons used in World War II." Israel has a big enough arsenal "to use a number of its nuclear weapons tactically, i.e., against military targets, during any conflict with its neighbors, while keeping a number of its weapons in reserve to threaten enemy cities." Israel even has the ability to deliver its warheads by ballistic missile, and not only against Arab states:

> Although Israel has never acknowledged the existence of the Jericho II, the missile is undoubtedly seen as a means for strengthening the country's undeclared nuclear force. . . . More disturbing is Israel's apparent rationale for building a longer-range version of the missile, which seemingly is directed not only at Baghdad, Benghazi, and Riyadh . . . but also at least in part at the Soviet Union. . . . Israeli officials have indicated in off-the-record interviews that the missile is intended in part to deter massive Soviet intervention on

behalf of Syria in any future conflict—a scenario that could all too easily escalate into a high-stakes U.S.-Soviet confrontation.[37]

Libya, Iraq, and Iran all appear to have nuclear ambitions, though apparently none will be able to make nuclear weapons in the near future. These states, as well as Egypt and Israel, already have potent strategic capabilities in the form of chemical weapons and have or soon will have ballistic missiles able to deliver them. Israeli planners worry about an Arab chemical attack in a future war and have publicly hinted that they might use nuclear weapons in retaliation, or perhaps even preemptively, to destroy Arab chemical warfare capabilities before they can be used against Israeli cities. Israel has already taken many steps to hamper Arab nuclear ambitions, in recent years by bombing an Iraqi nuclear plant and threatening to attack Saudi missiles that could reach Israeli cities. Seeking to forestall a threat to its own cities, the Soviet Union likewise warned Israel not to deploy the Jericho II missile.[38] Unlike the long-stalemated nuclear arms race between the superpowers, the regional nuclear-chemical strategic arms race in the Middle East (as in other volatile regions) poses real dangers.

Gideon Raphael, the former director-general of the Israeli Foreign Ministry and the former Israeli ambassador to the United Nations, writes that Syria's chemical warfare capabilities "could mean that the next war between Syria and Israel will degenerate into a contest between chemical and radiation weapons—with global implications." In 1984 and 1985 the Syrian defense minister stated that the Soviet Union had "guaranteed" that it would provide Damascus with nuclear warheads if Israel used nuclear weapons against Syria in a future war. Though the Soviet Union denied it, "other Soviet officials have reportedly told Western visitors that if Israel were to attack Syria itself—even if only with conventional armaments—Moscow would assist its ally with military force, including tactical nuclear weapons if necessary."[39]

Avishai and Cohen argue that despite Israel's great conventional military superiority,

> it is hard to see how an Israeli government would not consider using nuclear weapons to try to end [a war]. A longer, more drawn-out or inclusive regional war would mean thousands of Israeli casualties—a price the Israeli military will not want to pay. . . . If the IDF [Israeli Defense Forces] were to take heavy casualties on the Golan, or if, in the course of war with Syria, the Egyptians were to introduce a large armor force into the Sinai, what good choices would Israeli leaders be left with . . . particularly if the Syrians sur-

prised the IDF with chemical weapons carried by its own missiles? . . . And who, then, would be in control of Israel's nuclear arsenal? The army? The defense minister himself? The Cabinet as a whole, which has never been involved with matters of nuclear strategy? The tiny coterie of nuclear technocrats shaped by Yuval Neeman—the leader of the ultra-right Tehiya Party?

As Peter Pry observes, "an atomically armed Israel could inadvertently escalate the next Middle Eastern conflict into a global holocaust."[40]

As recent events graphically showed, the Persian Gulf likewise remains a potential nuclear flash point. The danger inherent in the Iraqi invasion of Iran greatly intensified when the United States intervened with a large nuclear-capable armada, ostensibly to protect Kuwaiti merchantmen. "If the United States is forced to retaliate in the event of an Iranian attack" on one of the U.S.-flagged Kuwaiti ships, the *New York Times* reported, "a number of Congressmen fear that the Russians could side with Iran, resulting in a direct American-Soviet confrontation." This logical concern did not dominate congressional criticism of the U.S. plan to protect Kuwaiti ships, since most discussions focused on American geopolitical interests. American warships, several Soviet merchant vessels, and an Iranian airliner were attacked, the United States fired on Iranian forces several times, and in at least one case, according to the Soviet press, "an Iranian frigate pointed its guns at a Soviet ship and made a hostile pass at a convoy under Soviet naval escort." In the closing stages of the war, the warships of *four* nuclear states—the United States, the Soviet Union, Britain, and France—plied the gulf. Many of these ships were equipped to fire nuclear weapons, and some probably had warheads aboard. The U.S.S. *Stark,* devastated by an Iraqi jet in the gulf, was unusual in *lacking* nuclear capabilities. The U.S.S. *Vincennes,* which shot down the Iranian airliner and engaged in combat with Iranian gunboats, *can* fire nuclear weapons—a significant fact that neither the Pentagon nor the U.S. news media brought to light during the intense news coverage of the ship's design and capabilities. As Christopher Paine notes, there is a clear American commitment to intervene in the gulf should U.S. interests appear to be threatened; "Soviet concern about developments in Iran, and Moscow's readiness to intervene militarily if necessary to prevent hostile forces from taking control along its southern borders, are matters of record." Consequently "there is a very great risk . . . of U.S. military intervention leading to confrontation with the Soviet Union which quickly threatens to become nuclear."[41]

We could cite other potential Third World nuclear flash points, and new ones are sure to erupt. The recent past offers little hope that the worst dangers are behind us. In the last few years *every* state known or presumed to have nuclear weapons has fought in the Third World: the United States in Grenada, Lebanon, Libya, and the Persian Gulf; the Soviet Union in Afghanistan; China in Vietnam; India in Sri Lanka and in clashes with Pakistan; Israel in the 1981 air attack on Iraq, the bombing of Tunis, and frequent ground, sea, and air attacks in Lebanon; Britain in the Falklands/Malvinas; France in Chad and the Pacific; South Africa in Namibia and Angola. Throughout the Third World, regional superpowers and major powers—such as China, India, Pakistan, Israel, South Africa, Brazil, and Argentina—already have or could soon have nuclear weapons, and as of this writing three of them (Israel, South Africa, and India) have regular troops fighting outside their borders. Nuclear danger, then, will hang over most future Third World conflicts.

## CHAPTER EIGHT

# What About the Cuban Missile Crisis?

In a Nuclear Age, Nations Must Make War Like Porcupines
Make Love—Carefully.
—*Sign outside Cuban missile crisis conference room at the*
*U.S. State Department, 1962*

AT THE BRINK: WHY?

On Tuesday morning, October 16, 1962, top officials of the U.S. government viewed photographs taken by Major Rudolph Anderson, of the Strategic Air Command, from a U-2 spy plane fourteen miles above the island of Cuba. They clearly showed Soviet technicians installing medium-range nuclear missiles. On Sunday morning, October 28, under an ultimatum from President Kennedy, Nikita Khrushchev agreed to remove Soviet nuclear missiles and bombers from Cuba. Kennedy vowed in return that America would never invade the island.[1]

As Robert Kennedy recalls, those thirteen days of the Cuban missile crisis saw "a confrontation between the two giant atomic nations . . . which brought the world to the abyss of nuclear destruction and the end of mankind." At the height of the crisis, on Saturday, October 27, Robert Kennedy told the Soviet ambassador: "We had to have a commitment by tomorrow that those [Soviet nuclear weapons] bases would be removed. . . . If they did not remove those bases, we would remove them. . . . Perhaps [the Soviet Union] might feel it necessary to take retaliatory action; but before that was over, there would be not only dead Americans but dead Russians as well." A huge invasion force of more than a hundred thousand U.S. troops and over a hundred ships stood ready. The president had even ordered the printing of five million leaflets in Spanish to be dropped over Cuba if the United States invaded.[2]

The United States had been on worldwide nuclear alert, the most urgent ever ordered, for a week. American Atlas and Titan missiles stood ready for launch. Polaris nuclear missile submarines left port and sailed underwater toward the Soviet Union. The B-52s of the Strategic Air Command took off over the Atlantic with their bomb-bay doors closed—a sign they were carrying full loads of fused nuclear bombs. Every time one bomber landed, another took off immediately to replace it. The total destructive power in the alerted Strategic Air Command forces alone "was over 7000 megatons—higher than the entire American strategic arsenal today." [3] Civil defense officials made frenzied plans to save key officials in case the worst happened.

David Detzer gives a graphic reconstruction: "Deep in the Pentagon's War Room, behind a green door, electronic consoles blink brightly. . . . Here and there in the room are unobtrusive Klaxon horns. If they should sound, President Kennedy has just signaled Def-Con 1 [Defcon I]. According to plans, one of the individuals in the room will instantly step forward, keys in hand, and unlock several padlocks on a small red box. Inside he will find plastic bags containing the proper coded message being sent at that moment to SAC bases around the world." [4]

In his famous speech of October 22, President Kennedy left no doubt about the risk he was running. He informed a horrified nation of the Soviet missiles in Cuba and said that his "unswerving objective" was "to secure their withdrawal or elimination from the Western Hemisphere. . . . action is required—and it is underway; and these actions may only be the beginning. We will not prematurely or unnecessarily risk the costs of worldwide nuclear war in which even the fruits of victory would be ashes in our mouth—but neither will we shrink from that risk at any time it must be faced." Kennedy thought at the time that the odds of war with the Soviet Union were "somewhere between one out of three and even." [5]

Americans have been led to believe that President Kennedy took this terrible risk to safeguard the physical security of the United States. His stated goal was the removal of "clearly offensive" Soviet nuclear weapons aimed at this country and based ninety miles off our coast. He told the American people that "the purpose of these bases can be none other than to provide a nuclear strike capability against the Western Hemisphere" and that "each of these missiles . . . is capable of striking Washington, D.C., the Panama Canal, Cape Canaveral, Mexico City, or any other city in the southeastern part of the United States, in Central America, or in the Caribbean area. . . . [This] constitutes an explicit threat to the peace and security of all the Americas." [6]

As I. F. Stone wrote several years after the crisis, "The public impression created by the government when the presence of the missiles in Cuba was verified is that they represented a direct threat to America's cities."⁷ The removal of that threat is widely considered to be John F. Kennedy's finest hour.

The missile crisis, then, may seem an exception to our argument in this book: the one instance in which a development in the nuclear arms race did destabilize the nuclear standoff and hence invited disaster. But by 1962 existential deterrence was already securely in place. The Cuban missiles in fact posed no new threat to the physical security of the United States and did not significantly change the nuclear balance of power. Kennedy and Khrushchev risked nuclear war over them, as we shall see, for other reasons.

## WHY THE CUBAN MISSILES DIDN'T MATTER

By 1962 both sides already had enough nuclear weapons to devastate each other. Neither could defend itself against nuclear attack. And neither stood any reasonable chance of disarming the other through a pre-emptive strike. Missiles in Cuba could not make either nation more vulnerable or less vulnerable; both were already totally vulnerable.

Consider the Soviet position first. Despite the Soviets' late start, relative underdevelopment, and losses in World War II, they had rapidly built a formidable nuclear arsenal. As early as 1955 an expert panel advised President Eisenhower that "the Soviet Union already had enough mid-range bombers and bombs of up to one megaton yield . . . to seriously damage the United States. . . . [We] would be vulnerable to a devastating and possibly decisive surprise attack." Later that year, after the Soviets had successfully tested a thermonuclear device with an explosive power far greater than the simple weapon that destroyed Hiroshima, "the USSR could seriously damage the United States even if only a few bombers managed to escape destruction and penetrate U.S. defenses."⁸

By the fall of 1962 the Institute for Strategic Studies in London estimated that the communist bloc possessed at least seventy-five intercontinental ballistic missiles, seven hundred medium-range ballistic missiles able to strike Western Europe, two hundred long-range and fourteen hundred medium-range bombers, and submarines able to deliver dozens of nuclear warheads to U.S. cities. More recent evidence suggests that some of those estimates may have been too large; but no matter what the actual numbers, without a doubt the Soviets had enough to decimate both Europe and the United States, and leaders on both sides knew it. A Soviet general recently said that Moscow had only about twenty intercontinental ballistic missiles at the time, leading to many sensational but inaccurate press reports that the Cuban deployments doubled or tripled the Soviet nuclear threat to the United States. Land-based missiles—no matter *what* their exact number—were a minor component of the Soviet strategic arsenal at the time compared with bombers and submarine-based missiles. Even if we someday learn that the Soviets had no operable intercontinental missiles in 1962, the strategic significance would be minimal, and so would the implications for our understanding of the missile crisis.[9]

The Soviets had far fewer nuclear forces than the United States, but what they had was sufficient. If the United States could be deterred, these forces would do it. Besides, as the president was reportedly told during the crisis, "the missiles in Cuba represented an inevitable occurrence: narrowing of the missile gap between the United States and U.S.S.R. It simply happened sooner rather than later."[10]

Still, some have suggested, the Soviet deterrent required urgent supplementation because of a growing American ability to pinpoint nuclear weapons bases inside the Soviet Union. Those were the days of "soft" missile and bomber sites; once the U-2s and orbiting satellites found them, they supposedly could be destroyed by a surprise American counterforce attack. After such an attack, the Soviets would theoretically have limited remaining forces, whereas the United States would have a large reserve. The president could then threaten to launch many missiles against Soviet cities for each Soviet weapon thrown at the United States in retaliation. Thus any Soviet counterattack would be suicidal and, according to this argument, would not take place, giving the United States a clean victory. Constructing a larger and less vulnerable ICBM and submarine force at home would be the permanent Soviet solution to this supposed problem, but it would take time. By quickly increasing the Soviet arsenal able to strike America, the argument goes, the Cuban missiles would have made Soviet retaliation more credible in the meantime.[11]

This clever scenario was far from political reality. The Soviets knew that an American president would be most unlikely to risk a nuclear attack on the basis of such a thin strategic theory. Any major counterforce attack would encounter so many uncertainties that the president could never be sure the United States and Europe would escape devastating retaliation. The existing Soviet deterrent sufficed to show any sane

American leader that a nuclear attack on the Soviet Union would result in immense damage to the United States as well.

The new missiles in Cuba could not have helped deter an American counterforce attack anyway. They were exposed and unprotected, on an indefensible island close to the U.S. mainland. In any U.S. first strike, the Cuban missiles and bombers would have been destroyed in short order. They would not have been around for the Soviets to use in retaliation and therefore could serve no deterrent function.[12] As Hagan and Bernstein concluded, "If one is considering the kind of ultimate intercontinental warfare that would constitute the last stage of a counterforce war or the first stage of a pre-emptive strike, hardly any conceivable amount of effort directed into Cuba could have tipped the balance in the Soviet Union's favor."[13]

It is even clearer that our own nuclear deterrent was secure and could not have rationally motivated the great risks President Kennedy took during the missile crisis. The United States was at the time so vastly superior to the Soviets in every measure of nuclear capability that there could be no serious thought of the Soviets' gaining an advantage in Cuba. By 1960 the Pentagon had already accumulated so much nuclear firepower and delivery capacity that President Eisenhower was "shocked and angered by the level of overkill envisioned" in the war plan. According to the official history of the Strategic Air Command, over 200 operational ICBMs were deployed on American soil, and over 100 U.S.-controlled missiles able to strike the Soviet Union were based in Britain, Italy, and Turkey. Several thousand strategic bombers could deliver over 500 Hound-Dog long-range air-to-surface nuclear missiles as well as thousands of megatons of nuclear gravity bombs to Soviet territory. Declassified Department of Defense documents show that the Polaris submarine fleet could fire almost 100 nuclear missiles against Soviet society from beneath the oceans. In 1962 the United States had 26,500 nuclear warheads—about the same number that we have today.[14]

No Soviet attack could have disarmed this frightful retaliatory arsenal with or without Cuban missiles and bombers. The Cuban weaponry was far too limited in range, accuracy, and controllability to pose a real threat to our dispersed, multifaceted, and redundant deterrent forces.[15] It is doubtful that *any* amount or kind of nuclear weapons in Cuba could have seriously threatened the American deterrent, especially the U.S. bomber force, a portion of which was kept safely airborne at all times, and the submarine-based missile force, which remains invulnerable to this day.[16]

In any case the Cuban weapons did not represent a *new* threat to the United States. It did not matter militarily that they were only ninety miles from our coastline, whereas home-based Soviet forces were thousands of miles away. The few minutes' difference in flight time would not change the result when the weapons landed. It would not even matter if, as some feared, the Cuban missiles opened the way for the Soviets to "surround" us with nuclear weapons emplaced wherever they could find a friendly government. In the missile age, geographical proximity does not count for much. And we were already surrounded at close quarters anyway by missiles on Soviet submarines in our coastal waters.

The U.S. officials who sat around the missile crisis conference table have acknowledged that they did not have self-defense on their minds. They would have a strong personal motive for defending their actions on such an unimpeachable basis. But they did not make this case then, and they have not done so since.

Robert McNamara, then secretary of defense, argued during the crisis that the Cuban missiles were of little consequence to our national defense given the nuclear firepower the Soviet Union could already deliver from its own territory. "A missile is a missile," he said. "It makes no great difference whether you are killed by a missile from the Soviet Union or Cuba." McNamara reportedly felt that the United States could accept the Cuban deployment without fear, even though it narrowed the American numerical advantage in missile power, because its military consequences were "minor": "seven to one missile 'superiority,' one to one missile 'equality,' one to seven missile 'inferiority'—the three positions are identical. What was identical was the unacceptability of the American casualties that could be inflicted from any of the three."[17]

McNamara's deputy secretary of defense, Roswell Gilpatric, concurred in a rare public admission during a national television interview on November 11, 1962. He stated that "the military equation was not altered" by the Soviet placement of nuclear missiles in Cuba. "I don't believe that we were under any greater threat from the Soviet Union's power, taken in totality, after this than before."[18]

Kennedy's presidential counsel during the crisis, Theodore Sorensen, wrote in his biography of the president, "To be sure, these Cuban missiles alone, in view of all the other megatonnage the Soviets were capable of unleashing upon us, did not substantially alter the strategic balance *in fact*." In an October 17 memo during the crisis, Sorensen stated that it was "generally agreed that these missiles, even when fully operational, do not significantly alter the balance of power—i.e., they do not significantly increase the potential megatonnage capable of being unleashed on American soil, even after a surprise American nuclear strike." [19]

McNamara, Gilpatric, Sorensen, and Kennedy's other top advisers at the time, McGeorge Bundy, George Ball, and Dean Rusk, recently reaffirmed that with or without nuclear weapons in Cuba, all understood that "nuclear war, already in 1962, would have been an unexampled catastrophe for both sides; the balance of terror . . . was in full operation." The president knew this. In a television interview several months after the crisis, he made clear that his concern about the Soviet missiles was "not that they were intending to fire them, because if they were going to get into a nuclear struggle, they have their own missiles in the Soviet Union." [20]

## DOMINANCE RITUAL

The important thing about the Cuban missiles, President Kennedy said, was that they changed the balance of power "politically." Sorensen confirms that Kennedy "was less concerned about the missiles' military implications than with their effect on the global political balance." As George and Smoke sum it up, the crisis was the grandest "in a series of increasingly ambitious efforts the two superpowers had been making to exploit their strategic armories for politico-diplomatic purposes." [21]

One such purpose, for Khrushchev, was the defense of Cuba. Khrushchev made a speech six weeks after the crisis declaring: "We stationed rockets in Cuba only for the defense of the Cuban Republic. . . . Cuba needed weapons as a means of containing the aggressors." Khrushchev's memoirs state, "Our goal was . . . to keep the Americans from invading Cuba, and, to that end, we wanted to make them think twice by confronting them with our missiles." [22]

Until recently, Americans generally dismissed this explanation as self-serving rationalization, but it is probably part of the truth. Almost from the victory of the Cuban Revolution, the United States had menaced Castro. America maintained an unwelcome naval base at Guantánamo and kept a visible military presence around the island. President Eisenhower ordered U.S. security agencies to organize, train, and arm hostile Cuban refugees only fifteen months after the revolution. In 1961 President Kennedy approved the ill-fated CIA-backed Bay of Pigs invasion. Reeling from that humiliation, the Kennedy administration later formulated Operation Mongoose, a high-level plan that attempted, among other things, the assassination of key Cuban leaders, including Castro. A top CIA agent named Theodore Shackley was assigned to develop a "vulnerability and feasibility study" of the Castro government. In 1962 he organized a massive military operation in Florida budgeted at over fifty million dollars and employing more than three hundred Americans and thousands of Cubans to support paramilitary strikes and assassination attempts inside Cuba. Only a few months before the missile crisis, the Cuban terrorist organization Alpha-66, based in Florida, mounted a speedboat strafing attack on a Cuban hotel near Havana frequented by Soviet military technicians, causing many deaths. Later raids targeted a British and two Cuban cargo ships just north of Cuba. In addition to many other actions, the CIA's Task Force W sabotaged Cuban sugar shipments and other exports. On the day before the missile crisis erupted, the Mongoose group decided to step up its sabotage operations, deciding "that all efforts should be made to develop new and imaginative approaches, with the possibility of getting rid of the Castro regime." Recent evidence shows that the U.S. government was seriously considering a massive outright invasion of Cuba just before the missile crisis.[23]

Around the same time, the U.S. Navy and Marines planned a major training exercise called Phibriglex 62. Four aircraft carriers, twenty destroyers, and fifteen troop carriers with a Marine brigade were to storm a small Puerto Rican island near Cuba. They had orders to overthrow a "fictional" leader named Ortsac, which can also be spelled backward.[24]

The real Castro told a French journalist that after becoming convinced an American invasion might be imminent, he told Khrushchev to "do anything that will convice the Americans that an attack on Cuba is tantamount to an attack on the Soviet Union." The Soviets reportedly replied that "the threat of conventional retaliation might not be enough to persuade America to think twice before invading Cuba."[25]

Thus, Khrushchev may have built the Cuban missiles in part as frontline doomsday weapons (discussed in Chapter 3) to ensure that any attack on Cuba would risk precipitating nuclear war. And Kennedy may have wanted the missiles removed partly to avoid that prospect so that the United States could maintain the option of invading the island. In these respects the Cuban missiles may have mattered—as all such doomsday weapons matter—not because they changed the nuclear balance of power but because they sat in a potential superpower battlefield.

The Cuban deployment perhaps also mattered because, as President

Kennedy remarked, although it could not change the nuclear balance *in fact,* "it would have appeared to, and appearances contribute to reality." U.S. intelligence had just exposed as fiction the famous "missile gap" supposedly favoring the Soviets. Khrushchev may have felt that he needed more nuclear hardware, even if militarily inconsequential, to ensure that Soviet foreign policy would not be stymied by an *appearance* of American nuclear superiority. Building long-range ICBMs at home and at sea was expensive and slow. Placing existing medium-range missiles and bombers in Cuba (what Garthoff terms "ersatz ICBMs") was cheap and fast. George and Smoke argue that Khrushchev wanted the missiles to put him "once more in a position to make use of strategic threats in support of a broad range of foreign policy goals, this time with even greater credibility than when he attempted to exploit American uncertainty over Soviet ICBMs."[26] As we discussed in Chapter 4, building militarily irrelevant weapons to impress others has been a common strategy.

Castro's fate and concerns over hypothetical misperceptions of the nuclear balance of power were linked to far larger stakes in the crisis: the quest for international credibility and prestige that, as we saw in Chapter 7, has frequently driven the superpowers into confrontation both before and after 1962. Khrushchev apparently saw the Cuban missiles as a way to dramatically demonstrate to the world that the Soviet Union would no longer act like a second-rate power but would challenge the United States for an equal role in managing world affairs. A direct challenge in, say, Berlin was too risky; it could easily lead to nuclear war, as the Soviets had learned so well in the prior few years. Khrushchev sought instead a decisive *symbolic* victory. He appears to have hoped that the Cuban missiles would become operational before they were discovered by U.S. intelligence. Then it would be too late for Kennedy to do much about them. Khrushchev would have showed the world that at his hands the United States was indeed a "paper tiger" (as the Chinese had claimed during the 1954 Quemoy-Matsu crisis), and that now the world truly had *two* superpowers.

Kennedy, however, was unwilling to give up the overwhelming U.S. dominance in the Cold War. When U.S. intelligence discovered the missiles during construction, he resolved to deny Khrushchev his symbolic victory at any cost. The Cuban missile crisis—not in essence a conflict over any limited prize like Cuba—was but the most titanic of the many symbolic superpower tests of wills that have set the nuclear dice in motion.

Maverick journalist I. F. Stone was one of the first to recognize that "the real stake was prestige. The question was whether, with the whole world looking on, Kennedy would let Khrushchev get away with it. The world's first thermonuclear confrontation turned out to be a kind of ordeal by combat between two men to see which one would back down first." [27]

At that time both men were under great pressure—personal and political—to demonstrate their nations' resolve to prosecute the Cold War ruthlessly. "It was the courage of John F. Kennedy which was in question," Stone alleges; staring down Khrushchev "was the best of therapies for Kennedy's nagging inferiority complex." Congressional elections would be held the following month, and the Republicans were scoring points against Kennedy's "do-nothing" policy about Castro. In the words of Roger Hilsman, "the United States might not be in mortal danger" from the Cuban missiles, "but the administration most certainly was." McNamara said during an October 16, 1962, meeting: "I don't believe it's primarily a military problem. It's primarily a, a domestic political problem." Robert Kennedy told his brother, "If you hadn't acted, you would have been impeached." [28]

Cuba was a sensitive issue for the Americans. It had been a cherished part of the American empire, with long historical, economic, and cultural ties to the mainland. Allowing it to become a Soviet nuclear weapons base seemed the ultimate humiliation. The president was already reeling from what he interpreted as multiple humiliations at the hands of the Soviets. The world, he thought, had seen him bullied by Khrushchev at the Vienna conference the year before. It had seen the United States defeated and embarrassed in the Bay of Pigs fiasco. And most important, it had seen Washington back down from confrontation in Berlin the year before.

After an interview with the president, James Wechsler of the *New York Post* said: "What worried [Kennedy] was that Khrushchev might interpret his reluctance to wage nuclear war [during the Berlin crisis] as a symptom of an American loss of nerve. Some day, he said, the time might come when he would have to run the supreme risk to convince Khrushchev that conciliation did not mean humiliation." In his speech to the nation announcing the discovery of the Cuban missiles, Kennedy left no doubt that the time had come: Khrushchev's "sudden, clandestine decision . . . cannot be accepted by this country, if our courage and our commitments are ever to be trusted again by either friend or foe." [29]

Indeed, leaders on both sides believed that the symbolic contest over the Cuban missiles would affect all the other Cold War conflicts of the time. President Kenendy, for example, worried that, if successful, Khrushchev's move would symbolize a grave weakening of American power in its own hemisphere and would thereby undermine U.S. political influence in the entire Latin region. Theodore Sorensen reports the president's view that "missiles on Soviet territory or submarines were very different from missiles in the Western Hemisphere, particularly in their political and psychological effect on Latin America." Herbert Dinerstein notes the American belief that the missiles would further Castro's "aggressive purposes." Roger Hilsman explains the fear that "in Latin America, other potential 'Castros' would be encouraged, American power would be less impressive and American protection less desirable, and some of the Latin American states would move in the Soviet direction even if their governments were not overthrown." [30] The principle of deterrence had less to do with nuclear war in 1962 than the principle of the Monroe Doctrine.

The Cuban test of wills, both sides apparently thought, would also help settle the fate of Berlin, and even of China half a world away. In 1963 Arnold Horelick wrote a Rand Corporation memorandum arguing that Khrushchev was deeply frustrated about his failure to compel "the West to accept a Berlin settlement on Soviet terms" and that he wanted a "breakthrough" to turn the tables. Richard Neustadt and Graham Allison agree that the Cuban missiles "seemed tied to the Soviet plan for action on Berlin." [31]

The superpowers had clashed just one year before, when the Berlin Wall was constructed. President Kennedy estimated the chances of nuclear war then at one in five, and he felt that he had strengthened Khrushchev's hand by backing down from the brink. Robert Kennedy reports his brother's fear that "if we did nothing . . . the Russians would move on Berlin and in other areas of the world, feeling the U.S. was completely impotent." Some argued that if Kennedy accepted the missiles, the United States "might not be able to persuade the Soviet Union that it was willing to run the risks of nuclear war to preserve Berlin." The president conjectured during the crisis that if he appeared weak on the missiles, "then they [would] start getting ready to squeeze us in Berlin." [32]

Horelick notes that at that time Khrushchev was also preoccupied with the disintegration of communist unity, especially China's increasing independence from Moscow. He argues that "the Chinese Communist attack on Khrushchev centered precisely on the unfavorable trend in the cold war which the Chinese attributed to Khrushchev's faulty and overcautious leadership." Roger Hilsman adds that from the Soviet perspective "a successful move in Cuba would cut the ground from under the Chinese Communists and go far toward convincing Communists everywhere that Soviet leadership was strong and Soviet methods in dealing with the 'imperialists' effective." [33]

As Richard J. Walton charges: "Kennedy again took the view that the issue was not primarily Cuba but another test of American determination. . . . Washington could not resist the conviction that any Soviet-American dispute was not limited to the question at hand but represented a fundamental test of American courage." Walton speaks the truth about the missile crisis forthrightly: "Kennedy embarked on a dangerous path with unforeseeable consequences not because of immediate physical danger but because missiles on Cuba 'would have politically changed the balance of power.' He took an unpardonable mortal risk without just cause. He threatened the lives of millions for appearances' sake." [34]

## WHY KENNEDY "HAD TO"
## RISK THE LIVES OF MILLIONS

Almost every Western commentator rightly condemns Khrushchev's attempt to deploy nuclear missiles in Cuba. Though he did not violate international law or do anything the United States had not done when it deployed nuclear weapons on the territory of allies near the Soviet Union, Khrushchev did raise the risk of nuclear war for symbolic political gain.

President Kennedy did the same thing. He may not have rattled the nuclear saber, but he drew it from its sheath, ordering the most urgent nuclear alert in history. Kennedy did not want nuclear war and would not have initiated one hastily. But he was willing to raise its likelihood dramatically. The alert was part of an effort to make the threat of nuclear war part of the Soviet calculation and is in this sense a clear act of nuclear diplomacy.

Some would argue that Kennedy *had* to alert American nuclear forces simply to ensure that procedures would be taken to protect them from a possible Soviet first strike, such as the dispersal of nonairborne nuclear bombers to over thirty civilian and military airfields. But there was no question that massive amounts of nuclear firepower—particularly in submarines at sea—would survive any Soviet attack even if U.S.

forces stood in their normal peacetime condition. The alert was not a military exigency but a political signal.[35]

Kennedy's speech to the nation on October 22 was not a direct threat to launch nuclear weapons if Khrushchev failed to meet the president's conditions but a more subtle attempt to make America's atomic arsenal count politically in the crisis. Kennedy emphasized, "We will not shrink from that risk [of 'worldwide nuclear war'] at any time it must be faced." He said, "I have directed the Armed Forces to prepare for *any* eventualities." He referred to "the world" as standing on "the abyss of destruction." And he stated his intention to employ "whatever action is needed."[36]

By demonstrating resolve and making nuclear war more likely if the crisis continued, Kennedy hoped to scare Khrushchev into terminating it. One must seriously doubt whether any "national interests," even physical defense, could make it ethically acceptable to a civilized people to take actions that could result in the killing of innocent millions, including many in other nations with no control over the decisions of the superpowers. But defense was not at stake, and the purely political objectives are undeniably trivial compared with nuclear war. Surely the missile crisis would not have gone down in history as an American triumph if there had actually been a nuclear war over militarily irrelevant weapons in Cuba. That Khrushchev took the first step down that road with an unprincipled provocation would be cold comfort to the American survivors.

Even if one assumes (as we do not) that the president has a right to pursue American political objectives right to the brink of global disaster, and even if the Cuban missiles posed a real threat to those objectives, far more responsible alternatives were available to President Kennedy in 1962. Kennedy could have stood up to Khrushchev without engaging in risky nuclear diplomacy. Instead of *invoking* nuclear weapons, Kennedy could have explicitly excluded them from any action he might take, even while forcefully demanding the removal of the missiles. This position does not imply weakness or capitulation: no sensible person would fault a statesman for trying to avoid nuclear conflict. By editing his speech, President Kennedy could have said something like the following (remarks from the real speech are in roman type; our suggested interpolations are in italics):

> This secret, swift, and extraordinary build-up of Communist missiles—in an area well known to have a special and historical relationship to the United States and the nations of the Western Hemisphere, in violation of Soviet assurances, and in defiance of American and hemispheric policy—this sudden,

clandestine decision to station strategic weapons for the first time outside of Soviet soil—is a deliberately provocative and unjustified change in the status quo which cannot be accepted by this country if our courage and our commitments are ever to be trusted again by either friend or foe.

*But I wish to emphasize, so that there may be no misunderstanding on the part of the Soviet Union, the other nations of the world, or our own brave people, that we shall not be the ones to initiate the use of nuclear weapons over this question.* We will not prematurely or unnecessarily risk the costs of worldwide nuclear war in which even the fruits of victory would be ashes in our mouth. . . .

. . . American citizens have become adjusted to living daily on the bull's eye of Soviet missiles located inside the U.S.S.R. or in submarines. In that sense missiles in Cuba add to an already clear and present danger. . . . *They will not panic us into an irrational response. We shall remain resolute in our determination to be responsible keepers of the great nuclear force, even though our adversaries, in their recent actions in Cuba, have shown themselves to be reckless adventurers, and unworthy of this great power.*

*To leave no doubt that this is the case, and to demonstrate to the world just how different we are from the men who have secretly sent nuclear weapons to Castro, I have ordered that the nuclear forces of the United States shall remain in their normal peacetime status. There will be no alert of these weapons, even as we prepare the rest of our armed forces to do whatever might be necessary in Cuba. Even in their peacetime state, no power on earth can sink our submarines beneath the oceans, destroy our aircraft patrolling overhead, or damage our missiles stored safely underground. I have also ordered that every precaution be taken to ensure that there can be no accidental or unauthorized use of any nuclear devices in our arsenal. I alone can order their use.*

*But if the Soviet Union should, at this time or ever in the future, threaten this nation's vital interests, there should be no doubt that we will respond with whatever means are necessary. We hope and pray that that time shall never come, and we believe that our strength as a nation and our reputation for decisive action are our best protectors against it. I will not rest until every nuclear weapon is removed from Cuba, and I promise you that this great nation will not make the mistake of taking a step that could rob our children of the future that all Americans have worked so hard to build.*[37]

Even if President Kennedy had scrupulously disavowed the nuclear option with such a speech, he would not have completely avoided the risk of nuclear disaster. Simply by confronting the Soviets militarily, he ran that risk, because any crisis can escalate out of control. As the preeminent theorist of war, Carl von Clausewitz, explained two centuries ago: "War is an act of force, and there is no logical limit to the application of that force. Each side, therefore, compels its opponent to follow suit; a reciprocal action is started which must lead, in theory, to extremes."[38]

According to Robert Kennedy, he and his brother understood that "neither side wanted war over Cuba . . . but it was possible that either side could take a step that—for reasons of 'security' or 'pride' or 'face'—would require a response by the other side, which, in turn, for the same reasons of security, pride, or face, would bring about a counterresponse and eventually an escalation into armed conflict." As Khrushchev told Kennedy in a personal letter during the crisis:

> If indeed war should break out, then it would not be in our power to stop it, for such is the logic of war. . . . We and you ought not to pull on the ends of the rope in which you have tied the knot of war, because the more the two of us pull, the tighter the knot will be tied. And a moment may come when that knot will be tied so tight that even he who tied it will not have the strength to untie it, and then it will be necessary to cut that knot, and what that would mean is not for me to explain to you, because you yourself understand perfectly of what terrible forces our countries dispose.[39]

President Kennedy's most responsible course would have been to emphasize that the Cuban missiles posed no new threat to the United States and to either let the matter rest or seek a diplomatic solution. As Richard Neustadt and Graham Allison ask: "Need Soviet recklessness have been matched in kind? Could Kennedy not have accepted their missiles in Cuba and announced to the world that Russian roulette was a game he would not play?"[40]

To suggest another alternative speech, Kennedy might have calmly reassured the American public about the meaninglessness of the missiles and thus avoided confrontation entirely:

> If I thought there was some reason to be concerned about them, I wouldn't be sleeping in this house tonight. They are there, but it is not that much of a change. You are in for a dime or in for a dollar. There has been no essential change in the strategic situation. The numbers don't change much. It is not a significant escalation. This isn't really anything new. I don't think they pose any particular threat at all.

Given that those nuclear missiles were stationed within miles of the U.S. shoreline, many may consider such a statement unfit for a strong, defense-minded, anticommunist administration. They should consult the newspapers of May 22 and May 23, 1984. Those exact words were uttered by President Reagan; his spokesman, Larry Speakes; his national security adviser, Robert McFarlane; and his chairman of the Joint Chiefs of Staff, General John W. Vessey, in response to a Soviet buildup of nuclear missile submarines in U.S. coastal waters.[41] These missiles were militarily almost an exact parallel to the ones placed in Cuba twenty-two years before. Like the Cuban missiles, they visibly added to the nuclear forces aimed at the U.S. mainland. They were based at an immodest distance from America's shores. And they could hit major U.S. cities and military installations on the East Coast in ten minutes' flight time—too fast for meaningful warning.

President Reagan could have reacted to this "threat" much as Kennedy did twenty-two years before. Borrowing Kennedy's stirring words, he could have condemned the Soviet action as a "deliberate provocation" and an "unjustified change in the status quo." He could have called the missiles "clearly offensive" and said that their purpose was "none other than to provide a nuclear strike capability against the Western Hemisphere." He could have emphasized that they were "capable of striking Washington, D.C., the Panama Canal, Cape Canaveral, Mexico City, or any other city in the southeastern part of the United States, in Central America, or in the Caribbean area." American warships could have been dispatched to warn off or fight off the rogue subs, and a nuclear alert could have been ordered to underline America's "courage and commitment." [42]

But Mr. Reagan deftly avoided making a crisis by refusing to be provoked, by yawning instead of blustering in response to something that posed no real threat. The nuclear perceptions game can be played several ways. One is to define a marginal Soviet move as unimportant, thereby making it so. Another is to call it a "definite threat to peace," thereby making it one.

Some will insist that nuclear missiles on Cuba are not comparable to those in the surrounding sea—that there is a special symbolic meaning to placing nuclear arms for the first time on land in the Western Hemisphere, a meaning independent of the actual military value of the weapons. Nuclear missiles were, in this view, a profound violation of the American "sphere of influence" in a way that hostile vessels in the ocean cannot be. We are, after all, land creatures. A race of fishes might see the situation differently, but solid earth is where nations seek their influence and draw their spheres.

There is some truth to the theory that the mutual respect of each other's spheres of influence helps prevent superpower confrontation. The best guarantor of peace would be a commitment by both to avoid foreign intervention. But if they are going to be interventionists, each side's clear knowledge of where it can act without fear of confrontation by the other, and where interference could bring on a crisis, at least reduces the probability that they will cross each other.

According to Neustadt and Allison:

It could be argued that, despite the risk inherent in the course of action President Kennedy chose, any other course would have meant greater risk. If, rather than challenging Khrushchev and demanding withdrawal of the missiles, he simply had accepted Khrushchev's move and minimized its importance . . . the 'rules of the precarious staus quo' . . . would have been seriously jeopardized. . . . Kennedy had tried to establish rules that would prevent either nation from miscalculating the other's vital interests and stumbling by misunderstanding into a confrontation from which neither could retreat. If Khrushchev's most serious infraction of these rules were disregarded, the rules would wear away.[43]

Kennedy arguably chose a good moment for enforcing the "rules," picking a spot where the United States had overwhelming conventional military superiority at a time when it still had some semblance of nuclear superiority. Compared, say, to a crisis in Berlin several years later, a confrontation in Cuba seemed a good way to make his point.

There are several problems with this kind of argument—the most sophisticated defense of the confrontive approach. The first is its hypocrisy. The United States had methodically stationed nuclear weapons on the territory of *its* allies on or near Soviet borders for some time—in Turkey, Italy, and Britain. The Soviets were doing nothing to the United States that it had not already done to them many times over. This fact had to be explained to President Kennedy, who said on October 26, in reference to Khrushchev's stationing of nuclear weapons in Cuba, "It's just as if we suddenly began to put a major number of MRBMs [medium-range ballistic missiles] in Turkey. Now that'd be goddam dangerous, I would think." "Well, we *did*, Mr. President," Bundy pointed out (leading Kennedy to respond, "Yeah, but that was five years ago").[44]

Indeed, as the Soviets must have noticed with some bitterness, on the very day Kennedy announced the blockade "the Jupiter [nuclear] missiles in Turkey were turned over to Turkish command."[45] True, the Soviets sent their missiles to Cuba secretly and in violation of explicit assurances that they would not. But deception by itself does not justify a risk of world war and nuclear incineration. It is also true that Turkey, Italy, and Britain did not have the long historical ties to the Soviet Union that Cuba did to the United States. But historical ties do not justify nuclear gamesmanship either. And in any case in 1962 Cuba was no more in America's sphere of influence than Britain was in the Soviets'.

The Soviets had definitively "violated" the U.S. sphere of influence already, if that is how one wishes to see it, four years earlier, when Castro took power and entered into a close politico-military relationship with them. That is when the United States lost political control of *land* in the Western Hemisphere, when the USSR gained military bases on *land* in North America, and when communism got a foothold on *land* within a hundred miles of our coast. There is no logical reason to see the placement of militarily irrelevant nuclear weapons there as a major shift in the military or political status quo, or to assume that if Kennedy had not defined it as important Khrushchev would have been emboldened to "violate" the U.S. sphere of influence on a regular basis.

Actually, no one could have known with confidence how Khrushchev's missiles or the American confrontation would be symbolically interpreted or what ripple effects they would have. *Any* symbolic interpretation was hypothetical. The international system is a seething, unpredictable, often chaotic interaction of many parties' actions and perceptions. These are not always consistent and not always rational. The real military and political interests of nations are hard enough to decipher. The symbolic ones are hopelessly complex. The men who ran the missile crisis may have believed that the long-term stabilizing benefits of denying Khrushchev his symbolic victory would counterbalance the short-term risks of both the naval blockade and the nuclear alert. But the short-term risks of confrontation were clear, the long-term benefits utterly hypothetical. To use facile, unprovable speculation to justify the deliberate risking of nuclear war is unconscionable, even if one accepts the legitimacy of endangering the world to advance the goals of the American state.

Things could have turned out differently. Khrushchev, for example, might have felt compelled to call Kennedy's bluff. If Kennedy had then been forced to invade Cuba to make good on his threat, would America definitely have emerged stronger? Is it not possible that the world would have seen the United States as an aggressor, attacking a tiny island to remove Soviet missiles when we had similar missiles on the Soviet border? Robert Kennedy thought so. "A surprise attack by a very large nation against a very small one," he said, "could not be undertaken . . . if we were to maintain our moral position at home and around the globe." During one of the meetings at which an invasion was discussed, he passed a note to his brother saying, "I now know how Tojo felt when he was planning Pearl Harbor." [46]

Alternatively, to avoid humiliation in the eyes of the world, Khrushchev might have decided that he had to make another, even bolder, move somewhere else—such as Berlin, where the United States had no conventional military option at all. As Fen Hampson points out, Kennedy's aggressive actions might in fact have sent "the wrong signal" rather than the one intended: "A naval blockade around Cuba did not prevent the Soviets from doing likewise with their land forces in Berlin. It almost invited it, and their previous behavior provided strong reasons for believing that this would be exactly how the Soviets would respond." Sorensen states: "Blockade was a word so closely associated with Berlin that it almost guaranteed a new Berlin blockade in response."[47]

Similar possibilities were endless. Once Kennedy decided to confront the Soviets, all the theories in the world could not rule out war or even guarantee that the United States would gain substantial political benefits. As Robert Kennedy candidly admitted, "Each one of us [on President Kennedy's advisory committee] was being asked to make a recommendation which would affect the future of all mankind, a recommendation which, if wrong and if accepted, could mean the destruction of the human race."[48]

Kennedy's symbolic stand in 1962 did not lead to war in the short run, but there is good reason to believe that it almost backfired disastrously eight years later in the 1970 "second Cuban missile crisis," recounted in Chapter 6. Even more than the 1962 missiles, the Soviet submarine base at Cienfuegos—the issue of the 1970 crisis—was inconsequential to the overall Soviet nuclear threat. Normally nuclear submarines can be serviced from surface vessels ("tenders") almost as well as from land bases such as the one being constructed in Cuba. Apart from cost-effectiveness and superior recreational facilities for the crew, remote shore facilities mainly decrease the time required for subs to transit to and from their firing stations for refueling and refitting. That increases the number of subs within firing range of the United States at any given time.[49]

But we have already seen how in 1984 the U.S. government stated that it did not *care* how many Soviet subs patrolled our coastline on station, that considering the overall Soviet nuclear threat more of them did not "pose any particular threat at all."[50] Yet Barry Goldwater interpreted the Soviet base, similar in purpose to American submarine bases elsewhere in the world, as evidence of a "serious Russian bid for world domination." Mike Mansfield was outraged because he thought they violated President Kennedy's statement after the first Cuban crisis that "offensive weapons must be kept out of the Western Hemisphere." They both failed to note that the Soviets already had enough nuclear missiles in the oceans of the Western Hemisphere to dominate or destroy as much as they could ever care to.[51]

According to George Quester, the main reason for the 1970 confrontation may have been nothing more than the need to live up to President Kennedy's symbolic commitment in 1962 to keep Soviet nuclear forces away from Cuba. Even though there were serious questions about the applicability of the 1962 agreement on land-based nuclear missiles to a submarine base that could serve different kinds of vessels, the Nixon administration apparently felt it could not appear to back away from the earlier U.S. demand. As Quester writes, Kennedy's " 'victory' thereafter committed the United States to maintaining these winnings, lest it seem to be weakening in comparison with the past. President Nixon might thus have cause to regret the position so handily captured by Kennedy." Indeed, Nixon may have "privately wished that American prestige had never been coupled to the denuclearization of Cuba." [52] How twisted are the webs we weave!

The Soviets backed down in 1970 as they had in 1962, halting construction of the base and forestalling a full-blown crisis. [53] Had they not, we might have found ourselves on the brink again over the presence of weapons that posed no threat. This possibility has been lost in the subsequent rapture over the outcome of the Cuban missile crisis. But it underscores how facile it is to rationalize the great risk Kennedy ran by the argument that it reduced future risks of similar crises.

In fact in May 1972, when a Soviet Golf-II class submarine *armed with nuclear ballistic missiles* paid a port visit to Cuba, the United States dispensed entirely with diplomatic protests and resorted directly to military action: "U.S. surveillance ships, aided by P-3 patrol aircraft (based at Guantánamo Bay in Cuba), made sonar contact and forced the submarine to surface. Several times at night this was repeated, with the Soviets even firing flares to discourage the P-3 aircraft, and with high-speed maneuvers by the Soviet and American ships; the submarine was repeatedly forced to surface until the Soviet formation was well into the Atlantic." Recall that this was a *nuclear ballistic missile submarine*. According to Garthoff, "This entire incident was not known to President Nixon, or to Dr. Kissinger, in orchestrating policy then or even long after the event!" [54]

Richard Walton persuasively argues that Kennedy had real, face-saving diplomatic means of quickly resolving the Cuban crisis short of armed confrontation, leading to the same trade-off that was later negotiated under the gun: the removal of the Soviet weapons from Cuba in return for a U.S. pledge never to invade the island. Hampson and others underline that aside from Kennedy's anxieties about his domestic political standing, there is no clear reason why he could not have attempted a diplomatic agreement with the Soviets before embarking on a perilous and illegal naval blockade, and nearly an outright invasion of Cuba. This is about as far as a critic such as Hampson can go, accepting as he does that "the missiles had to go." [55]

The Soviets explicitly offered another diplomatic opening late in the crisis: the removal of Soviet nuclear weapons from Cuba in return for the removal of the comparable American Jupiter missiles from Turkey. As Robert Kennedy reports, "The proposal . . . was not unreasonable and did not amount to a loss to the U.S. or to our NATO allies." The Jupiters were "clearly obsolete," and President Kennedy had tried to remove them unilaterally on several occasions, as recently as August 1962. According to Dean Rusk: "I remember we joked about which way the missiles would fly if they were fired. . . . I also remember being told that a tourist driving an automobile with a .22 caliber rifle could knock holes in the skins of these missiles." The president "did not want to involve the U.S. and mankind in a catastrophic war over missile sites in Turkey that were antiquated and useless." Nevertheless, he was unwilling to accept the Soviet offer, again not because of any tangible risk it would entail, but because it would *appear* weak to make concessions "under threat." [56]

He could have chosen otherwise, here as in the other crucial moments of the crisis. As Robert Jervis comments: "The NATO countries and presumably the USSR understood that these weapons had little value and probably knew that the United States was planning to dismantle them. Thus to grant the substance of the Soviet demand was hardly a concession at all." Kennedy's concern was that "others would interpret such a move as an index of the willingness of the United States to retreat under pressure even though the substance of the Soviet demand was almost completely irrelevant. If the Russians had asked the United States to change the color of its postage stamps the problem would have been essentially the same." [57]

SYMBOL WARS

Jervis's observation about the Jupiters applies to the entire crisis. The substance—the Cuban missiles—was in essence arbitrary, irrelevant. The missiles were only the *vehicle* of a historic struggle of the titans that would probably have occurred sooner or later over another issue anyway. Khrushchev could have chosen many other ways to try to humiliate Kennedy and improve the Soviet position in the Cold War. Indeed the Soviets do not speak of the "Cuban missile crisis," as we do, but of the "Carribean crisis" of 1962. For it was not really a crisis of the arms race at all.

Both sides arbitrarily *gave* militarily irrelevant Soviet nuclear weapons in Cuba an epic symbolic significance—Khrushchev by using them to make his break in the Cold War and Kennedy by sternly warning the Soviets the month before the missiles were discovered that the United States would not tolerate nuclear weapons in Cuba. Top U.S. officials have even expressed regret that the United States let itself be drawn into a challenge that would have meant little had Kennedy refused to play Khrushchev's symbolic game. In 1987 Theodore Sorenson openly admitted: "If we had known that the Soviets were putting 40 missiles in Cuba, we might . . . have drawn the line at 100, and said with great fanfare that we would absolutely not tolerate the presence of more than 100 missiles in Cuba."[58] During the crisis, on October 16, the president explicitly lamented, "Last month I should have said . . . that we don't care"—thus clearly acknowledging that the physical missiles in Cuba were not the problem, but rather that he endangered millions of lives essentially to follow through on a statement he regretted he had made. So much for Kennedy's "finest hour."

Those who still doubt the arbitrariness of the Kennedy administration's decisions about what was symbolically important enough to risk war over should consider the finale of the crisis. Even after Khrushchev accepted the American demand that all Soviet nuclear delivery systems in Cuba be removed, Kennedy balked over the presence of some elderly Soviet Ilyushin IL-28 light bombers on the island. Although these were not nuclear capable (except in the sense that a commercial airliner is, as Garthoff points out), the United States demanded that they be removed as part of the settlement. The quarantine of Cuba was not lifted until the Soviets agreed; the urgent Strategic Air Command nuclear alert was not canceled until the day after. General Maxwell Taylor and Treasury Secretary Douglass Dillon even urged the bombing of the Cuban airfields where the planes were based. Why all the fuss? Because "the president had publicly committed us to regard the IL-28s as part and parcel of a dangerous offensive arms buildup in Cuba in his quarantine speech of October 22, and that was why the IL-28s as well as the missiles must come out." The United States caused no trouble over more advanced Soviet aircraft in Cuba, notably MiG-21s. For "while the MiG-21s might be just as dangerous in potential, and while both the Ilyushins and the MiGs in fact represented no real threat so long as not armed

with nuclear weapons, nonetheless the United States had committed itself to regard the Ilyushin 'bombers' as dangerous, and had not so committed itself with respect to MiG fighter-bombers."[59] In other words,
the United States again risked war with the Soviet Union over hardware
with no importance other than that which Kennedy arbitrarily *gave* to it
in a speech.

It would be unrealistic to expect that such lunatic actions can be prevented by any technical means, such as controls over weapon deployments. The superpowers can decide to wage a symbolic and psychological contest over almost *anything*. Even if compelled by worldwide
public opinion to sign a START treaty or a nuclear freeze, or even to
reduce nuclear forces by 90 percent, either side could make a dangerous
move with nuclear weapons. The Soviets could sail a ballistic missile
submarine into New York harbor, or the Americans could send one to
Vladivostok, in both cases no doubt provoking a terrifying confrontation. The Soviets could put nuclear missiles in Nicaragua, or the United
States could put them in Afghanistan, with the same result. The oldest
and most decrepit missiles could cause the same crisis as the newest and
most powerful ones.

Stopping the arms race could eliminate some possible but unlikely
vehicles of a symbolic superpower collision (Star Wars, for example).
But it is far more important to discredit the widespread weaponitis that
allowed Kennedy to whip the public into a frenzy over meaningless missiles and that might allow a future leader to do the same.

Besides, there are infinite possible pretexts for a symbolic superpower
confrontation. The nuclear-armed states, as we have seen, can recklessly
commit their prestige to almost *anything*—whether insignificant Chinese islands, a defeated Egyptian army, or militarily meaningless nuclear missiles. We can perhaps ban new missiles, but we cannot ban Chinese islands, Egyptian armies, and all the other possible objects of
future superpower tests of will.

The danger of a recurrence of 1962 will remain so long as the
nuclear-armed states believe that a record of recklessness will help them
secure worldwide power by violent means. The danger will recede only
when concerned citizens organize to make that strategy unworkable—
restraining the aggression, intervention, and adventurism that prompts
the constant demonstrations of resolve, and preventing leaders from
pursuing those demonstrations to the brink of worldwide disaster.

# PART III

# The Politics of Survival

This stage on which we dance is filled with trap doors, shadow projections, fleeting mirages and colored curtains that rise and fall at the bidding of the [military industrial complex]. They even control the audience lights and sound system. We just dance.

—*Tom Atlee, "Who Owns the Game"*

## CHAPTER NINE

# What About Arms Control?

War stocks have not been hurt.
—New York Times, *after the announcement of the INF
treaty, 1987*

In Part I we argued that the arms race has little to do with the dangers of nuclear war today. Does that mean arms control is meaningless?

Arms control is certainly not the answer to the nuclear peril, and, *as currently practiced,* it probably will not make us any safer at all. Nor will it achieve another oft-cited goal: saving money now wasted on redundant weapons. Arms control *could* deliver some security and economic benefits *if* it seriously took on important problems, such as conventional weapons, nuclear proliferation, doomsday weapons, preventing nuclear accidents, and redirecting the vast sums wasted on the arms race to the urgent problems of our time.

Arms control to date has not noticeably reduced the danger of nuclear war or even slowed the cavalcade of expensive new weapons systems. Its most impressive accomplishment was probably the 1963 limited test ban treaty. Although of marginal military value, this treaty was an important environmental protection and public health measure because it outlawed atmospheric test explosions of nuclear weapons. The 1970 nuclear nonproliferation treaty might have made a real difference to the nuclear threat. But "it is hard to identify instances where the treaty has had any effect in slowing the spread of nuclear weapons." "Most of the countries of concern—India, Pakistan, Brazil, Argentina, Israel, and South Africa—are not parties to the treaty," the treaty's controls over signatory states such as Iraq and Libya are weak, and the treaty not only failed to limit but actually *encouraged* what is arguably the most important activity promoting nuclear weapons proliferation—

171

the transfer of "peaceful" nuclear technology and materials to non-nuclear signatory states. The 1972 ABM treaty concerned a category of weapons, antiballistic missiles, that both superpowers judged to be useless anyway and that, despite the pretensions of Star Wars, still are useless. The two SALT treaties, concerning offensive nuclear strike forces, have not "had any significant effect on the magnitude of damage that would be expected should a nuclear war occur, and it is doubtful if either has significantly enhanced deterrence or strategic stability."[1] They do not even appear to have constrained any major weapons programs on either side, the only clear case being the single U.S. Poseidon submarine decommissioned by the Reagan administration to remain within the SALT II limits.

In fact,

> arms control treaties have traditionally spurred efforts to develop nuclear weapons that were not covered by the treaties. . . . One month after SALT I was signed, the [U.S.] Department of Defense requested . . . an additional $20 million to develop long-range cruise missiles. Prior to this request the Defense Department had not worked on the development of long-range cruise missiles for over 10 years.

Unlike the SALT treaties, the 1987 INF treaty did lead to constraints on weapons, indeed to the destruction of some already deployed. But "history may repeat itself. Plans are already being made to develop and deploy new U.S. nuclear weapons in Europe" in the wake of that treaty.[2] INF will cause no perceptible changes in the consequences or risks of nuclear war. Neither will the much more dramatic START treaty, if successfully concluded. (We discuss both treaties later.) The American peace movement has not stopped a single new U.S. nuclear weapons system despite highly committed and courageous efforts to do so, nor has it achieved any of its more ambitious weapons-related goals, such as the comprehensive test ban or the nuclear freeze.

In this context, those seeking to avert a holocaust must confront "the possibility that many initiatives aimed at affecting arms, including arms control efforts, may be so diversionary as to be, on balance, pernicious, even though they may seem desirable from a narrow perspective."[3] Some types of arms control, though, could bring great benefits.

## THE WEAPONS THAT STATES REALLY USE

Anything that makes conventional state conflict and violence more likely or promotes their escalation could be highly dangerous, for the planet as a whole as well as for the immediate victims. For this reason, conventional weapons matter a great deal. Unlike nuclear arms, they are actually used—often—and their numbers, characteristics, and quality can make a great difference to the result. Controlling conventional weapons, particularly in the Third World, is a crucial task of our time.

Some of the most horrific incidents of this century have resulted from the unleashing of modern conventional weaponry on civilian populations. The killing in World War II of hundreds of thousands of defenseless people in Dresden, Tokyo, and other cities by high-intensity strategic bombing opened a ghastly era of mass destruction that soon shifted to the Third World. Weapons developments such as the cluster bomb, napalm, and the phosphorus bomb certainly mattered to the many thousands killed and maimed by them in places such as Vietnam, Afghanistan, and Lebanon.

Conventional weapons infusions from the United States, the USSR, and other arms exporters have made it possible for ruthless dictators to maintain power by destroying and terrorizing thousands of their own people in such places as El Salvador, Guatemala, Iraq, and Afghanistan. The great powers' use of advanced weaponry in the Third World and their promiscuous arms transfers to Third World states and movements have helped transform numerous national and regional conflicts, such as the Iran-Iraq war, from limited local disputes into high-tech carnages that draw in other states. The Third World is now the tinderbox for nuclear war; yet the superpowers and others seeking temporary political gain have been mindlessly pumping the bellows whenever they see a spark.

## THE NUCLEAR-ARMED CROWD

The diffusion of nuclear as well as conventional weapons to the Third World makes conflict there even more frightening. Nuclear arms races in the Third World certainly matter even though the one between the First World and the Second no longer does. As more Third World states acquire nuclear weapons, one of the many violent conflicts there could go nuclear even if the superpowers or European nuclear powers do not get involved. Controlling proliferation is another historic task for this generation.

Like the superpowers, nuclear-armed Third World states *may* challenge and confront each other more carefully when a nuclear war could result—but not carefully enough to avoid periodic crises that could endanger the planet. The historical record is not encouraging. Israel probably had nuclear weapons in 1973. Though Egypt and other states knew it, they still started a major war. Israel may have been a nuclear state even in 1970, which would mean that during the War of Attrition two nuclear states, Israel and the Soviet Union, briefly fought each other, as China and the Soviet Union had in 1969. (In 1985 Richard Nixon told *Time* magazine that at one point during the first two years of his administration the Soviet Union privately told him that it was considering a preemptive nuclear attack to destroy China's small nuclear weapons capability. This may have been a reference to the 1969 Soviet-Chinese border war. Nixon claims that he warned the Soviets that the United States might retaliate with nuclear weapons.) Nuclear arms did not make Israel too cautious to invade Lebanon in 1982, seriously provoking Soviet-backed Syrian forces there, nor did they deter Syria from engaging the invaders, and later the United States, in combat, risking an Israeli-Syrian war or worse. Argentina (soon, perhaps, to be a nuclear state itself) provoked a major nuclear power, Britain, into outright war when it seized the disputed Falklands/Malvinas islands in 1982. As Admiral Eugene Carroll observes: General "Galtieri invaded despite the fact that he was attacking the territory and citizens of a nuclear power. By this one action he demonstrated that nuclear superiority does not deter war and that fear of nuclear annihilation does not prevent fatal miscalculation." Press reports suggest that Britain may have actually issued a nuclear threat and may even have dispatched a nuclear missile submarine to the scene.[4] Other reports, as we have seen, suggest that Israel readied jets and missiles armed with nuclear weapons in 1973 in case the Arabs proved too successful on the battlefield. The Soviet Union evidently sent a ship loaded with nuclear devices of some kind to the Egyptian port of Alexandria around the same time.[5] Nuclear arms likewise did not prevent the 1979 China-Vietnam war (which entailed so much Soviet-Chinese tension that it could have ended in war between the two nuclear states) or direct French military intervention in the war between Chad and Libya.

The internationalization of the civilian nuclear energy industry has been the main bridge for the spread of nuclear materials and know-how to the Third World. Had "Atoms for Peace" been rejected years ago as the oxymoron it is, and had nuclear energy been abandoned, it might now be possible to keep uranium, plutonium, reactor cores, and nuclear reprocessing plants from spreading around the globe. Now the materials and knowledge needed to make nuclear explosives are widely available.[6]

And despite some useful efforts, the nuclear states have dealt with the problem half-heartedly at best—often putting political considerations of the moment before the critical goal of preventing the spread of nuclear weapons. The United States, for example, cut off aid to Pakistan (officially at least) in 1979 because of Pakistani nuclear activities but restored the aid shortly after the Soviet invasion of Afghanistan. Even as Pakistan was in the process of actually *crossing* the nuclear threshold, it rose to become the *third largest* recipient of U.S. foreign aid. Over many years the United States has likewise done little to challenge major nuclear weapons activities by the *largest* recipient of U.S. foreign aid, Israel, which reportedly has constructed a large nuclear arsenal, perfected weapons using the H-bomb principle, collaborated in nuclear weapons activities with South Africa, and even developed a ballistic missile able to reach the Soviet Union. Serious efforts to prevent the further spread of nuclear materials and knowledge could slow proliferation, and so remain essential.[7]

But "ultimately one must expect that most nations determined to acquire . . . a nuclear [weapons] capability will succeed."[8] Equally important, then, is reducing the conflict, violence, and intimidation that motivate states to seek nuclear weapons. U.S. nuclear saber-rattling, for example, apparently helped convince both the Chinese and the Indians that they should obtain their own nuclear arms. As Gordon Chang observes: "Washington's brandishing of the nuclear cudgel during the [1954–1955 Quemoy-Matsu] crisis [see Chapter 6] provoked not only potential disaster, but also a development that would later haunt the United States. Apparently, Eisenhower's threats helped convince the Chinese Communists that they needed nuclear weapons of their own. In January 1955, in the midst of the offshore crisis and under American pressure . . . Mao Zedong (Mao Tse-Tung) and other top Communist leaders decided to launch China's nuclear program." Raymond Garthoff observes that "the deployment of the U.S. nuclear-armed aircraft carrier task force during the [1971] Indo-Pakistani War, with its implicit threat to India, was a factor" in the Indian decision to seek nuclear weapons. "In debate in the Indian Parliament over the nuclear issue, proponents of an Indian nuclear capability repeatedly referred to the arrival of the American carrier in 1971 as a reason to attain such a capability."[9]

Bitter conflicts have driven numerous states to seek nuclear weapons—for example, South Africa, Israel, Iraq, and Pakistan. In contrast, many technologically advanced and affluent states seem to have forsworn the nuclear option, largely because they lack external threats or expansive political ambitions—for example, Australia, New Zealand, Canada, the Netherlands, and Switzerland. New Zealand in fact sacrificed a mutual defense treaty with the United States to enforce a nuclear-free policy at home.

As Gary Milhollin wrote in late 1987: "World attention will soon focus on the superpower summit meeting where a minor arms control pact [the INF treaty] will be signed. In the rest of the world, which is less stable, countries will continue to make bombs they really intend to use. Perhaps it is time to shift our gaze and watch the risks that count." [10]

## THE NUCLEARIZATION OF EVERYTHING

What doesn't matter, then, is the *nuclear* arms race between the powers that *already* have substantial nuclear arsenals. But, as we discussed in Chapter 3, one aspect of the superpower nuclear arms race—the nuclearization of conventional fighting forces—is truly dangerous. It potentially gives to a pilot, artilleryman, or ship's captain the power to ignite a holocaust, with or without authorization, in the heat of conventional battle or crisis.

While increases or decreases in warhead megatonnage, missile accuracy, or bomber penetrability are almost meaningless in a world of mutual existential nuclear vulnerability, the insertion of thousands of nuclear weapons into the firestorm of modern conventional warfare is not. A commonsense decision to keep nuclear warheads far from areas of war and crisis would eliminate one of the most likely paths to nuclear war.

Most changes in the numbers and types of these weapons, including the introduction of the neutron bomb, seem of little importance. What matters is, first, the number of potential combat situations into which nuclear weapons are brought and, second, the ease with which they might be used. On both counts the little-noticed but accelerating nuclearization of the oceans is an example of a development in the arms race that does matter.

The new U.S. sea-launched cruise missile (SLCM), for instance, first deployed in June 1984, is being installed in large numbers (in one nuclear and two conventional versions) on attack submarines and surface warships. The Center for Defense Information is one of the few public interest organizations to publicize the hazards.

Rear Admiral Larry Blose, Director of the Cruise Missile Project, noted in 1987 that with Tomahawk cruise missiles "the Navy is moving from 15 offensive strike platforms (aircraft carriers) to more than 195 strike platforms." The deployment of 3,994 SLCMs, of which 758 will be nuclear, by the mid-1990's on up to 198 battleships, cruisers, destroyers, and attack submarines changes the military picture at sea.

SCLMs, which, like other naval nuclear weapons, lack electronic locks, substantially widen the range of situations in which ship and sub commanders might be tempted to fire nuclear weapons.

SLCMs will be deployed on existing ships and submarines, warships designed primarily for non-nuclear warfare. . . . If a vessel engaged in a conventional battle is about to be destroyed, its commander may elect to use all his weapons, including his nuclear SLCMs, and thus a conventional battle could escalate to a nuclear war. Some of the SLCMs will be deployed on attack submarines with which communications are relatively poor. In critical situations, submarine commanders might believe that they do not have enough time to get authorization to launch their nuclear weapons and decide to use them. Poor judgment in such a case would result in a minor conflict escalating to a nuclear war. . . . In the precarious naval environment, it is unlikely that once the first nuclear salvo is fired, the conflict will be confined to the high seas. On the contrary, *there is strong evidence that it is U.S. policy, in the event of a nuclear conflict beginning at sea, to escalate that conflict to an all-out nuclear war.*[11]

U.S. land, air, and sea forces are highly nuclearized already. As of March 1983, "the nuclear armed ships of the U.S. Navy consisted of all 13 aircraft carriers, one battleship, all 28 cruisers, all 71 destroyers, 73 of 96 nuclear attack submarines, and 61 of 87 frigates." In the Air Force, numerous U.S.-based fighter interceptor squadrons are nuclear armed, as are tactical fighter wings based at home and abroad. Even Air National Guard planes are equipped to fire nuclear missiles. The Army fields a staggering arsenal of battlefield nuclear weapons, including air defense systems, land mines, and that mainstay of conventional battle, artillery, "almost all" of which "is now nuclear capable." The Marine Corps, whose main mission is foreign intervention, flies its own nuclear-armed air force and fields nuclear-capable artillery. Altogether, as of 1983, there were 722 U.S. military units certified for nuclear warfare.[12]

Although limiting or reversing the deployment of SLCMs is important, the real need is for a thorough denuclearization of combat units in

Europe, South Korea, and elsewhere, and especially of the troops and ships of mobile interventionary forces destined to fight in future Third World hot spots. This is the most meaningful and urgent form of nuclear arms control. As we noted in Chapter 3, battlefield nuclear weapons are useless for war fighting anyway, since detonating them inescapably risks escalation to a holocaust.[13] They should be abolished, unilaterally if necessary. If the United States wants to start or fight a nuclear war, it will have no trouble doing so at any time or place whether or not warheads are pre-positioned on the front lines of battle with bullets and rockets whizzing overhead. This is, after all, the missile age.

Amid the euphoria following the INF treaty, the United States made clear that its interest in arms control did not extend to battlefield nuclear weapons. Responding to a Warsaw Pact suggestion to limit the modernization of battlefield nuclear arms, and ultimately perhaps eliminate them, U.S. State Department spokesman Charles Redman noted that, "as a matter of policy, the United States opposes any nuclear-weapon-free zone in the NATO treaty area."[14]

Preoccupied with big strategic nuclear weapons, peace organizations have not seriously sought to denuclearize conventional fighting forces either, though some recent initiatives concerning sea-based tactical nuclear weapons are excellent steps in the right direction. Protesters have tried to exclude nuclear-armed U.S. warships from both foreign and domestic ports, for example, and New Zealand has banned such ships entirely.[15] In September 1987 retired Rear Admiral Gene La Rocque of the Center for Defense Information wrote a letter to the Pentagon urging the removal of nuclear weapons from American warships escorting Kuwaiti tankers in the Persian Gulf. And on June 10, 1987 (exactly two years after French secret agents sank the Greenpeace protest ship *Rainbow Warrior,* killing one of its crew), Greenpeace began its "Nuclear Free Seas Campaign," directed at the nuclear navies of the United States, the Soviet Union, Britain, France, and China. With 650,000 members, Greenpeace U.S.A. is larger than all the other arms control, peace, and disarmament organizations combined. Interestingly, as Robert Schaeffer reports, in these other groups "the reaction to the Greenpeace campaign was cool and skeptical," in part because these groups worry, as Spurgeon Keeny, president of the Arms Control Association, puts it, that the Greenpeace campaign could "divert attention" from what the other groups continue to regard as "the main issues: SDI, the weaponization of space, the demise of the ABM Treaty and collapse of SALT II."[16]

Although denuclearizing frontline combat units seems far and away the most urgent priority, a more sweeping denuclearization of conventional military forces, such as that proposed by Morton Halperin, would bring additional safety. Recognizing that the threat of uncontrollable escalation renders nuclear explosives useless for actually fighting wars, Halperin argues that they "cannot be regarded as weapons and should not be placed in the hands of the military." [17] Strategic as well as theater and tactical nuclear devices would be placed under a system of control divorced from the regular military command, thus officially separating conventional and nuclear fighting capabilities. Nuclear devices would be reserved for retaliation in case of nuclear attack on the United States. They would not be designed or deployed to fight wars. The military would be told to plan on the assumption that it will not receive permission to use nuclear weapons in any future conflict. As Halperin argues, such a policy is the only sane way to handle nuclear weapons and could reduce the risk of accident, unauthorized use, first strike, preemption, or miscalculation.

## THE DEADLY CONNECTION

We should reemphasize in this context that the "deadly connection" between Third World interventionism and nuclear war is not fundamentally a problem of the arms race, as many assume. Even the book that originally advanced this important concept describes it as "the possible links between the nuclear arms build-up and U.S. intervention strategies." Others also interpret it as "the relationship between U.S. intervention in the Third World and the US nuclear arms race." [18]

The rationale for this interpretation is that new strategic U.S. first-strike weapons or new firebreak-spanning weapons carried by conventional forces could actually serve, as planners hope, as a "cover," "shield," or "umbrella" for dangerous conventional interventions. But as we have seen, with only a few exceptions new weapons in fact change nothing; they cannot "cover" intervention (or anything else) any more than the existential deterrent already does. True, the planners still may hope to intimidate the Soviets and others by creating a *perception* that the United States is crazy enough to launch a first strike or set off neutron bombs if anyone challenges its Third World adventures. But, as we argued in Chapter 4, opposing new weapons is not a promising way to counter that strategy.

The real dangers today are intervention itself and the use of forces armed with nuclear weapons (of whatever age and type) to carry it out.

The "deadly connection" should be understood as an argument, first, for curbing conventional political and military actions that could ignite a crisis or war involving nuclear-armed powers and, second, for radically denuclearizing the forces that do the fighting.

## WHAT ABOUT ACCIDENTS?

Many assume that the continuing arms race raises the risk of an accidental nuclear war—whatever the effects of the arms race on first strike and the firebreak. This conclusion is not self-evident. Some innovations may add to the risk of accident—for example, weapons without electronic locks, such as the SLCM. But other innovations appear to lower the risk, for example, by modernizing electronic locks or by fixing other recognized problems of older systems that could lead to accidents. As noted in the *Nuclear Weapons Databook* (whose authors are not admirers of the Pentagon), "Development of new warheads incorporating upgraded safety, control, and security features is . . . a high [Pentagon] priority." [19]

Paul Bracken suggests that the conventional view is actually backward: "The more complex the warning and control system the less the chance of an inadvertent launch, because of the disproportionate increase in the number of checks and balances designed to prevent this from occurring. Against the discrete accident, malfunction, or operator error the total system is massively redundant. The more complex, the more redundant. I believe the likelihood of nuclear war by pure technical accident is much lower today than it was twenty years ago." Interestingly, Bracken notes that almost every step toward this end was taken unilaterally by each superpower, not through the bilateral arms control process. These unheralded forms of arms control, which focus not on numbers or performance characteristics of weapons but on the command system governing them, were "a greater arms control achievement than the SALT II agreement or any likely development in the START talks." Moreover, contrary to the view that reductions in the risk of nuclear war coincide with periods of "good relations" with the Soviets (a topic that we take up later), "these gains in reducing the probability of accidental war were made during a period of very poor Soviet-American political relations." [20]

In any case the greater threat is not a discrete technical malfunction but a compounded set of errors occurring during a crisis or war. As Bracken argues, "We approach wisdom on the subject of accidental/

inadvertent war when we consider accidents or inadvertent behavior during a tense high alert or limited war." This is only common sense, and the conclusion is obvious: "It may be best to concentrate our energy on *preventing* confrontations," as this book argues.[21]

Still, reforms in weapons and command systems could reduce the risk of unintended nuclear war, though slowing or even stopping the arms race would not *necessarily* do that. We mentioned several important steps earlier: removing doomsday nuclear weapons from the front lines of potential battles and from the warships routinely dispatched to crisis zones; installing secure self-destruct mechanisms on ballistic missiles so they can be destroyed if launched in error; installing electronic locks on the many nuclear warheads now lacking them; outlawing destabilizing nuclear alerts designed to "send a signal" in crises; and an unconditional decision by each side never to launch nuclear weapons before confirming actual nuclear explosions from an enemy attack, and even then never to launch hastily (putting aside the question of whether to launch at all).

## THE ECONOMIC AND SOCIAL
## EFFECTS OF ARMS CONTROL

As Bernard Brodie wrote in 1978, shortly before his death, "the greater utility of arms control agreements lies not in enhancing our security, which is usually beyond their power, but in helping to save both sides from wasteful expenditures."[22] In a world beset by starvation, disease, illiteracy, and environmental devastation, it is surely obscene to spend billions on redundant missiles, bombers, and submarines.

When treated as an economic and social issue, the nuclear arms race raises serious questions and problems not normally considered when it is opposed for military reasons. If the real goal is economic reallocation, the first question is how, as a practical matter, to free up military dollars for alternative uses. Perhaps surprisingly, neither arms control nor opposition to individual weapons systems (whether nuclear or conventional) necessarily saves money. Consider the INF treaty, which unlike previous treaties actually banned weapons systems already deployed by the superpowers. A revealing article in the business section of the *New York Times* shortly after the superpowers announced that an INF agreement seemed imminent noted: "Whatever it does for peace, an arms control treaty may actually benefit military contractors. . . . war stocks have not been hurt." Military analyst Douglas Lee points out one reason: "You don't free up any resources by taking apart things that have already been built." As the *Times* reported, "The military already has spent most of the $9 billion that was planned for buying Pershing 2 missiles, made by Martin Marietta, and ground-launched cruise missiles made by General Dynamics." Moreover, "now the weapons will be withdrawn from Europe, but the Pentagon only appears likely to seek more funds to buy tanks, artillery, and aircraft for the defense of Europe."[23]

The INF agreement, like others before it, creates direct political pressure for increased "compensatory" spending on both conventional forces and other nuclear weapons—even though, in the case of the INF treaty and in almost all other cases, there is actually no real military loss to compensate for. As Nicholas Wade observes, referring to a book by former intelligence analyst Bruce Berkowitz: "Limits on arms . . . play the same role as does natural selection in Darwinian theory. They spur the evolution of species that are not constrained. The SALT I treaty of 1972 limited missile launchers because silos and submarines are easy to count. But the constraint spurred the evolution of missiles with multiple warheads . . . and cruise missiles"—both extremely costly items. The same is true of conventional arms. As the *New York Times* reported, "According to Joshua M. Epstein, who analyzes military budgets for the Brookings Institution, after the Reykjavik summit talks, Congressional leaders such as Representative Les Aspin, the Wisconsin Democrat who is chairman of the House Armed Services Committee, 'have consistently called for increases in conventional forces in the aftermath of any arms controls.'"[24]

So has the military. In February 1988 the commander of American and allied forces in Europe, General John R. Galvin, "said on the record what senior officers have been saying privately . . . 'I would caution them [those who think arms control will save money] and everyone else that this is wrong'" because of highly expensive conventional and nuclear weapons "modernization" programs that must accompany any "arms control" treaties. As one congressional analyst said of the INF treaty, "Quite honestly, if anything there will be incentives to increase spending both on the conventional side and on the nuclear side, on other forces." Indeed, "the same companies that profited from producing the nuclear arms will profit from compensating for their withdrawal." Wolfgang Demisch, who analyzes military firms for the First Boston Corporation, pointed out that "Martin Marietta makes the Pershing 2, and the company is also a leading factor in the smart sensors and enhanced munitions that presumably will be needed to replace it." As Demisch told the *Times,* the economic bottom line of nuclear arms agreements is that "the relative complacency of the Street [Wall Street] is justified. Unless you develop, on the basis of arms control, a political consensus to reduce defense spending, it won't make any difference." [25]

That is the key point. In the United States, at least, the size of the overall military budget appears to be set politically—by making a decision to spend a given amount on the military, certainly not by adding up the costs of individual programs evaluated on their own merits. So even if money is rescued from a particular weapons program, it may well end up in another. Concerted anti–MX missile efforts by the peace movement and others helped limit MX deployment compared with what might have occurred otherwise; a great deal of money was in some sense saved but may have just been shunted to another weapons program. In fact, many in the mainstream (including Michael Dukakis during the 1988 presidential campaign) who agree with the peace movement that nuclear weapons spending should be reduced explicitly advocate the transfer of the savings to conventional military programs in Europe and elsewhere.

The straightforward way to attack the defense budget is to seek reductions in its politically established ceiling by persuading the public, and ultimately Congress, that less should be spent. But nuclear weapons spending, though huge in absolute terms, accounts for only about a quarter of the overall military budget. As Senator Sam Nunn, head of the Armed Services Committee, said during the discussion of INF, "Truth of it is, you're not going to save much money in any of these nuclear arms control discussions because the big money is not in nuclear weapons. The big money is in conventional weapons." [26]

In any case, cutting the military budget is only half the battle. Any economic and social benefits obviously depend on what happens to the money. The popular slogan that so many children could be fed or schools built for the cost of a single submarine or bomber applies only if the money is transferred to these purposes. Guns forgone do not automatically become butter. Military savings could end up merely as a reduction in the federal deficit (perhaps not a bad result but not an example of the progressive social reallocation of spending that the peace movement advocates). Savings could be used for bad purposes. They could be wasted. Or, perhaps most probable, they could vanish without a trace into the vast federal budgetary cauldron.

Activists, then, should not try to stop U.S. nuclear weapons systems

or promote negotiated arms control treaties on the dubious grounds
that the nuclear danger will then recede *or* on the equally dubious
grounds that money will automatically be saved, or if it is saved that it
will necessarily go toward better purposes. If those better purposes are
to feed children, clean the air and water, or build clinics, they should be
pursued directly with whatever money can be found—including the
funds now wasted on superflous missiles and bombers *when* such funds
can be clearly redirected. To take one example of a promising initiative,
in 1987 the Soviet Union was among 148 countries represented at a
United Nations conference on the relation between disarmament and
international economic development. The Soviets proposed an international fund to channel money saved on future arms control agreements to Third World needs. Though even the sharp reductions in strategic nuclear weapons contemplated in the START negotiations would
probably not lead to much if any savings (as we discuss later), at least
the Soviets supported the principle that the superpowers should actually
beat their nuclear swords into ploughshares. (The United States, in contrast, boycotted the U.N. conference. The United States has long insisted
that arms control and economic development should not be linked and
has refused to commit any money saved by future arms treaties to Third
World programs.)²⁷

Savings from either the nuclear or conventional parts of the military
budget would not *necessarily* benefit the macroeconomy any more than
they would automatically go toward social needs at home or abroad.
There is much debate about the economic purposes and consequences
of high military spending. Some (on both the right and the left) regard it
as a motor of the economy—military Keynesianism—providing a politically acceptable way for a capitalist state to inject huge sums of capital into privately owned high-technology companies and providing a
guaranteed market for tremendous industrial output that might otherwise go unsold in an American economy that is steadily losing ground
to Japanese, European, and even Third World producers. In this view,
the arms race is driven largely by broad corporate interests, shared perhaps by workers and communities that depend on corporate prosperity
for their own livelihood. Others claim that high military spending primarily benefits only the few giant corporations that build the weapons
and is in fact *ruining* the U.S. economy—reducing employment by emphasizing capital-intensive high technology and eroding competitive-
ness by draining from the civilian sector the bulk of the nation's scien-

tific and technical brainpower and its research and development capital. But whatever the interests behind high military spending and whatever economic benefits or damage it brings, one must be skeptical of all predictions about how a smaller military budget would ultimately affect overall employment, inflation, and other macroeconomic indices. Predictions about the complex capitalist macroeconomy are notoriously unreliable, and the results would obviously depend on what is done with money diverted from the military budget.

Gordon Adams is one of the few economists to acknowledge that the effects of reducing military spending are uncertain, and he argues that they might not be as dramatic as is often assumed. A review of relevant research by Adams and D. A. Gold at the Center on Budget and Policy Priorities concluded that "the economic impact of military spending is only marginally different from that of other forms of federal spending. It is not uniquely inflationary, has an unclear relationship to productivity and technological development, and does not create significantly different numbers of jobs." [28]

Macroeconomic goals, like social ones, can only be achieved if they are pursued directly—in this case by ensuring that any military savings are redirected specifically toward desired economic purposes. If they *are* wisely redirected, much good could probably be done. Barry Bluestone and John Havens, for example, studied the effects of a "Rebuild America" scenario: shifting thirty-five billion dollars from the military budget to infrastructure development, both physical (e.g., roads, bridges, and utilities) and human (e.g., education, health care, and social services). The results suggest that "while generalized spending on defense may not produce significantly different economic outcomes from generalized non-defense spending, the particular expenditure pattern embodied in rebuilding physical and human capital infrastructure is in fact expansionary in terms of GNP, total output, employment, and family disposable income . . . reducing the federal deficit while inducing more economic growth." Bluestone and Havens found that although "additions to GNP and output appear to be rather modest, the impact of the shift in spending on employment is anything but trivial. More than a quarter of a million (262,000) full-time equivalent jobs . . . are created." [29] Whether true in its details or not, this kind of analysis suggests again that socially and economically motivated efforts to cut military spending, either nuclear or conventional, are meaningful only if they divert money to productive social and economic ends within a broader program for progressive change. Savings in the abstract may bring little human benefit even if efforts to curb the arms race are successful—and that would be tragic.

The same holds at the microeconomic level. As Adams emphasizes, huge influxes of military spending create jobs and wealth for many workers and communities. Reducing this spending would doom many of these workers and communities to disaster, through new federal spending patterns might of course benefit other localities. Despite major efforts, it has not been easy to convert isolated plants or communities from military to civilian production and maintain standards of living and economic security, unless the local economy is already strong enough to absorb displaced military workers. Activists, then, should not "use the concept of economic conversion as a way out of the dilemma that stopping the arms race will deprive workers of jobs and communities of economic livelihood." Rather, as Adams argues, those genuinely concerned with economic reform should not simply oppose military spending, whether conventional or nuclear, but must "take economic issues seriously on their own terms." [30] That means not only reducing local reliance on military spending where that can help, but also helping communities and regions plan their overall economies to meet the needs of their populations rather than the needs of corporations or the Pentagon.

Nuclear arms control, then—whether unilateral or negotiated— *could* help redress the arms race's disgraceful channeling of massive public funds to giant private companies (in the Soviet Union, giant state bureaucracies), freeing resources for better social and economic uses. But, as we will see in Chapter 10, significant savings will require far more radical changes than even the START treaty envisions. And we must insist on specific mechanisms to ensure that any savings really reach those in need.


THE SYMBOLIC EFFECTS OF
ARMS CONTROL: THE INF TREATY

Many believe that nuclear arms control agreements are historic accomplishments *politically* even if the military and economic impact is minor. Arms control has in fact become the main public barometer of the prospects for peace and disarmament.

Though the ultimate political consequences of the INF treaty and the START treaty negotiations are not yet certain, history suggests that the superpowers' main interest in arms control may lie elsewhere: in public relations. The signing of the INF treaty, like others before it, did not noticeably reduce the nuclear danger, but it did lead to a spectacular political bonanza for both superpowers and for their leaders. As James G. Hershberg colorfully puts it, "In a virtuoso display of method acting, Reagan shed the role of Gary Cooper in *High Noon* and contracted for a surreal buddy movie with Gorbachev, in which both salved troubles on the home front by taking dramatic steps to dispel nuclear gloom and spotlight hopes for global peace."[31]

To see the political usefulness of treaties such as INF, imagine that the central symbol of planetary security was something more realistic, say, the number of people killed by the superpowers' troops and their allies and clients around the world. In that case, the signing of the 1972 SALT treaty might have seemed unimpressive in comparison to the enormous slaughter then occurring in Vietnam and, at lower levels, elsewhere around the world. The signing of the 1987 INF treaty likewise might have seemed a modest achievement in comparison to the wholesale devastation of Afghanistan and the many other bloody Third World conflicts then fully in progress. The editors of the *Bulletin of the Atomic Scientists* might not have dramatically rolled back the hands of their "doomsday clock"; Gorbachev and Reagan might not have been nominated for the Nobel Peace Prize. The INF treaty prompted both responses (and when we examine the actual significance of the treaty we will see how very remarkable that is).

Arms control provides a low-cost way for both superpowers periodically to convey a commitment to reducing the nuclear danger *without* necessarily forgoing the violent foreign policies that in fact produce the danger. Arms treaties are mutually advantageous devices for keeping the peace movements of the twentieth century, in the East and the West, at bay. In them, the superpowers have found a remarkably efficient way to allay worldwide popular alarm about nuclear war that might otherwise lead to serious political problems for both Moscow and Washington.

Still, even resounding ideological victories do not come without risk. By using nuclear arms control to project an image of peaceableness, the superpowers invite a widening public response that they may not be fully able to control. By loudly proclaiming to be "on the road" to nuclear disarmament and world peace, they risk that their audiences may take the slogan seriously and even seek to hold them to it. An analogy is the orchestration of contrived "demonstration elections" in Third World states to project an image of true democracy even when there is no intention of delivering it. Sometimes this works nicely, for a while at least, as in El Salvador. But in other cases, as in Haiti, it can backfire.[32]

Disarmament and peace, like democracy, are ideals with which states like to be associated, but they must be careful to limit the unintended consequences of their public relations operations. In nuclear arms control, there is no great danger that the superpowers will lose the reins. This could change, lending arms control an important political dialectic. Yet those genuinely concerned with disarmament or peace would be naive to continue to cheerlead for the superpowers' "game of disarmament," as Alva Myrdal called it.[33]

Consider in more detail the INF agreement. The *New York Times* acknowledged in a prominent editorial that "the military effect will be slight," noting (inaccurately) that "the agreement affects some 2,000 warheads in arsenals containing 25,000" (the combined superpower nuclear arsenal is actually about twice that big). The paper asserts, however, that "the political effect is enormous."[34] Why? "When the pact is readied for signature, it will demonstrate that the two leaders have learned what it takes to get a job done together," even though the job in this case has little inherent significance. Similarly the *Boston Globe* editorialized that INF represents "a giant step" toward superpower cooperation. Such statements had a surreal quality at the time, as large-scale conflicts involving the superpowers and their clients continued to rage in Afghanistan, Angola, Cambodia, and elsewhere. Using comparable logic, the family and friends of a divorcing couple might celebrate wildly because the couple finally agreed that he would get the flowery bedspreads while she kept the solid ones—even though they were viciously battling in court over the house, the dog, the bank accounts, and the children. Mary McGrory, one of the few incisive observers, described INF accurately as a "paltry accord."[35]

In any case, the *Times*'s argument would logically apply to *any* major superpower agreement. But because the press and most other observers play into the superpowers' public relations strategies, uncritically repeating their version of events, nuclear arms agreements receive special treatment, even compared to far more significant accords. The most important military agreements of the 1980s, such as those to end the huge wars in Afghanistan and the Persian Gulf—and perhaps to avert the maiming and death of hundreds of thousands of people—received less press coverage, political commentary, and praise than the INF agreement to dismantle missiles widely recognized as redundant.

In fact, the very week that the INF agreement (not yet signed) was announced, two far more significant agreements were actually signed but went comparatively unnoticed. On September 16, 1987, the *Times* reported on a U.S.-Soviet pact to reduce the risk of nuclear war—not through arms control, but through the establishment of "risk reduction centers" that would enable the superpowers to communicate more effectively about missile tests and other matters that could lead to avoidable tension or war. Though no giant step away from nuclear danger, the pact could help avert conflict at some moment of great international trouble and confusion. The next day the *Times* reported the conclusion of the Montreal Protocol for protecting the earth's ozone layer against pollution, which Deputy Assistant Secretary of State Richard E. Benedick termed "perhaps the most historically significant international environmental treaty." Two days later, on September 19, the *Times* ran a huge full-width banner headline—dwarfing those of the previous two stories—announcing the agreement "in principle" on the Euromissiles.[36]

The priorities are particularly absurd in the case of the ozone treaty. Not only the two superpowers but also over seventy nations agreed to it, and "many more—industrialized and developing countries alike—[were] expected to sign shortly and eventually ratify the agreement."[37] It is widely considered a path-breaking success in gaining multilateral action to address severe global environmental threats. If agreements between nations are politically or symbolically important because they show that normally hostile leaders "have learned what it takes to get a job done together," then by rational standards this was surely the big news of the week, if not the year.

The same is true many times over when we consider the simpler and less speculative standard of direct humanitarian and environmental benefits. These are essentially zero for the INF treaty. But "officials of the [U.S.] Environmental Protection Agency . . . said the agency's computer models indicated that if the actions required by the [ozone] protocol were observed, they would avert 132 million cases of skin cancer and 27 million deaths from skin cancer that would otherwise have occurred among people born before 2075. The data also showed that about 1.5 million cases of eye cataracts would be averted." Ozone depletion may prove even more devastating by altering the earth's environment, perhaps warming the planet and disrupting the food chain, a prospect that has led scientists to issue unusually urgent warnings. Atmospheric scientist F. Sherwood Rowland states that "at this point, one cannot eliminate catastrophe as one of the possible conclusions." Nevertheless, amid prominent, detailed coverage of Senate committee hearings on the INF treaty, the *Boston Globe* buried the Senate Foreign

Relations Committee's unanimous approval of the Montreal Protocol on page 75, which also featured stories about a new treatment for gallstones and the birth of a rare tortoise in a zoo in Hamburg.[38]

There are many variations on the theme of the political or symbolic benefits of arms control. The *Boston Globe*'s usually excellent military correspondent, Fred Kaplan, writes, "Nearly everyone acknowledges [that INF's] main impact is political. . . . [It is] the first treaty that actually cuts nuclear weapons." Deferring the question of whether such cuts really pave the way for nuclear disarmament, as many assume, we note that far larger cuts in nuclear weapons have quietly occurred over the history of the arms race and in political terms might be considered far more significant since they were done unilaterally, without difficult, drawn-out negotiations. According to the *Nuclear Weapons Databook,* in 1967 the U.S. nuclear stockpile comprised 32,000 warheads, shrinking to 26,000 by 1983. And "according to one official report [the 1984 Department of Defense Annual Report], 'the total number of megatons was four times as high in 1960 than in 1980.'"[39] That enormous cut, rarely applauded and almost unknown, marked a step not toward a less nuclear world but toward a modern arsenal of more accurate weapons. INF is a far smaller change but likewise does not reduce the military capabilities of either side. Like the drop in total megatonnage and earlier arms agreements, the removal of the Euromissiles occurs *because* it represents no real loss of military capability.

One often reads that INF will reduce the superpowers' nuclear arsenals by about 5 percent, a strange way to describe weapons that did not even exist on the American side a few years ago and were deployed under the rationale that they would stimulate an arms agreement to remove them forthwith. Some weapons of the 5 percent are considered obsolete and would have been phased out soon anyway. And the INF treaty does not actually require the elimination of *any* nuclear destruction capability. Although intermediate-range missiles and launchers will be destroyed, the warheads carried by those missiles will not be. (As U.S. Secretary of Defense Frank Carlucci told Congress, the decision to retain the warheads "basically was done at our behest.") Those warheads "can be modified to fit missiles that are not covered by the treaty," meaning that the real nuclear arsenals of the superpowers will be reduced not by 5 percent but by 0 percent.[40]

In fact, even as the superpowers proudly announce that they are cutting their nuclear arsenals, they are actually *expanding* those arsenals dramatically. Take one case in point. Shortly before the announcement of the "in-principle" INF agreement, a largely unnoticed news report by

Fred Kaplan revealed that the Pentagon was quietly reactivating the B-53 nuclear bomb. Packing nine megatons, it is "the biggest, dirtiest bomb in the U.S. arsenal," six and a half times more powerful than the second largest, the B-28. Each B-53 carries over seven hundred times the destructive power of the weapon that devastated Hiroshima. Built in the 1960s, it was deemed obsolete and deactivated in the early 1980s. It "does not provide the same degree of security and safety" as newer warheads.[41] The Air Force reportedly plans to deploy about 50 of the old behemoths on B-52 aircraft, making for a total of about 450 megatons of new destructive power.

In comparison, according to the *New York Times,* each of the 120 deployed Pershing II missiles (some operational and some spares) that are slated for removal under the INF agreement carries a warhead yielding between 5 and 50 kilotons; each of the 309 ground-launched cruise missiles to be scrapped under INF carries a warhead yielding 200 kilotons.[42] The destructive power to be removed, then, totals at most 67.8 megatons. Only 8 reactivated B-53s, then, will exceed the total U.S. megatonnage to be removed under INF. The 50 B-53s will introduce into the U.S. arsenal more than six times the destructive power of the missiles to be retired in Europe.

The B-53 is just one of several U.S. nuclear warhead deployments slated for the near future. Others include 3,000 warheads on D-5 missiles, most yielding 475 kilotons each, for Trident submarines; over 500 mobile Midgetman missiles carrying 500 kilotons each; and 500 warheads on 50 MX missiles yielding between 300 and 475 kilotons each. In Europe, as Dan Plesch reports, the United States and NATO plan to dramatically upgrade their nuclear forces following the INF treaty:

- The United States will deploy in European waters some 380 submarine-launched cruise missiles (SLCMs), with a 250-km range, by the mid-1990's.

- NATO plans to equip strike-aircraft based in Europe with around 1300 air-launched cruise missiles (ALCMs) having a range of 400 km.

- Under development are a new ballistic and a new cruise missile— both with a range of about 400 km. They are earmarked for use with the more than 600 Multiple Launch Rocket Systems (MLRS) on order for NATO nations.

- Following the recent deployment of some 200 new nuclear artillery shells for eight-inch guns will be an additional 400 to be produced and deployed in Europe for 155-mm artillery tubes. These systems will have double the range and explosive power of those they replace.

The Natural Resources Defense Council estimates that "U.S. cuts under INF represent only 90 days of warhead production."[43] As Mr. Reagan accepts wide praise for agreeing to "cut" nuclear weapons for the first time in history, a new era of rapid expansion of the U.S. and allied nuclear arsenals continues. That is a triumph of propaganda over fact.

Arms control advocates insist that INF is nevertheless symbolically significant because, even though other kinds of nuclear arms will have to await other treaties, this treaty sets a precedent by "eliminating an entire class of nuclear weapons." True, one narrow category of weapons—intermediate-range land-based nuclear missiles—will be abolished. But again on the American side this category did not even exist until several years ago. Perhaps the real precedent here is to invent new classes of weapons so they can later be abolished in politically popular arms control "breakthroughs."

More important, the *missions* of these missiles will not be abolished but simply reassigned to other weapons. As Diana Johnstone points out, "The Pentagon will transfer its cruise missiles to warships—in the North Atlantic, Baltic and Mediterranean (where they can be aimed to the South as well as the North)—where it meant to put them all along and where they will not draw the attention of protesting civilians." She cites a 1981 Library of Congress research report finding that cruise missiles were originally sent to Europe to save them from arms control, and that now that this goal has been accomplished the United States will follow the long-standing plan to, as British M. P. Robin Cook put it, "pepper the seas with sea-launched cruise missiles."[44] Another medium-range weapon, known as the jet aircraft, also stands ready in Europe to deliver nuclear warheads wherever they might be needed in time of war, as do ballistic-missile submarines lurking offshore and "strategic" missiles and bombers based in the United States.

The commander of the U.S. Strategic Air Command, General John T. Chain, made no secret of American intentions in an interview with the *New York Times* shortly before the signing of the INF treaty. As Richard Halloran reports, Chain said that "the Joint Chiefs of Staff had asked SAC to determine what weapons could cover Soviet targets after the United States removed . . . ground-launched cruise missiles and . . . Pershing 2 ballistic missiles from Europe." Chain observed that "we

could use B-52's, which could sit on alert here in the United States."
One hundred and fifty such aircraft are equipped to launch cruise missiles, with a range of 1,500 miles and high accuracy. SAC owns 1,700 of them. Chain added that FB-111 bombers (those used to attack Libya in 1986) could also fly such missions from bases in Europe or the United States. "Each of SAC's 61 FB-111's can carry 15,000 pounds of nuclear bombs at sea level at more than the speed of sound." Moreover, the targets covered by the Euromissiles "are the same types of targets that we could hold at risk from here in the United States" with intercontinental missiles. Attack submarines armed with cruise missiles, he noted, could also be used.[45] At the outbreak of any future nuclear war, millions of Eastern and Western Europeans will not be impressed that a "whole class" of weapons previously aimed at them had been abolished when they are about to be obliterated by ready substitutes.

### GETTING FRIENDLY: ARMS CONTROL AND SUPERPOWER RELATIONS

Another popular notion about the political or symbolic effects of arms agreements such as the SALT treaties and INF is that they can reduce the nuclear danger by promoting better relations between the superpowers. This idea has become so widespread that few feel the need to explicitly defend it. Two assumptions hide within the argument: (1) that better relations between the superpowers are a major factor determining the risk of nuclear war and (2) that nuclear arms agreements help establish better relations. Both premises deserve examination.

As we noted, each superpower bloc has wisely decided not to pose any direct military threat to the sovereignty of the other, knowing that to do so would probably result in the destruction of the planet. This kind of restraint does not require good relations but only an instinct for self-preservation. Since World War II superpower interventions have usually taken another form entirely—responses to *local* conflicts in Europe and the Third World. Such operations can and do continue in times of relatively warm cultural and diplomatic contacts between the United States and the Soviet Union. The American war in Vietnam, after all, proceeded with awful intensity despite détente because it was not directed against the Soviets in the first place. Similarly good relations with the United States would probably not have prevented the Soviet attack on Afghanistan, aimed as it was against a domestic Afghan threat to Soviet power in the country. Superpower violence in the Third World, the main contemporary trigger for nuclear war, is quite consistent with good relations between the superpowers themselves.[46]

Still, warm relations *could* make an important difference in some cases. One superpower must challenge the actions of the other to make a crisis, and détente might help discourage such challenges. But again the historical record should make us cautious about such predictions. Recall that the most dangerous nuclear confrontation since the Cuban missile crisis occurred in 1973, immediately after the June 1973 Nixon-Brezhnev Summit II, whose centerpiece, ironically, was the "Agreement Between the United States of America and the Union of Soviet Socialist Republics on the Prevention of Nuclear War." This was perhaps the height of détente. But the pursuit of important interests overrode any barriers to confrontation arising from détente. Nixon understood the profound limitations of détente in this regard:

> I evaluated the Soviet behavior during the Mideast crisis not as an example of the failure of détente, but as an illustration of its limitations—limitations of which I had always been keenly aware. . . . The Soviet Union will always act in its own self-interest; and so will the United States. Détente cannot change that. All we can hope from détente is that it will minimize confrontation in marginal areas and provide, at least, alternative possibilities in the major ones.

The shocking 1973 nuclear crisis did not even prevent the occurrence of Summit III in June 1974. Nixon reports Brezhnev's "willingness to pick up the dialogue of détente where it had left off before the Mideast crisis," a willingness he shared.[47]

In other circumstances, of course, particularly in what Nixon calls the "marginal areas," warm diplomatic relations may well discourage intervention and crisis by giving the superpowers something to lose should open conflict between them erupt. Détente may also help to resolve crises that do occur, though not necessarily. Kissinger's diplomatic access to Moscow in 1973, and the Soviets' willingness to rely on his solemn assurances, permitted him to double-cross the Russians and reignite the crisis by giving Israel permission to violate the cease-fire that he had just negotiated. In other circumstances, though, particularly in the case of an outright accident or mistake, cordial relations could help prevent a disaster by encouraging negotiations rather than military action. Moreover, détente may reduce the mutual popular paranoia that helps each superpower justify the subset of its international adventures that become publicly known and debated. To the extent that Gorbachev, for example, is perceived in the United States as a man of peace, the American government may have a more difficult time using the Soviet threat as a pretext for Third World intervention.

Whatever happens to the U.S.-Soviet relationship, the most meaningful barometer of change is not the warmth or coolness of rhetoric but the actual behavior of both states in the political conflicts that could lead to war. Better relations do not necessarily demonstrate progress. Less militarism in the Third World would.

Whatever the importance of superpower relations, it would be surprising if nuclear arms agreements of minimal military and economic significance profoundly improved them. Indeed, "on the record . . . there is no reason to believe that such improvements will be of long duration."[48] Arms treaties, like other negotiated agreements between states, particularly those between adversaries, are founded on self-interest, not trust or good will. True, any superpower agreement—not just those concerning nuclear weapons—can both reflect and promote better relations. But often they simply become another terrain of conflict and propaganda.

As Nicholas Wade writes: "The general pattern of arms accords is to cap the new weapons each side wants to build, scrap those that are obsolete, and leave problem weapons for the next agreement. That makes each new treaty harder to negotiate. Verification becomes trickier, which increases suspicions and charges of cheating, and worsens relations—just the opposite of what arms control is meant to achieve." "Wrongly designed," he adds, arms control "can spur new competition in dangerous technologies, foster accusations of cheating and speed the very tensions it seeks to avert." SALT II, for example, was initially hailed as a great leap forward for superpower relations but quickly degenerated into bitter superpower conflict—first over the U.S. Senate's failure to ratify it, later over alleged minor violations of it by both sides, and finally over the U.S. government's unilateral decision to violate it explicitly by deploying more cruise missiles than it allows. Similar conflicts developed over the ABM treaty regarding alleged cheating and the permissibility of the testing and deployment of Star Wars components. In 1986 a former chief of the U.S. delegation to SALT II and director of the U.S. Arms Control and Disarmament Agency, Ralph Earle II, wrote in *Foreign Policy* that "inadvertently or intentionally" the Reagan administration's "mishandling" of the nuclear treaty compliance issue "created an unnecessary and undeniable self-inflicted wound" that may do "irreparable damage" to "U.S.-Soviet relations."[49] In retrospect, no

one could seriously claim that ABM, SALT, or SALT II led to better relations in any sustained or basic sense, though each of course played a
role in the normal cycle of periodic upswings and downswings.

Did the INF treaty lead to better relations and a safer world in the
meaningful sense of reduced international conflict involving the superpowers? Certainly not right away. Indeed, the period immediately surrounding INF was one of unusually great superpower militarism, with
both nations engaged in their largest interventions of many years. The
Soviets continued their murderous occupation of Afghanistan, complete
with frequent attacks on U.S.-backed Pakistan, while the United States
continued to support segments of the Afghan resistance with large
quantities of weapons and other aid used for killing Soviet soldiers and
for terrorist attacks in Kabul and elsewhere, including advanced antiaircraft missiles used to down both military and civilian Afghan and Soviet planes. On the very day banner headlines hailed the INF signing in
the morning papers, a barely reported UPI dispatch stated, "A diplomat
quoted a senior Afghan medical officer as saying, 'more casualties were
being brought into Kabul' from [the Afghan cities] Khost and Kandahar
'than at any time during the war.'" Although the Afghan situation soon
changed dramatically, it had not yet done so when Gorbachev was being
toasted as a new Soviet man of peace around the world. The reasons for
the ultimate Soviet withdrawal can be traced not to INF, of course, but
to the fortunes of the battlefield, domestic discontent, and the huge cost
of the war, similar to the considerations that ultimately drove the United
States from Vietnam. In and around the Persian Gulf in the immediate
post-INF period, the United States continued its largest and most dangerous military intervention since the Vietnam War, undertaken despite
an urgent Soviet proposal for all foreign warships to stay clear of that
explosive war zone.[50] Even as the Central American peace treaty was
being enacted, the United States increased supplies to the Nicaraguan
contras (who in turn widely expanded terrorist attacks against Nicaraguan civilians), continued a devastating economic embargo (even block-
ing a convoy of American veterans bearing medical and other humanitarian aid), and kept up an unrelenting ideological campaign against
Managua. Prominent in this campaign was President Reagan's demand—
found nowhere in the Central American treaty—that the Nicaraguans
eject their Cuban and Soviet advisers, which would be comparable to a
Soviet demand that, say, Pakistan, not known for a commitment to democracy and human rights, expel American civilian and military officials. The United States continued to support the South African regime,

which in support of the Angolan rebels it sponsors invaded Angola outright shortly after the announcement of the nuclear treaty, killing not only many Angolans but also Cubans and possibly Soviets helping to defend the country from the apartheid state. Many other cases could be cited.

Even the routine hazards of superpower militarism seemed unchanged or intensified by unusual recklessness on both sides right after the treaty. On February 12, as the U.S. Senate debated INF, two American warships—the guided-missile cruiser *Yorktown* and the destroyer *Caron*—deliberately violated Soviet territorial waters by steaming to within ten miles of the sensitive Soviet coastline on the Black Sea. President Reagan, the Pentagon said, personally ordered the provocative operation to assert the right of "innocent" passage into other nations' territorial waters under an interpretation of international law disputed by the Soviet Union. According to the *New York Times,* the passages were "tense" and conducted with crews "at a high state of readiness." Fortunately they were not at too high a state of readiness. Apparently determined to assert Soviet rights with their own massive weapons platforms, the Soviets warned away the American vessels; when this tactic failed, Soviet frigates assumed a collision course and rammed the U.S. warships. As military researcher William Arkin sensibly noted: "That episode might have led to something more serious. It shows that this sort of routine intelligence-gathering and routine confrontation can lead to unintended crises." [51] The *Nuclear Weapons Databook* notes that all U.S. destroyers and all U.S. cruisers are equipped to carry and fire nuclear weapons. Arkin later published a study concluding that the *Caron* was on a spy mission, which would not qualify as permitted "innocent passage" under international law. Since 1980, Arkin added, the *Caron* had officially carried nuclear weapons six times. There was no way of knowing if they were on board during the ramming incident. [52]

Within a year of the INF treaty, several important Third World peace treaties were signed and some major conflicts there showed promise of being resolved (e.g., Afghanistan, the Iran-Iraq war, and Namibia and Angola). Improved superpower relations perhaps helped in some cases, such as southern Africa, though in other conflicts, such as the gulf war, they were probably irrelevant. More important—for Afghanistan particularly—has been Gorbachev's independent desire to disengage the Soviet Union from various Third World albatrosses and turn attention to domestic reform and the building of economic bridges to Western Europe. INF played no direct role in any of these decisions.

Only time will tell if Third World conflicts posing nuclear dangers will truly wind down, if new ones will take their place, and what role, if any, the new superpower relationship will play. Unlike the last round of détente, the new round may lead to real progress toward a safer and less violent world. If, as some believe, the end of the Cold War is at hand, the nuclear danger could decrease dramatically. The measure of progress, however, will not be whether further nuclear arms treaties follow INF but what Washington and Moscow actually do in the Third World.

## START: A FRESH START
## FOR ARMS CONTROL?

Perhaps the biggest factor in the INF treaty's popularity is the hope that it will pave the way for more dramatic arms control successes. The *Boston Globe* editorialized: "If it becomes the precedent for a strategic arms treaty," INF "will constitute the most substantive achievement yet" for Reagan and Gorbachev. Many hopes ride on what is widely regarded as the preeminent arms control goal of this historical period, the Strategic Arms Reduction Treaty (START), to dramatically cut strategic nuclear strike forces. What is its significance? As Fred Kaplan reported in the *Boston Globe,* "Officials have said that the treaty . . . would cut long-range strategic weapons on both sides by 50 percent."[53] But it turns out that where nuclear weapons are concerned, 50 percent does not really equal 50 percent, much as "reducing nuclear arsenals" actually meant increasing them at the time the INF treaty was signed.

In December 1987 a study published by the Natural Resources Defense Council (NRDC) reported something already understood by knowledgeable insiders: that the treaty actually under negotiation would reduce strategic weapons by only about 30 or 35 percent. Naturally a 50 percent cut sounds more dramatic and wins more political points—the main objective of the arms control exercise. START can be described this way only because of a strange "counting rule," which treats each nuclear bomber carrying only bombs and short-range attack missiles as one warhead even though it can actually deliver many. As Kaplan notes, START as currently understood "would limit each side to 6,000 strategic nuclear warheads. However, because of the counting rule, the United States could in fact end up with 9,200 warheads, since about 3,200 of those warheads—bombs and short-range attack missiles on bombers—would not be counted under the terms of the treaty."[54] Similarly the Soviets could end up with 7,100 warheads. Such blatant nuclear numerology causes little concern. The press continued to report START as "cutting in half" strategic arsenals even after the NRDC publicly revealed that this was not true.

In a prominent editorial at the time of the INF treaty signing, the *New York Times* raised the basic but rarely asked question about START: "Will it actually reduce the risks of war?" The editorialist insisted that "numbers *can* matter. Agreements *can* produce situations permitting a foe to plan a first strike." How this could happen is not explained, perhaps because it is impossible (see Chapter 2). An earlier story in the *Times* reported: "Reagan Administration officials have argued that an agreement on deep cuts in long-range arms would produce a more stable strategic balance because it would compel the Soviet Union to reduce its force of land-based missiles. The Administration has said that those missiles are the most suitable weapons for carrying out an attack on American missile silos." But Brent Scowcroft argues on the basis of the current American proposal that "by any of the measures commonly used, stability would be impaired."[55]

As usual, both viewpoints are off base. The effects on stability would be ambiguous but so slight as to be undetectable. With or without START, deterrence will remain as stable or as unstable as the balance of terror makes it, because START cannot change the terror that each side would feel in starting a nuclear war. The most realistic assessment is that "reductions in levels of strategic forces by 50% or so, as have been suggested in recent Soviet and American proposals, would not necessarily make much difference in the levels of damage to be expected in the event of war. Nor is there reason to believe that such cuts, even if they involve selective reductions in 'counterforce' weapons, would necessarily make much difference in the likelihood of nuclear holocaust."[56]

That conclusion is perhaps obvious, and it is strongly supported by a recent study by the Brookings Institution and the Lawrence Livermore National Laboratory. That study, as we mentioned in Chapter 2, found that with current forces numbering roughly 10,000 strategic warheads on each side, neither superpower can even begin to destroy enough of its enemy's nuclear weapons in a first strike to prevent utterly devastating retaliation. Even in a crisis, then, neither side has any incentive to launch a first strike. The same would be true, the study found, if both sides reduced their forces to roughly 6,000 strategic warheads—levels that, as we saw, are somewhat lower than those actually envisioned in the START treaty.

The study considered three possible 6,000-warhead scenarios: forces roughly similar in composition to current forces except for proportional numerical reductions across the board; forces designed for maximum invulnerability to attack; and heavily modernized forces designed for maximum ability to destroy the enemy's nuclear forces as well as for invulnerability. In each scenario, after absorbing the most devastating first-strike attack possible, either side "could readily strike" *all* of the 1,500–2,000 targets considered worth striking in retaliation, just as they can today.[57]

Little would change, in fact, if the superpowers' nuclear arsenals were reduced even further, to *half* the levels officially envisioned in START: 3,000 strategic warheads on each side, less than one-third of current levels. Both sides would almost certainly choose such reductions to maximize the invulnerability of their remaining forces. In that case, "target coverage in [either] first strike [or] retaliation is essentially identical for both sides and equal to" that achievable with current forces. Indeed, either side would still have residual strategic forces remaining unused after attacking all worthwhile targets, even after absorbing the worst possible first strike.[58]

Thus even if we assume, as many mainstream analysts do, that strong deterrence requires the ability to retaliate against the entire military apparatus of the enemy, START would not even begin to affect the risk of nuclear war. There simply are not enough important military targets to justify the number of weapons each side would retain even after the reductions contemplated in START. If we make the far more reasonable assumption that threatening the enemy's cities is more than sufficient to discourage a first strike, then even arms reductions to well below 3,000 warheads would not affect the risk of nuclear war, either. As Steinbruner points out, "500–2,000 warheads delivered in retaliation covers anything that might be considered a reasonable deterrent requirement under *any* of the prevailing opinions about that requirement."[59] Clearly START, which would leave each side with several times that number of warheads, means little.

Would deep strategic arms cuts at least reduce the number of casualties in the event of a nuclear war? Here again, the Brookings–Lawrence Livermore study verifies common sense: "civilian damage, measured in the number of deaths, does not appear very sensitive to levels of strategic forces." Nuclear weapons are so powerful that only a few are needed to wipe out whole populations. As Spurgeon Keeny explains, only 100 one-megaton weapons (or their equivalent) could "cause some 20 million–40 million Soviet prompt fatalities, and I am sure at least twice that many delayed fatalities from untreated casualties and secondary effects." One Trident 2 submarine carrying D-5 missiles "would have more than this amount of equivalent megatonnage on board."[60]

In fact the study projected that smaller forces could actually kill *more* people than current forces. For example, a simulated first strike with a modernized force of 3,000 U.S. strategic weapons killed *twice* as many Soviet people as a first strike with current forces of 10,000 U.S. weapons; a simulated American retaliation following a Soviet first strike likewise killed twice as many Soviets with 3,000 modernized weapons as with 10,000 current weapons.[61]

The reason for such disparities is that the main determinant of the amount of likely damage is not the number of available weapons but the way the weapons are *targeted* and, to some extent, their *size*. As we might expect, the Brookings–Lawrence Livermore study found that most fatalities would result from attacks on cities and that larger warheads would cause more deaths than smaller ones. Hence, "withholding attacks on [urban areas] or using lower-yield accurate weapons could do much to reduce immediate deaths."[62] Even with those steps, of course, a major nuclear war would be a cataclysm beyond history; all predictions of casualties are largely guesswork based on studies of the comparatively small nuclear attacks on Hiroshima and Nagasaki in 1945. Still, considering the number of lives potentially at stake, we must applaud any steps to reduce the anticipated damage of a nuclear war. Even dramatic cuts in strategic nuclear arsenals, however, would not necessarily do any good. And current arms control proposals, including START, do not deal with targeting or yield, both of which are perhaps unverifiable but could of course be changed unilaterally.

As General Jones, former chairman of the Joint Chiefs of Staff, explained to *Harper's* magazine: "People at both ends of the political spectrum expect too much from arms control. They tend to think the negotiations will somehow make all our problems go away. . . . Even if both sides scrapped 5,000 nuclear weapons tomorrow, the world would be no safer if tensions between the two countries remained the same." Perhaps inadvertently, the *Boston Globe* wrote the truth about the current phase of arms control in September 1987: "The superpowers have set the stage for hacking away at redundancies elsewhere in the thicket of nuclear deterrence."[63] So why is everyone excited about reducing redundancies, which by definition are meaningless?

The important aspect of START is that, as the NRDC study reported, "all the U.S. weapon systems now in development would be allowed to proceed." These include the Stealth bomber, the Trident II (D-5) submarine-launched missile, new cruise missiles, and a new gravity bomb, the B-83. Similarly, "almost all the Soviet weapon systems now being deployed or in development" could continue, including the SS-24 and SS-25 ICBMs, the Typhoon and Delta-4 submarines, the SS-N-20 and SS-N-23 submarine-launched missiles, the Tupolev bombers (known here as Bear and Blackjack), and the AS-15 air-launched cruise missiles. START "would also inspire a new generation of nuclear weapons. By reducing the number of missiles and warheads, START would fuel the race for super-accurate missiles with 'single-shot kill probability' systems and 'maneuvering re-entry vehicles' that could avoid missile defense systems." With fewer but far more accurate weapons, American and Soviet forces might actually pose a greater threat to each other's heavily protected targets like missile silos and command centers, and, hence, "might become even more lethal after START." [64] Even for those who believe such things matter, does this sound like a safer world?

It would not even be a cheaper world. As Michael Howard says of deep cuts in nuclear arsenals: "If the cuts applied to existing inventories [they would not] significantly reduce military expenditures. Size of inventories in itself bears no necessary relationship . . . to the cost of maintaining" the nuclear balance. Richard Halloran agreed in the *New York Times* in December 1987 that as long as weapons modernization proceeds, "such an arms agreement would apparently not produce much immediate financial saving because spending for costly nuclear weapons would continue." In February 1988 Halloran reported that "senior officers," including NATO chief General Galvin, concurred that neither INF nor a long-range nuclear arms treaty nor even a conventional weapons treaty would save money, because they would limit existing weapons that have already been paid for and could affect only their comparatively small operating costs. [65]

Even the SALT II treaty placed restrictions on the technological arms race, long regarded by arms control advocates as a far more fundamental concern than the aggregate sizes of nuclear stockpiles that will remain bloated in any case. By the standards of arms controllers, then, START would be a great leap backward, not forward. General Chain, the commander of the Strategic Air Command, told Halloran in December 1987 that he would not be surprised if "we end up with some type of agreement that reduces nuclear weapons." "That's fine with me," the general cheerfully added, "as long as I have modern nuclear weapons."[66] That says everything you need to know about the "historic" START treaty.

## WHAT ABOUT "MINIMUM DETERRENCE"?

What about reductions far more radical than START, toward the much-discussed "minimum deterrent"—the lowest level of nuclear forces consistent with maintaining the balance of terror? Opinions differ about how low that level is—whether a few thousand, a few hundred, or a few dozen nuclear weapons—but by definition it would preserve existential deterrence. Hence, even the most radical nuclear reductions seriously proposed short of total nuclear disarmament should not greatly alter the calculations of political leaders in considering the use of nuclear weapons or taking risks during crises. All of the superpowers' weapons in excess of the minimum deterrent are redundant. Removing them changes little.

As we have seen, even the amount of destruction in the event of a nuclear war might not change much should the superpowers slash their strategic arsenals by 90 percent or more. If the remaining weapons land on cities—and with so few weapons on hand, that is probably where they would be aimed—they might kill nearly as many people as today's arsenal would if used to attack the full range of military targets. A recent National Academy of Sciences study concluded that a few hundred weapons exploded over cities would immediately kill 20 million to 40 million people in the United States and 30 million to 50 million people in the Soviet Union; a full-scale attack against 2,000 military and economic targets, the study found, would kill roughly the same number of people.[67]

Still, if strategic arsenals were vastly reduced, a nuclear war *might* kill fewer people, and if the remaining weapons were not gigantic blockbusters, it would probably do much less damage to the earth's environment. From debatable assumptions, George Rathjens estimates that 90 percent cuts in 1985 strategic nuclear force levels could reduce expected fatalities in a large-scale nuclear war by a factor of two to ten.[68] The superpowers should certainly reduce their strategic arsenals to the minimum deterrent, unilaterally if necessary, if only for the *chance* of sparing the planet the total destruction that tens of thousands of warheads could wreak. A minimum deterrent, moreover, would probably mean an end to nuclear war–fighting doctrines that rely on large and varied nuclear arsenals and hence an end to the dangerous misperceptions about nuclear war those doctrines may spawn (see Chapter 4). But minimum deterrence would probably not help achieve the truly important task of our time: reducing the risk of nuclear war. Apart from banning doomsday weapons, as we discussed above, the only kind of nuclear arms control that can reduce that risk is total abolition, to which we now turn.

## WHAT ABOUT DISARMAMENT?

Considering the historical record, the violent character of states, and human passions and fallibility, we must expect a disaster sooner or later as long as nuclear weapons exist. Nuclear disarmament is possibly the most important task in history. But we must be realistic about the obstacles to it and about the ability of arms control to bring nuclear disarmament closer.

The Reykjavik summit and the INF treaty have led many, even on the left, to suppose that American and Soviet leaders may now be ready to consider the abolition of nuclear weapons. That is a naive assumption, particularly for the United States. Even most American officials who supported INF vehemently oppose the denuclearization of Europe, a logical first step toward general nuclear disarmament. Mr. Gorbachev has made some dramatic moves, such as the unprecedented unilateral Soviet moratorium on nuclear testing. But disarmament is a different matter.

In fact all the nuclear states would regard losing their ultimate weapons as a catastrophe. Deterrence does work to a degree—not nearly enough, as we have seen, to make the world safe, but well enough to make world leaders afraid to experiment with the alternative. Nuclear weapons provide their owners with at least some protection from and power over other nations. More important, the threat of a nuclear cataclysm helps deter a third world war that, even if fought with only conventional weapons, could far exceed the destruction of World War II.

Moreover, in a world without nuclear weapons "as crises developed, would we not have something akin to the mobilization that preceded World War I, and a period of great instability as the realization of nuclear weapons capabilities seemed imminent?"[69] The losing side would surely be tempted to make and perhaps use nuclear weapons. The fear of that might lead other states to do the same. In this one situation, a first strike might even seem appealing if one side thought it could knock out the other's production facilities or tiny, hastily produced arsenal (e.g., Israel's 1981 strike against an Iraqi reactor). Nuclear disarmament would of course bring enormous benefits for the nuclear states, particularly considering the likely alternative: more and more states acquiring nuclear arms and the constant risk of a catastrophe that would destroy everyone. But for now at least the nuclear states prefer the devil they know to the one they don't.

American and Soviet leaders endorse nuclear disarmament *in word* much as they praise other popular values like democracy and human rights, even as they regularly support the opposite in Afghanistan and El Salvador, Poland and South Africa. As the worldwide disarmament movement grows in strength and visibility, world leaders will continue to claim its goal as their own. But that is just a costless exercise in nuclear-age public relations.

Even if the superpowers someday reconsider, tremendous practical obstacles would remain. There is no way to disinvent nuclear weapons. Pending methods of verification not now available or even conceivable, neither side could be certain that the other had not secretly retained some warheads or the capability of quickly producing them. With about fifty thousand superpower weapons remaining in place, neither side could gain anything by squirreling away a few dozen intermediate-range missiles after INF, despite the hysteria about verification. But if nuclear stockpiles were reduced to zero or near zero, even a few hidden warheads could provide tremendous coercive power; each can level a city.

The problem multiplies manyfold as more states join the nuclear club and others line up at the door. How could disarmament be imposed on the dozen or so nuclear and near-nuclear nations and the others that could make nuclear weapons over the next few years if they chose to? How could disarmament be verified and policed when college students can design A-bombs and nuclear materials are scattered around the globe? Who could impose disarmament on states such as Israel and South Africa—highly sophisticated, widely distrusted, and determined to retain nuclear weapons? Who would believe these states even if they did comply?

The current superpowers and other nuclear states seem unlikely to tolerate even a small risk of cheating, though the risk would of course be inconsequential compared with the risk of total planetary destruction that we now face every day. As H. D. S. Greenway observes, "Neither the United States nor the Soviet Union is going to put itself in a position of military inferiority to Israel and India."[70]

Even those parts of the U.S. peace movement most committed to nuclear disarmament as a present-day focus of political work are beginning to recognize these problems. In June 1987, for example, a major conference of disarmament activists met in Ringwood, New Jersey, "to discuss the requirements and the plausibility of a long-term, unified campaign to eliminate all nuclear weapons worldwide. . . . The initial impetus for the conference was a 'Disarmament 2000' campaign proposal . . . focused primarily on nuclear weapons and on the mass movement building necessary to abolish nuclear weapons by the year 2000." But according to Rob Leavitt, "There was little consensus that nuclear disarmament by 2000 was possible." The participants concluded: "It is difficult to imagine that total nuclear disarmament is possible in the absence of a new world order," enjoying, among other changes, conventional disarmament and an end to military intervention.[71]

That conclusion may be too pessimistic. A huge global mass movement (ignited, perhaps, by a nuclear accident, a small nuclear war, or some other scare) could force nuclear disarmament on the nations of the world—if it is prepared to use civil disobedience on a huge scale and to endure the terrible state violence that would likely be unleashed against it in the West, the East, and the Third World alike. Whether a powerful enough movement could be organized, and whether it could succeed, no one can know. But it is probably the *only* way nuclear disarmament could be achieved prior to radical political changes in the world order.

We must surely abandon the hope that arms control as we know it is a promising strategy for pursuing nuclear abolition. Many insist that arms control is at least a "step in the right direction." One bumper sticker reads: "The Freeze: Step One." The communications director of the largest U.S. antinuclear organization, SANE/Freeze, said in reference to the INF treaty, "Our slogan is 2000 down, 48,000 to go."[72]

The metaphor is misleading, another reflection of weaponitis. The path to nuclear disarmament is not like a continuous road from here to there on which one makes gradual progress by taking step after step. It is more like a road interrupted by a vast canyon. States can indeed take gradual steps toward the edge of the canyon—the minimum deterrent. But once there they would quickly discover not only that they still faced the threat of nuclear annihilation but also that all the prior "steps in the right direction" had not brought nuclear disarmament any closer. That goal requires *crossing* the canyon—getting the most powerful states on a violent planet to relinquish their ultimate weapons with no guaranteed assurances that all others would do the same. That is an entirely different enterprise from junking redundant weapons that don't really matter anyway.

Deep cuts in nuclear arsenals might do some good at a purely symbolic level, suggesting that if reductions are good elimination would be even better. But the symbolism could cut both ways. Dramatic progress in arms control could in fact *hurt* the prospects for abolition by breeding complacency about the nuclear peril while doing nothing to undermine the real forces that motivate states to get and keep nuclear weapons.

Those forces must be confronted *directly* by restraining the illegitimate violence of our governments wherever we can. Considering the immense power and low moral standards of modern states, world peace will of course not come in a day. But reducing aggression and intervention by the leading states is probably a prerequisite for a long-run institutional solution to international violence, whether by means of world government, conventional disarmament, the "peace system" that some advocate, or other schemes.[73] In the meantime, we must do what we can to make sure we survive long enough to find out.

In short, peace is the path to nuclear disarmament, not the other way around. Paradoxically, a disarmament movement working to reduce the weapons that it seeks to abolish probably cannot establish the conditions under which abolition might be possible. That requires a peace movement.

## CHAPTER TEN

# U.S. Foreign Policy and Nuclear War

Crisis management . . . bears a disturbing resemblance to the
ancient art of alchemy. . . . The only good strategies are those
designed to prevent crises.
—*Richard Ned Lebow,* Nuclear Crisis Management:
A Dangerous Illusion

Nuclear arms control, as we have seen, can play only a limited role in
helping to prevent nuclear war, and as currently practiced it may do no
good whatsoever. Changes in foreign policy could do far more because,
as Part II shows, almost all actual nuclear danger points have resulted
from superpower recklessness and intervention in the Third World.

## CAN THE WORLD BE MADE SAFE
## FOR CONVENTIONAL STATE VIOLENCE?

Can we avoid nuclear danger *without* constraining the conventional
violence that is raging around the world? It is in the interests of the superpowers that we believe so. Moscow does not want its actions in
Afghanistan to go down in history as a reckless threat to humanity, just
as Washington would like those concerned about nuclear war to ignore
American actions in Lebanon and the Persian Gulf.

In the United States, at least, specialists pin great hopes on "crisis
management." Former U.S. defense secretary Robert McNamara claims
that "there is no longer any such thing as strategy, only crisis management." One of its most eminent proponents, William Ury of the Harvard Law School's Nuclear Negotiation Project, goes even further:
"Thanks to fire stations and fire hydrants, emergency exits and smoke
detectors, building regulations and fire drills in school, trained firefight-
ers and their modern equipment—in short, a comprehensive fire pre-

vention and firefighting system—we live in relative safety. The same approach can be taken with crises. . . . They can be effectively stopped before they go out of control." [1]

Can they really? Even a leader who *wants* to avoid escalation may not be able to do so because the opponent's actions can be difficult to control. Deterrence, based ultimately on filling the adversary with fear of nuclear war, can surely induce caution. But as Part I makes clear, its strength rests on the existential threat of mutual annihilation and cannot be greatly boosted by shifts in weapons or doctrine. The many examples we cited in Part II leave no doubt that the existential risk is often just not enough to do the job, because—to be blunt—leaders on both sides are willing to run it periodically for their purposes of the moment.

Even if more cautious and well-intentioned leaders could be found, they would be no more able than their predecessors to confidently prevent major blunders, mishaps, and miscalculations, such as the U.S. jet that blithely wandered into Soviet airspace—and onto Soviet nuclear attack warning radars—during the Cuban missile crisis. Progress can be made. But no one, not even the professors of crisis, can repeal Murphy's Law. There are no emergency exits from nuclear war, no fire hydrants to tap to put it out, no safe ways to play with matches near the oil fields of the Middle East or the massive ammunition dumps many Third World nations have become.

As a recent reminder of the many dangers, a conference on the occasion of the twenty-fifth anniversary of the Cuban missile crisis suggested that even a quarter century of exhaustive scholarship has not revealed the full magnitude of recklessness and foul-up during the worst nuclear crisis in history, long considered an early success for deterrence and an inspiring model of crisis management. As Seymour Hersh writes, "The risks were greater than anyone in Washington knew." For apparently President Kennedy and his aides thoroughly misinterpreted one of the most crucial incidents of the crisis—the downing of an American U-2 spy plane over Cuba at the height of the tension. Assuming that Khrushchev had ordered the attack to demonstrate Soviet resolve, the Kennedy team angrily escalated the crisis, issuing an ultimatum to the Soviets to remove their missiles or face an American invasion of Cuba. As then secretary of defense Robert McNamara said at the conference, "It seemed to me that the Soviets, who had some 40,000 troops on Cuba, would . . . suffer casualties and would have to respond somewhere else in the world. That carried with it the risk that nuclear weapons would be launched." Kennedy had given the Pentagon standing orders to strike any base in Cuba that launched an attack on a U-2; his decision not to retaliate immediately "became known at the operating level in the Pentagon barely in time to prevent a planned air strike on the probable offending air defense missile site."[2]

Newly available U.S. intelligence imformation, based partly on the 1964 breaking of a Soviet code in use in 1962, suggests not only that Kennedy's interpretation of the U-2 shoot-down was incorrect, but also that the whole crisis may have been far more complex and volatile than Americans had realized. Remarkably, the Soviet troops at the anti-aircraft site in question may have been attacked, presumably by Cuban soldiers, the night before. Intercepts from the commander of an adjacent Soviet naval base reportedly indicate that his unit was counter-attacking and had taken casualties. Hersh writes that U.S. analysts "were unable to exclude the possibility that the SAM [antiaircraft] site . . . may not have been fully under Soviet control when the U-2 was shot down the next morning." No evidence of an order by Khrushchev to attack the U-2 has been found. According to Hersh, a "senior intelligence official . . . who was at the top of an intelligence agency in 1962" said, "We'll never know whether it was shot down by Cubans or Russians. . . . I doubt if even Castro knows." In 1964, Hersh asserts, the only U.S. government official who knew of the new intelligence information and understood its significance was Daniel Ellsberg, then a Rand Corporation analyst, who revealed it without citing the source in 1986.[3]

On October 31, 1987, Ellsberg added in the *New York Times* that according to Khrushchev's speech writer Fyodor Burlatsky: "Khrushchev had given very strong, very precise orders that Soviet officers should make no provocation, initiate no attack in Cuba." But Castro, wrote Ellsberg, "was determined to defend the sovereignty of Cuban air space regardless of Soviet desires to avoid provoking American retaliation." Indeed, Castro told Tad Szulc in 1984: "It was we who gave the order to fire against the low-level flights. . . . We had simply presented our viewpoint to [the Russians], our opposition to low-level flights, and we ordered our batteries to fire on them." Robert Kennedy told Ellsberg: "If one more plane was destroyed, we would hit all the SAM's immediately, and probably the [nuclear surface-to-surface] missiles as well, and we would probably follow that with an invasion." Transcripts of White House meetings on October 27, 1962, confirm that this threat "conveyed accurately to the Russians the consensus of the White House discussions that afternoon." But when Robert Kennedy delivered the

U.S. ultimatum to the Soviets after the U-2 attack, he did not realize that "the warning was directed to the wrong party. . . . Mr. Khrushchev by this point had no influence over the Cuban antiaircraft artillerymen who threatened low-flying flights." Recognizing the danger of imminent catastrophe, Khrushchev gave orders to end the crisis by dismantling the Soviet nuclear missiles in Cuba. These orders, Ellsberg writes,

> arrived in Cuba between 1 and 3 A.M. Cuban time Sunday, according to my notes from 1964. The dismantling began at 5 A.M. The race to the radio station with the Soviet announcement, which bypassed even slower diplomatic channels, came a few hours later.
>
> It came just in time. At 9 Sunday morning, about the time Moscow Radio began its broadcast, the Joint Chiefs of Staff agreed "tentatively to schedule four low-level recon flights for late afternoon, and that aircraft would fly through any fire encountered."

Castro told Szulc: "I am absolutely certain that if the low-level flights had been resumed we would have shot down one, two, or three of these planes. . . . With so many batteries firing, we would have shot down some planes. I don't know whether this would have started the nuclear war." [4]

Sergei A. Mikoyan, whose father, Anastas, was Khrushchev's special emissary to Castro, denies that a Cuban-Soviet firefight took place but agrees that Kennedy totally misinterpreted the U-2 shoot-down. Asserting that "there was no command . . . from the supreme commander [Khrushchev]," he said the attack was ordered by a "small commander." Though claiming to know who the officer was, he would not reveal the name or say whether the officer was Cuban or Russian. In either case, it is clear that a small planet could be destroyed by a small commander during a crisis over a small matter.

General Rafael del Pino Diaz, a Cuban officer who defected to the United States in May 1987, later told the Associated Press that Soviet officers had in fact shot down the plane without authorization from Moscow. "They wanted to provoke a confrontation," del Pino said, because they were outraged that Khrushchev had ordered Soviet ships to turn back from Cuba after the United States blockaded the island. Mikoyan added, "I do not exclude that there could be some elements from abroad" involved in fighting with Soviet antiaircraft troops in Cuba during the crisis, such as Cuban counterrevolutionaries, who, in another bizarre twist, were normally under CIA control. [5]

The twenty-fifth anniversary of the Cuban crisis produced another revelation. Burlatsky claimed that Soviet officers overseeing the installa-

tion of the Cuban missiles failed to follow orders that they be camou-
flaged. Consequently U.S. spy planes were able to take clear photos of
the missiles, which otherwise might have remained secret until they
were operational and probably immune to U.S. attack. Asked how such
a thing could occur, Burlatsky reportedly laughed and said, "Because it
was Russian style. They try to plan all our society, but Russian people
usually don't plan one day in his life." If true, then like the dangerous
American actions that ended the crisis, the dangerous Soviet ones that
began it may have been surrounded by a web of human confusion and
foul-up unlikely to yield to the "techniques" of crisis management.

Raymond Garthoff recently revealed that when the Strategic Air
Command went on its unprecedented Defcon II nuclear alert, immediately after Kennedy's October 22 speech, the SAC commander in chief,
General Thomas Powers, took it on himself to transmit the orders un-
coded. Naturally, "Soviet communications personnel," to say nothing of
the leadership, "must have been shocked suddenly to hear all the alert
orders from Omaha and a steady stream of responses from bomber
units reporting their attainment of alert posture, including nuclear-
armed flights poised for attack on the Soviet Union." This provocative
action was not ordered, or even known, by the president, the secretary
of defense, or top military brass "as they so carefully calibrated and
controlled action in the intensifying confrontation." Powers, it seems,
"had been ordered to go on full alert, and he did so. No one had told
him *how* to do it, so he decided to 'rub it in.'" [6]

Khrushchev had his own problems with overzealous military men. At
the end of the crisis Soviet officers opposed withdrawing the missiles.
Khrushchev asked them if they could guarantee that World War III
would not be the result of holding firm. They looked at Khrushchev, he
said, "as though I was out of my mind or, what was worse, a traitor."
Khrushchev told journalist Norman Cousins: "I said to myself, 'To hell
with these maniacs.'" [7] We can only hope that the maniacs on both sides
do not get more of a hearing the next time around.

In 1987 Garthoff revealed perhaps the most bizarre and dangerous
incident of the whole affair. It could make any would-be crisis manager
consider early retirement. Immediately after President Kennedy's dramatic speech opening the crisis on October 22, the Soviets arrested an
American and British spy, Colonel Oleg Penkovsky of Soviet military
intelligence. Garthoff, then in government, was personally responsible
for evaluating Penkovsky's information and at that time was told the

following story in strict confidence by a CIA officer who helped manage Penkovsky's operations.

Apparently the CIA had given the highly placed spy several coded signals to use over the telephone in case of emergency. They didn't bargain for what they got: "When he was being arrested, at his apartment, he had time to send a telephonic signal—but chose to use the signal for an imminent Soviet attack!" "When he was about to go down," Garthoff speculates, "he evidently decided to play Samson and bring the temple down on everyone else as well." Normally, of course, "such an attempt would have been feckless. But October 22, 1962 was not a normal day," the president of the United States having just launched the worst Soviet-American crisis in history, complete with unprecedented— and public—preparations for nuclear attack on the Soviet Union. The president and his aides were watching closely for signs of how the Soviets would react. As the usually reserved Garthoff observes:

> What if Colonel Penkovsky's farewell signal had been taken seriously? The United States might well have then undertaken some further action (such as Defcon 1) that Moscow could have construed as preparation for immediate hostilities. The President's speech on Cuba might then have been seen, in suspicious Moscow intelligence, military, and even political circles, as a feint to cover American mobilization for a first strike. Soviet military doctrine in 1962 called for *Soviet* preemption if there was a positive indication that the United States was preparing imminently and irrevocably for a first strike. SAC doctrine also called for preemption if a Soviet attack was imminent. . . . The risk and danger to both sides could have been extreme, and catastrophe cannot be excluded.

Fortunately Penkovsky's "Western intelligence handlers, at the operational level, after weighing a dilemma of great responsibility, decided not to credit Penkovsky's final signal and suppressed it. Not even the higher reaches of the CIA were informed of Penkovsky's provocative farewell." [8]

Academics and politicians rarely acknowledge the severe limitations of crisis management, perhaps because the implication—that crises must be prevented by restraining state violence—is not politically palatable. An exception is political scientist and longtime student of international crisis Richard Ned Lebow:

> Crisis management in the United States bears a disturbing resemblance to the ancient art of alchemy. Alchemists of old sought to transmute base elements into gold by simple chemistry and magical incantation. They failed because

their quest was based on a false premise; elements cannot be transmuted by chemical processes. . . . Government officials, and many academic researchers, have embarked upon a similarly fruitless quest for the secret keys to nuclear crisis management. Convinced, as were the alchemists before them, that their goal is attainable, they search for the modern day equivalent of the philosopher's stone: the organizational structures and decision-making techniques that will transmute the dark specter of nuclear destruction into the glitter of national security. Once again, the task is hopeless. . . . Like transmutation, crisis stability is theoretically possible, but for the foreseeable future it lies beyond the power of political alchemists.[9]

Rather than blundering into crises under such illusions, "leaders must show more profile and less courage," Lebow continues. "They must be less concerned with 'winning' and more concerned with controlling crises, because the principal danger is no longer that the adversary will get his way but that one or both of the protagonists will set in motion a chain of events that will lead to an undesired and catastrophic war." Yet

political leaders and their advisors still give every indication of believing that crisis management consists of controllable and reversible steps up a ladder of escalation, steps taken to moderate an adversary's behavior. Even as well known a "dove" as Edmund Muskie, who played the president in a nationally televised crisis game in 1983, demonstrated his willingness to threaten the Soviet Union with nuclear weapons and, presumably, to carry through on the threat if necessary. This is precisely the kind of behavior which, whether by accident or design, increases the likelihood of war.[10]

Lebow believes that "*the . . . most important objective of policies aimed at war prevention must be to try to prevent acute crises altogether. . . .* There is unlikely to be any such thing as good nuclear crisis management. The only good strategies are those designed to prevent crises."[11]

One reason for the tendency to ignore Lebow's warning is the widespread feeling that, whatever the dangers of political conflict and war, they cannot be eliminated for the foreseeable future. True, peaceful coexistence among nationalities, races, states, and classes is still inconceivable. There is little hope that the leading states will renounce violence as a means to maintain and extend their political power wherever they feel it can succeed.

But neither nuclear arms *nor* war—which together produce the nuclear threat—is likely to disappear soon. The only sensible question to ask is whether chipping away at them can make a difference to the danger. Incremental steps toward the abolition of nuclear weapons, as we have emphasized, are almost meaningless considering the absolute de-

structive potential and uncontrollability of those that remain. The same
is not true of efforts to prevent war and other forms of conventional political violence. Successful incremental steps in this direction matter a
great deal—both to those who would have been maimed and killed and
to the rest of us, who are thereby spared one more occasion on which
events could slip out of hand and terminate civilization. Today George
Kennan's proposed 50 percent across-the-board cut in nuclear arms
would mean little. A 50 percent cut in superpower military intervention
and nuclear risk taking in the Third World might save the planet and
would certainly save many lives.

The long-term visions of a nonnuclear world and of a world beyond
war should not be cast aside. Ultimately they may be the only chance for
planetary survival, and they are certainly the only chance for a decent
way of life. But we must accept that neither goal can be reached easily or
rapidly, and that they may never be reached. We must take what steps
we can to reduce the nuclear threat now. Otherwise there may be no
long run to worry about.


FOREIGN POLICY: THE REAL
BATTLEGROUND OF THE NUCLEAR ISSUE

One conclusion at least should be uncontroversial: reducing the risk
of nuclear war requires that states take that risk into account when
planning foreign policy much more than they have so far. In democ-
racies such as the United States, that means serious public debate about
the nuclear risks of government actions around the world. Considering
the stakes, one would expect front-page newspaper stories, prominent
statements by the president and other politicians, debate in scholarly
journals, prime-time television coverage, and so on. With few exceptions, these now appear only in the most extreme cases, such as the
1962 and 1973 crises, and then only after a crisis has already erupted.

Anyone unwilling to accept the need for such debate must deny either the nuclear risks of Third World intervention or the necessity of
publicly debating those risks in a democracy. An editor at the *Boston
Globe,* for example, told one of the authors that there is "zero risk" of
nuclear war arising from regional conflicts and U.S. military interventions outside of Europe, Japan, and the Middle East. Presidents Eisenhower, Kennedy, Johnson, and Nixon did not entertain such happy illusions. *Some* risk is surely entailed when U.S. marines go to Lebanon in
the aftermath of an invasion and fighting between U.S. and Soviet client

states, when U.S. jets bomb Libya, a Soviet client, or when a huge U.S. armada intervenes in a complex Persian Gulf war on the Soviet Union's doorstep. Certainly if the Soviets committed large forces on the U.S. doorstep, say, in the Gulf of Mexico, few here would doubt the dangers.

Others may acknowledge the risk but justifiably fear that openly debating it would hobble foreign policy by reducing public support for U.S. military intervention. The "serious war scare" that Nixon sought to avoid through secrecy in (among others) the 1970 Cuban crisis could sweep the country in future Third World operations should the dangers become widely known.[12] The general population evidently lacks the stomach for its leaders' nuclear risk taking. Surely in a democracy the proper role of such risk taking in foreign policy is not something for a handful of officials to decide in secret.

That is the minimalist message of our book: even those who admire American foreign policy should have the honesty to think about its nuclear risks and to debate them openly. Those who still support or condone potentially dangerous military actions, such as the 1987–1988 Persian Gulf intervention, should openly say why they are willing to run the gamble and why the United States or any other state has the right to run even small risks of nuclear war to further its foreign policy of the moment.

## THE ULTIMATE ENVIRONMENTAL IMPACT STATEMENT

A small first step might be to take a cue from the environmental movement, extending the application of environmental impact statements to the evaluation of foreign and military policy. If the environmental impact of power plants and dams deserves to be weighed in advance, then the risk factors for nuclear war—the ultimate environmental catastrophe—certainly do too.

If done with an honest appreciation of how easily things can go wrong, such statements could raise serious questions about the dozens of ongoing U.S. Third World operations, including outright military interventions (e.g., the Persian Gulf), "secret" wars (e.g., Afghanistan, Cambodia, Angola), proxy wars (e.g., Nicaragua), the military backing of states engaged in civil or extraterritorial wars or military occupations (e.g., El Salvador, Israel, Chad), and many covert actions at lower levels of violence. Such evaluations would surely be speculative and open to interpretation, but given the record and the stakes, shouldn't we in a democracy consider and debate them?

## WHY DOES THE UNITED STATES ROLL THE NUCLEAR DICE?

Moving beyond the obvious need for debate about nuclear risk taking, we must ask what this risk taking is all about. Our discussion will focus on the role of the United States. Though it certainly does not cause all international conflict and violence, it contributes often enough, through its foreign policy, through arms transfers, through direct military intervention, and through its vast network of Third World client states, many highly despotic and violent.[13] More to the point, Americans can influence their own government more than any other, particularly because it is a democracy with opportunities for public influence over foreign policy. Criticizing the Soviets is easy but usually ineffectual. Doing so while ignoring American actions is hypocritical. No one would listen to a wife beater who denounced his neighbor for the same crime. Even if the United States were responsible for only 1 percent of the political conflict and violence that could flare into nuclear war, the first moral duty of concerned Americans would be to understand and oppose their own nation's contribution to the problem.

The historical record shows that the American contribution to the nuclear threat has come mostly from intentional political choices, not intellectual error or ignorance. Despite the myth and confusion about the sources of nuclear risk documented throughout this book, American leaders have generally understood, crudely at least, the hazards accompanying their conduct of foreign policy. As the memoirs cited in Part II reveal, they have been well aware that their more reckless foreign adventures could flare into nuclear confrontation. They are simply willing to run the risk, and in some cases actually *want* to do so to intimidate enemies.

This behavior gives the lie to the common notion that everyone is against nuclear war. Certainly every sane person would prefer that nuclear war not occur. But many are willing, and on occasion eager, to run significant *risks* of nuclear war to advance the goals of the state to which they pledge loyalty. This is the real political difference between those who are truly committed to avoiding nuclear danger and those who are not—the false difference being whether or not one supports the MX missile or the nuclear freeze. Mainstream American politicians, both Republicans and Democrats, do not mind rolling the nuclear dice over militarily meaningless missiles in Cuba, a beaten and surrounded Egyptian army, or a few Kuwaiti tankers. That, in the real world, makes them nuclear hawks, whatever their views on Star Wars and the START treaty. Authentic nuclear doves, rare among the American political elite, do not regard periodically endangering the planet as a legitimate way to pursue American objectives in the world.

Even national self-defense would not justify the killing of millions of innocents any more than an individual citizen has the right to spray machine-gun fire indiscriminately into a crowd to protect himself from a mugger. In any case, no nuclear state has faced a serious foreign threat to its physical or political survival *except* for nuclear war.[14] A policy of strict self-defense would have avoided *every* nuclear crisis—including Hiroshima and Nagasaki, which the United States incinerated well after the war in Europe was over and Japanese offensive military power had been destroyed.

If self-defense has not been the motive for nuclear risk taking, then what has? The question has political importance: if the goals turned out to be extraordinarily noble, some would deem the risks justifiable (although the generations whose future was permanently risked might not agree). In addition to self-defense, U.S. military operations are commonly justified as either (1) humanitarian missions for democracy, freedom, human rights, or other lofty moral goals or (2) necessary, if sometimes unpleasant, rescue operations to save weak peoples from Soviet aggression or expansionism. Taking these in turn, let us see if they account for the most significant instances of U.S. nuclear risk taking since the Cuban missile crisis.

Moral considerations certainly played no great role, as they rarely do in the conduct of powerful states. In 1967, during the Six-Day War, the most dangerous incidents followed Soviet threats to intervene after Israeli forces posed a threat first to the Egyptian heartland and then, far more seriously, to the capital of Syria. Regardless of one's views of Arab versus Israeli responsibility for the war itself (an issue we cannot take up here), Johnson's provocative military actions seem far out of proportion to any legitimate political purpose, particularly given his belief that they involved significant nuclear risks. By the standards of modern international affairs, it would be hard to question the legitimacy of superpower efforts to deter an attack on the capital of an ally by invading enemy forces, particularly when the invading forces are violating a cease-fire agreement. According to Wells, Rusk and Johnson both believed that Israeli actions "gave Moscow a 'legitimate' reason for intervention."[15]

In 1973 the Arab states started the war. Again if we abstract away from the political issues, the circumstances of superpower confrontation were remarkably similar: after Israel (having turned the tables) struck deep into Arab territory, the Soviet Union told the United States that it "could not be indifferent to threats to Damascus." Later, after the Israelis violated a cease-fire agreement, the Soviets threatened to intervene if Israel continued its destruction of the Egyptian Third Army, in the process posing "a potential threat to Cairo itself." Kissinger acknowledged that the Soviets "could not possibly hold still while a cease-fire they had cosponsored was turned into a trap for a client state." At the time Kissinger reportedly said: "My God, the Russians will think that I have double-crossed them. And in their shoes, who wouldn't?" In fact, "if [Kissinger] had communicated the importance of an immediate cease-fire to Tel Aviv, the [nuclear] crisis never would have occurred." [16] Nevertheless, the U.S. alerted its nuclear weapons worldwide and prepared airborne troops for a ground intervention that could have led to the first (and possibly final) major U.S.-Soviet combat of the nuclear age. Kissinger was not concerned that he had actually authorized Israeli cease-fire violations while in Tel Aviv (see Chapter 6); that he almost certainly could have compelled the Israelis to halt their attacks sooner, thereby ending the crisis; or that the United States had previously refused Sadat's request for *joint* superpower intervention to stop the fighting.

Moral considerations certainly did not influence the Nixon-Kissinger "tilt toward Pakistan" in the 1971 Indo-Pakistani war, a policy described elsewhere as "tilting toward massacre." As Kalb and Kalb put it, "The United States found itself siding with a corrupt Pakistani dictatorship against the world's most populous democracy." In what one commentator described as "the most massive calculated savagery that has been visited on a civil population in recent times," the Pakistani government brutally suppressed dissent by East Pakistani Bengalis, 98 percent of whom had voted for autonomy in the free elections held in December 1970. Moreover, Pakistan dragged India into the conflict by bombing eight Indian airfields around West Pakistan and rolling armored columns into Indian Kashmir. Kissinger acknowledges in his memoirs that "Pakistan had unquestionably acted unwisely, brutally, and even immorally"—somewhat of an understatement considering that an estimated one million East Pakistani civilians were killed during the civil war, many by West Pakistani atrocities. McConnell and Calhoun agree that "from the beginning of the crisis in March, the U.S. was painfully aware of the poor moral position in which the Pakistanis had put themselves and their supporter." Yet for them, as for Kissinger, morality was not the point: "The Pakistanis had to be saved from themselves." The Bengalis, however, were not to be saved from the Pakistanis. [17]

Regarding the 1970 War of Attrition crisis too, Kissinger explicitly called attention to some ethical difficulties of U.S. actions: "Our agencies blamed Israel for the tension along the Suez Canal, arguing—not without evidence—that Israel had provoked the Soviet reaction by its deep penetration raids," which again posed a threat to the Egyptian heartland and capital. George agrees that "many U.S. officials tended to the view that Israeli belligerence had provoked Soviet intervention. Besides, it dawned on American policymakers that they could not really object to direct Soviet assistance limited to preventing the collapse of its Egyptian ally." Yet the Nixon administration had "condoned, if it did not tacitly support," the Israeli deep penetration attacks. Kissinger "took pleasure in anticipating that the Israeli air raids would demonstrate to the Egyptian leader that his superpower ally could not render effective assistance and that this lesson would lead Nasser eventually to contemplate a rapprochement with the United States."[18]

Jordan's Black September crisis of the same year may seem an exception to the rule, since Syrian armor reportedly crossed the frontier into Jordan to fight alongside the Palestinians resisting King Hussein's efforts to use the Jordanian Army to expel them. Arguably, any direct Israeli or U.S. intervention would have been to protect the Jordanian government from an invader. But, as we saw, the Syrian "invasion" may have been an Israeli fabrication. The United States did not know what was going on. Many believed that reports of the Syrian intervention were only a "pretext" for the involvement of U.S. or Israeli forces.[19] Whatever one's view of this complex crisis, it was not an obvious case of unprovoked outside aggression resisted by a superpower protector.

To mention one recent example, in the U.S. Persian Gulf intervention of 1987–1988 U.S. warships defended shipping against attacks by one of the combatants, Iran, while ignoring many attacks on commercial ships and even an American warship by the other, Iraq. Iraq happens to have started both the war—by invading Iran in 1980—and the practice of attacking tankers (not to mention the use of chemical weapons on civilians); it attacked far more ships than Iran and caused many more casualties among seamen. Again, unsurprisingly, politics rather than morality was the motive for violence that could escalate in unpredictable ways in a sensitive region near the USSR.

In addition to moral justifications, the standard rationale for U.S. nuclear risk taking and military intervention in general is that it has been necessary to prevent global Soviet aggression. It is clear, however, that U.S. nuclear risk taking in the most serious crises since 1962 has not been in response to Soviet efforts to "expand" or even to instigate Soviet

allies to do so. The Soviets have certainly acted aggressively and brutally, for example, in Hungary, Czechoslovakia, and particularly Afghanistan. But they have usually been careful to *avoid* expansive actions
beyond their border regions that could lead to superpower crisis and nuclear confrontation—within limits working to prevent such crises even
at considerable political cost and, if unsuccessful, to de-escalate and contain them. This pattern of course implies nothing benign about the Soviet
dictatorship beyond a rational desire to avoid planetary incineration.

Secretly moving nuclear arms to Cuba in 1962 after Kennedy had
said that he would not permit it was a reckless Soviet provocation that
could have led to nuclear war—a major exception to Soviet nuclear caution. Referring to comparable U.S. deployments in Turkey and elsewhere on the periphery of the Soviet Union, however, Khrushchev notes
in his memoir that he was "doing nothing more than giving [the Ameri-
cans] a little of their own medicine."[20] And once the crisis ignited, as
Kaplan emphasizes, unlike Washington, "the Kremlin refrained from
provocative military activities. Moscow even allowed Soviet submarines
joining Russian freighters en route to Cuba to suffer U.S. Navy harassment. . . . The only really provocative military action directed against
the United States during the crisis was the shooting down over Cuba of a
U-2 aircraft by a SAM missile," which, as we have seen, may not have
been the work of the Soviet leadership at all.[21]

In neither 1967 nor 1973 did the Soviets appear to encourage an
Arab-Israeli war, though like the United States they provided weapons.
Under complex circumstances Israel, not the Soviet-backed Arab states,
started the 1967 war.[22] And the Soviets strictly limited their threat of
intervention to the defense of their allies' capitals—not an aggressive or
expansionist aim, whatever one's judgment of it. As Anthony Wells
notes:

> The course of the war showed . . . that the Russian commitment [to Arab
> clients] did not extend to the territorial integrity of the Arab countries but
> only to "the vital centers and existing regimes of its sponsored states." . . .
> Thus, while the seizure of the Sinai did indeed produce a Soviet threat to in-
> tervene, the Soviets dropped that threat when the Israelis stopped at the Suez
> Canal. The threat to intervene was raised again—intensively—when the Syr-
> ian forces collapsed as the Israelis stormed the Golan Heights on June 9, a
> collapse that left the road to Damascus virtually undefended.

As President Johnson was no doubt aware, the attack on the Golan
Heights violated an agreed cease-fire. And, as Jabber and Kolkowicz
note, "the Soviet Union refrained from any demonstration of force. . . .

For the most part, the Soviet eskadra [of naval forces]—the only instrument available to the Russians for the regional projection of military power between June 5 and 10, 1967—behaved as if no Middle East war were under way." With the exception of one incident of harassment of an American ship, "Soviet naval behavior seems, in fact, to have been deliberately orchestrated to reassure the United States that the Mediterranean Squadron did not intend to take part in the crisis." "A few minor adjustments in routine procedures" by the Soviets "were negligible compared with the extensive American use of naval forces during the war." [23]

Commenting on the 1973 Arab attack, Stephen Roberts notes: "Arab testimony suggests that, in 1971 and 1972 at least, Moscow did not want its clients to go to war; and even in 1973, when the U.S.S.R. resumed arms supply, its central motive may have been not to incite war but to maintain some influence over a policy of war already resolved upon by Egypt regardless of the availability of Soviet assistance." Sadat, one should remember, had expelled most Soviet advisers from Egypt in 1972. George points out that "as many specialists on Soviet policy in the Middle East have recognized, Soviet leaders tried for several years to discourage Sadat from resorting to force. Although important facts remain obscure and unverified, it appears that at first the Soviets did withhold military equipment and supplies deemed necessary by Sadat for a major Arab attack. The Soviets also counseled Sadat to seek his objectives through diplomacy rather than force. Kissinger was quite aware of the Soviets' actions at the time." According to Bruce Porter, not one to overlook Soviet aggressiveness, "The historical record argues that the Soviet leadership did not want the October war." He quotes Sadat that "the U.S.S.R. persisted in the view that a military battle must be ruled out and that the question must await a peaceful conference." He also supports Sadat's claim that the Soviets were not even informed about the plans for war until October 3, and not about the details until October 4, two days before the attack. Interestingly, according to George, the Soviet Union's decision "reflected its expectation that the Arab states would suffer another quick defeat if they attacked Israel. In that event the Soviet Union would be faced once again, as in 1967 and 1970, with the difficult task of bailing the Arabs out, thereby risking a military confrontation with Israeli forces if not also with the United States." Not a bad call. [24]

The Soviets actually warned the United States that Sadat might attack if rapid diplomatic progress were not made. As George notes, at the June 1973 summit Brezhnev "hammered at" Nixon about the danger and delivered more warnings through other channels; "but as so often happens, the recipient of the warning did not regard it as credible."[25] Immediately after learning that an Arab attack was forthcoming, Moscow quickly retreated from the impending trouble, evacuating Soviet advisers and their dependents from Egypt and Syria and sending major elements of its Mediterranean squadron out to sea. "To the Arabs, these measures conveyed the unmistakable message that Moscow was washing its hands of the entire affair." As Porter notes, even after the war broke out the Soviets evidently tried to end it quickly. He cites evidence that "Moscow made a serious effort to contain the conflict in its first four days, before concluding that a military supply bridge would be necessary." And he observes, "The Soviet Union made cautious and calculated responses to U.S. actions throughout the conflict. There is every evidence to indicate that the Kremlin wanted to contain the conflict and to avoid an overt confrontation with Washington."[26]

Referring to the 1970 Black September crisis, Abram Shulsky notes that "the Soviets had much to lose and relatively little to gain." King Hussein "was somewhat sheltered by a temporary alliance he had made with Nasser, who remained the chief Soviet client in the Middle East." Shulsky found it "difficult to determine the extent of the Soviet role in the original Syrian decision to invade Jordan."[27] William Quandt writes that "although the Soviet Union has not revealed much about its role in the Jordanian crisis, it did not seem to feel that any major Soviet interests were at stake. Washington's view that the U.S.S.R. was intimately involved in the Syrian intervention is certainly an exaggeration." Indeed, "as early as September 18 the U.S.S.R. had reportedly sent Nixon a moderate message that it would not intervene and that it would restrain Syria. . . . All in all, the U.S.S.R. must have felt the United States was deliberately overreacting by placing a large share of the blame on it." Quandt also reports an interview in which "a high-ranking Jordanian official" claimed that "the Jordanians learned after the crisis that the U.S.S.R. did try to restrain the Syrians and urged them to withdraw their forces." Similarly, Mahmoud Riad, then the Egyptian foreign minister, ridicules Kissinger's claims of deep Soviet involvement: "The only role played by the U.S.S.R. during the events of Jordan, as proved by its communications with us in Egypt and by its contacts with the Syrians and Iraqis, was to urge the containment of the crisis rather than accelerate it."[28]

As George Breslauer observes of other events that year, "The Soviets neither instigated nor encouraged Nasser's launching of the War of Attrition. According to Heikal, in May 1969, Soviet leaders 'begged Nasser to use every effort to halt the "war of attrition" across the Suez Canal.'" Ultimately the Soviet military role was large but, as in other crises, defensive; its purpose was, as Dismukes observes, to "salvage a key client *in extremis.*" As a result of the Israeli deep penetration air raids, the Soviets became "concerned with the security of Egypt's vital center—and perhaps even the survival of the Nasser regime itself." Indeed, since "Israeli politicians . . . spoke of their intention to bring Egypt to its knees and to topple the Nasser regime," one can hardly accuse the Soviets of expansionism for executing "the earlier Soviet decision to defend Egypt against Israeli saturation bombing." They "made some efforts to persuade the United States to curb the Israeli deep penetration air operations" and warned that they would "see to it" that the Arab states could defend their territory. Many U.S. officials "felt that Israel [had] brought on the Soviet response by a reckless bombing campaign and irresponsible rhetoric aimed at the Nasser regime's existence." [29]

Initially the Soviets were extremely careful to intervene only for direct defense of the Egyptian interior and even then to avoid initiating combat.

> They had deployed interceptor aircraft from their air defense forces not ground attack aircraft that could directly threaten the Israelis in the Sinai. . . . Their flight operations showed extraordinary circumspection. In the initial period they did not threaten, much less attack, Israeli aircraft intruding deep into Egyptian airspace. . . . It is difficult to avoid the conclusion that at this early stage Soviet pilots were under orders that, at a minimum, prevented them from firing unless fired upon and may well have directed them to avoid contact with Israeli aircraft entirely. . . . The Soviets unquestionably hoped that their objectives—the first and controlling of which was the restoration of the security of the Egyptian heartland—could be achieved without combat.

Later, after withering Israeli air attacks, the Soviets moved antiaircraft batteries up to defend the Canal zone and, as we described in Chapter 6, Soviet-Israeli combat developed. But the Soviets did not threaten Israeli territory. [30]

The Soviets apparently did not encourage the 1971 Indo-Pakistani war either. According to McConnell and Calhoun, "all the evidence suggested that Moscow did not want war and repeatedly cautioned the Indians against launching one." Once hostilities were in progress, "it . . . seems unlikely that Moscow wanted to stage a demonstration of support for India against Pakistan, let alone actually intervene on Delhi's behalf. . . . The U.S.S.R. had no incentive to intervene. Rather, her great fear was of possible intervention by other outsiders, and she wanted to avoid taking steps that would help others justify their involvement." [31] Hall asserts that "in private conversations with Indian officials, Soviet officials tirelessly advocated military nonintervention in the civil war." As Garthoff notes, "Virtually no Western (or Pakistani) historian now, or political analyst at the time, would characterize India as having been a proxy for the Soviet Union. Nor would students of Soviet policy." And "there is . . . no evidence that the Soviets had at any time pushed the Indians toward aggrandizement or military action"—a view the U.S. State Department and the CIA shared at the time. [32]

## THE REAL POLITICS OF
## NUCLEAR WAR AND PEACE

It is difficult to avoid the conclusion that U.S. leaders have run calculated nuclear risks not for self-defense, high moral principles, or the protection of weak countries from the Soviets, but to further U.S. power—to shore up friendly despots engaged in internal massacres in Jordan and Pakistan, to prevent the Soviets from defending the capitals of their own friendly despots in Egypt and Syria, and to twice seek hazy psychopolitical gain over militarily irrelevant weapons in Cuba. These crises were not isolated or idiosyncratic. They grew from long-standing U.S. foreign policies that if unchanged will probably continue to imperil the planet.

The decisions to rush to the aid of King Hussein and General Kahn, for example, did not spring from love of these men or admiration for the massacres they were presiding over, but from the key roles assigned to Jordan and Pakistan in American plans for the Middle East and Asia. The United States might run similar risks today in support of Hussein or the late General Zia's successor in Pakistan. Pakistanis still worry about "a repetition of 1971." [33] Everyone worries about another Middle East war that could engulf King Hussein. [34]

Americans concerned about the nuclear peril can stop studying the details of the arms race and begin learning about the history, character, and driving forces of their government's political and military role in the world, large topics we cannot take up here. They will want to ask at least two basic questions that would be at the heart of a reasonable inquiry by Americans into the politics of nuclear war and peace: (1) To what degree has the United States been responsible for the international tensions and conflicts that could have led to nuclear war? and (2) Were the goals and results of hazardous U.S. actions worth the terrible risks? Such an inquiry may lead to unpleasant realizations—not only that this country has often used and promoted violence and instability in the Third World's many potential nuclear tinderboxes, but also that with few exceptions U.S. behavior in the Third World has no more been motivated by self-defense, altruism, or Soviet "containment" than it was in the crises discussed in this book.

The United States has consistently acted in the nuclear age much as leading states did in the prenuclear one (including states with significant elements of internal democracy, such as ancient Athens and imperial Britain): seeking wealth and power wherever possible, a process requiring much violence, sometimes against big-power competitors but usually against indigenous populations. Formerly the inevitable military disasters of great powers—the fall of ancient Rome, the British defeat by American revolutionaries, the Ottoman collapse in the First World War, the defeat of Nazi Germany in the second—might ravage an empire or, in the last case, a continent and more. Today it could destroy the planet. What threatens the world today is not nuclear weapons per se—the nuclear danger would be small, though real, if nuclear states pursued peaceful foreign policies—but an ancient pattern of aggressive political behavior mindlessly carried forward by the United States, the Soviet Union, and others into the nuclear era.

As illustrations of the motives, character, and consequences of post–World War II U.S. intervention in the Third World, briefly consider two cases now largely forgotten by all but participants and academic specialists: the American installation of client governments by force in the Dominican Republic and Guatemala. In 1965, shortly after the supposedly sobering shock of the 1962 Cuban crisis, the United States invaded the Dominican Republic to defeat a "populist uprising," led by constitutionalist military officers, that had "widespread popular support." The U.S. force ultimately comprised 23,000 troops, with several thousand more waiting offshore with a Navy task force "almost half as large as the one then engaged in a full-scale war in Vietnam." This massive intervention—"almost universally opposed around the world" and "in direct defiance of international law"—did not occasion a superpower standoff because the Soviets did not interfere. In the standard view, "the prospect that the USSR would have committed itself to the protection of a radical government in the Dominican Republic, in the face of a firm U.S. threat to take military action to prevent a new Cuba [*sic*], must be considered as nil." But "it is of course easier to be confident of such an assessment in retrospect, for the USSR did in fact remain on the sidelines throughout the crisis."[35]

Again the United States faced no conceivable security threat from the tiny country, intervened on the side of the opponents (not the supporters) of human rights and democracy, and was opposing communist expansionism only in propaganda. According to the *Wall Street Journal*'s Philip Geyelin, who had access to official records and cables, within the first day of the rebellion "the Santo Domingo [U.S.] Embassy had clearly cast its lot with the 'loyalist' military cabal and against the rebellion's original aim: The return of [elected president] Juan Bosch." U.S. officials evidently encouraged the bombing and shelling of Santo Domingo itself, actions that led to "widespread hatred" of the Air Force commander, Wessin. Bosch was no Communist, but the United States had become "increasingly disenchanted with [his] nationalism; with his determination to engage in substantial social reform measures, which alienated Dominican businessmen, landowners, and the Catholic church; and, most important, with his refusal to crack down on radical groups." As for the quality of U.S. motives for military intervention, Slater cites the desire to maintain "a general position of predominance throughout the Central American Caribbean area," to protect "U.S. prestige and credibility around the world" and, "psychologically," the U.S. role in Vietnam, to protect President Johnson's domestic political fortunes, and to safeguard the careers of lower-level foreign policy specialists in the U.S. government fearful of being charged with "losing" the Dominican Republic.[36]

The U.S. ambassador, John Bartlow Martin, had earlier been "informed by the CIA that there were 'not more than one hundred well-trained, fully-committed, and fully-disciplined' Dominican communists" and that they were split between Moscow- and Peking-oriented factions. "Martin was convinced that the communists, weak and divided as they were, did not constitute a threat to the government." Indeed, "there was no organized communist or leftist guerrilla movement." As Barnet notes, "The threat was not that the communists had taken over [the rebellion] but that events were out of control and might lead to a nationalist, anti-U.S. regime that could look to Castro or to Moscow for help. As Slater emphasizes, "A genuinely indigenous revolution was in fact a far cry from international Communist aggression," and even if successful "would in fact almost certainly be independent of Moscow, Peking, or Havana."[37]

Ambassador Martin unilaterally established an interim government under Antonio Imbert, a leader of "known opportunism, predilection for power, and widespread unpopularity in the Dominican Republic." "Predictably enough, Imbert immediately set out to form a military dictatorship and to destroy the constitutionalists and any other opposition, imprisoning, torturing, and even murdering hundreds of Dominicans." The actions of the Dominican police and military have been accurately described as "terrorism," and "although the Johnson administration had proclaimed as one of the principal reasons for the intervention the need to save lives in a bloody civil war, most of the estimated 3,000 Dominican deaths occurred after the intervention, some of them in clashes between the constitutionalists and U.S. troops and the rest at the hands of a Dominican military that the United States had rescued from probable annihilation in April and thereafter helped protect and rebuild." In May, in one particularly brutal operation the United States supported, Imbert's troops engaged in a "brutal slaughter of hundreds of constitutionalists and innocent civilians," even though "the constitutionalists were helpless anyway in the face of 23,000 American troops and a rebuilt Dominican police and military, and they knew it." Slater comments, "In such circumstances, to have taken lives deliberately in exchange for slight political advantage was morally questionable, to put it as mildly as possible." He concludes that "a decade later there is very little democracy in the Dominican Republic. The country is not a 'showcase' of anything." Indeed, Amnesty International reported that in the early 1970s an average of one person "disappeared" in the country each day, while the infamous La Banda death squad was "openly tolerated and supported by the National Police." [38]

In another "morally questionable" Third World operation, the United States intervened in Guatemala in 1954 to topple the government of Jacobo Arbenz Guzman, who had won democratic elections in 1951 with nearly twice as many votes as all the other candidates combined. Like Bosch, Arbenz was certainly not a Communist but a mild social reformer, and there was no serious "communist threat" in the country. Indeed, "there were perhaps as many as three thousand Communist-party members or active sympathizers in a country of three million," and most "were scarcely under the discipline of Moscow," with the leadership "split between Moscow-oriented and nationalist factions." Guatemala "was receiving no aid from the Soviet Union [and] indeed had [no] relationship with the communist bloc." [39] But trying to relieve the crushing poverty and despair among the vast bulk of the peasant population, Arbenz incurred the wrath of the United States by a modest program of land and social reform, including the expropriation of several hundred thousand acres of uncultivated land owned by United Fruit Company (which owned much of the country). Arbenz offered to compensate United Fruit at exactly the value the company had claimed for the land in tax statements to the Guatemalan government, but the company refused.

Instead, the CIA arranged for a coup, which, as Stephen Schlesinger observes from U.S. government documents obtained under the Freedom of Information Act, "was conceived of and run at the highest levels of the American Government in closest cahoots with the United Fruit Company and under the overall direction of Secretary of State John Foster Dulles, backed by President Eisenhower." The CIA established bases for an invasion force in Honduras and Nicaragua led by a Guatemalan colonel named Castillo Armas. When the attack began, American pilots bombed Guatemala City. In case anyone should doubt the official U.S. role in this adventure, at one point the American ambassador, John Peurifoy, "strapped a .45 to his belt and began to lead the operation." The ambassador's plane later flew Colonel Armas to the capital to assume leadership of the country, which he did, by jailing thousands of political prisoners, destroying the labor movement (killing over two hundred union leaders), abolishing the secret ballot, and disenfranchising the "illiterate masses," 70 percent of the population.[40]

Even though the Soviet Union's main response to the coup was to ask the United Nations to dispatch a peacekeeping force, the United States dramatically flew nuclear-armed heavy bombers from the Strategic Air Command to Nicaragua, presumably to signal its commitment to the success of the operation in the unlikely event of Soviet interference.[41] Once again, the planners were well aware that even the "safest" operations have wider dangers.

Guatemala quickly became one of the most violent and miserable countries in the world, with tens of thousands murdered and "disappeared" by the government and allied right-wing organizations, and hundreds of thousands dead of malnutrition and avoidable disease. "Death squad murders averaged almost ten a day through the first half of the 1970's," and as Amnesty International noted, "it is invariably reported in the Guatemalan press that [death squad victims] show signs of having been tortured and mutilated before death." In the early 1980s, the *Boston Globe* reported that the Guatemalan army and police turned the nation into "the hemisphere's heart of darkness," with comparisons to "the Uganda of Idi Amin or the Cambodia of Pol Pot." At the time of the 1987–1988 Arias peace plan for Central America, although all nations in the region were obliged to release political prisoners, Guatemala could not comply: since the U.S.-backed coup that plunged the little nation from an experiment in democracy into unending terror in 1954, "the thousands abducted had all been killed."[42]

If these are the sorts of "interests" for which the United States frequently intervenes, then no gut-wrenching moral choices are necessary to choose between safeguarding the planet from nuclear war and safeguarding it from conventional aggression and exploitation. We can and must do both by opposing the militarism of the United States and, to the extent we can, of the Soviet Union and others.

## THE FUNCTIONS OF WEAPONITIS AND THE POLITICS OF SURVIVAL

Weaponitis persists, while the real sources of nuclear peril are ignored, partly because of an error in thought—the incorrect diagnosis of the arms race as the main danger of the nuclear age. The error, however, is useful; weaponitis serves important interests of the parties to the nuclear debate.

Weaponitis most obviously benefits those who profit from the continual arms buildup it legitimates: the huge defense corporations that build the weapons, the military bureaucracies that buy and control them, and the professional military strategists and intellectuals who make their livings and their reputations by rationalizing and planning the arms race. To acknowledge that the arms race no longer matters to the security and power of the United States would be bad business for military contractors and bad politics for the military. Corporate executives want to increase, not undermine, the market for their products, just as military officers want to command more, not fewer, nuclear weapons systems and new ones rather than old ones.

Similarly, to dominate the nuclear debate after existential deterrence took hold in the 1950s, the experts on throw weight, hard target kill capability, and the like had to make it appear that such matters continued to be important. They erected an imposing edifice of deterrence theory and related historical lore that only the specialists can fully master and that makes the details of the hardware seem vitally important. Looking at the nuclear problem from a different, more political, point of view would cede the issue to other intellectual approaches—and to other intellectuals.

Moreover, if intellectuals in government, private think tanks such as the Rand Corporation, and academia want to stay friendly with the powers that be and remain on their lucrative contract lists, they must frame inquiry into the nuclear issue, like other issues, in an ideologically acceptable manner. Weaponitis does the job nicely, even when disagreements about technical details emerge within the paradigm. Denouncing, say, road-mobile ICBMs in favor of rail-mobile ones may at worst annoy government officials holding a different view. Denouncing American foreign policy, beyond narrow limits, can get one blacklisted.

For the government itself, and for those who support the essentials of its long-standing, bipartisan foreign policy, weaponitis has an irresistible virtue: in a society deeply alarmed by the possibility of nuclear war, it diverts attention from Third World U.S. military interventionism and toward the far less important nuclear arms competition. Arms control plays a particularly important role in this process, as we noted in Chapter 9. It is a widely popular, seemingly progressive, and highly visible activity that the state can use to show its commitment to reducing the nuclear danger. The executive branch manages the negotiation process and the information flow about it. The Soviets can be blamed for problems even when the Americans are balking. Years can be spent working out treaties on minor issues such as the Euromissiles, with tremendous public relations bonanzas at the end if the efforts succeed. And all the while Soviet and American leaders can bomb Third World countries, support unstable dictatorships, arm belligerents, pursue foreign policy as usual, and still receive relatively good press on the nuclear question because of their "commitment to arms control." This manipulation cleverly coopts the peace movement's critique of the arms race into a slick government public relations tool. It is an effective way to manage an issue that could explode into serious popular dissent and unrest if the public grasped where the real hazards lie.

For American politicians, particularly in the large political center, arms control is a uniquely comfortable politics. It provides a popular, nearly risk-free agenda for "addressing" the nuclear problem. Liberal arms control supporters earn much political support this way, even from progressives, while countenancing and sometimes actively encouraging military interventions in Afghanistan, Lebanon, Cambodia, and the Persian Gulf in a time of enormous public concern about war and peace.

The downside of weaponitis for the politicians is an occasional peace movement victory, perhaps the scaling back or someday even the cancellation of a weapons system, and a few arms control treaties concluded under public pressure. In most cases the actual result is programs to build enormously costly nuclear systems with a cleaner political bill of health, such as the purportedly stabilizing Midgetman missile to "replace" the MXs not built, or the variety of conventional and nuclear arms destined to "compensate" for the Euromissiles banned under INF. These are all small potatoes. They do not greatly affect American foreign policy or American power in the world.

The real threat of the anti–nuclear war movement has always been that it might politicize and encourage a mass revolt against American militarism in the Third World. This could well occur if the U.S. population realized that the victims include not only Salvadorans, Nicaraguans, Lebanese, Libyans, Grenadans, Angolans, and so on, but potentially themselves and their families as well. As long as concerned citizens busy themselves with learning MX missile throw weights and Pershing II flight times, demonstrating at nuclear weapons bases, and pressuring Congress about Star Wars, this threat is coopted.

These functions of weaponitis have not gone completely unnoticed within the anti–nuclear weapons movement. Activist Tom Atlee observes that weapons systems and arms control proposals—technically complex and easily multiplied year after year—are ideal for keeping the opposition busily ineffective. He asks, "Could it be that our friends in the Military Industrial Complex Establishment (let's call them MICE, shall we?) long ago figured out how to keep us (in the peace movement) hopping around on their playing field, dutifully following their game plan—without us realizing we were being manipulated?" The method is simple. "The MICE entice us into debates about weapons systems. . . . The catch is that even when we 'win' one of these debates, the MICE always come up with new weapons systems . . . for us to argue about. And since it takes the American public months or years just to figure out what each debate is about, the MICE have plenty of time to start a new development before the old one runs out of steam. So we never catch up to the MICE. . . . It is their game and they rig it in their favor."

Writing in mid-1986, Atlee catalogs some of the recent acts of this political drama. "To counter our predeployment opposition to Euromissiles, the MICE came up with the zero/zero [theater nuclear forces arms control proposal] option. . . . Brilliantly the MICE framed the debate—and we obliged, arguing the faults of zero/zero." After the Soviets rejected it and walked out of the talks, "we peace people, without realizing what a trap we were walking into, tried to make 'Reagan's lack of [arms control] talks' an election issue. Reagan let the issue blossom and then invited the Soviets back to talk. Perfect: if they agreed, he'd be a peacemaker; if they turned him down, that just proved they were the bad guys. And so it goes."

Similarly, "let's suppose that the MX is, at this point, nothing more than a decoy. Let's suppose that the MICE know the MX is a losing proposition—but also know that by holding it up and shaking it, they can get us to shoot at it, thus absorbing our energy." Then comes the next act: Star Wars. "Right on cue, we are flocking to the microphones and mimeograph machines and, backed by panels of impressive scientists, we're telling how it can't work without even noticing that the MICE have led us into another canyon ambush."

Atlee is aware that "our whole focus on arms control ties us into the MICE's game plan." He notes a *Washington Post* report that Assistant Secretary of Defense Richard Perle "favors talking to the Soviets, in part because negotiations help maintain political support for military spending in the West." These talks simply become another forum for enticing the peace movement into endless (and largely ineffective) antiweapons campaigns. Atlee concludes: "This stage on which we dance is filled with trap doors, shadow projections, fleeting mirages and colored curtains that rise and fall at the bidding of the MICE. They even control the audience lights and sound system. We just dance."[43]

The peace movement obligingly dances in part because of a sincere belief that the weapons matter, but also, one must admit, because it too enjoys definite functions of weaponitis. The same depoliticization of the nuclear issue that shields the state and mainstream politicians from criticism of America's behavior in the world offers similar advantages to an opposition movement seeking wide public support, including that of the elites.

Each new nuclear monster such as MX is a fat easy target. Large segments of the population, the media, and the Congress can be mobilized against these monsters. Funds can be raised; elections can be affected. The nuclear freeze drew the support of three-quarters of the population and the U.S. House of Representatives. The idea that bloated nuclear arsenals must be reduced is attractive and saleable; in many circles the arms race is now a dirty word.

Changing strategy to highlight political questions about American foreign policy, many fear, might undermine a remarkably comfortable position for an opposition mass movement in American politics—meaning fewer members, less money, less favorable press. Attracting support for the movement, some activists told us, is the necessary first step in galvanizing public opposition to the nuclear threat. If weapons are powerful mobilizing symbols, they are also a valid strategy for opposing nuclear war. Many believe that giving up a focus on weapons would mean abandoning the entire effort to avert a cataclysm. As one European peace researcher and activist told us in response to the argument that the weapons themselves do not much matter, "You are analytically correct, but politically I am not so sure."

That seems an unrealistic fear. The real triumph of the anti–nuclear war movement was awakening people to the nuclear danger by relentlessly showing how destructive nuclear war would be. That educational task could have been accomplished without promoting the theory that the nuclear danger comes chiefly from the arms race. This "weapons strategy" was a political choice. The American people could have understood and acted on the "nuclear war is unwinnable and must never be fought" message even if they had not been bombarded as well by the "arms race is the problem" message.

Continuation of the weapons strategy by those who understand the near-irrelevance of the arms race would amount to a calculated deception—something no democratic movement should tolerate and few activists would support. It is unconscionable to cause people to fear that they and their children face grave new dangers when the first MX missiles are deployed or when arms talks break off without an agreement. There are surely enough real problems to worry about today without terrifying people about false ones. It would be better for the movement in the long run to mobilize fewer people around the real issues than more around the false ones—if that is the choice.

And it may not be. Insisting on the falsehood that the arms race is the problem could actually damage the peace movement's ability to mobilize populations in the long run regardless of how the political battles over weapons systems turn out.

A major movement victory such as the freeze—literally the end of the arms race—could destroy public concern through complacency even though the risk of nuclear war would not change. It has happened before. As Carl Conetta observes of the first big phase of American anti–nuclear war popular organizing, in the late 1950s, "The 1963 Partial Test Ban Treaty effectively ended that movement." He worries that the second phase, which began in 1980, may suffer a similar fate: "Today, peace activists are claiming the recent U.S.-Soviet INF agreement as a movement victory. But does this victory, like the Partial Test Ban before it, mean that the disarmament movement will enter a long period of quiescence?" Similarly, historian Paul Boyer notes that before the 1963 treaty and, to a lesser extent the 1972 SALT I treaty, "there was enormous public concern about testing and nuclear war, but afterwards there was an immediate decline in public concern about these issues. Much the same thing may happen in the wake of an INF treaty," which could "take the wind out of the sails of the peace movement." [44] By periodically "just saying yes" to central but inconsequential movement demands about weapons, the state can easily unbalance its adversaries without conceding anything of importance.

Major antiweapons campaigns will probably continue to fail, however, as they usually have in the past, because of the many powerful interests supporting the arms race. In this case too the movement risks demobilization—through despair—as in the European peace movement after the defeat of massive campaigns to prevent the deployment of the Euromissiles and in the American one after the failure to achieve the bilateral freeze or to defeat even one new weapons system. As Michael Howard writes:

> It cannot be wise to encourage the belief that security lies only in the achievement of an unattainable goal or in the conclusion of agreements which, even if they could be reached, would do little or nothing in themselves to produce a more peaceful world. These false expectations engender unnecessary and debilitating fears, fears which find expression in such phrases as "the next round of arms talks will provide the last opportunity for mankind to get the arms race under control," or that failure to achieve a "breakthrough" will be catastrophic. . . . The higher the expectations aroused by governments responding to (or exploiting) public opinion, the greater will be the disappointment when they are not fulfilled, the more bitter will be the mutual recrimination, and the worse the international climate as a result.[45]

True, many businesspeople, professionals, workers, and others in the American political mainstream might defect from the movement if it criticized American foreign policy rather than American missile policy. One former activist with Physicians for Social Responsibility told us that when he tried to turn the organization's attention to more political issues, he was informed that the doctors who supported the group financially would not tolerate the change. The neurosurgeons and cardiologists were happy to oppose the arms race, but not American actions in El Salvador and Lebanon. A politicized peace movement might find a less friendly reception in Congress, the press, and liberal foundations as well; the already highly political parts of the peace movement, notably those opposing U.S. intervention in Central America, certainly do.

That is not surprising, nor is it a valid reason for preserving weap-onitis. A movement that opposes the aggressive foreign policies of the nuclear states will inevitably face greater hostility than one working for politically respectable goals such as arms control. That is simply the price of not accepting the establishment's invitation to dance.

If basic changes do not occur, history suggests that we may be head-ing for disaster. But there is also reason for hope. With large numbers of people alarmed about the nuclear peril in the United States and around the world, the nuclear powers could find that their populations will no longer permit them to endanger everyone in pursuit of power and wealth.

An organized movement able to call millions into the streets could seriously inhibit the reckless state actions that have long constituted the prime threat to human survival. What Scott Sagan derisively calls the "noise" of domestic opposition could rise to painful levels. Dur-ing the next tense Third World crisis, citizens can ensure that John Foster Dulles was correct to worry that "a negative public opinion" might prevent national leaders from using nuclear weapons. We can transform the universal fear of nuclear war into the public revolt against brinksmanship that so haunted Richard Nixon.[46] We can ensure that leaders are not free of public pressure when plotting aggression, inter-vention, and adventurism throughout the world. These are the real chal-lenges for democracy in the nuclear age.

# Notes

INTRODUCTION

1. Jonathan D. Auerbach, "'Nuclear Freeze' at a Crossroads," *Boston Globe*, June 22, 1986, p. A19; Senator Jim Sasser of Tennessee, quoted in Council for a Livable World literature, November 1987.

2. Bernard Brodie, ed., *The Absolute Weapon* (New York: Harcourt Brace, 1946).

3. Harold Freeman, *This Is the Way the World Will End, This Is the Way You Will End, Unless* (Cambridge, Mass.: Schenkman, 1982), pp. 12–13, 2–4, 7–8.

4. Ibid., pp. 19–20; Barbara G. Levi, Frank N. von Hippel, and William H. Daugherty, "Civilian Casualties from 'Limited' Nuclear Attacks on the USSR," *International Security* 12, no. 3 (Winter 1987–1988), p. 189 (emphasis added).

5. Albert Einstein, quoted in Ralph E. Lapp, "The Einstein Letter That Started It All," *New York Times Magazine*, August 2, 1964.

6. *New York Trust Co. v. Eisner*, 256 U.S. 345, 349 (1921).

7. George Santayana, *The Life of Reason*, vol. 1, *Reason in Common Sense* (New York: Dover, 1980).

8. Freeman, *This Is the Way the World Will End*, p. 33.

9. Noam Chomsky provides the clearest and most extensively documented accounts of the Cold War and the U.S. role in the Third World. His many books on these topics include *The Political Economy of Human Rights*, with Edward Herman, 2 vols. (Boston: South End Press, 1979); *Towards a New Cold War* (New York: Pantheon, 1982); *Turning the Tide* (Boston: South End Press, 1985); and *On Power and Ideology* (Boston: South End Press, 1987).

10. Bernard Brodie, "The Development of Nuclear Strategy," in *Strategy and Nuclear Deterrence: An "International Security" Reader*, ed. Stephen E. Miller (Princeton: Princeton University Press, 1984), pp. 4, 3, 7 (first published

in *International Security* 2, no. 4 [Spring 1978]; Quarles, quoted in Lawrence Freedman, *The Evolution of Nuclear Strategy* (New York: St. Martin's Press, 1982), p. 156.

11. Paul Bracken, *The Command and Control of Nuclear Forces* (New Haven: Yale University Press, 1983), p. 1.

12. Albert Carnesale et al., *Living with Nuclear Weapons* (Cambridge: Harvard University Press, 1983), p. 67.

13. "Three Harvard Professors Argue for New Way to Reduce Nuclear War Risk," *Boston Globe*, May 31, 1985, p. 16; Graham T. Allison, Albert Carnesale, and Joseph S. Nye, Jr., eds., *Hawks, Doves, and Owls: An Agenda for Avoiding Nuclear War* (New York: Norton, 1985), pp. 223–246.

14. See Robert Jervis, *The Illogic of American Nuclear Strategy* (Ithaca: Cornell University Press, 1984).

15. George Rathjens, "First Thoughts About Problems Facing EXPRO" (Boston, 1985, photocopied). A revised version of this paper was published as EXPRO Paper No. 5 (Chestnut Hill, Mass.: Exploratory Project on the Conditions of Peace, 1986), available from EXPRO, Department of Sociology, Boston College, Chestnut Hill, MA 02167.

16. Michael Howard, "Is Arms Control Really Necessary?" (lecture delivered to the Council for Arms Control, London), excerpted in *Harper's* 272, no. 1632 (May 1986): 13–14. Matthew Melko of Wright State University also argues that the arms race may be nearly irrelevant to war and peace in our time, though his reasoning differs from ours; see his "What If the Arms Race Did Not Matter?" (paper presented at the North Central Sociological Association meeting, Cincinnati, April 1–14, 1987), as well as his forthcoming book.

17. Joseph Gerson, ed., *The Deadly Connection: Nuclear War and U.S. Intervention* (Philadelphia: New Society Publishers, 1986).

CHAPTER ONE

1. The term *weaponitis* was used by political scientist Samuel Huntington during a speech at a Boston College Graduate Student Association symposium on the arms race and nuclear war, October 12, 1983. See William A. Schwartz, "U.S. Nuclear Policies Increase Threat of War," Boston College *Heights*, October 17, 1983, but note that the author suffered from weaponitis himself at the time.

2. Bernard Brodie, *Strategy in the Missile Age* (Princeton: Princeton University Press, 1959), p. 147.

3. Harold Freeman, *This Is the Way the World Will End, This Is the Way You Will End, Unless* (Cambridge, Mass.: Schenkman, 1982), p. 10.

4. As Thomas Schelling correctly argues, the ability to devastate a society's inner core without first defeating its armed forces, not the raw ability to devastate populations, is what is fundamentally new about nuclear arms. During earlier periods it was surely possible for a victor to kill every inhabitant of a conquered land, if necessary by cutting every throat in turn. The key element of the nuclear revolution is not the increase in efficiency or speed with which this killing can be done—matters of real but secondary importance—but rather the

ability to do it without defeating the defender's military forces first. See Thomas Schelling, *Arms and Influence* (New Haven: Yale University Press, 1966), chap. 1.

5. McGeorge Bundy, "To Cap the Volcano," *Foreign Affairs* 48, no. 1 (October 1969): 9–10; Herbert York, "Nuclear Deterrence: How to Reduce the Overkill," in *Pacem in Terris III*, ed. Fred Warner Neal and Mary Kersey Harvey (Santa Barbara: Center for the Study of Democratic Institutions, 1974), 2:26, cited in Alva Myrdal, *The Game of Disarmament* (New York: Pantheon, 1982), p. 117; Michael Howard, "Is Arms Control Really Necessary?" (lecture delivered to the Council for Arms Control, London), excerpted in *Harper's* 272, no. 1632 (May 1986): 14.

6. Bernard Brodie, *The Absolute Weapon* (New York: Harcourt Brace, 1946), p. 31; James Schlesinger, "Rhetoric and Realities in the Star Wars Debate," *International Security* 10, no. 1 (Summer 1985): 5.

7. See Paul Bracken, *The Command and Control of Nuclear Forces* (New Haven: Yale University Press, 1983); John Steinbruner, "National Security and the Concept of Strategic Stability," *Journal of Conflict Resolution* 22, no. 3 (September 1978): 411–428, and "Nuclear Decapitation," *Foreign Policy* (Winter 1981–1982), reprinted in *Search for Sanity*, ed. Paul Joseph and Simon Rosenblum (Boston: South End Press, 1984), pp. 181–192; Daniel Ford, *The Button* (New York: Simon & Schuster, 1985); Desmond Ball, "Can Nuclear War Be Controlled?" Adelphi Paper No. 169 (London: International Institute for Strategic Studies, 1981).

8. Steinbruner, "National Security," p. 421; Ball, "Can Nuclear War Be Controlled?" p. 36; Colin S. Gray, "Targeting Problems for Central War," *Naval War College Review* 33, no. 1 (January–February 1980): 7. Gray is one of the most intelligent and fascinating of the right-wing nuclear theorists. In his acute diagnosis of the contradictions and impracticality of the mainstream approach to nuclear strategy and weapons development, he argues that they have caused little if any advance over the early days of massive retaliation. He is right. His prescription, a doctrine and weapons sufficient to ensure victory in nuclear war, is absurd. But he has accurately shown that they would be a logical condition for the meaningfulness of strategy and hardware development over the past quarter century.

9. Howard, "Is Arms Control Really Necessary?" p. 14.

10. Bernard Brodie, "The Development of Nuclear Strategy," in *Strategy and Nuclear Deterrence: An "International Security" Reader*, ed. Stephen E. Miller (Princeton: Princeton University Press, 1984), p. 7 (first published in *International Security* 2, no. 4 [Spring 1978]).

11. Public Agenda Foundation, *Voter Options on Nuclear Arms Policy* (New York: Public Agenda Foundation, 1984), table 13, p. 20; table 38, p. 49; table 53, p. 64; table 10, p. 17.

12. McGeorge Bundy, "The Bishops and the Bomb," *New York Review of Books* 30, no. 10 (June 16, 1984): 3–8.

13. Ibid.

14. Ibid.; George Kennan, "A Modest Proposal," in *Search for Sanity*, ed.

Paul Joseph and Simon Rosenblum (Boston: South End Press, 1984), pp. 577–583 (first appeared as a paper, "Proposal for International Disarmament," 1981).

CHAPTER TWO

1. Daniel O. Graham and Gregory A. Fossedal, "First Strike and You're Out," *American Spectator* 18, no. 7 (July 1985): 12, 10; Keenen Peck, "First Strike, You're Out," interview with Daniel Ellsberg, *Progressive* 49, no. 7 (July 1985): 34; Howard Moreland, "Are We Readying a First Strike?" *Nation* 240, no. 10 (March 16, 1985): 297, 299.

2. Kosta Tsipis, *Arsenal: Understanding Weapons in the Nuclear Age* (New York: Simon & Schuster, 1983), p. 238. Tsipis notes that each side might be able to destroy *some* enemy subs, but not enough to make a difference.

3. Ibid., pp. 138, 142, 144, 145.

4. Interview.

5. Frank N. von Hippel, Barbara G. Levi, Theodore A. Postol, and William H. Daugherty, "Civilian Casualties from Counterforce Attacks," *Scientific American* 259, no. 3 (September 1988): 36–37.

6. Thomas C. Schelling, "Abolition of Ballistic Missiles," *International Security* 12, no. 1 (Summer 1987): 179–180.

7. Michael M. May, George F. Bing, and John D. Steinbruner, *Strategic Arms Reductions* (Washington, D.C.: Brookings Institution, 1988), pp. 15–17.

8. Ibid., pp. 22, 5–6; George F. Kennan, "Zero Options," *New York Review of Books*, May 12, 1983, p. 3.

9. For a concise and authoritative discussion of command system vulnerabilities, see Kurt Gottfried and Bruce G. Blair, eds., *Crisis Stability and Nuclear War* (New York: Oxford University Press, 1988), chap. 6.

10. John D. Steinbruner, "The Purpose and Effect of Deep Strategic Force Reductions," in *Reykjavik and Beyond: Deep Reductions in Strategic Nuclear Arsenals and the Future Direction of Arms Control*, ed. Committee on International Security and Arms Control, National Academy of Sciences (Washington, D.C.: National Academy Press, 1988), p. 16.

11. Gottfried and Blair, *Crisis Stability and Nuclear War*, pp. 87, 95–96.

12. Frank von Hippel, quoted in William M. Arkin, "Sleight of Hand with Trident II," *Bulletin of the Atomic Scientists* 40 (December 1984): 5–6; Gottfried and Blair, *Crisis Stability and Nuclear War*, p. 87.

13. Richard K. Betts, "Surprise Attack and Preemption," in *Hawks, Doves, and Owls: An Agenda for Avoiding Nuclear War*, ed. Graham T. Allison, Albert Carnesale, and Joseph S. Nye, Jr. (New York: Norton, 1985), pp. 57, 60. Even Betts, who generally attributes importance to technical factors in determining the risk of a first strike, acknowledges that "without dramatic [that is, highly unlikely] increases in the vulnerability of forces or in strategic defense, marginal differences in the balance of forces could only be a straw to break the camel's back—something that would tip a decision that was already only a millimeter away from being made for other reasons" (p. 67).

14. Stansfield Turner, "Winnowing Our Warheads," *New York Times Maga-*

*zine,* March 27, 1988, p. 69; Richard Ned Lebow, *Nuclear Crisis Management: A Dangerous Illusion* (Ithaca: Cornell University Press, 1987), pp. 61–62, 64.

15. Even if we were to grant that the vulnerability of command and control created incentives for preemption, the number and characteristics of the weapons on hand should not make those incentives much stronger or weaker. Command and control networks (like almost everything else) can be destroyed even by primitive, inaccurate nuclear weapons. The command systems of both superpowers have been at risk since at least the 1960s, and short of near disarmament they will remain at risk regardless of what weapons the superpowers create or what arms control treaties they sign. As Steinbruner notes, "Since only modest numbers of weapons are required to threaten the U.S. command system, increases beyond that level have little effect."

With the command system in such dire peril, the vulnerability of weapons is relatively inconsequential even if one believes such vulnerabilities matter. Even with *no* first-strike capability, one side might preemt if war seemed inevitable for the small chance that damage could be limited by disrupting command and control. As Steinbruner writes, preemptive decapitation "precludes the worst case destruction which would occur from a fully coordinated, fully committed [enemy] attack," and "it offers some slight chance of escaping with very low damage should effectively isolated [enemy] force elements fail to retaliate." This possibility, "however slight, is probably the only imaginable route to decisive victory in nuclear war." Indeed, as Stephen M. Meyer argues: "If Soviet leaders had great confidence in the reliability of their strategic warning and believed nuclear war was unavoidable, then preemption might look attractive quite apart from damage control. If one cannot avoid nuclear war there is no advantage to launching second."

Conversely, if both sides had enough first-strike weapons to destroy *all* the enemy's missiles and bombers on the ground, the logic is no different. Invulnerable enemy submarines would still pose a threat of total destruction to the attacker, and again, the only possible hope would be the minute chance that with command disrupted, the submarines would not fire. Once again, as Lebow writes, "for no more than a miniscule chance of preventing retaliation, policy makers would make nuclear war a certainty and deprive themselves of any prospect of ending it short of the exhaustion of both sides."

See John Steinbruner, "Nuclear Decapitation," *Foreign Policy* (Winter 1981–1982), reprinted in *Search for Sanity,* ed. Paul Joseph and Simon Rosenblum (Boston: South End Press, 1984), pp. 186, 184; Stephen M. Meyer, "Soviet Perspectives on the Paths to Nuclear War," in *Hawks, Doves, and Owls,* ed. Allison, Carnesale, and Nye, p. 200; Lebow, *Nuclear Crisis Management,* p. 53. We have generalized Steinbruner's statements about preemption, which refer specifically to Soviet preemption. The logic is evidently the same for American preemption. Meyer suggests that the amount of expected damage limitation, and thus the technical characteristics of the opposing arsenals, might figure into a Soviet preemption decision made on the basis of ambiguous warning of an impending U.S. nuclear attack. If they could not be sure that war was inevitable, Meyers argues, the Soviets would base a preemption decision in part on how much relief from nuclear devastation they could reasonably expect to achieve.

That sounds plausible, but it is misleading. There really is no such thing as damage limitation in modern nuclear war, especially for the Soviets, who would face a virtually unlimited supply of nuclear megatonnage based undersea in invulnerable U.S. submarines *regardless* of how much land-based nuclear firepower they destroyed. If damage limitation were possible at all, it would arise from disrupted command and control, not from the physical destruction of weapons. Each side will always have enough warheads to effectively destroy the other, regardless of who strikes first. The only question is whether those warheads will be used and how they will be targeted. But as we have noted, destruction of command and control, though easy, does not guarantee restraint. The consequences could be exactly the opposite, with isolated commanders launching far more weapons on their own authority than an intact central command would have ordered. And even if one does believe that command and control targeting is a rational damage-limiting strategy, its feasibility is for the most part independent of the weapons in place on either side.

16. Gottfried and Blair, *Crisis Stability and Nuclear War,* pp. 85, 89 (emphasis added).

17. Ibid., p. 88.

18. Lebow, *Nuclear Crisis Management,* p. 175. Interestingly, Lebow is one of the seventeen analysts who contributed to *Crisis Stability and Nuclear War.* The preface to that book says that all seventeen contributors agree with the book's main findings. It seems odd that Lebow, whose earlier book, *Nuclear Crisis Management,* spelled out the irrationality of a prompt launch so clearly, would endorse the conclusions of *Crisis Stability and Nuclear War* on this point.

19. See Morton H. Halperin, *Nuclear Fallacy: Dispelling the Myth of Nuclear Strategy* (Cambridge, Mass.: Ballinger, 1987). The arms race and arms control (with the exception of very radical proposals like Halperin's) should not much affect the risk of a hasty nuclear launch, even if leaders were insane enough to consider it. The only weapons-related factor of any importance is how fast decapitation could be accomplished, and hence how much time leaders would have to mull over the option of launching promptly after receiving warning of an enemy attack. Standard ballistic and cruise missiles can destroy nodes of command and control very quickly. Certain weapons, such as Pershing II missiles near the central front in Europe and Soviet submarines hugging the U.S. Atlantic coast, can in theory do the job slightly faster. Many believe that such weapons may lead to itchier trigger fingers in Washington and Moscow, where leaders will have several fewer minutes to interpret mysterious radar blips. Perhaps. But the insane risks of launch on warning are not affected by the length of the warning. In the missile age, the arms race and arms control can affect warning time by at most several minutes. And the real impact of decreased warning time is perhaps not obvious. It might just reduce the interval in which national leaders or lower-level commanders could convince themselves that an enemy attack was under way, panic, and launch the missiles.

Moreover, as one former high-level nuclear planner told us, if Soviet radar screens ever signal a possible attack in progress, the identity and technical characteristics of the weapons suspected of making the blips would be the last thing on the leaders' minds. The Soviets would have little idea of what was actually coming at them and little confidence they understood what particular weapons would actually do if they hit, given the artificiality of peacetime testing and military intelligence. The horrifying suspicion that a swarm of enemy missiles was screaming toward their country—not unreliable assessments of the missiles' performance characteristics—would be their overwhelming concern. Desmond Ball notes that "the Soviet attack characterization and assessment systems, which are technically quite inferior to their American counterparts, would have great difficulty distinguishing a major counterforce strike from a more general attack, even if it were considered meaningful in Soviet strategic doctrine to attempt such differentiation." Despite its greater technical sophistication, the United States in fact would have a similar difficulty.

Can technical improvements in command and control reduce the "incentives" for a prompt launch? *If* the United States completes its massive current command and control upgrade program and *if* Soviet strategic forces remain roughly as they are today (which on both counts "may be overly optimistic"), the seventeen analysts estimate that the U.S. command system would become less vulnerable—but not by much. The Soviets might have to fire more weapons to destroy it, but still only a tiny fraction of their arsenal. The new command system might also survive longer after an attack, but at most for hours; "contrary to a widespread impression . . . the improved system will *not* have the endurance required to conduct 'controlled' or 'protracted' nuclear war unless the Soviets were to spare U.S. command, and structured their attacks to make that intention immediately evident." Obviously we must take such predictions with a large grain of salt.

Even if we assume that in the event of a nuclear war the improved command system would actually survive more than a few minutes, the strategic implications are debatable. The standard view is that the improvements would reduce the incentives for a prompt launch by providing greater confidence that the command system would survive. Perhaps so. But a prompt launch is insane, and the most important task by far is to keep that fact absolutely clear. If leaders should accept the strategic analysts' view that command vulnerability justifies prompt launch, they might rush into a launch anyway, since "the endurance of the improved system, while surpassing that of today, would still be too short-lived to provide full confidence that the attack could be absorbed and still allow coordinated retaliation following thorough attack assessment." In fact, the command improvements contemplated by the United States might make leaders *more* tempted to launch the missiles precipitously. The seventeen analysts believe that today leaders may "harbor some doubts" about the American ability to accomplish the difficult task of detecting and assessing an enemy attack, communicating with top leaders, deciding on and ordering retaliation, and actually launching weapons within a few minutes. The planned improvements in command and control will apparently make a sudden launch more technically feasible—and possibly more tempting—than it is today: the upgrade program "will improve the prompt-launch capability whether or not the enhancement of that capability is an explicit aim of modernization." See Desmond Ball, "U.S. Strategic Forces: How Would They Be Used?" in *Strategy and Nuclear Deterrence: An "International Security" Reader,* ed. Stephen E. Miller (Princeton:

Princeton University Press, 1984), p. 224 (first published in *International Security* 7, no. 3 [Winter 1982–1983]); Gottfried and Blair, *Crisis Stability and Nuclear War*, pp. 97–98, 92, 86–87.

CHAPTER THREE

1. On NATO's favorable position, see, for example, Jane M. O. Sharp's letter "The Myth of Warsaw Pact Superiority Debunked," *New York Times,* November 9, 1986; Joshua M. Epstein's op-ed "Preserving Security in Europe," *New York Times,* November 14, 1986; Tom Wicker, "Don't Fear for NATO," *New York Times,* February 8, 1988, p. A19; and, for more detail, Center for Defense Information, "NATO and Warsaw Pact Forces: Conventional War in Europe," *The Defense Monitor* 17, no. 3 (1988). On NATO responses to any Warsaw Pact conventional advantages, see, for example, General Bernard W. Rogers, "The Atlantic Alliance: Prescriptions for a Difficult Decade," *Foreign Affairs,* Summer 1982, pp. 1145–1156; and *Strengthening Conventional Deterrence in Europe,* Report of the European Security Study (New York: St. Martin's Press, 1983).

2. Earl C. Ravenal, "Counterforce and Alliance: The Ultimate Connection," *International Security* 6, no. 4 (Spring 1982): 36. Ravenal believes that higher levels of credibility may be required for political reasons, even if they are irrelevant to extended deterrence: "It takes more credibility to keep an ally than to deter an enemy" (p. 36).

3. Allan S. Krass and Matthew Goodman, "Nuclear Rationality: The Clausewitzian Strategies of the Superpowers" (photocopied); Colin Gray and Keith Payne, "Victory Is Possible," *Foreign Policy,* no. 39 (Summer 1980).

4. Earl C. Ravenal, "Counterforce and Alliance," p. 32.

5. Robert Endicott Osgood, *Limited War: The Challenge to American Strategy* (Chicago: University of Chicago Press, 1957), p. 242.

6. Paul Bracken, *The Command and Control of Nuclear Forces* (New Haven: Yale University Press, 1983), pp. 164, 163–164, 136.

7. Ibid., pp. 167, 168.

8. Ibid., pp. 170–171, 177–178, 176, 177.

9. "Who Could Start a Nuclear War?" *Defense Monitor* 14, no. 3 (1985): 1, 2, 4, 6.

10. Lori Esposito and James A. Schear, *The Command and Control of Nuclear Weapons,* Workshop Report (Aspen, Colo.: Aspen Institute for Humanistic Studies, 1985), pp. 15, 3, 17 (emphasis added). In Europe, they note, "there would . . . be immediate pressure for dispersal [of nuclear weapons], especially of longer-range INF systems, if hostilities seemed imminent." Moreover NATO might well "consider the prospect of conditional delegations of release authority" to fire nuclear weapons (p. 16).

11. Barry R. Posen, "Inadvertent Nuclear War? Escalation and NATO's Northern Flank," in *Strategy and Nuclear Deterrence,* ed. Miller, p. 98 (emphasis in original; first published in *International Security* 7, no. 2 [Fall 1982]).

12. Ibid., p. 86.

13. Michael T. Klare, "Securing the Firebreak," *World Policy Journal* 2, no. 2 (Spring 1985): 229–230; Alain C. Enthoven, "American Deterrent Policy," in

*Problems of National Strategy: A Book of Readings,* ed. Henry Kissinger (New York: Praeger, 1965), p. 124, cited in Klare, "Securing the Firebreak," p. 232.

14. Klare, "Securing the Firebreak," pp. 234, 240. Klare cites General Louis Wagner's testimony before the House Armed Services Committee, March 11, 1980 (p. 239). The firebreak concept actually applies to all types of nuclear weapons, not only those at the low end of the destructive spectrum. Just as there are tactical conventional weapons that tactical nuclear weapons can come to resemble, there are also strategic conventional weapons that strategic nuclear weapons can come to resemble. Old-style ICBMs, with their huge warheads and inaccurate delivery, obviously differed from conventional strategic weapons systems. Though the ashes of Dresden and Tokyo showed that nonnuclear strategic bombing can rapidly extinguish hundreds of thousands of lives, no one could mistake a conventional American air attack on the Soviet Union with a barrage of old Titan II missiles, which carry 9-megaton warheads about 450 times more powerful than the bomb that leveled Hiroshima. A modern Minuteman III/ Mk-12 ICBM, in contrast, carries a 0.17-megaton warhead, 50 times smaller than the Titan II, and (in theory at least) delivers it about six times more accurately. The most modern strategic missile systems, such as MX and the submarine-based Trident II/D-5, can supposedly deliver warheads reliably to within 400 feet of the target. Such weapons may appear able to conduct surgical nuclear strikes—say, against Soviet missile silos—that would not be altogether different from conventional bombing. Indeed, the major trend in strategic nuclear weapons systems, as in tactical ones, has been to refine them so that they can do the jobs of conventional ones, destroying military targets without decimating huge areas. In theory it is more tempting to leap the firebreak with a few well-aimed, low-yield Minuteman III/Mk-12 warheads than with monstrous multimegaton Titan IIs that could easily fall far off target and would almost certainly be the opening shot of an orgy of mass destruction. One day, conventional warheads mounted on strategic delivery systems (such as super-accurate long-range cruise missiles) may even be able to do at least some of the jobs now given to their nuclear counterparts. Then strategic missiles would be dual-capable too.

All technical data on nuclear weapons in this section are from Thomas B. Cochran, William M. Arkin, and Milton M. Hoenig, *Nuclear Weapons Databook,* vol. 1, *U.S. Nuclear Forces and Capabilities* (Cambridge, Mass.: Ballinger, 1984).

15. Complete destruction is unlikely at least in comparison to nuclear war and over a relatively short period of time. Casualties in Vietnam, for example, ran to the millions and included the decimation of the agricultural economic base, the ecology, and much of the social system. Some have said that the Vietcong did not fear nuclear weapons, since conventional ones were already doing so much damage. But despite the monstrous conventional attacks it suffered, Vietnam exists physically and socially. That might not be true had nuclear weapons been used. Another large-scale conventional war involving the superpowers, if by some miracle it remained conventional, might leave both societies alive. That cannot be said of a large-scale nuclear war.

16. McGeorge Bundy, "To Cap the Volcano," *Foreign Affairs* 48, no. 1 (October 1969): 9–10.

17. Societies can defend themselves—partially but effectively—against con-

ventional weapons, and they can bring conventional war to a halt long before they suffer or inflict complete destruction. True, conventional munitions can wreak total destruction, but only over a period of time long enough for the conflicts to resolve. As Thomas Schelling notes: "Against defenseless people there is not much that nuclear weapons can do that cannot be done with an ice pick. . . . Something like the same destruction always *could* be done. With nuclear weapons there is an expectation that it *would* be done" (Thomas C. Schelling, *Arms and Influence* [New Haven: Yale University Press, 1966], pp. 19, 23; emphasis in original).

18. Robert S. McNamara, "The Military Role of Nuclear Weapons: Perceptions and Misperceptions," *Foreign Affairs* 62 (Fall 1983), pp. 71–72.

19. Klaus Knorr, "Controlling Nuclear War," *International Security* 9, no. 4 (Spring 1985): 92, 89; Leon Wieseltier, "When Deterrence Fails," *Foreign Affairs* 63, no. 4 (Spring 1985): 847; General Jones, quoted in *Washington Post,* June 19, 1982, p. A3. In principle some weapons could occupy an intermediate place in the hierarchy of destructiveness, spanning the gap between the conventional weapons of normal warfare and the unconventional weapons of total destruction. Because of this ambiguity, both credibility and the firebreak might be affected by how such weapons evolve. Some argue that today's chemical and biological weapons already hold this middle ground.

20. All technical data on nuclear weapons systems in this section are from Cochran, Arkin, and Hoenig, *Nuclear Weapons Databook,* vol. 1.

21. Desmond Ball, "Can Nuclear War Be Controlled?" Aldephi Paper No. 169 (London: International Institute for Strategic Studies, 1981), p. 37 (emphasis in original); Krass and Goodman, "Nuclear Rationality," p. 29.

22. Ronald Reagan, quoted in *Boston Globe,* March 30, 1980; Gordon H. Chang, "To the Nuclear Brink: Eisenhower, Dulles, and the Quemoy-Matsu Crisis," *International Security* 2, no. 4 (Spring 1988): 107–108.

23. Ball, "Can Nuclear War Be Controlled?" pp. 35, 37; Esposito and Schear, "Command and Control," p. 17.

24. Barry M. Blechman and Douglas M. Hart, "The Political Utility of Nuclear Weapons: The 1973 Middle East Crisis," in *Strategy and Nuclear Deterrence,* ed. Miller, p. 294 (first published in *International Security* 7, no. 1 [Summer 1982]).

25. Blechman and Hart, "Political Utility," pp. 294–295 (emphasis in original); Esposito and Schear, "Command and Control," p. 15; Strobe Talbott, *Deadly Gambits* (New York: Alfred A. Knopf, 1984), p. 187.

26. See Thomas C. Schelling, *Arms and Influence,* pp. 36–43; H. R. Haldeman, *The End of Power* (New York: Times Books, 1978), pp. 82–83, cited in Daniel Ellsberg, "A Call to Mutiny," in *The Deadly Connection: Nuclear War and U.S. Intervention,* ed. Joseph Gerson (Philadelphia: New Society Publishers, 1986), pp. 56–57.

27. For other discussions of the competing effects, see Glenn Snyder, "The Balance of Power and the Balance of Terror," in *The Balance of Power,* ed. Paul Seabury (San Francisco: Chandler, 1965); Ravenal, "Counterforce and Alliance," p. 27; and Peter J. Liberman and Neil R. Thomason, "No-First-Use Unknowable," *Foreign Policy,* no. 64 (Fall 1986): 17–36.

CHAPTER FOUR

1. Steven Kull, "Nuclear Nonsense," *Foreign Policy,* no. 58 (Spring 1985): 28–52.

2. Warner Schilling, "U.S. Strategic Nuclear Concepts in the 1970's," in *Strategy and Nuclear Deterrence: An "International Security" Reader,* ed. Stephen E. Miller (Princeton: Princeton University Press, 1984), p. 201 (first published in *International Security* 6, no. 2 [Fall 1981]). On megatonnage see Carnesale et al., *Living with Nuclear Weapons* (Cambridge, Mass.: Harvard University Press, 1983), p. 76. On warheads see Thomas B. Cochran, William M. Arkin, and Milton M. Hoenig, *Nuclear Weapons Databook,* vol. 1, *U.S. Nuclear Forces and Capabilities* (Cambridge, Mass.: Ballinger, 1984), p. 15. To appreciate the hypocrisy of current official concern about Soviet numerical advantages in throw weight and the like, one must examine the history of U.S. nuclear planning, which clearly shows that deliberate decisions were made at various times to limit U.S. nuclear forces when there was no possible military benefit to adding more warheads or launchers. As Arkin explains, some of the reductions occurred because of the greatly increased capability of more modern weapons, which could operationally replace more than an equivalent number of older, cruder warheads.

3. Howard Moreland, "Are We Readying a First Strike?" *Nation* 240, no. 10 (March 16, 1985): 297.

4. Michael T. Klare, "Securing the Firebreak," *World Policy Journal* 2, no. 2 (Spring 1985): 229–230.

5. Schilling, "Strategic Nuclear Concepts," p. 202.

6. Dean Rusk, Robert McNamara, George W. Ball, Roswell Gilpatric, Theodore Sorensen, and McGeorge Bundy, "The Lessons of the Cuban Missile Crisis," *Time,* September 27, 1982, p. 85.

7. Marc Trachtenberg, "The Influence of Nuclear Weapons in the Cuban Missile Crisis," *International Security* 10, no. 1 (Summer 1985): 147–148.

8. Trachtenberg argues that "Soviet policy was very much influenced by the strategic balance," even though American policy was not. He asserts that "the Soviets seem to have been profoundly affected by their 'strategic' inferiority.' . . . They probably took American ideas about 'damage limitation' and 'discriminate and controlled general war,' and the [weapons] capabilities with which they were linked, far more seriously than the Americans did." His conclusion that "the strategic balance mattered in 1962" may seem to damage our case about perceptions. But there is a great difference in the quality of both evidence and argument between Trachtenberg's claims about American and Soviet perceptions. In the American case, he relies on newly released transcripts of actual White House meetings in which key decisions were made. This strong documentary evidence completely supports other evidence from key decision makers that was already available.

In the Soviet case, however, Trachtenberg did not cite a single source of direct evidence on how the strategic balance influenced Soviet leaders in the crisis. He acknowledges that his case about the Soviets is "somewhat speculative." Indeed, it rests entirely on an *interpretation* of one undisputed fact: while the

United States initiated a massive conventional and nuclear military alert, the Soviets made no real effort to ready their military machine for war. Trachtenberg assumes that Soviet perceptions of the strategic situation can be reasonably inferred from this inaction. He argues that the Soviets feared an alert might provoke the United States into a nuclear preemption and "quite possibly" that the key factor in their fears was "the disparity in force levels and in degrees of force vulnerability." Thus, in Soviet thinking, the U.S. advantage in nuclear hardware made it more likely that America would strike first given the provocation of a Soviet military alert.

This is a highly simplistic picture of Soviet motivation and at best an arbitrary selection among many possible explanations. A simpler and more plausible one is that the Soviets had no desire for general war with the United States, and certainly not one over the limited issue of missiles in Cuba. Unlike the Americans, they were not prepared to increase the risk of war by a provocative alert—not because of some calculation of warhead power, but because of the obvious existential reality that general war would visit unacceptable devastation on both nations. Thus an appreciation of existential reality and of the irrelevance of the strategic balance is just as consistent with the evidence of the absent Soviet military alert as Trachtenberg's theory that for the Soviets the balance mattered. Trachtenberg's theory of Soviet perceptions is just that—a theory unsupported by any genuine evidence.

In our view it is implausible that Khrushchev avoided alerting his forces out of fear of a first strike by superior U.S. forces. If this were his outlook, what accounts for Khrushchev's numerous challenges to the United States, most dramatically in Berlin only the year before? As Trachtenberg notes: "Khrushchev had tried over the past few years to extract political advantages by brandishing the specter of nuclear war . . . [and] tended to . . . overlook the ways in which the tactic of exploiting the nuclear threat could backfire." No profound *strategic* changes had occurred in the interim, so how can the strategic balance reasonably explain Khrushchev's uncharacteristic military restraint in the Cuban crisis? *Political* factors, not strategic ones, had changed: Kennedy was now willing to go to, and perhaps over, the brink. See Trachtenberg, "Cuban Missile Crisis," pp. 137–163. See also excerpts from the newly available transcripts Trachtenberg quotes in the same journal, pp. 164–203.

9. Richard Nixon, *RN: The Memoirs of Richard Nixon* (New York: Grosset & Dunlap, 1978), p. 922. For a brief account of these events, see Barry M. Blechman and Douglas M. Hart, "The Political Utility of Nuclear Weapons: The 1973 Middle East Crisis," in *Strategy and Nuclear Deterrence,* ed. Miller, pp. 273–297 (first published in *International Security* 7, no. 1 [Summer 1982]).

10. Nixon, *RN,* pp. 920–943.

11. Blechman and Hart, "Political Utility," pp. 287–288, 291; Richard K. Betts, *Nuclear Blackmail and Nuclear Balance* (Washington, D.C.: Brookings Institution, 1987), p. 125.

12. McGeorge Bundy, "The Unimpressive Record of Atomic Diplomacy," in *The Nuclear Crisis Reader,* ed. Gwyn Prins (New York: Vintage, 1984), p. 51; Raymond L. Garthoff, *Reflections on the Cuban Missile Crisis* (Washington, D.C.: Brookings Institution, 1987), p. 113. Noting the origins of the window-

of-vulnerability hysteria in the Reagan campaign strategy, Bundy adds that "the notion of a new vulnerability to nuclear diplomacy was unreal; perhaps we were dealing instead with a little atomic politics" (pp. 51–52).

13. Henry Kissinger, *Years of Upheaval* (Boston: Little, Brown, 1982), p. 1175; Center for Defense Information, "First Strike Weapons at Sea: The Trident II and the Sea-Launched Cruise Missile," *The Defense Monitor* 16, no. 6 (1987): 3; Bundy, "Atomic Diplomacy," p. 53.

14. Bundy, "Atomic Diplomacy," p. 44.

15. Betts, *Nuclear Blackmail*, pp. 144, 145, 147, 149.

16. Ibid., pp. 150–151, 153, 155, 156; Steven Kull, *Minds at War: Nuclear Reality and the Inner Conflicts of Defense Policymakers* (New York: Basic Books, 1988), p. 6.

17. Betts, *Nuclear Blackmail*, pp. 158, 159, 173; Kull, *Minds at War*, pp. 6–7, 249.

18. Garthoff, *Cuban Missile Crisis*, pp. 112–114.

19. McGeorge Bundy, "To Cap the Volcano," *Foreign Affairs* 48, no. 1 (October 1969): 11.

20. Barry M. Blechman and Stephen S. Kaplan, with David K. Hall, William B. Quandt, Jerome N. Slater, Robert M. Slusser, and Philip Windsor, *Force Without War: U.S. Armed Forces as a Political Instrument* (Washington, D.C.: Brookings Institution, 1978), pp. 127–129, 527. These authors use a simple measure of the strategic balance: force loadings, or the number of nuclear warheads available. Even using a different measure, the number of delivery vehicles, they could establish no connection between the strategic balance and outcomes of military incidents involving both superpowers.

21. See the famous article by Richard Pipes, "Why the Soviet Union Thinks It Could Fight and Win a Nuclear War," *Commentary* 64, no. 1 (July 1977). For opposing views, see, for example, George Kennan, *The Nuclear Delusion* (New York: Pantheon, 1983); McGeorge Bundy, "A Matter of Survival," *New York Review of Books* 30, no. 4 (March 17, 1983): 3–6; David Holloway, *The Soviet Union and the Arms Race* (New Haven: Yale University Press, 1984).

22. Robert L. Arnett, "Soviet Attitudes Towards Nuclear War: Do They Really Think They Can Win?" *Journal of Strategic Studies* 2, no. 2 (September 1979): 182–183; Holloway, *Soviet Union*, quoted in Bundy, "Matter of Survival"; Bundy, "Matter of Survival," p. 4.

23. Leon Wieseltier, *Nuclear War, Nuclear Peace* (New York: Holt, Rinehart & Winston, 1983), p. 35.

24. Dusko Doder, "A Comeback by Ex-Soviet Military Chief," *Boston Globe*, July 18, 1985, p. 13; "Is Arms Control Obsolete?" *Harper's* 271, no. 1622 (July 1985): 44.

25. Steven Kull, "Conventionalizing Nuclear Weapons" (photocopy).

26. Kull, *Minds at War*, pp. 305, 312, 57, 184, 77, 116.

27. Ibid., pp. 272, 275.

28. George W. Rathjens and Laura Reed, *Neither MAD nor Starstruck— And Doubts, Too, About Arms Control* (Cambridge: Center for International Studies, Massachusetts Institute of Technology, 1986), pp. 15–16.

29. Bernard Brodie, *Strategy in the Missile Age* (Princeton: Princeton Uni-

versity Press, 1959), p. 171; John Steinbruner, "Beyond Rational Deterrence," in *Power, Strategy, and Security*, ed. Klaus Knorr (Princeton: Princeton University Press, 1983), p. 118 (first published in *World Politics* 28, no. 2 [January 1976]).

30. Bernard Brodie, "The Development of Nuclear Strategy," in *Strategy and Nuclear Deterrence: An "International Security" Reader*, ed. Stephen E. Miller (Princeton: Princeton University Press, 1984), pp. 20–21 (first published in *International Security* 2, no. 4 [Spring 1978]).

31. Ibid., p. 21.

32. This explanation raises the question whether additions might eventually lead to a meaningful military advantage for one side if the other, taking the irrelevance of nuclear hardware to heart, unilaterally stopped building more. One former high-level political official we interviewed, for example, felt sure that such an advantage was possible, even though he understood that the normal give and take of the arms race has not led to any significant change to date. Even in this extreme scenario we seriously doubt that one side could develop a meaningful nuclear superiority.

Consider that during the Cuban missile crisis the United States had about as much nuclear superiority as either side could possibly attain; yet it was irrelevant. Similarly, imagine that France underwent a profound political shift and allied itself with the Soviets, re-aiming its submarine-based nuclear missiles at America. Clearly the United States would enjoy an advantage in every possible measure of nuclear weapons capability. But since France's small arsenal could destroy the United States anyway, does anyone seriously believe that the United States would underestimate the danger of a Franco-American war?

33. Kull, "Nuclear Nonsense," p. 36.

34. Robert Jervis, "Why Nuclear Superiority Doesn't Matter," *Political Science Quarterly* 94, no. 4 (Winter 1979–1980), p. 631; Donald C. Daniel, "Issues and Findings," in *International Perceptions of the Superpower Military Balance*, ed. Donald C. Daniel (New York: Praeger, 1978), pp. 185, 188, 189; Ronald D. McLaurin, "Arab Perceptions of the Regional Superpower Military Balance," in ibid., pp. 178–179; Kull, "Nuclear Nonsense," p. 36.

35. Joseph Gerson, "What Is the Deadly Connection?" in *The Deadly Connection: Nuclear War and U.S. Intervention*, ed. Joseph Gerson (Philadelphia: New Society Publishers, 1986), p. 14; Kull, *Minds at War*, pp. 162–163.

36. Richard H. Kohn and Joseph P. Harahan, eds., "U.S. Strategic Air Power, 1948–1962: Excerpts from an Interview with Generals Curtis E. LeMay, Leon W. Johnson, David A. Burchinal, and Jack J. Catton," *International Security* 12, no. 4 (Spring 1988): 78–95.

37. Army manual cited in Kull, *Minds at War*, p. 13.

38. Daniel, "Issues and Findings," p. 187; *Time*, August 1981, quoted in Kull, "Nuclear Nonsense," p. 46.

39. Richard K. Betts, "Innovation, Assessment, and Decision," in *Cruise Missiles: Technology, Strategy, Politics*, ed. Richard K. Betts (Washington, D.C.: Brookings Institution, 1981), p. 17.

40. George Rathjens, "First Thoughts About Problems Facing EXPRO" (Boston, 1985, photocopied). A revised version of this paper was published as

EXPRO Paper No. 5 (Chestnut Hill, Mass.: Exploratory Project on the Conditions of Peace, 1986), available from EXPRO, Department of Sociology, Boston College, Chestnut Hill, MA 02167.

41. Robert Scheer, *With Enough Shovels: Reagan, Bush and Nuclear War* (New York: Random House, 1982), p. 261.

42. Schilling, "Strategic Nuclear Concepts," p. 203.

CHAPTER FIVE

1. Isaac Asimov, fund-raising letter for Americans for Democratic Action, n.d.; Harrison Brown, "Star Wars Once Funny, Now Frightening," *Bulletin of the Atomic Scientists* 41, no. 5 (May 1985): 3.

2. Robert Jastrow, citing *Nature* in "The War Against Star Wars," *Commentary* 78, no. 6 (December 1984): 20; Gary Thatcher, "Big Powers Maneuver on Both Nuclear and Conventional Fronts," *Christian Science Monitor,* January 16, 1986, p. 36.

3. See *New York Times,* March 24, 1983; letter cited in Ellen Goodman, "Star Wars Comeback," *Boston Globe,* April 4, 1985, p. 19.

4. James Schlesinger, "Rhetoric and Realities in the Star Wars Debate," *International Security* 10, no. 1 (Summer 1985): 3–12; McGeorge Bundy, George F. Kennan, Robert S. McNamara, and Gerard Smith, "The President's Choice: Star Wars or Arms Control," *Foreign Affairs* 63, no. 2 (Winter 1984–1985): 266; Schlesinger, "Rhetoric and Realities," p. 5.

5. Bundy et al., "President's Choice," p. 267; "The Crack in Star Wars," *Boston Globe,* July 20, 1985, p. 14. On software problems see, for example, Herbert Lin, "The Development of Software for Ballistic-Missile Defense," *Scientific American* 253, no. 6 (December 1985): 46–53; Jonathan Jacky, "The 'Star Wars' Defense Won't Compute," *Atlantic* 255, no. 6 (June 1985): 18–30. For a more balanced view see Warre Meyers, "The Star Wars Software Debate," *Bulletin of the Atomic Scientists* 42, no. 2 (February 1986): 31–36.

6. Bundy et. al., "President's Choice," p. 267.

7. Schlesinger, "Rhetoric and Realities," p. 5; Bundy et al., "President's Choice," p. 268.

8. Ashton B. Carter, *Directed Energy Missile Defense in Space: Background Paper* (Washington, D.C.: U.S. Congress, Office of Technology Assessment, 1984), pp. 69–70; Fred Kaplan, "Snag Seen for 'Star Wars' Defense," *Boston Globe,* February 3, 1986, p. 1. Fred Hoffman claims that the Soviets would not expand their offensive forces to overcome a Star Wars defense and even that this idea "has been refuted by reality." How? Because "the United States drastically cut its expenditures on strategic defense in the 1960's and 1970's while the Soviets tripled their expenditures on strategic offense. After we abandoned any active defense against ballistic missile attacks even on our silos, the Soviets deployed MIRVs for the first time and increased them at an accelerating rate." This is a creative historical comparison. The question is whether an American *buildup* of nuclear defenses would impel the Soviets to an offensive missile *buildup,* but the example cited is different: an American *reduction* of efforts on the impractical nuclear defenses of the time. The same people who increased

their forces in the face of a decreasing threat to their survival will let their forces decline in the face of an increasing threat? What Hoffman's example really shows is that in the post–Cuban missile crisis era the Soviets were determined to build up their massively inferior nuclear arsenal to rough parity with the United States, regardless of U.S. decisions about deployments of nearly meaningless "defenses."

The relevant historical case is the American response to the Soviet development of a ballistic missile defense system in the mid-1960s. As Schlesinger reports: "The final judgment . . . was that the United States would counter the Soviet ABM by greatly expanding the number of warheads that we could throw against the Soviet Union. Indeed, by the time I left Rand, we were already talking about some 50,000 warheads to overcome Soviet defenses . . . we were going to expand our offensive capabilities geometrically to deal with Soviet defense." As Bundy et al. put it, "It is preposterous to suppose that Star Wars can produce anything but the most determined Soviet effort to make it fruitless. . . . That is what we would do, and that is what they will do." (Fred S. Hoffman, "The SDI in U.S. Nuclear Strategy," *International Security* 10, no. 1 [Summer 1985], p. 22; Schlesinger, "Rhetoric and Realities," p. 3; Bundy et al., "President's Choice," p. 272).

9. NBC, "Meet the Press," April 27, 1983; Schlesinger, "Rhetoric and Realities," p. 5; Carter, *Missile Defense,* p. 70.

10. Bundy et al., "President's Choice," p. 265; Carter, *Missile Defense,* p. 81; Abrahamson and DeLauer, quoted in Bundy et al., "President's Choice," pp. 266–267; Tina Rosenberg, "The Authorized Version," *Atlantic* 257, no. 2 (February 1986): 26–30. Charles Townes, then adviser to Secretary Weinberger and leader of two Pentagon groups studying MX missile basing modes, also acknowledged that perfect defense is "quite impractical. There is no technical solution to safeguarding mankind from nuclear explosives." Reagan's former science adviser, George Keyworth, admitted that in response to a workable Star Wars system, the Soviets would "shift their strategic resources to other weapons systems." Thus "by this acceptance he is conceding that even if Star Wars should succeed far beyond what any present technical consensus can allow us to believe, it would fail by the President's own standard."

Journalist Tina Rosenberg shows that the Reagan administration's internal classified studies of Star Wars reached far more pessimistic conclusions about the feasibility of population defense than the administration has attributed to them. The report of the sixty-seven-member Fletcher Commission, for instance, is repeatedly cited as prestigious technical support for Reagan's claims about SDI—for example, by Caspar Weinberger, who told the National Press Club in May 1984 that "they found the dream to be indeed possible"; by George Keyworth, who told the Brookings Institution in 1984 that according to the Fletcher Commission "the President's objective is not an unrealistic goal and they concluded it probably could be attained"; and by General Abrahamson, who writes that "the Fletcher panel has identified ways to counter every counter-measure the offense may choose to make." Yet, as Rosenberg demonstrates, the report actually said none of that. According to Theodore Postol, a former assistant to the chief of naval operations, "If you read volume seven [on countermeasures] first, you wouldn't bother reading the rest of the report. It presents an overwhelming case against the possibility of a hope of mounting something useful. It quite unambiguously indicates the problem was insolvable unless certain things were solved that no one knew how to address." The original draft of the report, reflecting the panel members' views, was first "smoothed" to the satisfaction of the panel's chairmen and then underwent "further transformations" by top Pentagon officials who had not participated in the study. The result was that, according to retired Major General John Toomay, deputy chairman of the Fletcher Commission, "the Administration in its public documents chose to interpret what the commission found out in a way that pleased them. A lot of technical people on the panel emphasized problems . . . [that] the Administration tended not to emphasize." Similarly, the public summary of the Hoffman report, often cited in defense of SDI, discussed "the possibility that nearly leakproof defenses may take a very long time, or may prove to be unattainable in a practical sense against a Soviet effort to counter the defense." According to Rosenberg, "What the Hoffman report in fact endorsed was not SDI but a limited system of traditional ABM missiles" (Townes, quoted in *New York Times,* April 11, 1983; Keyworth, quoted in Bundy et al., "President's Choice," pp. 268–269; Rosenberg, "Authorized Version," pp. 26–30).

11. See Paul Bracken, "Accidental Nuclear War," in *Hawks, Doves, and Owls,* ed. Graham T. Allison, Albert Carnesale, and Joseph S. Nye, Jr. (New York: Norton, 1985); Carter, *Missile Defense,* p. 76. For a fuller, less sanguine discussion of nuclear arms in the Third World, see Aaron Karp, "Ballistic Missiles in the Third World," *International Security* 9, no. 3 (Winter 1984–1985): 166–195.

12. George Rathjens and Jack Ruina, "BMD and Strategic Instability," *Dædalus: Journal of the American Academy of Arts and Sciences* 114, no. 3 (Summer 1985): 251; "Is There a Way Out," *Harper's* 270, no. 1621 (June 1985): 36–47; Sherman Frankel, letter to the editor, *New York Times,* February 24, 1988. The Department of Energy has actually *cut* its funding requests for nuclear safeguards and security programs. See Fred Kaplan, "Nuclear Safety Programs Victims of Budget Cuts," *Boston Globe,* January 26, 1986, p. 10.

Is it possible that an imperfect Star Wars might also "work," as the *Economist,* for example, contends, because "cities may be defensible with space technology . . . if there are restraints on the quantity and quality of the attacking forces"? Not unless the "restraints" meant something approaching nuclear disarmament. In any case, the Soviet response to a partial defense would probably be a massive *buildup* of offensive forces to assure penetration of the defensive net. Some argue that by reducing the utility of Soviet offensive forces, Star Wars will *reduce* the incentive to acquire them. But assuring penetration, and thereby the integrity of the Soviet strategic deterrent, will almost certainly be the overriding Soviet concern, not the abstract "utility" of their offensive missiles. Others contend that if the United States can learn to shoot down a Soviet missile for less money than it costs to put it up, then economics will ultimately force the Soviets to give up the offensive arms race or at least submit to U.S. superiority. But the real economics will almost certainly dictate otherwise. There are ways for the Soviets to deliver their nuclear warheads that Star Wars does not address, and one can reasonably expect the Soviets to work to retain the integrity of their deterrent at almost *any* cost, as the United States would ("Talks, too," *Economist,* September 28, 1985, p. 30).

13. Fred S. Hoffman, "The SDI in U.S. Nuclear Strategy," pp. 16, 19; Sidney D. Drell and Wolfgang K. H. Panofsky, "The Case Against Strategic Defense: Technical and Strategic Realities," *Issues in Science and Technology,* Fall 1984, pp. 45–65, reprinted in Herbert M. Levine and David Carlton, *The Nuclear Arms Race Debated* (New York: McGraw-Hill, 1986), pp. 226–242.

14. Senate Committee on Foreign Relations, *Strategic Defense and Anti-Satellite Weapons,* 98th Cong., 2d sess., April 25, 1984, p. 179.

15. Schlesinger, "Rhetoric and Realities," p. 6.

16. Zbigniew Brzezinski, "A Star Wars Solution," *New Republic* 193, no. 2 (July 8, 1985): 16–18; "The Case for Star Wars," *Economist,* August 3, 1985, p. 11.

17. Dolnick, "Star Wars," p. 47; William H. Taft IV, cited in Carter, *Missile Defense,* p. 65; Karl O'Lesskar, review of Robert Jastrow, *How to Make Nuclear Weapons Obsolete* (New York: Little, Brown, 1985), *American Spectator* 18, no. 9 (September 1985): 38; Robert Jastrow, "Reagan vs. the Scientists: Why the President Is Right About Missile Defense," *Commentary* 77, no. 1 (January 1984): 23–32.

18. Schlesinger, "Rhetoric and Realities," p. 10; "Is There a Way Out," *Harper's* 270, no. 1621 (June 1985): 36–47; Stanley Hoffmann, "Fog Over the Summit," *New York Review of Books,* January 16, 1986, p. 24.

19. John Kogut and Michael Weissman, "Taking the Pledge Against Star Wars," *Bulletin of the Atomic Scientists* 42, no. 1 (January 1986): 27–30; Union of Concerned Scientists, "Appeal by American Scientists to Ban Space Weapons" (n.d.); Robert Bowman, cited in Mobilization for Survival, "The Nightmare of 'Star Wars'" (n.d.); Benjamin Spock, fund-raising letter for Mobilization for Survival (n.d.). President Reagan himself said that "if paired with offensive systems" a defense screen "can be viewed as fostering an aggressive policy." As Richard Nixon put it in the *Los Angeles Times* in 1984, "Such systems would be destabilizing if they provided a shield so that you could use the sword." Charles A. Zraket, a Defense Department consultant and executive vice president of Mitre Corporation, a major defense contractor, was reported in the *Boston Globe* in 1985 as arguing that "if a highly effective defensive system were developed and one side started to deploy it . . . there would be a strong incentive for the other side to strike first to destroy the system before it was operational" (*Los Angeles Times,* July 1, 1984; David L. Chandler, "Pentagon Consultant Questions Space-Based Arms Plan," *Boston Globe,* June 26, 1985).

20. The most promising ABM is a "terminal" defense that attacks incoming Soviet warheads as they near their targets. But that is not "where the emphasis presently is in SDI. It is rather on boost-phase, post–boost-phase, and mid-course defense. Thus the SDI R&D program is ill-designed to the extent that the objective is to 'enhance deterrence'" (G. W. Rathjens, "The Technical (In)feasibility of SDI [remarks presented at symposium on SDI, Virginia Military Institute, April 8, 1986, photocopied], edited version published in S. W. Guerrier

and W. C. Thompson, *Perspectives on Strategic Defense* [Boulder, Colo.: West-view, 1986]).

21. Charles L. Glaser, "Do We Want the Missile Defenses We Can Build?" *International Security* 10, no. 1 (Summer 1985): 32–33.

22. E. P. Thompson, "Folly's Comet," in *Star Wars*, ed. E. P. Thompson (Harmondsworth: Penguin, 1985), pp. 103–104.

23. George Rathjens, "The Imperfections of 'Perfect Defense,'" *Environment* 26, no. 5 (June 1984): 38; Rathjens and Ruina, "BMD and Strategic Instability," pp. 254, 245; Glaser, "Missile Defenses," p. 35.

24. "SDI Lasers May Become Offensive Arms: Study," *Boston Globe*, January 13, 1986.

25. Ashton Carter, "Satellites and Anti-Satellites," *International Security* 10, no. 4 (Spring 1986): 47–88.

26. Robert English, "Offensive Star Wars," *New Republic* 194, no. 8 (February 24, 1986): 14.

27. Bundy et al., "President's Choice" (emphasis added).

28. Richard K. Betts, "Surprise Attack and Preemption," in *Hawks, Doves, and Owls*, ed. Allison, Carnesale, and Nye, p. 77.

## CHAPTER SIX

1. David Alan Rosenberg, "'A Smoking Radiating Ruin at the End of Two Hours': Documents of American Plans for Nuclear War with the Soviet Union, 1954–1955," *International Security* 6, no. 3 (Winter 1981–1982). See also Rosenberg, "The Origins of Overkill: Nuclear Weapons and American Strategy, 1945–1960," in *Strategy and Nuclear Deterrence: An "International Security" Reader*, ed. Steven E. Miller (Princeton: Princeton University Press, 1984), pp. 143–144 (originally published in *International Security* 7, no. 4 [Spring 1983]).

2. Noam Chomsky, "Which Way for the Disarmament Movement? Interventionism and Nuclear War," in *Beyond Survival: New Directions for the Disarmament Movement*, ed. Michael Albert and David Dellinger (Boston: South End Press, 1983), pp. 253–254.

3. Thomas H. Etzold and John Lewis Gaddis, *Containment: Documents on American Foreign Policy and Strategy, 1945–1950* (New York: Columbia University Press, 1978), p. 414. The full text of NSC 68 is also in *Naval War College Review* (May–June 1975) and in *Foreign Relations of the United States, 1950* (Washington, D.C.: Government Printing Office, 1977), vol. 1.

4. Richard H. Kohn and Joseph P. Harahan, eds., "U.S. Strategic Air Power, 1948–1962: Excerpts from an Interview with Generals Curtis E. LeMay, Leon W. Johnson, David A. Burchinal, and Jack J. Cotton," *International Security* 12, no. 4 (Spring 1988): 82–83; Daniel Ellsberg, "A Call to Mutiny," in Joseph Gerson, ed., *The Deadly Connection: Nuclear War and U.S. Intervention* (Philadelphia: New Society Publishers, 1986), pp. 40, 57; Richard K. Betts, *Nuclear Blackmail and Nuclear Balance* (Washington, D.C.: Brookings Institution, 1987), pp. 32, 34.

5. Ibid., p. 36.

6. Eisenhower, cited in Ellsberg, "Call to Mutiny," pp. 53–54.

7. Betts, *Nuclear Blackmail*, pp. 38, 41, 46, 47.

8. Ibid., pp. 43, 47. The Korean conflict brought other danger points as well, such as the October 1950 U.S. bombing, supposedly accidental, of a Soviet airfield near Vladivostok, the September 1950 attack by a Soviet aircraft on a U.N. fighter patrol just after a U.S. fighter strafed an airfield in Manchuria, and defensive operations by Soviet air units in Manchuria against U.S. planes, including one case of combat with unmarked Soviet aircraft flying out of the USSR (Stephen S. Kaplan et al., *Diplomacy of Power: Soviet Armed Forces as a Political Instrument* [Washington, D.C.: Brookings Institution, 1981], pp. 91, 92).

9. Betts, *Nuclear Blackmail*, p. 49.

10. See Ellsberg, "Call to Mutiny," pp. 40, 55, 56; Betts, *Nuclear Blackmail*, p. 52.

11. Gordon H. Chang, "To the Nuclear Brink: Eisenhower, Dulles, and the Quemoy-Matsu Crisis," *International Security* 2, no. 4 (Spring 1988): 99. In the Mandarin *pinyin* romanization the islands are known as Jinmen and Mazu.

12. Ibid., pp. 96, 97, 98.

13. Ibid., pp. 100, 107.

14. H. W. Brands, Jr., "Testing Massive Retaliation: Credibility and Crisis Management in the Taiwan Strait," *International Security* 12, no. 4 (Spring 1988): 141; Chang, "To the Nuclear Brink," p. 106; Brands, "Testing Massive Retaliation," p. 142.

15. Chang, "To the Nuclear Brink," p. 112; McGeorge Bundy, *Danger and Survival: Choices About the Bomb in the First Fifty Years* (New York: Random House, 1988), p. 280.

16. Chang, "To the Nuclear Brink," p. 113.

17. Associated Press, "Eisenhower Approached 'Nuclear Brink,'" *Patriot Ledger* (Quincy, Mass.), March 26, 1988, p. 2; Betts, *Nuclear Blackmail*, p. 56.

18. Chang, "To the Nuclear Brink," p. 107; Brands, "Testing Massive Retaliation," p. 142; Chang, "To the Nuclear Brink," p. 107; Brands, "Testing Massive Retaliation," p. 150; Chang, "To the Nuclear Brink," pp. 107–108; Brands, "Testing Massive Retaliation," p. 142.

19. Chang, "To the Nuclear Brink," p. 108; Brands, "Testing Massive Retaliation," pp. 128, 129, 139–140, 129.

20. Brands, "Testing Massive Retaliation," p. 143; Chang, "To the Nuclear Brink," p. 116.

21. Chang, "To the Nuclear Brink," pp. 116, 121.

22. Brands, "Testing Massive Retaliation," p. 125, 146; Chang, "To the Nuclear Brink," pp. 116, 117–118; Brands, "Testing Massive Retaliation," p. 147.

23. Brands, "Testing Massive Retaliation," pp. 147, 148; Kaplan, *Diplomacy of Power*, pp. 93–96. See also Alexander L. George and Richard Smoke, *Deterrence in American Foreign Policy: Theory and Practice* (New York: Columbia University Press, 1974), chap. 12; Ellsberg, "Call to Mutiny," p. 40; and Morton Halperin, *The 1958 Taiwan Straits Crisis: A Documented History*, RAND Corporation research memorandum RM-4900-ISA, December 1966 (formerly top secret).

24. Kaplan, *Diplomacy of Power*, pp. 154–155; Betts, *Nuclear Blackmail*, pp. 63, 65 (emphasis in original).

25. William B. Quandt, "Lebanon, 1958, and Jordan, 1970," in *Force Without War*, ed. Barry M. Blechman and Stephen S. Kaplan (Washington, D.C.: Brookings Institution, 1978), pp. 237, 256; Morton H. Halperin, *Nuclear Fallacy: Dispelling the Myth of Nuclear Strategy* (Cambridge, Mass.: Ballinger, 1987), pp. 32–33; Betts, *Nuclear Blackmail*, p. 66.

26. Quandt, "Lebanon, 1958, and Jordan, 1970," p. 238 (emphasis in original); Ellsberg, "Call to Mutiny," p. 40; Kaplan, *Diplomacy of Power*, p. 158.

27. Robert McNamara, *Blundering into Disaster* (New York: Pantheon, 1986), p. 9; Raymond Garthoff, *Reflections on the Cuban Missile Crisis* (Washington, D.C.: Brookings Institution, 1987), p. 30; McNamara, *Blundering into Disaster*, pp. 10–11.

28. Richard E. Neustadt and Graham T. Allison, afterword to Robert F. Kennedy, *Thirteen Days: A Memoir of the Cuban Missile Crisis* (New York: Norton, 1969), p. 112.

29. Lebow, *Nuclear Crisis Management*, p. 136 (emphasis added). Potentially dangerous post-1962 incidents not discussed in this book include the October 1967 sinking of an Israeli destroyer by a Soviet-supplied Egyptian patrol boat in the tense aftermath of the devastating June war, leading the Soviets to immediately send warships to Port Said in anticipation of a possible Israeli military response; the 1968 seizure of the USS *Pueblo* by North Korean patrol boats, leading President Johnson to deploy Strategic Air Command nuclear bombers to the western Pacific and the largest U.S. naval force since the Cuban missile crisis to the Sea of Japan, where they engaged in potentially dangerous incidents with two Soviet warships; the 1969 downing of a U.S. Navy EC-121 reconnaissance plane by North Korea, to which both superpowers fortunately responded with restrained actions; the 1975 seizure of a U.S. commercial container vessel, the *Mayaguez*, by Khmer Rouge forces in Cambodian waters, leading to a bloody U.S. military "rescue" operation; and the Angolan conflict, in which both superpowers, China, South Africa, and Cuba are substantially involved. See Kaplan, *Diplomacy of Power*, pp. 168, 105, 106, 403, 195–199.

30. McNamara, *Blundering into Disaster*, p. 13; Lyndon Baines Johnson, *The Vantage Point: Perspectives of the Presidency, 1963–1969* (New York: Holt, Rinehart & Winston, 1971), p. 288.

31. Anthony R. Wells, "The June 1967 Arab-Israeli War," in *Soviet Naval Diplomacy*, ed. Bradford Dismukes and James M. McConnell (New York: Pergamon, 1979), p. 166; Paul Jabber and Roman Kolkowicz, "The Arab-Israeli Wars of 1967 and 1973," in Kaplan, *Diplomacy of Power*, p. 433.

32. Johnson, *Vantage Point*, p. 300; "Sect. Rusk and Sect. of Defense McNamara Discuss Vietnam and Korea on 'Meet the Press,'" *Department of State Bulletin* 63, no. 1496 (February 26, 1968): 271, cited in William L. Ury, *Beyond the Hotline: How We Can Prevent the Crisis That Might Bring on a Nuclear War* (Boston: Houghton Mifflin, 1985), p. 22; Wells, "Arab-Israeli War," p. 167; James E. Ennes, *Assault on the Liberty* (New York: Random House, 1979), p. 78, cited in Noam Chomsky, *The Fateful Triangle* (Boston: South End Press, 1983), pp. 449–450; Johnson, *Vantage Point*, pp. 300–301.

33. Leonard S. Spector, *The Undeclared Bomb* (Cambridge, Mass.: Ballinger, 1988), p. 176; McNamara, *Blundering into Disaster,* p. 13 (see also Jabber and Kolkowicz, "Arab-Israeli Wars," pp. 435–436); Johnson, *Vantage Point,* p. 302; Wells, "Arab-Israeli War," p. 166. In *Decade of Decisions* (Berkeley and Los Angeles: University of California Press, 1977), William B. Quandt writes that "other participants in the events have judged Johnson's version overly dramatic" (p. 43).

34. Jabber and Kolkowicz, "Arab-Israeli Wars," p. 436; Johnson, *Vantage Point,* pp. 302, 303.

35. Wells, "Arab-Israeli War," p. 166; McNamara, *Blundering into Disaster,* p. 13; Johnson, *Vantage Point,* p. 304; Betts, *Nuclear Blackmail,* p. 128.

36. Marvin Kalb and Bernard Kalb, *Kissinger* (Boston: Little, Brown, 1974), p. 190; Dismukes and McConnell, *Soviet Naval Diplomacy,* p. 227; Quandt, "Lebanon, 1958, and Jordan, 1970," p. 258; Kalb and Kalb, *Kissinger,* p. 190; Bradford Dismukes, "Large-Scale Intervention Ashore: Soviet Air Defense Forces in Egypt," in *Soviet Naval Diplomacy,* ed. Dismukes and McConnell, pp. 226, 221, 222.

37. Henry Kissinger, *White House Years* (Boston: Little, Brown, 1979), pp. 570–571; Kalb and Kalb, *Kissinger,* pp. 190–191.

38. Kissinger, *White House Years,* pp. 568, 572, 574, 581–582.

39. Alvin Z. Rubinstein, "Air Support in the Arab East," in Kaplan, *Diplomacy of Power,* p. 475; Dismukes, "Large-Scale Intervention," pp. 232–233.

40. Peter Pry, *Israel's Nuclear Arsenal* (Boulder, Colo.: Westview, 1984), p. 29.

41. Kalb and Kalb, *Kissinger,* pp. 197, 199.

42. Quandt, "Lebanon, 1958, and Jordan, 1970," p. 257; Richard M. Nixon, *RN: The Memoirs of Richard Nixon* (New York: Grosset & Dunlap, 1978), p. 477; Seymour M. Hersh, *The Price of Power: Kissinger in the Nixon White House* (New York: Summit, 1983), p. 238.

43. Kalb and Kalb, *Kissinger,* p. 200.

44. Hersh, *Price of Power,* pp. 244, 245.

45. Ibid., p. 244.

46. Quandt, "Lebanon, 1958, and Jordan, 1970," p. 272 (see also Kaplan, *Diplomacy of Power,* pp. 181–183); Kalb and Kalb, *Kissinger,* p. 198; Quandt, "Lebanon, 1958, and Jordan, 1970," pp. 269, 279; Kissinger, *White House Years,* pp. 609, 614.

47. Nixon, *RN,* p. 483; Hersh, *Price of Power,* 246. See also Fred Kaplan, *The Wizards of Armageddon* (New York: Simon & Schuster, 1983), p. 370.

48. Kissinger, *White House Years,* pp. 621, 622; Kalb and Kalb, *Kissinger,* pp. 201–202.

49. Kalb and Kalb, *Kissinger,* pp. 202–203, 204.

50. Ibid., pp. 204, 205.

51. Ibid., pp. 205–206 (emphasis added).

52. Kissinger, *White House Years,* pp. 624–625.

53. Ibid., p. 625; Quandt, "Lebanon, 1958, and Jordan, 1970," p. 271; Kissinger, *White House Years,* p. 625. Quandt adds that "these contingency ar-

rangements were subject to review," which may be the basis of the ambiguity over whether Nixon authorized Israeli ground operations.

54. Kalb and Kalb, *Kissinger*, pp. 205–207 (emphasis in original).

55. Quandt, "Lebanon, 1958, and Jordan, 1970," pp. 271, 268.

56. Elmo R. Zumwalt, Jr., *On Watch: A Memoir* (New York: Quadrangle, 1976), pp. 300–301, cited in Abram N. Shulsky, "The Jordanian Crisis of September 1970," in *Soviet Naval Diplomacy*, ed. Dismukes and McConnell, p. 176.

57. Shulsky, "Jordanian Crisis," p. 176, cited in Desmond Ball, "Nuclear War at Sea," *International Security* 10, no. 3 (Winter 1985–1986): 7.

58. Quandt, "Lebanon, 1958, and Jordan, 1970," p. 271.

59. Hersh, *Price of Power*, p. 250; Kissinger, *White House Years*, p. 594.

60. Ibid., pp. 252, 253.

61. Nixon, *RN*, pp. 220–221; Kissinger, *White House Years*, p. 634; Kalb and Kalb, *Kissinger*, p. 210.

62. Nixon, *RN*, p. 486.

63. Kissinger, *White House Years*, pp. 641, 643; Nixon, *RN*, p. 488; Garthoff, *Cuban Missile Crisis*, pp. 33–34; Kalb and Kalb, *Kissinger*, p. 211; Kissinger, *White House Years*, pp. 645, 647.

64. Nixon, *RN*, p. 488; Kalb and Kalb, *Kissinger*, p. 211; Nixon, *RN*, p. 489.

65. Kalb and Kalb, *Kissinger*, p. 211; Szulc quoted in Hersh, *Price of Power*, p. 255.

66. Kissinger, *White House Years*, p. 651.

67. Kalb and Kalb, *Kissinger*, p. 257.

68. Nixon, *RN*, p. 526.

69. David K. Hall, "The Laotian War of 1962 and the Indo-Pakistani War of 1971," in *Force Without War*, ed. Blechman and Kaplan, pp. 177, 178.

70. Kalb and Kalb, *Kissinger*, p. 259; Kissinger, *White House Years*, p. 904; Nixon, *RN*, p. 528.

71. Nixon, *RN*, p. 526; Kalb and Kalb, *Kissinger*, p. 260; Kissinger, *White House Years*, p. 905; Hall, "Indo-Pakistani War," p. 188; Halperin, *Nuclear Fallacy*, pp. 41–42; CIA, cited in Hall, "Indo-Pakistani War," p. 201, and Kaplan, *Diplomacy of Power*, p. 184.

72. James M. McConnell and Anne Kelly Calhoun, "The December 1971 Indo-Pakistani Crisis," in *Soviet Naval Diplomacy*, ed. Dismukes and McConnell, pp. 183, 191.

73. Hall, "Indo-Pakistani War," pp. 193–194.

74. Kissinger, *White House Years*, pp. 909–910; Nixon, *RN*, p. 527.

75. Kissinger, *White House Years*, pp. 910, 912; Hall, "Indo-Pakistani War," pp. 202, 195; Nixon, cited in Halperin, *Nuclear Fallacy*, pp. 41–42; Hersh, *Price of Power*, p. 457.

76. Hall, "Indo-Pakistani War," pp. 192–194, 200, 221 (emphasis in original).

77. From Westmoreland's memoirs, cited in Ellsberg, "Call to Mutiny," p. 55.

78. Halperin, *Nuclear Fallacy,* p. 40.

79. From H. R. Haldeman's memoir, *The End of Power* (New York: Times Books, 1978), pp. 82–83, cited in Ellsberg, "Call to Mutiny," pp. 56–57; Ellsberg, "Call to Mutiny," p. 48.

80. Hersh, *Price of Power,* pp. 128, 129.

81. Ibid., pp. 124–125.

82. Ibid., pp. 368–369.

83. See Nixon, *RN,* p. 591. Kissinger comments: "Considering that we were bombing Hanoi and Haiphong four days before my visit to Moscow, this was restraint of a high order. What was significant was not that the criticism stopped well short of a protest but that Moscow maintained its invitation even in the face of an unprecedented assault on its client" (Kissinger, *White House Years,* p. 1122).

84. The Arabs achieved almost complete surprise despite numerous long-standing warnings by the Arab states and by the Soviet Union that such a war was inevitable unless captured Arab territory was returned by Israel. "Sadat had made his intentions so open that they came to be generally disbelieved," and Gromyko, in a typical Soviet statement, told the U.N. General Assembly on September 20 that "the fires of war could break out at any time, and who could tell what consequences would ensue" (Raymond L. Garthoff, *Détente and Confrontation: American-Soviet Relations from Nixon to Reagan* [Washington, D.C.: Brookings Institution, 1985], pp. 362, 365–366). Kissinger acknowledges in his memoirs that "Sadat boldly all but told what he was going to do and we did not believe him" (Henry Kissinger, *Years of Upheaval* [Boston: Little, Brown, 1982], p. 459). The United States bears substantial blame for making it possible for Israel to refuse to compromise over the territories they captured in 1967 despite the widespread understanding that their position made another war almost inevitable and with it the clear danger of the perilous superpower confrontation that did in fact occur.

85. Pry, *Israel's Nuclear Arsenal,* p. 31; "How Israel Got the Bomb," *Time,* April 12, 1976, cited in Pry, *Israel's Nuclear Arsenal,* pp. 31–32.

86. Amos Perlmutter, Michael Handel, and Uri Bar-Joseph, *Two Minutes over Baghdad* (London: Corgi Books, 1982), pp. 46–48; Spector, *The Undeclared Bomb,* p. 177. Perlmutter, Handel, and Bar-Joseph provide no documentation for their claims; Spector cites his interviews. According to Spector, the U.S. officials he interviewed said that Israel's readying of its nuclear weapons was not "necessarily in conjunction with the [Jericho] missiles." Spector adds that "Egypt was apparently aware of the possibility that Israel might use nuclear arms during the conflict" and that "some Israeli scholars believe that Israel's nuclear capabilities played a far more important role in the conflict than has been acknowledged" (pp. 177, 396).

87. Garthoff, *Détente and Confrontation,* p. 369.

88. Kissinger, *Years of Upheaval,* pp. 508, 509–510.

89. Ibid., p. 508; Zumwalt, *On Watch,* pp. 446–447, cited in Kaplan, *Diplomacy of Power,* p. 186; Stephen S. Roberts, "The October 1973 Arab-Israeli War," in *Soviet Naval Diplomacy,* ed. Dismukes and McConnell, pp. 196, 199–201; Kaplan, *Diplomacy of Power,* p. 188.

90. Kissinger, *Years of Upheaval*, pp. 517–520.

91. Kaplan, *Diplomacy of Power*, p. 188; Kissinger, *Years of Upheaval*, pp. 559–560.

92. Kissinger, *Years of Upheaval*, pp. 561, 569 (emphasis in original); Garthoff, *Détente and Confrontation*, p. 372.

93. Garthoff, *Détente and Confrontation*, p. 374; Roberts, "Arab-Israeli War," p. 202; Kissinger, *Years of Upheaval*, p. 575.

94. Garthoff, *Détente and Confrontation*, p. 375; Kissinger, *Years of Upheaval*, p. 580.

95. Kissinger, *Years of Upheaval*, p. 581.

96. Ibid., p. 582.

97. Ibid., p. 583; Barry M. Blechman and Douglas M. Hart, "The Political Utility of Nuclear Weapons: The 1973 Middle East Crisis," in *Strategy and Nuclear Deterrence: An "International Security" Reader*, ed. Stephen E. Miller (Princeton: Princeton University Press, 1984), pp. 279–280 (first published in *International Security* 7, no. 1 [Summer 1982]).

98. Scott D. Sagan, "Nuclear Alerts and Crisis Management," *International Security* 9, no. 4 (Spring 1985): 122.

99. But as Jabber and Kolkowicz observe: "It was not clear whether this [mobilization] was primarily connected with the contingency of possible Soviet intervention or was a precautionary move taken once it appeared that an early cease-fire was not in the cards. Apparently U.S. decisionmakers were not alarmed by the move. It was not immediately reported by the media, and U.S. officials made no allusion to it" ("Arab-Israeli Wars," p. 447). Indeed, on October 12 Kissinger had praised the Soviets for restraint in the crisis.

100. Blechman and Hart, "Political Utility," pp. 277–279.

101. Garthoff, *Détente and Confrontation*, p. 378; Kissinger, *Years of Upheaval*, pp. 587–588.

102. Kissinger, *Years of Upheaval*, pp. 589, 591; Sagan, "Nuclear Alerts and Crisis Management," p. 125; Garthoff, *Détente and Confrontation*, p. 379. For a review of the evidence that Nixon was excluded from these decisions and then lied about it later, in his memoirs and elsewhere, see Garthoff, *Détente and Confrontation*, pp. 378–379. McGeorge Bundy also alludes to "the short [nuclear] alert called in President Nixon's name on October 24, 1973" ("The Unimpressive Record of Atomic Diplomacy," in *The Nuclear Crisis Reader*, ed. Gwyn Prins [New York: Vintage, 1984], p. 50).

103. Sagan, "Nuclear Alerts and Crisis Management," p. 125; Blechman and Hart, "Political Utility," p. 283; Kissinger, *Years of Upheaval*, p. 589.

104. Blechman and Hart, "Political Utility," p. 281; Kissinger, *Years of Upheaval*, p. 590.

105. Garthoff, *Détente and Confrontation*, p. 379. Most accounts of the 1973 crisis suggest, apparently inaccurately, that Nixon ordered the nuclear alert and managed the crisis.

106. Nixon, *RN*, pp. 939–940, Kissinger, *Years of Upheaval*, pp. 594–595.

107. Blechman and Hart, "Political Utility," pp. 284–285.

108. Kissinger, *Years of Upheaval*, pp. 607, 604–605, 607, 608, 611.

109. Roberts, "Arab-Israeli War," pp. 204, 210.

110. Blechman and Hart, "Political Utility," pp. 295–296.

111. Kaplan, *Wizards of Armageddon,* pp. 370–371.

112. Garthoff, *Détente and Confrontation,* pp. 828, 829, 841.

113. Ibid., pp. 829–830, 832, 836–837.

114. Ibid., pp. 837, 842 (emphasis in original).

115. Zbigniew Brzezinski, *Power and Principle: Memoirs of the National Security Adviser, 1977–1981* (New York: Farrar, Straus, Giroux), pp. 351–352.

116. *Le Monde,* June 11, 1982, cited in Chomsky, *Fateful Triangle,* p. 27; Chomsky, *Fateful Triangle,* p. 450.

117. See Ned Temko, *Christian Science Monitor,* June 23, 1982; Claudia Wright, *New Statesman,* June 18, 1982; both cited in Chomsky, *Fateful Triangle,* p. 450.

118. AP, "Soviet Embassy Heavily Damaged by Israeli Shells," *New York Times,* July 8, 1982; *New York Times, Christian Science Monitor,* December 2, 1982; all cited in Chomsky, *Fateful Triangle,* p. 450. As Chomsky notes, these sources do not make clear whether the Israelis killed the eleven Soviets during or before the Lebanon war.

119. Cited in Noam Chomsky, "Patterns of Intervention," in *Deadly Connection,* ed. Gerson, pp. 60–61.

120. William A. Schwartz, "Nuclear Weapons in Lebanon?" (Chestnut Hill, Mass., 1983). Given the particular vessels deployed to Lebanon, determined from newspaper accounts, and the known nuclear capabilities of each ship in the U.S. Navy, it was possible to compile a long list of nuclear weapons potentially on site. One must say "potentially" because the Navy does not confirm or deny the presence of nuclear warheads on its ships at any time. But on the basis of interviews with people familiar with nuclear weapons procedures, it seems clear that at least some of these ships, especially the carriers, almost certainly brought warheads along. Such vessels were actively engaged in combat, with Soviet forces stationed nearby. Most of the major U.S. newspapers refused to publish the article documenting these facts, submitted as an Op-Ed article in the midst of the 1983 crisis.

121. Ury, *Beyond the Hotline,* pp. 20–21.

122. Selig S. Harrison, "Afghanistan: Soviet Intervention, Afghan Resistance, and the American Role," in *Low Intensity Warfare: Counterinsurgency, Proinsurgency, and Antiterrorism in the Eighties,* ed. Michael T. Klare and Peter Kornbluh (New York: Pantheon, 1988), p. 183.

123. On Afghan and Soviet attacks on Pakistan, see, for example, AP, "1,500 Soviet Troops Start Afghan Pullout," *Boston Globe,* October 16, 1986, p. 6; AP, "Afghans Raid 2 Border Villages in Pakistan; 35 Reported Dead," *Boston Globe,* February 27, 1987, p. 68; AP, "Afghan Jets Hit Village," *Boston Globe,* March 24, 1987, p. 3; Reuters, "13 Dead as Afghans Hit Pakistani Areas," *Boston Globe,* May 3, 1988, p. 8; Richard M. Weintraub, "Afghan Rebels Hit Soviet Arms Site," *Boston Globe,* September 2, 1988, pp. 1, 12; Colin Nickerson, "Amid Afghan Raids, Pakistanis Assail US," *Boston Globe,* September 3, 1988, p. 3. On dogfights, see AP, "Afghans Shoot Down a Pakistani F-16," *Boston Globe,* April 30, 1987, p. 8; Reuters, "Kabul Says Pakistan Downed 2 Aircraft," *Boston Globe,* November 4, 1988, p. 10. On the report of

the Afghan defectors and the capture of the Soviet pilot, see UPI, "Pakistan Jets Hit Afghan Warplane," *Boston Globe*, September 8, 1988, p. 12; on the 1984 report, see John Prados, *Presidents' Secret Wars: CIA and Pentagon Covert Operations from World War II Through Iranscam* (New York: Quill, 1986), p. 360.

124. Ahmed Rashid, "Pakistanis Want an Afghan Peace," *Nation*, January 31, 1987, p. 112.

125. On U.S. patrols, see John H. Cushman, Jr., "Pakistan Says It May Request Air Patrols by U.S.," *New York Times*, October 16, 1986, p. A12; John H. Cushman, Jr., "U.S. Seeking AWACs for Pakistan," *New York Times*, October 17, 1986, p. A6. On possible Pakistani and Afghan rebel terrorist attacks, see AP, "Afghans Say Pakistan Hit Civilian Plane," *Boston Globe*, April 1, 1987, p. 3; UPI, "Kabul Says Guerillas Down Plane, Killing 29," *Boston Globe*, April 11, 1988, p. 7; "Afghans Say Rebels Downed Plane, 53 Died," *Boston Globe*, June 12, 1987, p. 3; UPI, "Afghan Rebels Down Plane, Killing 43, Westerners Say," *Boston Globe*, June 24, 1987, p. 8; AP, "Pakistan Car Bomb May Have Killed 72," *Boston Globe*, October 14, 1987, p. 13; Reuters, "Four Rockets Launched by Guerillas Explode in Afghanistan Capital," *Boston Globe*, November 30, 1987, p. 4. On rebel attacks on Soviet territory, see David B. Ottaway, "Soviets Say Afghan Rebels Inflicted Casualties in Attack on USSR Hamlet," *Boston Globe*, April 13, 1987, p. 7. Ottaway cites conflicting reports on whether the rebels actually entered the Soviet Union or just fired rockets across the border. He also mentions the rebel Islamic party's statement that the group attacked the USSR to show that "we are not only fighting to free our territory but to free land taken from us by force and our Moslem brothers under the control of communism"—that is, to liberate Afghan territory seized by czarist Russia. The leader of the Islamic party has publicly called for the "liberation" of the Soviet Muslim-dominated republics.

126. Laurence Martin, *The Changing Face of Nuclear Warfare* (New York: Harper & Row, 1987), pp. 90–91.

127. Spector, *Undeclared Bomb*, pp. 129, 133, 135, 142–143.

128. Lawrence Lifschultz, "New U.S. Spy Flights from Pakistan," *Nation* 243, no. 18 (November 29, 1986): 593, 606, 608, 610.

129. Harrison, "Afghanistan," pp. 205–206.

130. Spector, *Undeclared Bomb*, pp. 130–131, 132.

131. John Walcott and Tim Carrington, "CIA Resisted Proposal to Give Afghan Rebels U.S. Stinger Missiles," *Wall Street Journal*, February 16, 1988, p. 1.

132. Ibid., pp. 1, 31; Harrison, "Afghanistan," p. 201.

133. Walcott and Carrington, "CIA Resisted Proposal," p. 31; Rashid, "Pakistanis Want an Afghan Peace," p. 114; Harrison, "Afghanistan," p. 203; "Pakistan Expects Rising Pressure as Fighting Grows in Afghanistan," *New York Times*, April 6, 1987, p. A9.

134. On Brzezinski, see Garthoff, *Détente and Confrontation*, pp. 974–975. Some American press reports said Brzezinski actually fired the weapon, but Garthoff considers them "exaggerated." On the press backgrounder, see David Woods, January 18, 1980, p. 1, cited in Ellsberg, "Call to Mutiny," pp. 37–38.

## CHAPTER SEVEN

1. McGeorge Bundy, *Danger and Survival: Choices About the Bomb in the First Fifty Years* (New York: Random House, 1988), pp. 517, 542, 590.

2. Ibid., pp. 593, 595, 596, 598. Bundy adds, in qualification, that Europe is safe from nuclear danger "as long as the countries of that region are self-confident and the tradition of mutual trust between them and the United States is maintained" (p. 598).

3. Paul Bracken, *The Command and Control of Nuclear Forces* (New Haven: Yale University Press, 1983), pp. 52, 68.

4. Barry R. Posen, "Inadvertent Nuclear War? Escalation and NATO's Northern Flank," in *Strategy and Nuclear Deterrence,* ed. Miller, p. 109 (first published in *International Security* 7, no. 2 [Fall 1982]).

5. Robert Kennedy, *Thirteen Days: A Memoir of the Cuban Missile Crisis* (New York: W. W. Norton, 1969), pp. 47–49.

6. Details on these incidents are from Scott D. Sagan, "Nuclear Alerts and Crisis Management," *International Security* 9, no. 4 (Spring 1985), pp. 106–122.

7. See Desmond Ball, "Nuclear War at Sea," *International Security* 10, no. 3 (Winter 1985–1986), p. 20.

8. Sagan, "Nuclear Alerts and Crisis Management," pp. 118–121.

9. Ibid., pp. 121–122; Raymond L. Garthoff, *Reflections on the Cuban Missile Crisis* (Washington D.C.: Brookings Institution, 1987), pp. 78–79. Some of this information had not been revealed before the publication of Garthoff's important book.

10. Stephen S. Kaplan, *Diplomacy of Power: Soviet Armed Forces as a Political Instrument* (Washington, D.C.: Brookings Institution, 1981), p. 58; Barry M. Blechman and Stephen S. Kaplan, *Force Without War: U.S. Armed Forces as a Political Instrument* (Washington, D.C.: Brookings Institution, 1978), pp. 28, 47; Ball, "Nuclear War at Sea," p. 28.

11. Ball, "Nuclear War at Sea," pp. 6–8.

12. Ibid., pp. 5–6.

13. Ibid., pp. 13, 29. Ball cites several other factors besides those we mention, such as the U.S. Navy's antisubmarine warfare strategy, as risk factors for unintended nuclear war at sea. This article is required reading for all serious students of how nuclear war might begin.

14. Johnson, cited in Richard Ned Lebow, *Nuclear Crisis Management: A Dangerous Illusion* (Ithaca: Cornell University Press, 1987), pp. 218–219; Gerald R. Ford, *A Time to Heal: The Autobiography of Gerald R. Ford* (New York: Harper & Row and the Reader's Digest Association, 1979), p. 136. We do not know if the reports were true. The important thing is that such an action by Schlesinger would be quite plausible.

15. Robert Jervis, *The Logic of Images in International Relations* (Princeton: Princeton University Press, 1970), p. 7; Henry Kissinger, *Years of Upheaval* (Boston: Little, Brown, 1982), p. 246.

16. Gordon H. Chang, "To the Nuclear Brink: Eisenhower, Dulles, and the Quemoy-Matsu Crisis," *International Security* 12, no. 4 (Spring 1988): 99; H. W. Brands, Jr., "Testing Massive Retaliation: Credibility and Crisis Man-

agement in the Taiwan Strait," *International Security* 12, no. 4 (Spring 1988): 124, 138.

17. I. F. Stone, "The Brink," in *The Cuban Missile Crisis,* ed. Robert A. Divine (Chicago: Quadrangle, 1971), p. 156 (first published in *New York Review of Books,* April 14, 1966, pp. 12–16); Lebow, *Nuclear Crisis Management,* p. 16.

18. Richard M. Nixon, *RN: The Memoirs of Richard Nixon* (New York: Grosset & Dunlap, 1978), pp. 481–482, 485 (emphasis added); Henry Kissinger, *White House Years* (Boston: Little, Brown, 1979), pp. 596–597, 616; Marvin Kalb and Bernard Kalb, *Kissinger* (Boston: Little, Brown, 1974), p. 202; William B. Quandt, "Lebanon, 1958, and Jordan, 1970," in Blechman and Kaplan, *Force Without War,* p. 281.

19. Kissinger, *White House Years,* pp. 641, 886, 895, 898, 903, 914, 916; Nixon, *RN,* p. 527.

20. Kissinger, *Years of Upheaval,* pp. 468, 520, 521, 536.

21. Lebow, *Nuclear Crisis Management,* pp. 71–72.

22. Daniel Ellsberg, "A Call to Mutiny," in *The Deadly Connection: Nuclear War and U.S. Intervention,* ed. Joseph Gerson (Philadelphia: New Society Publishers, 1986), pp. 36, 39 (emphasis in original); Blechman and Kaplan, *Force Without War,* pp. 47–49.

23. Kaplan, *Diplomacy of Power,* pp. 54–60; Garthoff, *Cuban Missile Crisis,* p. 41; Sagan, "Nuclear Alerts and Crisis Management," pp. 129–130.

24. Barry M. Blechman and Douglas M. Hart, "The Political Utility of Nuclear Weapons: The 1973 Middle East Crisis," in *Strategy and Nuclear Deterrence: An "International Security" Reader,* ed. Stephen E. Miller (Princeton: Princeton University Press, 1984), p. 296; Blechman and Kaplan, *Force Without War,* p. 531.

25. Cited in Raymond L. Garthoff, *Détente and Confrontation: American-Soviet Relations from Nixon to Reagan* (Washington, D.C.: Brookings Institution, 1985), p. 974. For the original, see *Presidential Documents* 16 (January 28, 1980).

26. See Ellsberg, "Call to Mutiny," pp. 37–39, 45. At this writing, commentators such as Charles Krauthammer are citing the Carter Doctrine to justify the Reagan administration's intervention of nuclear-armed U.S. Navy ships in the Iran-Iraq war—even though there is no connection between the two. The Carter Doctrine refers specifically to defense against an "outside force"; the Iran-Iraq war is a conflict between gulf states in which the United States is the outside force.

27. Christopher Paine, "On the Beach: The Rapid Deployment Force and the Nuclear Arms Race," in *Deadly Connection,* ed. Gerson, pp. 113, 117; Ellsberg, "Call to Mutiny," p. 44.

28. Joseph J. Kruzel, cited in Kaplan, *Diplomacy of Power,* p. 55 (from "Military Alerts and Diplomatic Signals," in *The Limits of Military Intervention,* ed. Ellen P. Stern [Sage, 1977], p. 89); Sagan, "Nuclear Alerts and Crisis Management," pp. 99, 130, 132, 135–136.

29. Sagan, "Nuclear Alerts and Crisis Management," p. 131; Lebow, *Nuclear Crisis Management,* p. 103.

30. Kissinger, *Years of Upheaval,* p. 536.

31. David Woods, *Los Angeles Times*, March 17, 1982, cited in Noam Chomsky, *Turning the Tide* (Boston: South End Press, 1985), pp. 171–172. According to Chomsky, "Lehman said he envisioned a conventional rather than a nuclear global war with the USSR—conceivable, but hardly likely."

32. Leonard S. Spector, *The Undeclared Bomb* (Cambridge, Mass.: Ballinger, 1988), pp. 69–70, 91, 147.

33. Peter Hayes, Walden Bello, and Lyuba Zarsky, "Korean Tripwire," *Nation* 245, no. 8 (September 19, 1987), p. 256; see also their *American Lake: Nuclear Peril in the Pacific* (New York: Penguin, 1986), pp. ix, 1, 2. *American Lake* is a crucial study of the Pacific's many nuclear dangers.

34. "Who's Who, and Why, in Angola," *Economist*, June 14, 1986, p. 33.

35. Spector, *Undeclared Bomb*, pp. 288, 293, 284.

36. Bernard Avishai and Avner Cohen, "Time to Heed the Nuclear Threat in the Middle East," *Boston Globe*, April 3, 1988; Pranger and Tahtinen, quoted in Taysir N. Nashif, *Nuclear Warfare in the Middle East: Dimensions and Responsibilities* (Princeton: Kingston Press, 1984), p. 60.

37. Spector, *Undeclared Bomb*, pp. 164, 180, 32, 162.

38. Ibid., pp. 186–187; Perlmutter, Handel, and Bar-Joseph, *Two Minutes over Baghdad*; Avishai and Cohen, "Nuclear Threat," p. 67.

39. Spector, *Undeclared Bomb*, pp. 179–180, 162.

40. Avishai and Cohen, "Nuclear Threat," p. 67; Pry, *Israel's Nuclear Arsenal*, p. 1.

41. *New York Times*, June 24, 1987; "Iranian Guns Aimed at Soviet Convoy," *Patriot Ledger* (Quincy, Mass.), November 20, 1987, p. 4; Thomas B. Cochran, William M. Arkin, and Milton M. Hoenig, *Nuclear Weapons Databook*, vol. 1, *U.S. Nuclear Forces and Capabilities* (Cambridge, Mass.: Ballinger, 1984), pp. 244–278; Joshua Handler and William M. Arkin, *Nuclear Warships and Naval Nuclear Weapons: A Complete Inventory*, Neptune Papers No. 2 (Washington, D.C.: Greenpeace and the Institute for Policy Studies, 1988), pp. 39–73; Paine, "On the Beach," p. 119.

CHAPTER EIGHT

1. We have drawn general historical information on the Cuban missile crisis from a variety of sources, especially Ellie Abel, *The Missile Crisis* (Philadelphia: Lippincott, 1966); Robert F. Kennedy, *Thirteen Days: A Memoir of the Cuban Missile Crisis* (New York: Norton, 1968); David Detzer, *The Brink* (New York: Crowell, 1979); Theodore Sorensen, *Kennedy* (New York: Harper & Row, 1965); Herbert Dinerstein, *The Making of a Missile Crisis* (Baltimore: Johns Hopkins University Press, 1976); and Richard Walton, *Cold War and Counterrevolution* (Baltimore: Penguin, 1972).

2. Kennedy, *Thirteen Days*, pp. 1, 86; Raymond L. Garthoff, *Reflections on the Cuban Missile Crisis* (Washington, D.C.: Brookings Institution, 1987), p. 45.

3. Scott D. Sagan, "Nuclear Alerts and Crisis Management," *International Security* 9, no. 4 (Spring 1985): 109n.

4. Detzer, *Brink*, pp. 164–165.

5. John F. Kennedy's address of October 22, 1962, quoted in Kennedy, *Thirteen Days*, pp. 155–156; Sorensen, *Kennedy*, p. 705.

6. John F. Kennedy, quoted in Kennedy, *Thirteen Days*, pp. 153–154. President Kennedy acknowledged in this speech that the nuclear threat to U.S. cities was not entirely new: "American citizens have become adjusted to living daily on the bull's eye of Soviet missiles located inside the U.S.S.R. or in submarines. . . . In that sense missiles in Cuba add to an already clear and present danger." (p. 155). But this admission did not change the thrust of his almost panicky speech—that the Cuban missiles posed a direct threat to U.S. population centers.

7. I. F. Stone, "The Brink," in *The Cuban Missile Crisis*, ed. Robert A. Divine (Chicago: Quadrangle, 1971), p. 156 (first published in *New York Review of Books*, April 14, 1966, pp. 12–16).

8. David Alan Rosenberg, "The Origins of Overkill," in *Strategy and Nuclear Deterrence: An "International Security" Reader*, ed. Stephen E. Miller (Princeton: Princeton University Press, 1984), pp. 148, 150 (first published in *International Security* 7, no. 4 [Spring 1983]).

9. Roger Hagan and Bart Bernstein, "Military Value of Missiles in Cuba," *Bulletin of the Atomic Scientists* 14, no. 2 (February 1963): 8–13. Declassified Pentagon studies were made available to us by the Institute for Defense and Disarmament Studies, Brookline, Mass. We are grateful to Matt Goodman, Burton Wright, and David Meyer of the institute for their generous help in compiling and assessing strategic force data. On news coverage of the new claims about the number of Soviet intercontinental ballistic missiles, see, for example, Dan Fisher, "Soviets Had Warheads in Cuba, Conferees Told," *Boston Globe,* January 29, 1989, p. 1; Bill Keller, "Warheads Were Deployed in Cuba in '62, Soviets Say," *New York Times,* January 29, 1989, p. 1.

10. Richard E. Neustadt and Graham T. Allison, afterword to Kennedy, *Thirteen Days*, pp. 123–124, paraphrasing statements reportedly made by Robert McNamara, then secretary of defense.

11. See Hagan and Bernstein, "Missiles in Cuba," for a discussion of this "short-circuit" theory of Soviet motivations.

12. Some might argue that nuclear missiles and bombers in Cuba would have complicated a coordinated American first strike, making its success less certain and thereby helping to deter it. Although Cuban weapons would be highly vulnerable, ensuring their destruction while at the same time eliminating all important nuclear arms bases in the Soviet Union would be more complex and uncertain than simply attacking Soviet targets. Timing simultaneous attacks of near and distant targets while ensuring surprise might be particularly problematic. But if, improbably, Soviet home-based nuclear forces were indeed vulnerable to preemptive destruction, such "complications" could not fundamentally invalidate a U.S. first strike. Given the long lead times needed to launch Soviet missiles and bombers of the time, complete surprise and simultaneity of attack would not be required. Destroying Cuban bases would be the easiest part of a preemptive raid and would not have to be completely coordinated with the intercontinental strikes at the Soviet Union. Therefore Cuban weaponry could not significantly add to the Soviet deterrent against a U.S. first strike.

13. Hagan and Bernstein, "Missiles in Cuba," p. 12.

14. Rosenberg, "Origins of Overkill," p. 175; J. C. Hopkins, *The Development of the Strategic Air Command* (Omaha: Strategic Air Command, Office of the Historian, 1981); Robert McNamara, declassified Department of Defense statement, 1966, substantiated by 1967 statement; Thomas B. Cochran, William M. Arkin, and Milton M. Hoenig, *Nuclear Weapons Databook*, vol. 1, *U.S. Nuclear Forces and Capabilities* (Cambridge, Mass.: Ballinger, 1984), table 1.6, p. 15.

15. Some argued that the Cuban weapons would add to a Soviet first-strike capability against U.S. nuclear forces. In the purely academic sense that they would enable the Soviets to knock out more American nuclear forces than was previously possible, this may be true. But given the immense U.S. retaliatory arsenal, in a practical sense it would be meaningless. As Raymond Garthoff, then a State Department official, wrote in memoranda to President Kennedy's Ex-Comm (Executive Committee of the National Security Council) during the crisis, even under a worst-case calculation the surviving American nuclear arsenal "could still cause considerable destruction in a U.S. retaliatory strike, the Soviets could not rely on the degree of surprise assumed in the above [first-strike] calculation, and it is very unlikely that the Soviets would be tempted toward resort to war by the change in the military balance" (Raymond L. Garthoff, "The Meaning of the Missiles," *Washington Quarterly 5*, no. 4 [Autumn 1982]: 78–79). The nuclear forces in Cuba were, moreover, vulnerable to American attack and, being liquid fueled, would take many hours to ready for launch. As we noted earlier, it would be impossible to maintain surprise while coordinating a strike by weapons in Cuba and by those thousands of miles away in the Soviet Union. The different flight times involved would give the United States ample warning before one of the two sets of weapons reached U.S. soil. The idea that the Soviets could mount a first strike against the United States with or without Cuban missiles in that era of overwhelming U.S. nuclear advantage is hardly credible.

16. Even with all the Cuban weapons operational, and under assumptions most unfavorable to the United States, after any Soviet attack we would have retained enough nuclear weapons to retaliate in any manner called for by the American strategic doctrine of the time (see Hagan and Bernstein, "Missiles in Cuba"). Even if by some stretch of the imagination the nuclear weapons in Cuba did pose a direct military threat to the United States, we had our own nuclear weapons systems in Turkey and elsewhere that would pose a parallel threat to the Soviet Union. The close symmetry between the Soviet missiles in Cuba and the U.S. missiles that had long been based on the borders of the Soviet Union is often ignored, but it reinforces the conclusion that the Cuban missiles could in no way have turned the United States into a nuclear hostage of the Soviets.

17. Richard Neustadt and Graham Allison, in Kennedy, *Thirteen Days*, pp. 124, 123–124.

18. *New York Times*, November 12, 1962.

19. Sorensen, *Kennedy*, p. 678; box 48, folder "Cuba. General. 10/17/62–10/27/62," Sorensen Papers, Kennedy Library, cited in Marc Trachtenberg,

"The Influence of Nuclear Weapons in the Cuban Missile Crisis," *International Security* 10, no. 1 (Summer 1985): 148. Trachtenberg claims that Sorensen's statement was "simply wrong" and that in fact "there was no consensus on the issue of whether the deployment of the missiles really mattered in strategic terms." He cites an October 16 statement by McGeorge Bundy that the Joint Chiefs of Staff felt that the Cuban missiles changed the strategic balance "substantially." The CIA reportedly held a similar view. According to Trachtenberg, both were particularly concerned that the Cuban deployment might be an opening wedge for a much larger one that might be sufficient to "blunt a retaliatory attack" and thereby threaten the United States with a first strike. Given the overwhelming U.S. nuclear advantage of the time, one must wonder about the motives of those who tried seriously to mount this argument. That some military and intelligence officials may have mistakenly attributed strategic importance to the Cuban missiles does not detract from our main point here: that President Kennedy and the other top U.S. political officials actually making the decisions were not worried about or motivated by any threat to deterrence or to U.S. physical security. Then secretary of defense McNamara, for example, explicitly rejected his joint chiefs' concern about the military significance of the Cuban missiles and bombers. Trachtenberg acknowledges that "neither President Kennedy nor anyone else at the [ExCom] meeting . . . seemed much concerned with how such a deployment would affect the vulnerability of America's strategic forces" (pp. 148–150).

More important, Trachtenberg goes on to question whether the president and his top advisers were completely clear about the strategic irrelevance of the nuclear deployments in Cuba. He notes that "Kennedy did seem concerned that the initial deployment might be followed by a more massive one"; that Kennedy was unconcerned about the Soviet bombers in Cuba but very concerned about the missiles; and, overall, that one "has the sense that President Kennedy's feelings on this issue had not really taken definite shape; it was as though he was groping for answers" (pp. 150–151). But none of Trachtenberg's quotations and evidence provides a concrete reason to doubt the conclusion, well supported by the evidence we have cited, that Kennedy and his aides considered the missiles politically but not militarily important. Obviously Kennedy was *concerned* about the Cuban missiles—that is the reason he risked incinerating the planet to remove them. The question at issue is *why*.

20. Dean Rusk et al., "The Lessons of the Cuban Missile Crisis," *Time*, September 27, 1982, p. 85.

21. John F. Kennedy, "The Nuclear Balance of Power," in *Cuban Missile Crisis*, ed. Divine (first published in *Public Papers of the Presidents: Kennedy, 1962* [Washington, D.C., 1963], pp. 897–898); Sorensen, *Kennedy*, p. 683; Alexander L. George and Richard Smoke, *Deterrence in American Foreign Policy: Theory and Practice* (New York: Columbia University Press, 1974), p. 448.

22. Nikita Khrushchev, speech to the Supreme Soviet, December 12, 1962, quoted as "In Defense of Cuba," in *Cuban Missile Crisis*, ed. Divine; Nikita Khrushchev, *Khrushchev Remembers*, ed. and trans. Strobe Talbott (Boston: Little, Brown, 1970), p. 496.

23. Raymond Garthoff, *Reflections on the Cuban Missile Crisis* (Washing-

ton, D.C.: Brookings Institution, 1987), pp. 16–17; Detzer, *Brink*, p. 34; Charles A. Radin, "US Was Set to Attack Cuba Before Crisis," *Boston Globe*, February 15, 1989, p. 1.

24. For details on the paramilitary campaign against Castro, see Detzer, *Brink*, pp. 30–38.

25. Jean Daniel, "Unofficial Envoy: An Historic Report for Two Capitals," *New Republic*, December 14, 1963, pp. 18–19. No conventional military buildup could prevent the United States from overrunning an indefensible island ninety miles from our coastline. And U.S. leaders knew that the Soviet Union's central nuclear arsenal would not plausibly be launched just to defend Castro, given almost certain American nuclear retaliation against the Soviet homeland. But to Khrushchev local nuclear missiles represented a more plausible threat. In this thinking, America would know that the Soviets might initiate a limited local nuclear war to preserve Castro even though they would be unlikely to start a global nuclear exchange to do so. The United States had long used a similar logic, stationing nuclear weapons on the territory of allies around the globe to discourage Soviet aggression without relying on the implausible threat of an intercontinental nuclear attack.

26. Kennedy, "Nuclear Balance of Power," p. 113; Garthoff, *Cuban Missile Crisis*, p. 25; George and Smoke, *Deterrence in American Foreign Policy*, 463.

27. Stone, "The Brink," p. 156.

28. Ibid., p. 157; Ronald Steel, *Imperialists and Other Heroes* (New York: Random House, 1964), p. 119; McNamara, declassified Department of State document, 1966; Kennedy, *Thirteen Days*, p. 114.

29. Arthur M. S. Schlesinger, Jr., *A Thousand Days: John F. Kennedy in the White House* (Boston: Houghton Mifflin, 1965), p. 391; John F. Kennedy, cited in Kennedy, *Thirteen Days*, p. 155.

30. Sorensen, *Kennedy*, p. 683; Dinerstein, *Missile Crisis*, pp. 182–183; Roger Hilsman, *To Move a Nation* (Garden City: Doubleday, 1967), excerpted as "The Missile Gap," in *Cuban Missile Crisis*, ed. Divine, p. 120.

31. Arnold Horelick, "The Soviet Gamble," in *Cuban Missile Crisis*, ed. Divine, pp. 138–139 (first published as "The Cuban Missile Crisis: An Analysis of Soviet Calculations and Behavior," *World Politics* 16 [April 1964]: 363–377); Neustadt and Allison in Kennedy, *Thirteen Days*, p. 116.

32. Kennedy, *Thirteen Days*, p. 14; Neustadt and Allison, in ibid., p. 116; "Off-the-Record Meeting on Cuba, October 16, 1962, 6:30–7:55 P.M.," JFK Library, p. 13, cited in Fen Osler Hampson, "The Divided Decision Maker: American Domestic Politics and the Cuban Crises," *International Security* 9, no. 3 (Winter 1984–1985): 138.

33. Horelick, "Soviet Gamble," p. 138; Hilsman, "Missile Gap," p. 120.

34. Walton, *Cold War and Counterrevolution*, pp. 122–123.

35. Sagan, "Nuclear Alerts and Crisis Management," *International Security* 9, no. 4 (Spring 1985), p. 109. Some will also argue that the "nuclear alert" was largely just a by-product of the general *conventional* military alert Kennedy ordered. He ordered the conventional one at least partly to preserve his option of launching a large-scale conventional military operation against Cuba on short notice and to prepare for a conventional war should that occur. We are

not experts on military alert procedures, but it seems inconceivable that the president did not have the option of specifically leaving nuclear forces on a non-alert status while readying the conventional military. Given the stakes involved, even a major violation of normal alert processes (which alert conventional and nuclear forces in tandem) would seem a minor price to pay for keeping nuclear weapons unambiguously out of Kennedy's actions.

36. John F. Kennedy, cited in Kennedy, *Thirteen Days*, pp. 156–158 (emphasis added).

37. The direct quotations from President Kennedy's address of October 22, 1962, are cited in Kennedy, *Thirteen Days*, pp. 153–159.

38. Carl von Clausewitz, *On War*, ed. and trans. Michael Howard and Peter Paret (Princeton: Princeton University Press, 1966), p. 77.

39. Kennedy, *Thirteen Days*, pp. 40, 65, 67–68.

40. Neustadt and Allison, in Kennedy, *Thirteen Days*, p. 114.

41. The fabricated speech is an amalgam of exact quotations from these top officials, drawn from "White House Plays Down Soviet Sub Threat," *New York Times*, May 22, 1984, p. 13; and "Transcript of President's News Conference," ibid., May 23, 1984, p. A22. On the increased deployment of Soviet ballistic missile submarines, see also "Soviet Said to Add New Subs off U.S.," ibid., May 21, 1984, p. 1; and Tom Wicker, "The End of Arms Control," ibid., May 25, 1984, op. ed.

42. All quotations are from President Kennedy's speech to the nation about the Soviet missiles in Cuba, October 22, 1962, cited in Kennedy, *Thirteen Days*, pp. 153–159.

43. Neustadt and Allison, in Kennedy, *Thirteen Days*, p. 115.

44. Cited in Trachtenberg, "Cuban Missile Crisis," p. 151.

45. Garthoff, *Cuban Missile Crisis*, p. 37.

46. Kennedy, *Thirteen Days*, pp. 16–17, 9.

47. Fen Osler Hampson, "The Divided Decision-Maker: American Domestic Politics and the Cuban Crises," *International Security* 9, no. 3 (Winter 1984–1985): p. 138; Sorensen, *Kennedy*, pp. 687–688.

48. Sorensen, *Kennedy*, p. 22.

49. See George H. Quester, "Missiles in Cuba, 1970," *Foreign Affairs* 49 (April 1971): 494–496.

50. See note 41. Moreover, on the basis of official American nuclear policy, in 1970 as well as now, a robust force of Soviet nuclear submarines, on station and within firing range of the United States, should be considered *good*. Since land-based nuclear bombers and missiles have become increasingly vulnerable to preemptive attack, invulnerable undersea-based nuclear forces on both sides are considered stabilizing. As long as neither side has reason to fear that it might be fully disarmed by an enemy surprise attack, neither's finger should become itchy on the nuclear trigger. This is the logical basis of the official nuclear doctrine, which explicitly renounces any effort to develop an ability to preemptively destroy all Soviet retaliatory nuclear forces for fear that it would lead the Soviets to a launch-on-warning policy. As George Quester said of the blustery U.S. response in 1970, "With the American stress on assured second-strike deterrents for each side, how could we insist on Russian submarines being kept out of fir-

ing range of the United States?" (Quester, "Missiles in Cuba," p. 495). The hypocrisy of this position is even clearer now that it has become official policy to "drive the Soviets into the sea," meaning a combination of deployments and arms control measures designed to motivate the Soviets to move away from heavy land-based missile forces and to invest more in submarine-based nuclear forces (see House Committee on Armed Services, hearings, Part 2, Strategic Programs, 98th Cong., 1983, especially the "Report of the President's Commission on Strategic Forces," the so-called Scowcroft Commission report).

51. Henry Kissinger, *White House Years* (Boston: Little, Brown, 1979), p. 648. Fen Hampson estimates that the Soviets had at the time about 224 sub-based ballistic missiles that could be brought within range of the United States and therefore that the number actually threatening the United States at any given time would be lower, since all subs are not on station at the same time. Even if only 20 percent were on station, that would mean over 40 ballistic missiles able to strike at U.S. cities from the sea, in addition to the overwhelming threat posed by Soviet home-based bombers. The sea-based missiles were more than enough to terrorize the United States, should that be the goal, and totally inadequate for launching a disarming attack. So to increase the number by a factor of two or three or even more would have no great practical consequence.

Hampson suggests that although the Cienfuegos base might not pose an immediate strategic problem, it could in the long run. "In the context of the rapid expansion of the Soviet [strategic submarine] force that took place in the seventies (by 1980, for example, the total force numbered 71), the base *would* . . . have had important long-term strategic implications." Evidently President Reagan and the Pentagon did not realize this in 1984 when they stated that it was irrelevant how many subs the Soviets ran into the Atlantic. See Hampson, "Divided Decision-Maker," p. 152.

52. Quester, "Missiles in Cuba," p. 500.

53. To be more exact, they backed down twice in 1970, since, as we noted in Chapter 6, the United States suddenly added ludicrous new restrictions even after the Soviets had agreed not to construct a submarine base in Cuba—thus prolonging the crisis and raising again the risk of direct confrontation. What was the problem? According to Kissinger, the Soviets were running submarine tenders out of normal Cuban ports to service submarines in the open ocean. Even this, which bears no relation at all to the 1962 agreement on "offensive weapons in Cuba," was sufficient to produce stern warnings from Kissinger, who ended the crisis only after the Soviets had remarkably agreed not to run unarmed tenders out of Cuba. Imagine the outcry here if the Soviets issued an ultimatum barring U.S. submarine bases from allied nations such as Britain (e.g., the Holyloch base) and even banning from them the surface maintenance vessels used to service U.S. subs!

54. Garthoff, *Cuban Missile Crisis*, pp. 101–102. The incident was kept secret until the commander of the U.S. patrol revealed it in 1980.

55. Walton, *Cold War and Counterrevolution;* Hampson, "Divided Decision-Maker," pp. 134–149, 145.

56. Kennedy, *Thirteen Days*, pp. 72–73; Garthoff, *Cuban Missile Crisis*, p. 43; Eric Pace, "Rusk Tells a Kennedy Secret: Fallback Plan in Cuba Crisis," *New York Times*, August 28, 1987, pp. 1, 73.

57. Robert Jervis, *The Logic of Images in International Relations* (Princeton: Princeton University Press, 1970), pp. 178–179. In 1987 Dean Rusk stated for the first time that the day before the Soviets agreed to remove the Cuban missiles President Kennedy finally decided that the Turkish missiles should not stand in the way of a peaceful settlement. Kennedy reportedly drafted a statement to be read by U.N. Secretary General U Thant "proposing the removal of both the Jupiters and the missiles in Cuba." Only the president and a U.N. official named Andrew Cordier knew of the statement, according to Rusk; Cordier was to hold it in secret and deliver it to U Thant only if Kennedy gave the signal. Since of the three only Rusk is still alive, the report cannot be confirmed. Rusk said that the plan "was not all that much of a big deal; it was simply an option that would have been available to President Kennedy had he wanted to use it." If it really existed, the "Cordier ploy" would demonstrate that Kennedy might not have gone to war over the obsolete Turkish missiles. But one still has to ask why he did not just agree to the swap when the Soviets proposed it, thus avoiding all the terrible dangers that ensued. See Pace, "Rusk Tells a Kennedy Secret," pp. 1, 73.

58. "Proceedings of the Hawk's Cay Conference on the Cuban Missile Crisis," Marathon, Florida, March 5–8, 1987, p. 53, cited in Garthoff, *Cuban Missile Crisis*, p. 19.

59. Garthoff, *Cuban Missile Crisis*, pp. 65–73.

CHAPTER NINE

1. George W. Rathjens and Laura Reed, *Neither MAD nor Starstruck—And Doubts, Too, About Arms Control* (Cambridge: Center for International Studies, Massachusetts Institute of Technology, 1986), pp. 14–15.

2. Center for Defense Information, "After the INF Treaty: U.S. Nuclear Buildup in Europe," *Defense Monitor* 17, no. 2 (1988): 5.

3. Rathjens and Reed, *Neither MAD nor Starstruck*, p. 5.

4. *Time*, cited in Morton H. Halperin, *Nuclear Fallacy: Dispelling the Myth of Nuclear Strategy* (Cambridge, Mass.: Ballinger, 1987), p. 41; Rear Admiral Eugene J. Carroll, in *The Nuclear Crisis Reader*, ed. Gwyn Prins (New York: Vintage, 1984), p. 11; "The Belgrano Cover-Up," *New Statesman* (London), August 31, 1984, cited in Joseph Gerson, "What Is the Deadly Connection?" in *The Deadly Connection: Nuclear War and U.S. Intervention*, ed. Joseph Gerson (Philadelphia: New Society Publishers, 1986), p. 13.

5. See Amos Perlmutter, Michael Handel, and Uri Bar-Joseph, *Two Minutes over Baghdad* (London: Corgi Books, 1982), pp. 46–48. See also Raymond Garthoff, *Détente and Confrontation: American-Soviet Relations from Nixon to Reagan* (Washington, D.C.: Brookings Institution, 1985), p. 379. Citing one detailed study, Garthoff rejects the theory that the Soviets were supplying nuclear warheads.

6. See Leonard S. Spector, *The Undeclared Bomb* (Cambridge, Mass.: Ballinger, 1988).

7. Ibid., pp. 120–148, 159–189, 294–296; Rathjens and Reed, *Neither MAD nor Starstruck*, p. 20.

8. Rathjens and Reed, *Neither MAD nor Starstruck*, p. 20.

9. Gordon Chang, "To the Nuclear Brink: Eisenhower, Dulles, and the Quemoy-Matsu Crisis," *International Security* 2, no. 4 (Spring 1988): 121; Garthoff, *Détente and Confrontation,* p. 287.

10. Gary Milhollin, "New Nuclear Follies?" *New York Times,* November 25, 1987, p. A27.

11. Center for Defense Information, "First Strike Weapons at Sea: The Trident II and the Sea-Launched Cruise Missile," *Defense Monitor* 16, no. 6 (1987): 5–7 (emphasis in original).

12. Thomas B. Cochran, William A. Arkin, and Milton M. Hoenig, *Nuclear Weapons Databook,* vol. 1, *U.S. Nuclear Forces and Capabilities* (Cambridge, Mass.: Ballinger, 1984), pp. 244, 84–88, 89–91, 82. In 1974 the Air Force reportedly removed nuclear warheads for air-to-air missiles from Air National Guard units nationwide after allegations that two Air National Guard fighter pilots were involved in drug trafficking (UPI, "Removal of Nuclear Weapons from Guard Units Revealed," *Boston Globe,* October 24, 1988, p. 5).

13. See, for example, essays by Rear Admiral Eugene J. Carroll, Admiral Noel Gayler, and Lieutenant General A. S. Collins, in *Nuclear Crisis Reader,* ed. Prins, and references cited in Chapter 3 of this book.

14. James M. Markham, "Soviet Bloc Seeks Battlefield Nuclear-Arms Talks," *New York Times,* January 6, 1988, p. A3. An interesting exception to the trend is Paul Nitze's unexpected informal proposal for a superpower treaty to ban nuclear-armed sea-based cruise missiles, depth charges, torpedoes, and possibly bombs carried by aircraft on ships. If done thoroughly, such a change could eliminate the sea-based tactical nuclear arsenals that, as we have seen, pose one of the most worrisome threats of nuclear escalation during conventional hostilities. The motive for this unusual proposal probably has less to do with reducing the risk of unintended escalation than with eliminating what many regard as a serious threat to the U.S. Navy in time of war. In our interviews, several ranking Navy officers complained that on balance tactical nuclear weapons at sea benefit the Soviets, one reason being that the United States has far more to lose if both fleets are destroyed in a nuclear war at sea. Nevertheless, unlike other arms control ideas, such a proposal could actually reduce the risk of nuclear war. See Michael R. Gordon, "U.S. Aide Offers Plan to Cut Arms at Sea," *New York Times,* April 6, 1988.

15. For unusual press coverage of these activities, see Charles Scheiner, "Atlantic Activists Meet, Seek to Close Down Huge Ocean Arsenals," *Guardian,* October 21, 1987, p. 14.

16. See David Corn and Jefferson Morley, "A Nuclear Gulf," *Nation,* October 3, 1987, p. 331; Robert Schaeffer, "Making Waves," *Nuclear Times* 6, no. 2 (November–December 1987): 23, 24. La Rocque reportedly focused not on the risk of the weapons' coming into unauthorized use but on the problems we would face if they were lost at sea or if their radioactive materials were scattered into the environment in conventional combat. Greenpeace's campaign has drawn criticism not only for focusing attention on tactical rather than strategic nuclear weapons, but also for opposing *all* sea-based nuclear weapons, including the strategic ones on ballistic-missile submarines, widely considered the most secure and stabilizing strategic weapons platforms.

17. Halperin, *Nuclear Fallacy*, p. 55.

18. Bishop Thomas J. Gumbleton, foreword to *Deadly Connection*, ed. Gerson, p. vii; Christine Wing and Frank Brodhead, "Peace Movements East and West," *Resist*, no. 205 (April 1988).

19. Cochran et al., *Nuclear Weapons Databook*, p. 14.

20. Paul Bracken, *The Command and Control of Nuclear Forces* (New Haven: Yale University Press, 1983), p. 53; Paul Bracken, "Accidental Nuclear War," in Graham T. Allison, Albert Carnesale, and Joseph S. Nye, Jr., eds., *Hawks, Doves, and Owls: An Agenda for Avoiding Nuclear War* (New York: Norton, 1985), pp. 44–45.

21. Bracken, "Accidental Nuclear War," pp. 29, 49 (emphasis in original).

22. Bernard Brodie, "The Development of Nuclear Strategy," in *Strategy and Nuclear Deterrence: An "International Security" Reader*, ed. Stephen E. Miller (Princeton: Princeton University Press, 1984), p. 9 (first published in *International Security* 2, no. 4 [Spring 1978]).

23. John H. Cushman, "War Stocks and the Weapons Pact," *New York Times*, September 27, 1987, business section, p. 1.

24. Nicholas Wade, "The Hazards of Arms Control," *New York Times*, February 10, 1988, p. A30; Cushman, "War Stocks," p. 1.

25. Richard Halloran, "NATO Chief Assails Notion That Arms Pacts Save Money," *New York Times*, February 8, 1988, p. A2; Wolfgang Demisch, cited in Cushman, "War Stocks," p. 1.

26. Cushman, "War Stocks," p. 1.

27. Paul Lewis, "Soviet Proposes Shift of Arms Cash to Third World," *New York Times*, August 26, 1987, p. A9.

28. G. Adams and D. A. Gold, "The Economics of Military Spending: Is the Military Dollar Really Different?" Defense Budget Project, Center on Budget and Policy Priorities, 1985, cover page, p. 2.

29. Barry Bluestone and John Havens, "Reducing the Federal Deficit Fair and Square" (paper delivered at the Symposium on the Fortieth Anniversary of the Joint Economic Committee, "The American Economy in Transition: From the Second World War to the 21st Century," Washington, D.C., January 16–17, 1985), p. 24. See also Barry Bluestone and John Havens, "How to Cut the Deficit and Rebuild America," *Challenge* 29, no. 2 (May–June 1986): 22–29.

30. Gordon Adams, "Economic Conversion Misses the Point," *Bulletin of the Atomic Scientists* 42, no. 2 (February 1986): 24–25, 27.

31. James G. Hershberg, "National Insecurity: How the Red Menace Derailed the Contragate Probe," *Boston Phoenix*, February 3, 1989, p. 10.

32. See Edward S. Herman and Frank Brodhead, *Demonstration Elections: U.S.-Staged Elections in the Dominican Republic, Vietnam, and El Salvador* (Boston: South End Press, 1984).

33. Alva Myrdal, *The Game of Disarmament: How the United States and Russia Run the Arms Race* (New York: Pantheon, 1982).

34. "To the Summit, and Beyond," *New York Times*, September 20, 1987, p. 26. For another prominent acknowledgment that the INF treaty has little military significance, see Graham Allison and Albert Carnesale, "Why Say No to 1,500 Warheads?" *New York Times*, November 15, 1987.

35. "An Arms-Control Precedent," *Boston Globe,* November 30, 1987, p. 16; Mary McGrory, "New View, Old Habits," *Boston Globe,* December 9, 1987, p. 21.

36. David K. Shipler, "U.S. and Russians Sign Pact to Limit Nuclear War Risk," *New York Times,* September 16, 1987, p. 1; Philip Shabecoff, "Dozens of Nations Approve Accord to Protect Ozone," *New York Times,* September 17, 1987, p. 1; "Reagan and Gorbachev to Meet This Year to Sign Missile Pact, Now Nearly Complete," *New York Times,* September 19, 1987, p. 1.

37. Dianne Dumanoski, "Ozone, Arms and Politics," *Boston Globe,* September 20, 1987, p. A25.

38. Shabecoff, "Accord to Protect Ozone," p. 1; Dianne Dumanoski, "Scientists Fear Fallout from Ozone Loss," *Boston Globe,* March 21, 1988, p. 3; Dianne Dumanoski, "Ozone Pact Clears Hurdle to Senate Ratification," *Boston Globe,* February 18, 1988, p. 75.

39. Cochran, Arkin, and Hoenig, *Nuclear Weapons Databook* 1:15, 5.

40. Center for Defense Information, "After the INF Treaty: U.S. Nuclear Buildup in Europe," *Defense Monitor* 17, no. 2 (1988): 2.

41. "The Dirtiest Bomb," *Boston Globe,* August 15, 1987, p. 14; Cochran, Arkin, and Hoenig, *Nuclear Weapons Databook* 1:58.

42. *New York Times,* January 24, 1988, p. 12. Cochran, Arkin, and Hoenig, *Nuclear Weapons Databook,* give a yield of only 10–50 kilotons for the cruise missiles (1:182).

43. Kaplan, "U.S. to Take Its Most Powerful Nuclear Bomb out of Mothballs," *Boston Globe,* August 6, 1987, p. 3; Dan Plesch, "NATO's New Nuclear Weapons," *Defense and Disarmament Alternatives* 1, no. 3 (May 1988): 2. The United States does plan to retire many obsolete nuclear weapons—bombs, artillery shells, and Lance missiles—from Europe as new ones are deployed, perhaps leading to reductions in the total number of U.S. warheads there. But as the commander of American and allied forces in Europe, General John R. Galvin, acknowledges, such reductions would be unilateral, would have nothing to do with the INF treaty, and would in no way weaken military capabilities. Like earlier warhead reductions in Europe and in the United States, such reductions would simply reflect modernization, which allows fewer, more advanced weapons to surpass the capabilities of larger numbers of obsolete weapons. See Richard Halloran, "NATO Chief Sees a New Reduction in Warheads," *New York Times,* August 11, 1988, p. A7. See also Natural Resources Defense Council, "A New Improved Nuclear Arms Race?" (advertisement), *New York Times,* December 6, 1987, p. 31.

44. Diana Johnstone, "Strategic Realignment," *Nuclear Times,* September–October 1987, p. 14.

45. Richard Halloran, "U.S. Weighs Effect of New Arms Pact," *New York Times,* December 6, 1987, p. 17.

46. The views we expressed in "Arms Control: Misplaced Focus" (*Bulletin of the Atomic Scientists* 42, no. 3 [March 1986]: 39–44) have been misinterpreted as a call for improved relations with the Soviet Union. See the letter by Howard Moreland, in the *Bulletin of the Atomic Scientists* 43, no. 2 (March 1987): 61.

47. Richard M. Nixon, *RN: The Memoirs of Richard Nixon* (New York: Grosset & Dunlap, 1978), pp. 941–942.

48. Rathjens and Reed, *Neither MAD nor Starstruck,* pp. 17–18.

49. Nicholas Wade, "Hazards of Arms Control," p. A30; Ralph Earle II, "America Is Cheating Itself," *Foreign Policy,* no. 64 (Fall 1986): 16.

50. United Press International, "Afghan City Reported Under Siege; Many Dead," *Boston Globe,* December 9, 1987, p. 28; Philip Taubman, "Moscow Proposes Foreign Warships Quit Persian Gulf," *New York Times,* July 4, 1987, p. 1.

51. See "2 Soviet Warships Reportedly Nudge U.S. Navy Vessels," *New York Times,* February 13, 1988, p. 1; "Soviet Vessels Bump Two US Navy Warships," *Boston Globe,* February 13, 1988, p. 1; "Moscow Blames U.S. for Incident Between Warships in Black Sea," *New York Times,* February 14, 1988, p. 1; "Soviets See a Setback in Collision of Ships," *Boston Globe,* February 14, 1988, p. 8. Neither the *Times* nor the *Globe* reported the nuclear weapons capabilities of the American ships involved.

52. Cochran, Arkin, and Hoenig, *Nuclear Weapons Databook* 1:244; "Bumped US Ship Was Spying, Report Says," *Boston Globe,* April 22, 1988, p. 3.

53. "An Arms-Control Precedent," *Boston Globe,* November 30, 1987, p. 16; Fred Kaplan, "Questions Raised on Scope of Treaty Plan," *Boston Globe,* December 2, 1987, p. 13.

54. Ibid.

55. "The Treaty After the Treaty," *New York Times,* December 9, 1987, p. A34; Michael R. Gordon, "Reagan's Missile Cut Offer Throws Open 'Window of Vulnerability' Debate," *New York Times,* December 7, 1987, p. A20.

56. Rathjens and Reed, *Neither MAD nor Starstruck,* p. 21.

57. Michael M. May, George F. Bing, and John D. Steinbruner, *Strategic Arms Reductions* (Washington, D.C.: The Brookings Institution, 1988), p. 6.

58. Ibid., p. 54. In the other two 3,000-warhead scenarios—proportional reductions from current forces and modernized forces designed for attacking enemy missiles as well as for invulnerability—target coverage for retaliation after absorbing a first strike "falls off for the lower-priority targets." Nevertheless, even in these improbable scenarios, the victim of a first strike could strike most of the important military and industrial targets of its attacker and could of course utterly destroy the attacker's cities even if the victim waited until the attack was over before launching any weapons in retaliation (ibid., p. 54).

59. John D. Steinbruner, "The Purpose and Effect of Deep Strategic Force Reductions," in Committee on International Security and Arms Control, National Academy of Sciences, *Reykjavik and Beyond: Deep Reductions in Strategic Nuclear Arsenals and the Future Direction of Arms Control* (Washington, D.C.: National Academy Press, 1988), p. 14 (emphasis added).

60. May, Bing, and Steinbruner, *Strategic Arms Reductions,* p. 7; Spurgeon M. Keeny, Jr., "The Impact of Defenses on Offensive Reduction Regimes," in Committee on International Security and Arms Control, *Reykjavik and Beyond,* p. 23. Indeed, both sides could probably threaten the amount of damage Keeny describes even if *all* strategic weapons were abolished. The United States and the Soviet Union each have many weapons systems that are not considered "strategic" but that could in fact be used to deliver nuclear warheads to the other's territory. For example, as Alexander Flax notes,

All military aircraft—including all of our fighters—are tanker-refueled many times when they are flown to Europe. That is how they get there. Thus, they have intercontinental range. . . . tactical transport aircraft like the C-141, C-5, and the C-130 . . . . have cargo doors in the rear that open for parachute extraction so that loads can be dropped to troops in the field. Those doors are also very good for extracting cruise missiles. They are also good for extracting anything else . . . even space-launch vehicles, which originally were all converted ballistic missiles, are perfectly good ICBMs. And one can test all of the elements except the reentry vehicle by conducting a space launch.

Sea-launched cruise missiles could also be used to deliver nuclear warheads to enemy cities from the oceans and with modifications could "fly from Europe to the Soviet Union." As we emphasize throughout this book, short of near-total nuclear disarmament there is simply no way for either side to avoid the possibility of appalling damage, if not total destruction, in the event of a nuclear war. See Alexander H. Flax, "The Impact of New Technologies and Noncentral Systems on Offensive Reduction Regimes," in Committee on International Security and Arms Control, *Reykjavik and Beyond*, pp. 30–32.

61. May, Bing, and Steinbruner, *Strategic Arms Reductions*, pp. 67–68. The authors note that the high 3,000-warhead Soviet fatality rates we cite result from one assumption: that the United States equips its Trident submarines with D-5 missiles, which have a much higher yield than current Poseidon and Trident C-4 submarine-based missiles.

62. Ibid., pp. 68–69.

63. "Is Arms Control Obsolete?" *Harper's* 271, no. 1622 (July 1985): 50; "An Arms-Race Precedent," *Boston Globe*, September 19, 1987, p. 14.

64. John B. Judis, "Would Long-Range Arms Treaty Be a False START For Peace?" *In These Times*, December 16–22, 1987, p. 3. Judis, like Kaplan, is referring to the NRDC study.

65. Michael Howard, "Is Arms Control Really Necessary?" (lecture delivered to the Council for Arms Control, London), excerpted in *Harper's* 272, no. 1632 (May 1986): 14; Halloran, "New Arms Pact," p. 17; Halloran, "Arms Pacts," p. A2. Even strategic arms cuts far deeper than START would not necessarily save money. One reason is that both sides would probably feel the need to restructure their forces, at great cost, to avoid concentrating their remaining warheads in a few of the giant delivery platforms they now use today. Flax writes: "Because of the relatively small numbers of launch platforms that may be involved as we go to 3,000 warheads and below, we really have to consider modifying our launch platform concepts. We probably do not want Trident submarines carrying 24 missiles. We probably do not want big bombers carrying 20 cruise missiles. . . . It could be that we will end up with a force of one-third the size of our current force, costing roughly what the present strategic force costs." See Flax, "Impact of New Technologies," in Committee on International Security and Arms Control, *Reykjavik and Beyond*, pp. 32–33.

66. Halloran, "New Arms Pact," p. 17.

67. Steinbruner, "Deep Strategic Force Reductions," p. 13.

68. George Rathjens, "The Conditions for Complete Nuclear Disarmament: The Case for Partial Nuclear Disarmament," in *A New Design for Nuclear Disarmament*, ed. William Epstein and Toshiyuki Toyoda (Nottingham: Spokes-

man, 1977), cited in Rathjens and Reed, *Neither MAD nor Starstruck*, p. 21; Rathjens and Reed, *Neither MAD nor Starstruck*, pp. 21–22.

69. Rathjens and Reed, *Neither MAD nor Starstruck*, p. 23.

70. H. D. S. Greenway, "Nuclear-Poor, Not Nuclear-Free," *Boston Globe,* December 11, 1987, p. 23.

71. Rob Leavitt, "Vision Quest," *Defense and Disarmament News* (Institute for Defense and Disarmament Studies), August–September 1987, p. 7.

72. "Activists Greet Arms Pact with Guarded Optimism," *Guardian,* October 14, 1987, p. 6.

73. Information on the concept of the peace system is available from EXPRO, Department of Sociology, Boston College, Chestnut Hill, MA 02167.

## CHAPTER TEN

1. Robert McNamara, quoted in William L. Ury, *Beyond the Hotline: How We Can Prevent the Crisis That Might Bring on Nuclear War* (Boston: Houghton Mifflin, 1985), epigraph; Ury, *Beyond the Hotline*, p. 7.

2. Seymour Hersh, "New Light on the Cuban Missile Crisis: USSR May Not Have Been in Control," *Boston Globe*, October 11, 1987, p. 18; Associated Press, "They Feared the Worst in Cuban Missile Crisis," *Patriot Ledger* (Quincy, Mass.), October 14, 1987, p. 8; Raymond L. Garthoff, *Reflections on the Cuban Missile Crisis* (Washington, D.C.: Brookings Institution, 1987), p. 63.

3. Hersh, "New Light," p. 18. Strangely enough, the new data also surfaced during a review of Soviet forces in Cuba during the 1979 pseudo-crisis the Carter administration provoked over the Soviet "combat brigade" in Cuba (see Chapter 6).

4. Daniel Ellsberg, "The Day Castro Almost Started World War III," *New York Times,* October 31, 1987, p. 27.

5. Richard Bernstein, "Meeting Sheds New Light on Cuban Missile Crisis," *New York Times,* October 14, 1987, p. A10; Associated Press, "Cuban Leader Felt Betrayed by Soviets, Realized He Was Pawn," *Patriot Ledger* (Quincy, Mass.), October 22, 1987, p. 18; Fred Kaplan, "'62 Missile Crisis: Key Soviet Slip Suggested," *Boston Globe*, October 14, 1987, p. 1. Garthoff raises another possibility, that "someone in the Soviet leadership, necessarily high in the military or able to give an order to the military, was responsible for creating an incident in an unsuccessful attempt to forestall Khrushchev's efforts to arrange a compromise." See Garthoff, *Cuban Missile Crisis*, p. 53.

6. Garthoff, *Cuban Missile Crisis*, pp. 37–38 (emphasis in original).

7. Norman Cousins, "The Cuban Missile Crisis: An Anniversary," *Saturday Review,* October 15, 1977, p. 4, cited in Garthoff, *Cuban Missile Crisis*, p. 48.

8. Garthoff, *Cuban Missile Crisis,* pp. 39–41, 109 (emphasis in original).

9. Richard Ned Lebow, *Nuclear Crisis Management: A Dangerous Illusion* (Ithaca: Cornell University Press, 1987), p. 18.

10. Ibid., pp. 17–18.

11. Ibid., p. 167 (emphasis in original). Lebow's views differ from ours in that he attributes far more importance to crisis instabilities generated by the structure of nuclear forces and command systems produced by decades of arms racing. He appears to believe that in principle crises could become manageable

if profound changes were made in "force structure, strategic doctrine, and targeting policy" (p. 22). We see no reason for such optimism, for the reasons spelled out in Part I. Lebow also focuses only on the worst crises, such as the Cuban missile crisis, implying that lesser ones, such as those reviewed in Chapter 6, do not carry nuclear dangers. Again his optimism seems misplaced. It may derive from his overemphasis on strategic factors in the production of crisis instability, which seem more significant in crises so deep that leaders can imagine them escalating to all-out war. But all substantial superpower crises are unstable, not so much because of missile or command center vulnerabilities but because once nations begin to rally their forces they always risk being backed into a corner they feel they must shoot their way out of and also risk spontaneous war through miscalculation, error, or exceeded authority in the field.

12. See Chapter 6 and Richard M. Nixon, *RN: The Memoirs of Richard Nixon* (New York: Grosset & Dunlap), p. 488.

13. Contrary to Americans' common belief, the United States, Israel, and South Africa use military force outside their borders far more frequently than any of the other presumed nuclear states. The others certainly do so, but relatively rarely. Britain and France long ago abandoned most of their imperial ambitions and fight abroad only in the occasional leftover imperial hot spots such as the Falklands/Malvinas, Northern Ireland, Chad, and the Pacific islands. Foreign intervention by Chinese, Indian, and Pakistani forces is also relatively rare, though it poses greater nuclear dangers than military action by the European nuclear states. Examples include Chinese involvement in the Korean War, the 1979 Chinese invasion of Vietnam, Pakistani involvement in the Afghan war, and various Indo-Pakistani conflicts. Apart from brutal civil interventions in Hungary and Czechoslovakia and the invasion of Afghanistan, the Soviet Union has engaged its forces abroad only occasionally and with restraint—though of course the nuclear dangers are always real, as in the 1970 War of Attrition. The United States, in contrast, intervenes in the Third World regularly, often with substantial forces—in the fifteen years since the pull-out from Vietnam, for example, attacking Cambodia (in the Mayaguez incident), invading and occupying Grenada, bombing, shelling, and landing marines in Lebanon, bombing Libya, and engaging Iranian forces and destroying an Iranian airliner in the Persian Gulf. Israel and South Africa fight abroad constantly, as they have for many years. In addition to violence in the occupied territories, for example, in recent years Israel has bombed Tunisia and Iraq and invaded Lebanon, where it engaged Syrian forces and still occupies territory and stages regular ground attacks and air strikes. South Africa recently invaded Angola, which is defended by Cuban soldiers, and fights on in Namibia.

14. This lack of external threats to physical or political survival should be uncontroversial for the United States, the USSR, China, Britain, France, and India, as well as other states that may be assumed to be nuclear or near-nuclear, such as Pakistan and South Africa (some of which face serious *internal* threats to the political status quo, as in the revolt against apartheid). Israel may be a partial exception, having faced a major attack in 1973, when it appears to have possessed nuclear weapons. Rapid and surprising Arab advances, coupled with

the depletion of Israeli weapons and ammunition stocks, may have produced a brief moment of fear that the country might be overrun. This is probably the closest a nuclear power has ever come to facing a genuine military threat, but it should not be exaggerated. The war aims of Sadat and the other Arab leaders probably did not extend to the political or physical destruction of Israel, and probably not even to the liberation of the occupied territories. The reason is simple: they knew those goals were far beyond their military means, as Israel's rapid (though costly) reversal of the war ultimately confirmed. The Arab leaders were probably also deterred from threatening Israel itself by the prospect of possible Israeli nuclear retaliation. This may have been a key factor in the U.S. decision to rush conventional weapons and supplies to Israel. See Amos Perlmutter, Michael Handel, and Uri Bar-Joseph, *Two Minutes over Baghdad* (London: Corgi Books, 1982). As we noted in Chapter 6, these authors report that after the initial Arab advances the Israelis may have actually put thirteen nuclear warheads on alert and readied both Jericho missiles and jet fighter-bombers equipped to deliver them.

15. Anthony R. Wells, "The June 1967 Arab-Israeli War," in *Soviet Naval Diplomacy*, ed. Bradford Dismukes and James M. McConnell (New York: Pergamon, 1979), p. 166.

16. Stephen S. Roberts, "The October 1973 Arab-Israeli War," in *Soviet Naval Diplomacy*, ed. Dismukes and McConnell, p. 202; Henry Kissinger, *Years of Upheaval* (Boston: Little, Brown, 1982), p. 575; Scott D. Sagan, "Lessons of the Yom Kippur Alert," *Foreign Policy*, no. 36 (Fall 1979): 167, 176.

17. Noam Chomsky and Edward S. Herman, *The Washington Connection and Third World Fascism* (Boston: South End Press, 1979), pp. 105–106; Marvin Kalb and Bernard Kalb, *Kissinger* (Boston: Little, Brown, 1974), p. 257; John P. Lewis, op. ed., *New York Times*, December 9, 1971, cited in Chomsky and Herman, *Third World Fascism*, p. 106; Garthoff, *Détente and Confrontation*, pp. 263, 265; Henry Kissinger, *White House Years* (Boston: Little, Brown, 1979), p. 914; David K. Hall, "The Laotian War of 1962 and the Indo-Pakistani War of 1971," in *Force Without War*, ed. Barry M. Blechman and Stephen S. Kaplan (Washington, D.C.: Brookings Institution, 1978), p. 177; James M. McConnell and Anne Kelly Calhoun, "The December 1971 Indo-Pakistani Crisis," in Dismukes and McConnell, *Soviet Naval Diplomacy*, p. 185.

18. Kissinger, *White House Years*, pp. 570–571; Alexander L. George, "Missed Opportunities for Crisis Prevention: The War of Attrition and Angola," in *Managing U.S.-Soviet Rivalry: Problems of Crisis Prevention*, ed. Alexander L. George (Boulder: Westview, 1983), pp. 196–197.

19. See, for example, Mahmoud Riad, *The Struggle for Peace in the Middle East* (London: Quartet, 1981), p. 162: "Nasser decided that the situation needed a joint concerted Arab effort to stop hostilities in Jordan, especially as US military movements pointed to a possible American military intervention which would inevitably enlist Israeli army support, the pretext for which would be the danger of Syrian involvement in the fighting in Jordan."

20. Nikita Khrushchev, *Khrushchev Remembers*, 2 vols. (Boston: Little, Brown, 1970, 1974), cited in Garthoff, *Cuban Missile Crisis*, p. 6. As Garthoff

notes, the authenticity of these memoirs, sometimes called into question, was established by comparing the voice prints of the tapes on which they are based with those of known Khrushchev verbal statements.

21. Stephen S. Kaplan, *Diplomacy of Power* (Washington, D.C.: Brookings Institution, 1981), p. 131.

22. Officially the Israeli attack was a "preventive" action against impending Arab attack and followed provocations by the Arab states such as the closing of the Strait of Tiran, the ejection of U.N. peacekeeping troops, and the massing of Egyptian troops along the Israeli frontier. But the reality was more complex, with Arabs fearing that Israel was preparing to attack. Menachem Begin stated: "In June 1967, we again had a choice. The Egyptian Army concentrations in the Sinai approaches do not prove that Nasser was really about to attack us. We must be honest with ourselves. We decided to attack him" (cited in Noam Chomsky, *The Fateful Triangle* [Boston: South End Press, 1983], p. 100, with other supporting material).

23. Wells, "Arab-Israeli War," p. 165; Paul Jabber and Roman Kolkowicz, "The Arab-Israeli Wars of 1967 and 1973," in *Diplomacy of Power: Soviet Armed Forces as a Political Instrument,* ed. Stephen S. Kaplan et al. (Washington, D.C.: Brookings Institution, 1981), pp. 435–438.

24. Stephen S. Roberts, "The October 1973 Arab-Israeli War," in *Soviet Naval Diplomacy,* ed. Dismukes and McConnell, p. 193; Alexander L. George, "The Arab-Israeli War of October 1973: Origins and Impact," in *Managing U.S.-Soviet Rivalry,* ed. George, p. 140; Bruce Porter, *The U.S.S.R. in Third World Conflicts: Soviet Arms and Diplomacy in Local Wars, 1945–1980* (Cambridge: Cambridge University Press, 1984), pp. 142, 118n, 124; George, "Arab-Israeli War," p. 140. George notes that "the Soviet Union's policy of restraining Sadat was not without serious diplomatic and political costs for the U.S.S.R.'s position in the Middle East" (p. 140). He also adds that "though Soviet leaders still hoped that Sadat would not plunge into war, this possibility could not be excluded, and at some point they appear to have given reluctant approval for Egypt's use of force, if necessary, to recover its territory" (p. 145).

25. George, "Arab-Israeli War," p. 146. George reports several possible, but ambiguous, Soviet warnings of the Arab attack. One was their evacuation of Soviet civilians from Egypt just before the attack, which given Soviet obligations to their allies was "noteworthy." Several reports also "allege that Soviet ambassador Dobrynin advised Kissinger on October 5 that the Arab attack would be launched on the following day" (see pp. 145–147).

26. Jabber and Kolkowicz, "Arab-Israeli Wars," p. 442; Porter, *U.S.S.R. in Third World Conflicts,* pp. 126, 140.

27. Abram N. Shulsky, "The Jordanian Crisis of September 1970," in *Soviet Naval Diplomacy,* ed. Dismukes and McConnell, pp. 169–171. He adds, "At the very least, the fact that Soviet military advisers were present in Syria suggests that the Soviets probably had some knowledge of the Syrians' intentions" (pp. 170–171), which of course is not the same thing as instigating or encouraging them.

28. William B. Quandt, "Lebanon, 1958, and Jordan, 1970," in *Force*

*Without War,* ed. Blechman and Kaplan, pp. 280–281, 279, 280n; Riad, *Struggle for Peace,* p. 165.

29. George W. Breslauer, "Soviet Policy in the Middle East, 1967–1972: Unalterable Antagonism or Collaborative Competition?" in *Managing U.S.-Soviet Rivalry,* ed. George, p. 77; Bradford Dismukes, "Large-Scale Intervention Ashore: Soviet Air Defenses in Egypt," in *Soviet Naval Diplomacy,* ed. Dismukes and McConnell, pp. 221, 226; Breslauer, "Soviet Policy," p. 76; George, "Missed Opportunities," p. 191; William B. Quandt, *Decade of Decisions* (Berkeley and Los Angeles: University of California Press, 1977), p. 95.

30. Dismukes, "Large-Scale Intervention," pp. 229–230. The Soviet movements did violate the cease-fire. But although the Egyptians may be accused of duplicity, the Soviets cannot be, at least technically. As Quandt notes, the Soviets had not signed the cease-fire agreement: "One might have wondered what obligation the Soviet Union had to respect the terms of an American-arranged cease-fire to which it had not been a party. The Soviet bid for a cooperative approach had been rebuffed in early June, and the United States had proceeded unilaterally. The Soviet Union was not violating any agreement to which it was a party." Quandt also notes that according to the *New York Times* Israel had reinforced its own canal positions and thereby violated the agreement as well. See Quandt, *Decade of Decisions,* p. 108.

31. McConnell and Calhoun, "Indo-Pakistani Crisis," pp. 186, 184. They argue, however, that "the U.S.S.R. had followed a course that made war possible." Such a course hardly qualifies as aggression or expansionism and could be said of both superpowers in 1971 and most other Third World wars.

32. David K. Hall, "The Laotian War of 1962 and the Indo-Pakistani War of 1971," in *Force Without War,* ed Blechman and Kaplan, p. 197; Raymond L. Garthoff, *Détente and Confrontation: American-Soviet Relations from Nixon to Reagan* (Washington, D.C.: Brookings Institution, 1985), p. 279.

33. Mazhar Ali Khan Malik, letter to the editor, *New York Times,* March 10, 1988, p. A30.

34. Moreover, the same drive for power in the Third World that led to the overt crises discussed in this book underpins everyday American foreign policy and has fostered dozens of other military interventions and threats that ran some incalculable risk of erupting into superpower confrontation. Most, of course, did not become crises, in many cases simply because the Soviets did not seriously challenge American actions. A few became pseudo-crises destined for historical footnotes, as we mentioned in Chapter 6. The great majority will not be recorded as nuclear danger points at all. That is an error, because like any low-probability event, nuclear crisis usually does not happen when the risk is run. One does not usually fall and break a hip when walking on an icy road either, but only the foolhardy conclude that they are immune to the danger. A comparable mentality justifies the continuation of American foreign policy as usual, even in the face of urgent historical warnings.

Many previous operations by both superpowers were once deemed safe but turned out otherwise. Khrushchev presumably did not expect to see the United States at Defcon III when he planned nuclear shipments to Cuba. Nor did

Eisenhower and Kennedy expect an atomic showdown when they tried to topple the Cuban revolutionary government through assassination, sabotage, subversion, and ultimately invasion of the Bay of Pigs. Kissinger did not realize that his casual permission for Israel to violate the cease-fire he had just negotiated in Moscow would also end at Defcon III in 1973. Nor did Johnson and Nixon foresee this in 1967–1973, when they provided Israel with enormous quantities of arms without pressing for the return or independence of the Arab territories captured in 1967, even though the occupation was widely understood to make another Arab-Israeli war, with all its dangers, almost inevitable. And so on. A full discussion of the nuclear risks of U.S. foreign and military policy since 1962 is beyond the scope of this study, though it would be a vitally important contribution to the nuclear debate and to a meaningful history of the nuclear age. Basic changes are required if routine militarism is not to crash-land in superpower confrontation in the future, as it periodically has in the past.

35. See Jerome N. Slater, "The Dominican Republic, 1961–66," in *Force Without War*, ed. Blechman and Kaplan, pp. 306, 315, 335, 336.

36. Philip Geyelin, cited in Richard J. Barnet, *Intervention and Revolution* (Cleveland: World, 1968), pp. 169–170; Slater, *Dominican Republic*, pp. 326–327, 303, 307–308.

37. Barnet, *Intervention and Revolution*, pp. 161, 174; Slater, *Dominican Republic*, p. 338.

38. Slater, *Dominican Republic*, pp. 321–322, 339, 342; Amnesty International, *Report on Torture*, cited in Edward S. Herman, *The Real Terror Network: Terrorism in Fact and Propaganda* (Boston: South End Press, 1982), p. 118.

39. Barnet, *Intervention and Revolution*, pp. 229–230.

40. Noam Chomsky and Edward S. Herman, *The Political Economy of Human Rights*, vol. 1, *The Washington Connection and Third World Fascism* (Boston: South End Press, 1979), p. 276; Barnet, *Intervention and Revolution*, pp. 234–235; Chomsky and Herman, *Political Economy of Human Rights*, p. 274.

41. Blechman and Kaplan, *Force Without War*, pp. 48, 51.

42. Herman, *Real Terror Network*, p. 118; "The Dark of Guatemala," *Boston Globe*, March 17, 1988, p. 16.

43. All Tom Atlee quotations come from "Who Owns the Game?" *Thinkpeace* 2, no. 3 (May–June 1986): 5–6. Atlee includes, along with weapons systems and arms control, specific U.S. foreign adventures as items that the MICE cook up to keep the peace movement ineffectively occupied. We have omitted the references to these because this part of the argument is far-fetched. The United States normally intervenes for specific reasons of foreign policy and sometimes to whip up broad public support for the administration. In any case, it is precisely these interventions that the government considers critical and tries to shield from protest. Atlee is correct in suggesting that the peace movement cannot merely oppose *individual* acts of military intervention by the United States, but must attack the ideologies and interests that produce them. But unlike nuclear weapons systems, each specific intervention normally results in death and injury to many innocent people in the victimized country and some-

times either sustains or emplaces unpopular governments that rule by terror and force after the United States withdraws.

44. Carl Conetta, "Nuclear Protest at an Impasse," *Zeta Magazine*, February 1988, p. 83; Robert Schaeffer, "The 5% Solution," *Nuclear Times*, September–October 1987, p. 26.

45. Michael Howard, "Is Arms Control Really Necessary?" (lecture delivered at the Council for Arms Control, London), excerpted in *Harper's* 272, no. 1632 (May 1986): 14.

46. Scott D. Sagan, "Nuclear Alerts and Crisis Management," *International Security* 9, no. 4 (Spring 1985): 137; H. W. Brands, "Testing Massive Retaliation: Credibility and Crisis Management in the Taiwan Strait," *International Security* 12, no. 4 (Spring 1988): 150; Nixon, *RN*, pp. 486, 488.

# Index

Auerbach, Jonathan D., 1
Avishai, Bernard, 142–144

Ball, Desmond, 16, 39, 40, 129, 130–131, 243 n.19
Ball, George, 48–49, 152
Bar-Joseph, Uri, 109
Barnet, Richard J., 227–229
Begin, Menachem, 282 n.22
Bello, Walden, 140–141
Benedick, Richard E., 189
Bernstein, Bart, 150
Betts, Richard K., 25–26, 50, 52, 63, 78, 84–85
Bidault, Georges, 85
Bing, George F., 23–24, 199–201
Bismarck, Prince Otto Eduard Leopold von, 26
Black September crisis: motives for U.S. actions in, 220, 223; nuclear dangers during, 96–100
Blair, Bruce G., 25, 26, 27, 243 n.19
Blechman, Barry M.: on 1973 Arab-Israeli war, 50, 113–114, 115, 116; on dangers of nuclear threats, 137; on frequency of U.S. nuclear threats, alerts, and signaling, 136; on frequent use of nuclear-armed U.S. warships in world conflicts, 130; on irrelevance of nuclear balance of power to actual superpower conflicts, 53–54; on nuclear credibility, 40–41
Blose, Rear Admiral Larry, 177
Bluestone, Barry, 185
Boumedienne, Houari, 94
Bowie, Robert, 87
Bowman, Robert, 74
Boyer, Paul, 235
Bracken, Paul, 8, 32–33, 128, 180–181
Brands, H. W., 87–89, 132
Breslauer, George W., 223–224
Brezhnev, Leonid I., 94, 113
Brodhead, Frank, 179
Brodie, Bernard: on "absolute weapon," 3; on difficulty of defending against nuclear weapons, 16; on irrelevance of nuclear superiority, 7; on "marginal thinking," 58; on nuclear schizophrenia, 57; on potential benefits of arms control, 181; on revolutionary nature of nuclear weapons, 14
Brown, Harold, 138
Brown, Harrison, 67
Brzezinski, Zbigniew, 73, 118, 125
Bulganin, Nikolai, 90
Bundy, McGeorge: on 1973 Arab-Israeli war, 261 n.102; on 1979 superpower

conflict over Soviet troops in Cuba, 117; on crisis over Quemoy and Matsu, 87; on Cuban missile crisis, 48–49, 152, 162; on deadly connection, 126–127; on "existential deterrence," 17–18; on irrelevance of nuclear balance of power to actual superpower conflicts, 53; on leaders' recognition that nuclear superiority is unattainable, 55; on modest requirements of nuclear deterrence, 15; on nuclear danger in Europe, 127, 264 n.2; on questionable benefits of Euromissiles for NATO, 51; on Star Wars, 69, 71, 77; on "window of vulnerability," 50, 248–249 n.12
Burchinal, General David A., 61, 62
Burlatsky, Fyodor, 210, 211–212
Burt, Richard, 42, 137
Bush, George, 64

Calhoun, Anne Kelly, 105, 219, 224–225, 283 n.31
Cambodia, 140
Carlucci, Frank, 190
Carnesale, Albert, 72
Carrington, Tim, 123–124
Carroll, Admiral Eugene, 174
Carter, Ashton, 69–70, 71, 77
Carter, Jimmy, 117–118, 137
Carter Doctrine, 137–138, 265 n.26
Castro, Fidel, 153, 210–211
Catton, General Jack J., 83
Center for Defense Information, 33–34, 51, 172, 177, 190
Chad, 174
Chain, General John T., 192–193, 202–203
Chang, Gordon, 86–89, 175
Chiang Kai-shek, 89
Chomsky, Noam, 81–82, 119, 219, 229, 237 n.9, 266 n.31
Church, Frank, 117–118
Cienfuegos crisis (Cuba 1970): demonstrating U.S. resolve during, 133; hypocrisy of U.S. position in, 271–272 n.50, 272 n.53; and irrelevance of Soviet submarine base to deterrence, 272 n.51; nuclear dangers in, 100–103; relation of, to Cuban missile crisis, 164–165
Clausewitz, Carl von, 159
Cochran, Thomas B., 177, 180, 190, 191
Cohen, Avner, 142–144
Colson, Charles, 107–108
Command, Control, Communications, and Intelligence (C³I), 40. *See also*